The Mexican Transpacific

CRITICAL MEXICAN STUDIES

CRITICAL MEXICAN STUDIES
Series editor: Ignacio M. Sánchez Prado

Critical Mexican Studies is the first English-language, humanities-based, theoretically focused academic series devoted to the study of Mexico. The series is a space for innovative works in the humanities that focus on theoretical analysis, transdisciplinary interventions, and original conceptual framing.

Other titles in the series:
   The Restless Dead: Necrowriting and Disappropriation,
       by Cristina Rivera Garza
   History and Modern Media: A Personal Journey, by John Mraz
   Toxic Loves, Impossible Futures: Feminist Living as Resistance,
       by Irmgard Emmelhainz
   Drug Cartels Do Not Exist: Narcotrafficking in US and Mexican Culture,
       by Oswaldo Zavala
   Unlawful Violence: Mexican Law and Cultural Production,
       by Rebecca Janzen
   *Monstrous Politics: Geography, Rights, and the Urban Revolution in
       Mexico City*, by Ben A. Gerlofs

The Mexican Transpacific
Nikkei Writing, Visual Arts, and Performance

Ignacio López-Calvo

VANDERBILT UNIVERSITY PRESS
Nashville, Tennessee

Copyright 2022 Vanderbilt University Press
All rights reserved
First printing 2022

Library of Congress Cataloging-in-Publication Data

Names: López-Calvo, Ignacio, author.
Title: The Mexican transpacific : Nikkei writing, visual arts, and
   performance / Ignacio López-Calvo.
Description: Nashville : Vanderbilt University Press, [2022] | Series:
   Critical Mexican studies | Includes bibliographical references and
   index.
Identifiers: LCCN 2022010469 (print) | LCCN 2022010470 (ebook) | ISBN
   9780826504937 (paperback) | ISBN 9780826504944 (hardcover) | ISBN
   9780826504951 (epub) | ISBN 9780826504968 (pdf)
Subjects: LCSH: Mexican literature—Japanese authors—History and
   criticism. | Japanese in literature. | Art, Mexican—Japanese
   influences. | Japanese—Mexico—Ethnic identity. |
   Japanese—Intellectual life—Mexico. | LCGFT: Literary criticism.
Classification: LCC PQ7134.J37 L67 2022 (print) | LCC PQ7134.J37 (ebook)
   | DDC 860.9/8956072—dc23/eng/20220930
LC record available at https://lccn.loc.gov/2022010469
LC ebook record available at https://lccn.loc.gov/2022010470

To my loving mother, María Teresa Calvo Matesanz,
who would cry every time I went to the airport.

Contents

Acknowledgments		ix
A Note on Translation		xi
Foreword		xiii

INTRODUCTION. Nikkei Cultural Production and Transpacific Studies from a Latin Americanist Perspective   1

PART I: IMMIGRANT, LITERARY NEGOTIATIONS OF NATIONAL IDENTITY

1. Nonaka's Memoir: From *Captain in the Mexican Revolution* to Enemy of the State   41
2. Challenges to *Nihonjinron* in Nakatani's Memoirs   67
3. Strategic Essentialism in Akane's Performative *Tanka*   96

PART II: JAPANESE MEXICAN VISUAL AND PERFORMANCE ARTS

4. Resignifying *Yamato-damashii* and Utopian Socialism in the Manga *Los samuráis de México*   129
5. Nishizawa's Bicultural Dialectics and the Critical Stereotyping of His Art   147
6. The Transpacific in Akiko's Theatrical Performance   166

CONCLUSION. Another Past Is Possible   193

Notes	199
Work Cited	233
Index	245

Acknowledgments

I would like to express my gratitude for the University of California MEXUS-CONACYT collaborative research grant that I, along with my colleague Emma Nakatani, received in 2017. I would also like to thank Martín Camps, Selfa Chew-Smithart, Aiko Chikaba, Irene Akiko Iida, Lucero Estrella, Hugo López-Chavolla, Paulina Machuca, Emma Nakatani, Jaime Ortega, Víctor Hugo Pacheco, Laura Torres-Rodríguez, Cristina Rascón, Miyuki Sakai, the Asociación México-Japonesa, Ignacio Sánchez-Prado, Ana Valenzuela, and Juan Villoro for their kind support to my research, and especially José I. Suárez, who proofread the manuscript, and Randy Muth, Seth Jacobowitz, Juan E. de Castro and Nicholas Birns, who provided valuable feedback. I would also like to thank Vanderbilt University Press editors Gianna Mosser and Zack Gresham for their support throughout the writing process.

A Note on Translation

Whenever possible, I used published translations of the original quotations, which are acknowledged after the quotation and included in the works cited. Otherwise, the translation is mine and, for that reason, has no page numbers and does not appear in the works cited.

Spelling of several Okinawan and Japanese words, particularly for long vowels, changes from author to author and from text to text, as authors often try to transcribe phonetically terms that they learned at home.

Foreword

I first heard about Ignacio López-Calvo, a scholar of Asian–Latin American cultural production, in 2010 through another colleague. In my first written contact with him, he kindly asked me for a copy of my undergraduate thesis, which contextualized my Japanese grandfather's memories and presented them as a historical document. Without hesitation, I sent him an electronic file with my undergraduate thesis, which I presented at Universidad Iberoamericana in 2002. After he thanked me, we lost contact until 2016, when Ignacio asked me to participate in a project sponsored by a University of California MEXUS-CONACYT collaborative research grant. The project's aim was to interview Mexican artists and writers of Chinese and Japanese ancestry. As a historian, I was somewhat unfamiliar with such an objective; however, I saw it as an opportunity to delve into an unknown world. At last, in 2017, he and I met in person.

    I am elated that this study is partially based on those years of collaboration and, particularly, by two of its components. First is a detailed and careful literary analysis of my grandfather Yoshihei Nakatani's memoirs. As a historian of the Nikkei community in Mexico, I have spent over twenty years reading, contextualizing, interpreting, and analyzing these memoirs, which as a teenager studying history I happened to find in a drawer at home. Having read my grandfather's memoirs numerous times since, it was refreshing and motivational for me to revisit the document through López-Calvo's reflective and analytical perspective. This new reading has raised questions that I will try to answer in the near future. Second, reading this book was a unique personal experience. At times, I paused to reflect on the fact that, for the first time in my life, I deeply identified as a Nikkei.

Although I am the granddaughter of a Japanese immigrant and my family has always kept my grandfather's memory alive through Japanese traditions (especially those related to food and singing), the truth of the matter is that my contact with Mexico's Japanese community has not been constant. It is perhaps for this reason that I grew up without a clear consciousness of or attachment to my Japanese origins. It was not until after my grandfather's demise, along with my subsequent thesis on his memoirs and the history of the Japanese colony in Mexico, that I began to see with greater clarity what it means to be Nikkei. However, I must confess that I still tended to view the concept in distant and alien terms. In this context, I found López-Calvo's study truly evocative, because it forced me reflect on my Mexican and Japanese roots.

My personal and emotional reflections notwithstanding, readers are presented with a work that is innovative in several ways. As López-Calvo points out in the introduction, it has been only in recent years that the history of the Japanese Mexican community has begun to receive the scholarly attention it deserves, yet this is the first study to focus on its cultural production. It features the autobiographical writings of Issei Kingo Nonaka, Yoshihei Nakatani, and Akane; the contemporary Nisei Irene Akiko's theatrical performance; the renowned painter Luis Nishizawa Flores's artwork; and a manga dealing mostly with the history of the famous Enomoto Colony, a work translated and published by the Japanese Mexican Association.

These six diverse case studies demonstrate how an ethnic community can be studied through its cultural production. In López-Calvo's words, these memoirs, poems, manga, visual artworks, and theater pieces reflect the Japanese Mexican community's individual and collective self-image. These works also reflect the group's diasporic nature, as its Japanese culture is altered upon coming into contact with the host society. Consequently, this book interprets identity as a dynamic element that evolves in various ways and for different reasons.

López-Calvo manages to shed light on several other key issues regarding Nikkei cultural production in Mexico: the emergence of transpacific studies, a field that addresses socioeconomic and cultural relations among regions along the Pacific Rim; the conceptualization of Asian–Latin American literature; racism and xenophobia as inextricable elements of migration studies that take on greater relevance in light of current events; the remembering and forgetting that shape immigrant identity; and the visibility and empowerment of an ethnic group that, despite its relatively small number, has had a profound impact on Mexican culture. Finally, I want to express my deeply felt gratitude to Ignacio López-Calvo for giving me the opportunity to be part of this project. Meeting Mexican writers and artists of Chinese and Japanese ancestry has enriched my understanding of these immigrant groups and their descendants. I also want to thank him for allowing me to write this foreword to a study that, I am sure, will reveal new ways of seeing, studying, and understanding the Nikkei community in my country, Mexico.

Mexico City, June 2021
Emma Nakatani (Department of History,
Centro de Investigación y Docencia Económicas)

Introduction
Nikkei Cultural Production and Transpacific Studies from a Latin Americanist Perspective

Most studies about the transnational Japanese, or Nikkei, diaspora in Mexico have traditionally ignored cultural production, thus missing out on the community's self-definition. In this introduction, I theorize transpacific literary and cultural production from the perspective of Latin American studies, but first I draw attention to other cultural manifestations that are also discursively meaningful. Indeed, another way to recover this ethnic heritage in Mexico is through material culture, which could be considered, in Marxist terms, as the base (production forces, materials, resources that generate goods needed by society) on which the superstructure (culture, identity, ideology, social institutions) rests, at times justifying it.

Cultural memory scholar Marita Sturken maintains that "cultural memory is produced through objects, images, and representations. These are technologies of memory, not vessels of memory in which memory passively resides so much as objects through which memories are shared, produced, and given meaning" (1997, 9). Let us then start with objects and images as technologies of memory, and more specifically, with the narrative exploration of the agency of objects as a productive starting point for analyzing Japanese Mexican cultural production. Because the agency of objects affects human beings, the literary scholar Héctor Hoyos suggests, for an analysis of what he terms the "human-nonhuman continuum," "the task is to think of the past through the prism of things" (2019, 74, 65). In his view, "nonhumans give and they receive; they domesticate us, we, them—intention is beside the point. Thus, a desire for sweetness informs our relationship with apples; for beauty, with tulips; and for intoxication, with marijuana" (47). From this perspective, cultural production by Asian immigrant communities and their descendants reflects, through the representation of their own chronotopes and symbolic objects, the sociality of their emotions.

The expression of affect in Chinese Latin American narratives tends to present the image of the Chinatowns, *cafés de chinos*, or Chinese-owned shops as the quintessential loci of the immigrant experience. Likewise, in my opinion, in Latin America, Nikkei writing—by *Nikkei* I refer to Japanese living overseas or living outside Japan who have one or more ancestors from that country, for example, first-generation Issei, second-generation Nisei, third-generation Sansei, fourth-generation Yonsei, and fifth-generation Gosei—embodies a sui generis blend of nostalgia, cultural pride, and self-exoticization.[1] Its collective structures of feeling include, in the natural world, cherry blossoms, or *sakura*, like the cherry tree planted by Akane in one of her poems; material culture such as the kimono, the *ofuro* (a Japanese bathtub that originated with short, steep wooden sides), the bento box (single-portion takeout or home-packed meal), and the *butsudan* (Buddhist altar); food and drink such as sushi, miso soup, and sake; traditional cultural practices such as haiku writing, *hanami* (flower viewing), ikebana (the art of flower arrangement), origami (the folk art of folding paper), *sadō* (the traditional tea ceremony), and *tanomoshi* (a rotating credit association), as well as sumo, kendo, and other sports and martial arts; and traditional musical instruments such as the *shamisen* or *taiko* drums. Each chronotope, traditional object, or cultural expression functions as a symbolic repository of memories and identities that, even though it is meant to be transmitted from generation to generation, inevitably loses emotional value over the years. However, the analysis of material culture, just like that of literary (self-)representation, may be useful to the goal of restoring the cultural memory of disappearing or erased communities.

Consider the following examples of transcultural Mexican material culture that contain traces of folk Asianness. First, the most emblematic example of Asian material culture coming to Mexico during colonial times is the *china poblana* dress, associated with the city of Puebla and characterized by a short-sleeved sequin-embroidered shawl, a blouse, slippers covered with green or red silk, and a two-part skirt: the upper part made of green silk and the lower part often embroidered with flowers, birds, or butterflies. Various stories explain its origin. In one story, an enslaved princess from India (not China, despite the garment's name) named Mirnha is abducted by pirates, taken to Macao, then Manila, and, once in Mexico, is bought by Spaniards in Puebla. It is said that people there called her *china*—this generic label is unfortunately still common in Spain and throughout Latin America, with the exception of Brazil, where Asians are instead

Nipponized as *japonês*. (Tellingly, in Spanish, India ink in *tinta china*.) Later, the Sosa de Puebla family purchased Mirnha and changed her name to Catarina de San Juan. Her outfits, it is believed, inspired local women to blend, in transcultural fashion, the traditional clothing styles from India with Mexican indigenous ones, which resulted in the renowned *china poblana* dress. Yet Tatiana Seijas, in her 2014 *Asian Slaves in Mexico: From Chinos to Indios*, clarifies that "in reality, we do not know who designed the costume. Catarina surely had no part in this creation" (27).

The emblematic Fuente del Risco, at the Casa del Risco Museum in Mexico City, located in the former home of Isidro Fabela (1882–1964), a Mexican politician, historian, lawyer, and diplomat, represents another link to the material heritage of Japanese and Chinese cultural influences in Mexico. This stunning fountain, over eight meters tall, built during the latter part of the eighteenth century, was joined to a wall in the courtyard by an unknown artist. Its international and eclectic decorations respond to the then-common practice of using broken pieces of expensive tableware as ornament. Among these pieces (*riscos* in Spanish, hence the fountain's name) are red, blue, and green *imari* porcelain from Japan as well as Chinese fragments, including three plates from the Ming and Qing dynasties that were brought to the then Spanish colony in a Manila galleon (also known as the *nao de China*).[2] Shockingly, this gem of Mexican ultrabaroque art was used as a latrine after the house's abandonment toward the end of the Mexican Revolution (1910–1920).

The historian Paulina Machuca has studied the importation of the Philippine coconut palm to early modern Mexico (250 plants were introduced), along with the introduction of the production techniques of *tuba* (a spirit made from palm sap) and *vino de coco* (coconut wine) by Filipinos on the western coast of New Spain—Colima, Motines, Zacatula, and Acapulco (2018, 20).[3] This Philippine distillation technique and the Asiatic stills (used to make alcoholic beverages for religious ceremonies devoted to Philippine ancestor and nature spirits and deities called *anitos*) were imported during colonial times, for the production of mescal, which often replaced coconut wine.[4] Some of the so-called *indios chinos* (Chinese Indians) from what today is the Philippines, China, India, Borneo, Indonesia, New Guinea, and Sri Lanka who were brought to colonial Mexico, and particularly to Colima, became wealthy thanks to coconut wine production (Machuca 2018, 179). Later, the need for additional workers demanded that the colony's indigenous labor force join the industry, some of whom eventually became master *vinateros* (vintners).

Likewise, Ana G. Valenzuela Zapata, Aristarco Regalado Pinedo, and Michiko Mizoguchi have studied East Asian influences in the production of mescal along the coast of Jalisco. As they explain, by the seventeenth century, "the two distillation processes (the Arabic and the Asiatic) arrived in Mexico (probably via different routes) and were used throughout the Pacific coast to make spirits," including coconut in Colima and agave in New Galicia.[5] They argue that some types of *shōchū* (a Japanese beverage that typically contains 25 percent alcohol by volume and is distilled from rice, barley, sweet potatoes, buckwheat, or brown sugar) are produced on the islands of Kyūshū and Okinawa by the same distilling technique used to produce a type of mescal known as *raicilla* in El Tuito and Zapotitlán de Vadillo, as well as *mescal de olla* from Manzanilla de la Paz, all in today's Jalisco. This distillation technique, the Asiatic still, known in Mexico as *huichol*, is called *kabutogama chiki* in Japan. The authors argue that distillation, introduced by the Spanish to Mexico, was implemented using different methods, not just the coconut wine model. They add that those individuals who were familiar with Asian distilling techniques and used different materials along the Mexican Pacific coast were not necessarily Asian themselves. This Eastern technique, simpler than the Arabic *alambique*, still survives in Mexico and in Asia.[6]

Another icon of Nikkei cultural heritage in Mexico are jacaranda trees that the Japanese immigrant Tatsugoro Matsumoto, founder of the original Flor Matsumoto flower shop in Mexico City, brought to Mexico from Brazil and Paraguay. Mexico's president Pascual Ortiz Rubio requested that the Japanese government donate cherry trees to be planted along the Mexican capital's main avenues as a symbol of friendship between the two countries. Thereupon, Japan's foreign minister asked Matsumoto about the feasibility of planting cherry trees in the city. Matsumoto, who happened to be growing jacaranda trees in his greenhouse, responded that cherry trees were not most appropriate and recommended that jacaranda be planted instead. Thanks to Matsumoto's advice, Mexico City and other Mexican cities that followed its example enjoy the blooms of stunning jacaranda trees in early spring, which have become a symbol of Mexico.[7]

Likewise, in San Luis Potosí, which has had a Japanese Mexican community for several generations, people use the word *yuki* ("snow" in Japanese) instead of the usual *raspado* or *granizado* to refer to shaved ice sweetened with flavored syrups; those who sell this treat are *yukeros*.[8] According to Ricardo Pérez Otakara, his grandfather Fusaichi Otakara first brought the *yukeras* (shaved-ice shops) to northern Mexico. Fusaichi was a descendant of a samurai who immigrated to Mexico in 1907, at the age of seventeen, and worked as a day laborer, a miner, and a cook. Having been trained as a samurai, he became, like many other of his countrymen, an anonymous soldier of the Mexican Revolution and served as a cavalry captain under Francisco I. Madero and Francisco "Pancho" Villa. Years later, Fusaichi made a living in Nuevo León selling *yukis*. He also founded the Asociación México-Japonesa del Noreste, or Mexican Japanese Association of the Northeast).

In yet another example of transculturation, "Japanese peanuts" (*cacahuates japoneses*) were invented in 1945 in Mexico City by the Japanese immigrant Yoshigei (Carlos) Nakatani (1910–1992) and were first sold in the La Merced market.[9] Before immigrating to Mexico in 1932, Nakatani had worked at a candy factory in his hometown of Sumoto, which made *mamekashi* (seeds covered with flour and condiments). Years after his arrival, Nakatani decided to take advantage of his experience in Japan: he coated peanuts with a thick, crunchy coat of wheat flour and soy sauce—today Mexicans often mix them with chili powder and lime juice. Pressed to feed his eight children—the future visual artist Carlos Nakatani (1934–2004) and the singer Gustavo "Nakatani" Nakatani (1949–2020) among them—he sold his "Japanese" peanuts at La Merced, and it is said that consumers would yell "¡Ahí viene el japonés!" (Here comes the Japanese man!). Nipón, the company created by Nakatani and led today by one of his granddaughters, dominated the Japanese peanut market until 1980, when brands like Sabritas and Barcel became competitors since Nakatani had never sought a patent. Unsurprisingly, *cacahuates japoneses*, now exported to Japan, are known there as Mexican peanuts, often sold in a bag sporting a mariachi with a sombrero and moustache. This raises the recurrent issue of how these terms of ethnic or national origin (Japanese, Japanese Mexican) often have no fixed meaning in Latin America: depending on the speaker and context, the term can mean Japanese, Japanese Mexican, or simply Mexican.

A third transcultural example of Nikkei communities' long impact on Mexico is *chamoy*, also known as *miguelito*, a Mexican powder or liquid condiment made of dehydrated fruit, chili pepper, salt, sugar, and water.[10] It is believed to have originated from *umeboshi*, a traditional Japanese dish made from pickled *ume* (Japanese apricot) with red coloring added. The condiment was created in Mexico during the 1950s by Teikichi Luis Iwadare, a Japanese immigrant who decided to produce *umeboshi* with apricots, plums, or mangos and name it *chamoy*. According to Aiko Chikaba, Tsutomu Kasuga, who worked for Iwadare as an apprentice, was developing chamoy around the same time (2016, 173).

A final example of Japanese heritage in Mexico City is the Museo del Juguete Antiguo (Antique Toy Museum), a private collection of more than a million toys owned and managed by Nisei architect Roberto Shimizu (1945–), located since 2008 in Colonia Doctores. Shimizu, supported by his children, conceives of his toy collection, which he has declared the largest in the world, as part of the history, popular culture, and even economic history of Mexico, because many of the pieces were created from 1920 to 1960, when the country was the fifth largest toy manufacturer in the world. The industry eventually disappeared because of Asian competition.[11] One of the most emblematic pieces in the collection exhibits is a figure of the Japanese superhero Ultraman fighting monsters with the aid of the *luchador enmascarado* (masked wrestler) El Santo (Rodolfo Guzmán Huerta, 1917–1984), who was transformed in film and comics into the greatest folk Mexican superhero.[12] In the comment section of a YouTube video about this museum, visitors praise the effort of these "japoneses." In another comment, they are referred to as "foreigners" and "Chinese" in the same sentence, although in the video, Shimizu explains that it was his parents who were immigrants—not even his native Mexican Spanish prevents the collector, with an Asian phenotype, from being considered a foreigner in his own country.

It is also noteworthy that not every object brought on the Manila Galleon has remained popular in Mexico. Thus, while the *mantón de Manila* (Manila shawl), a silk shawl originally made with chinoiserie-style motifs in China and derived from the *Filipino pañuelo*, was popular in colonial Latin America, it failed to remain so. In Spain, it is still today considered a quintessentially traditional Spanish garment, worn, for example, by flamenco dancers and Andalusian women during festivities. The *mantón de Manila* is also believed to have influenced the designs of the Latin American *rebozo*, a long, flat garment handwoven from cotton, wool, silk, or rayon, like a shawl, and worn by Mexican women. All of these objects tell us about "connected histories," to use Sanjay Subrahmanyam's (1997) term: they help us to interpret networks of cultural contacts and economic exchanges between distant populations and, simultaneously, they reflect historical changes, at small and large scales, that challenge nation-based historiographical approaches. Material evidence of human circulation, distilling methods, goods, and manufacturing methods paints a rich history of those global networks that have long found Mexico to be a principal connecting hub, thereby contributing to the decentering of European modernity. These Asian or Asian-influenced objects and traditions represent micronarratives that metonymically push us toward more encompassing, global macronarratives. They encourage us to rethink Mexican history beyond its national borders and from a different vantage point, looking instead at the often-silenced cross-cultural connections and clashes (e.g., slavery, human exploitation, racism, predatory extractivism), intercontinental economic connections, and immigration. Consequently, Mexican history becomes inextricably linked to China, Japan, Korea, and the Philippines.

THE TRANSPACIFIC FROM A LATIN AMERICANIST PERSPECTIVE AS AN ALTERNATIVE HEURISTIC LENS

In his 1998 essay collection *What Is in a Rim? Critical Perspectives on the Pacific Region Idea,* historian Arif Dirlik questions the meaning of often-used geopolitical terms, such as *Pacific Rim, Pacific Basin,* and *Asia-Pacific*:

> The immediate reference is obviously physically geographic: Pacific Rim (or Pacific Basin) refers to societies situated on the boundaries of the Pacific Ocean and within it. Discussions of the Pacific Rim, however, rarely account for all the societies thus situated, more often than not referring primarily to societies of the northern hemisphere and sometimes using the term euphemistically as a contemporary substitute for what used to be called East Asia.
>
> The terms sometimes include societies technically outside the physical boundaries of the Pacific Ocean even as some of the societies situated on the Rim or within it are left out. These usages problematize the geographic reference of the term(s). (1998, 3)

Dirlik concludes that we should switch our focus from economic connections (abstract relations between capital and commodities, or across physical borders) to the peoples and human exchanges that have shaped the region. Indeed, terms that may at first seem all-encompassing, such as *Pacific Rim,* may turn out to be exclusionary. On this matter, Viet Thanh Nguyen and Janet Hoskins argue that "transpacific studies exists at the juncture of area studies, American studies, and Asian American studies ... [it] draws from all these approaches while focusing less on the limits of a particular place or a people and stressing the movements of people, culture, capital, or ideas within regions and between nations" (2014, 24). Conspicuously absent from this definition, though, is Latin American studies—despite Latin America's Pacific coastline, a long history of exchange with Asia, and tradition of both free (voluntary) and coerced immigration from Asia to Peru, Mexico, and other countries. In fact, in both transatlantic and transpacific studies the focus has noticeably been on wealthier countries, the Global North. This oversight must be corrected, as transpacific studies and Latin American studies undoubtedly can benefit from a fruitful dialogue and exchanges of theories, methods, and knowledges. Regarding cultural production analyses by and about

Mexican Nikkeijin, a transpacific approach will help decenter teleological, nation-focused narratives of Mexicanness.

In this context, for the past few years, a group of researchers from different academic disciplines has been studying transpacific cross-cultural experiences between Asia and Latin America from a new perspective: rather than seeing Asia–Latin America as a region to be studied, as is typical in area studies, it has been reconceived as an epistemological position, that is, as a lens for analyzing and comparing these sophisticated networks. Inspired by Kuan-Hsing Chen's *Asia as Method: Toward Deimperialization*, the literary scholar Junyoung Verónica Kim argues that this critical intervention troubles the ideological constraints of traditional ethnic studies, which are mostly focused on immigration to the United States and on US understandings of race (emerging from the civil rights movement), and of area studies, which emerged from Cold War ideology and US hegemony:

> Asia–Latin America can be a method precisely insofar as "Asia" or "Latin America" is not taken as putatively natural givens but instead is conceived as a site of struggle and dissensus. Asia–Latin America as method involves negotiating and juxtaposing different systems of knowledge that bear on it and, by so doing, intends to shed light on the subjectivities that arise through such encounters. (2017, 101)

This transdisciplinary methodological approach involving populations in movement, diasporic and transnational processes, and negotiations among different knowledge systems challenges fixed categories, established divisions, and theoretical issues, including those dealing with the performance of national and diasporic belonging, citizenship, and identities.

In the field of literary studies, when considering immigrants writing in Mandarin or Japanese in Latin America, are we dealing with Asian, Latin American, or Asian–Latin American literature (see Chapter 3)? Does the answer change if first-generation immigrants choose to write in Spanish or Portuguese, or if they engage in bilingual writing? What about the Spanish- or Portuguese-language cultural production by Latin American *dekasegi* (temporary workers) of Japanese ancestry who began moving to Japan in the 1990s to work in medium-sized factories? In such cases when the lines blur between disciplines and nation-states, a transpacific method is more productive and appropriate. Furthermore, as Kim points out, this transpacific approach contributes to displacing Europe and the United States as the traditional hegemonic sites where knowledge production takes place, focusing instead on new geopolitical connections and fluxes that end up (re)centering former peripheral areas. Previously silenced hybrid worldviews and alternative modernities emerge from these contested contact zones, thereby contributing to the historical recovery of the Asian presence and heritage in Latin America and the Caribbean.

Yet the term *transpacific* should be used with caution. After all, transpacific studies are not always entirely transpacific. The Asian and Asian American studies scholar Lisa Yun affirms the implicit contradiction in the term:

> Historically, the "transatlantic" and the "transpacific," often perceived of as discrete epistemological geographies, meet in the history of the slave and coolie. In fact, "transpacific" is actually a misnomer for essentializing Asian migration, since many Asians (including coolies) also came via transatlantic routes and were situated within transatlantic colonial and maritime systems. (2004, 41)

Indeed, in many cases, using the names of oceans to discuss regional or national issues is problematic. Maritime voyages of Japanese emigrants to Brazil, for instance, included the transatlantic crossing, which is erased by *transpacific*: the ship carrying the first immigrants, the *Kasato-Maru*, left the port of Kobe on April 29, 1908, for Singapore, then rounded the Cape of Good Hope, and arrived at the Brazilian port of Santos, in São Paulo state. Likewise, ships that transported Chinese indentured workers to Cuba and the rest of the Caribbean, like the *Oquendo* and the *Duke of Argyle* in 1847, crossed the South China Sea, the Indian Ocean, and finally the Atlantic Ocean. An older example of a transpacific and transatlantic trip was the Keichō Embassy (1613–1620), which traveled from Japan to Spain and Italy, through New Spain (see Chapter 6). The concept of transpacific, then, should not be uncritically applied to all cases of modern Asian migration to the Americas. By contrast, in the cases of Nikkei immigration to Mexico and the Chinese who had arrived in San Francisco but emigrated to northern Mexico after the Chinese Exclusion Act of 1882 (approximately five thousand of these so-called *chinos californianos* migrated again to Cuba), their trip was indeed entirely transpacific.

As the historian Jeffrey Lesser elucidates, "Real and imagined geography is critical to the construction of ethnic identity" (2007, xxv). Today, the imagined geographies of Latin America have once again incorporated Asia into their sphere, as was done during the times of the Manila galleons. And since Latin America has returned to Asia, Latin American studies should also reconsider the traditional preeminence of transatlantic approaches and continue to incorporate transpacific threads into cultural, economic, and sociopolitical fields. In the words of Peter Gordon and Juan José Morales, coauthors of *The Silver Way: China, Spanish America and the Birth of Globalisation, 1565–1815*, "Latin America, like much of the world, is currently experiencing a 'pivot to Asia,' or perhaps it's really a pivot back" (2017, 75).

ASIAN–LATIN AMERICAN LITERATURE AS WORLD LITERATURE

I have proposed elsewhere that Asian–Latin American literature should be considered an alternative type of world literature.[13] Following the ideas of "worlding" and decolonizing the literary world-system, I suggest that the worldliness of a literary text cannot be reduced to simple matters of improvement when translated into English or of global circulation and marketing processes. If we examine the unequal power relations between Western cores and non-Western peripheries, then Asian–Latin American cultural production—peripheral and marginal even in the context of its own national markets—cannot be considered world literature, as it lacks the symbolic and cultural capital provided by translation and global circulation. If instead of looking at literature as a market commodity, we focus on writing and reading practices exhibiting a decolonizing, planetary consciousness that overcomes national and Eurocentric worldviews, then this "minor" literature has a chance to be considered part of the world republic of letters, to use literary critic Pascale Casanova's (2007) term. After all, as Homi Bhabha points out: "The study of *world literature* might be the study of the way in which cultures recognize themselves through their projections of 'otherness.' Where once the transmission of national traditions was the major theme of a world literature, perhaps we can now suggest that transnational histories of migrants, the colonized, or political refugees—these border and frontier conditions—may be the terrains of world literature" (1994, 12). In this sense, much of Japanese Mexican cultural production can certainly be considered part of these important transnational histories, and Mexican identity can be better understood by looking at how it projects feelings of otherness toward Mexico's own Asian communities.

Instead of taking a geographical look at the global patterns of textual mobility or the global distribution of physical books, we can consider an active, conceptual circulation of ideas—beyond the local, the national, the Eurocentric. In this case, we will find examples of Asian–Latin American literature characterized by a decolonial axiology and non-Eurocentric and (rooted) cosmopolitan border thinking. These works tend to display what the philosopher Anthony Appiah has called "rooted cosmopolitanism," that is, a situation in which one "can be cosmopolitan—celebrating the variety of human cultures; rooted—loyal to one local society (or a few) that you count as home; liberal—convinced of the value of the individual; and patriotic—celebrating the institutions of the state (or states) within which you live" (1997, 633). Hence, as a type of transnational, transpacific, hybrid literature, an important part of Asian–Latin American writing fulfills the prerequisites of world literature as conceived by Karl Marx and Friedrich Engels's early definition in *The Communist Manifesto* in 1848: "And as in material, so also in intellectual production. The intellectual creations of individual nations become common property. National one-sidedness and narrow-mindedness become more and more impossible, and from the numerous national and local literatures, there arises a world literature" (2005, 11).

In some Asian–Latin American texts, one can perceive ways of thinking that can be traced back to both a heritage culture and the Latin American country's culture, as the author tries to make readers aware of alternative modes of perception, all while building symbolic bridges between East and West. It is precisely the East-West or East-South cross-cultural encounter and negotiation of knowledges that make this cultural production distinctive.[14] Asian–Latin American literature also fits within the range of world literature proposed by theorist and literature scholar Pheng Cheah, who defines *world literature* as "an active power of world making that contests the world made by capitalist globalization: that is, world literature is reconceived as a site of processes of worlding and as an agent that participates and intervenes in these processes" (2014, 303). Indeed, a considerable part of Asian–Latin American writing, as I have explained elsewhere, does include authors and texts with transnational, postnational, cosmopolitan, globally oriented sensitivities and consciousness beyond Eurocentrism and the expectations of a traditional, national readership.[15] Many Asian–Latin American texts often include both Western and Eastern literary settings and worldviews, while sidestepping essentialist approaches related to the notion of multiculturalism, and they deploy protagonists who negotiate different and evolving national, transnational, and transcultural identities throughout their lives, sometimes entering and leaving Asianness according to the sociopolitical and economic circumstances. After all, as Stuart Hall pointed out, "Cultural identities come from somewhere, have histories. But like everything which is historical, they undergo constant transformation. . . . [Cultural identity] is a matter of 'becoming' as well as of 'being.' It belongs to the future as much as to the past" (1999, 225).

In this sense, regarding the Asian Mexican community's performance of national identification according to the sociopolitical circumstances, the historian Julia María Schiavone Camacho states:

> The complex ties Mexicans and Chinese formed in northern Mexico during the late nineteenth and early twentieth centuries and the integration of Chinese men into local communities led to racial and cultural fusion and over time to the formation of a new cultural identity—*Chinese Mexican*. Racially and culturally hybrid families straddled the boundaries of identity and nation. They made alternating claims on Chineseness and Mexicanness during their quest to belong somewhere, especially as social and political uproar erupted in Mexico, the United States, and China. (2012, 3)

Chinese Mexican families deported to China from Sonora and Sinaloa in 1931, many of whom genuinely loved Mexico, "claimed Mexicanness strategically to leave China during a time of intense social and political turmoil" (Schiavone Camacho 2012, 1). In this view, they became truly Mexican only after their deportation to China, where they developed a strategic, diasporic, Mexican identity based on the memory of an imagined Mexican homeland (6). As I explained in *Japanese Brazilian Saudades: Diasporic Identities and Cultural Production* (2019), the same may be said of Brazilian *dekasegi* who had proudly identified as Japanese while living in Brazil but adopted a more Brazilian and Latin American identification once they felt rejected as *gaijin* (foreigners) in Japan, where they began moving en masse in the 1990s.

Like these real-life examples, racialized authors and their characters also engage in entering and leaving Asianness, at times to challenge Orientalist stereotypes or presumed fixed, stagnant identities that are often related to the "yellow peril" and "model minority" stereotypes. They also resort to this strategy to claim their belonging within the nation, even if they simultaneously assert their cultural differences or refuse to acclimate to mainstream societal values. Asian–Latin American writing offers a critique of hegemonic Western modernity and the nationalist epistemic violence that, since the inception of Asian immigration to Latin America and the Caribbean, has occasionally tried to erase these individuals' worldviews and modes of being in the world. In the case of Japanese Mexicans, the (self-)historicization of their experience is not just a path to demanding a place within the national imaginary but also a suggestion about new ways to rethink, for instance, national history, the historical and racial memory of the US border, or ways of conceiving race in Mexico. Their writing may, therefore, be a symbolic intervention into nation-making processes.

At the very least, Asian–Latin American cultural production has the potential to improve the self-esteem of these historically silenced minority communities and to inspire readers' and viewers' empathy with Asian and Asian Latin American cultures, an outcome that could generate better cross-cultural understanding, tolerance, and social justice. This storytelling may not only enrich Asian Mexicans' individual and collective self-perception but also inform new ways of visualizing Mexicanness. And therein lies the possibility of considering Asian–Latin American literature as world (non-Eurocentric, decolonial) literature. Finally, this corpus of works and performances collectively complements the re-membering and revision of the social history of Asian communities in Mexico carried out by recent historical studies.

Some Asian–Latin American authors attempt to offset Orientalist portrayals of Asianness displayed through the exoticizing lens of the Western gaze, avoiding, for example, masculinist colonial fantasies about the purportedly exotic geisha always willing to accept Western male advances, the submissive Asian wife, or the inscrutable and mysterious Asian man. Likewise, in Latin American works by authors who are not of Asian descent, Asian characters tend to signify Otherness—if not the direct opposite of Mexicanness, Latin Americanness, or the Western world—embodied in vampires and other monsters, or in secret societies and mafias. In contrast, Asian–Latin American authors provide a more realistic and naturalized image of Asian immigrants and their descendants.[16]

It is noteworthy, however, that even in texts and performances by Asian immigrants and their descendants, it is not uncommon to find an imagined, romanticized, or idealized East or "Orient," at times disguised as cultural authenticity. These authors may also strategically associate with the prestige of their ancestral homeland. For instance, during the 1990 Peruvian presidential elections, the Nisei then candidate Alberto Fujimori at times dressed as a samurai to be associated with the economic and technological achievements of postwar Japan. Paradoxically, other times he dressed as an indigenous Andean peasant to distance himself from the perceived whiteness of his political opponent, the celebrated novelist and future Nobel laureate Mario Vargas Llosa. Fujimori even called himself "El Chino" during the campaign. His tactical ambivalence, though, ultimately proves that ethnic identities are not fixed; they can change dramatically according to the circumstances, from person to person and from one generation to the next.

Ultimately, "'cultural' difference is no longer a stable exotic otherness; self-other relations are matters of power and rhetoric rather than of essence. A whole structure of expectations about authenticity in culture and in art is thrown in doubt" (Clifford 1988, 14). From this perspective, Asian–Latin American authors sometimes appropriate the millenary cultural traditions of their ancestors as a strategic tool to mark their social group's cultural difference, often signaling an epistemological privilege that prevents their non–Asian Latin American readers or viewers from having access to part of their ethnic knowledges—this same inheritance of ancient Asian cultures may be evoked as a source of ethnic pride, sometimes approaching the rhetoric of cultural nationalism.

Likewise, the presence of recurrent cultural translations in Asian–Latin American cultural production should not necessarily lead us to assume that these authors, particularly when they are not first-generation immigrants, are proficient in Asian cultural and literary traditions, or that they share Chinese or Japanese worldviews. In this sense, the literary scholar Debra Lee-DiStefano warns: "The critic should be aware that culturally many Americans of Asian descent have no ties to their migratory past or pay little attention to it, whereas others are very close to it and make several efforts to keep the connection alive. Assuming cultural connections based on ethnic ties is a slippery slope because it repeats the center/margin power relationship. The critic could be extending the marginalization process, which defeats the traditional reason for the investigation" (2012, 21). For the same reason, being a Latin American of Asian descent does not necessarily prevent an author from having Eurocentric views, from sharing the same Orientalist outlook of numerous Latin American authors (either in Edward Said's sense or in a more benign one) since Rubén Darío and the *modernistas*, or even from displaying anti-Asian racial prejudice. As Kim clarifies, "periphery-periphery relations, or in this case East-South relations, cannot be understood as free of unequal dynamics. That is to say, the West as trope does not magically disappear by juxtaposing Asia to Latin America" (2017, 107).

Asian communities in Latin America have resorted to different strategies to attain the symbolic capital of cultural authenticity and belonging. One of these is to identify with indigenous populations, such as the Nahuatl in Mexico, the Guaraní in Brazil, or the Quechua in Peru. This is evident in the following passage by the Mexican historian Moisés González Navarro (1994): "Mexico was seen as a place of great hope because of its vast territories, mild climate and friendly attitude toward the Japanese, in addition to the fact that there was no racial prejudice against them. It was often said that both peoples belonged to the same ancestral family."[17] By contrast, elsewhere these communities have strived to distance themselves from other Asian ethnicities; for example, Chinese nationals in Peru, in fears of being confused as Japanese during World War II, placed Chinese flags in front of their shops and even cooperated with the US Federal Bureau of Investigation as it was deporting Japanese nationals to American internment camps—their objective was to eliminate competition and to take over Japanese shops.[18]

HISTORICAL CONTEXTUALIZATION OF JAPANESE IMMIGRATION TO MEXICO

The presence of racialized Asians in Mexico can be traced to the sixteenth century, when the global silver trade led by the yearly or biannual round-trip voyages (two or more until 1593, then one afterward) of the Manila galleons turned Mexico City into one of the most cosmopolitan places in the world. The galleon trade, which lasted from 1565 through 1815, mostly enabled the exchange of silver from Mexico and Peru (silver coins minted in Mexico became currency in East Asia) for Chinese and Japanese silk fabrics, exotic spices, porcelain, lacquer, ceramics, sculpted ivory, and other luxury products. The trade is considered one of the starting points of modern globalization, as the long commercial route linked Asia, the Americas, and Europe economically as well as culturally. Gordon and Morales maintain that "the Manila galleon provided the missing link in the world's trade network: for the first time, all the maritime routes—Atlantic, Pacific and Indian Ocean—were now operational in both directions, knitting Europe, the Americas, Asia and Africa together" (2017, 31). Along with these commodities, the galleons also transported books, art, religious artifacts, and other cultural items.

Most Filipinos arrived in Mexico either enslaved or as sailors and never returned home. The galleons would yearly bring between sixty and seventy enslaved Filipinos to the Americas (Braccio 2009, 69). Today, many Mexicans have Filipino ancestry because of that importation of humans. Reflecting this history, Mexican immigration law continues to grant special status to Filipinos (approximately 1,200 Filipino nationals reside in Mexico). Asian emigration to Mexico continues to this day, with many Chinese immigrants arriving in the early 2000s.

After the arrival of the first Chinese indentured workers, or "coolies" (originally a racial slur and today considered offensive in English) to Spanish Cuba in 1847, 250,000 unfree Chinese would be brought, often against their will or swindled, to work in quasi-slavery conditions—the same type of exploitation was also taking place in an already-independent Peru.[19] Fifty years after these workers arrived in Cuba, other Chinese immigrants would reach Mexico, but, as in Panama, for example, the majority were then free immigrants, often entrepreneurs, who nonetheless suffered oppression and persecution. With time, the suffering and death of these racialized bodies would be regarded as mere collateral damage in the framework of the nation's modernization prospects and of the economic growth that was related to global capitalism's expansion.

Fifty years after the inception of the so-called coolie trade (also known as the yellow trade), which imported Chinese contract laborers to Latin America, Japanese immigrants began to arrive in Mexico, Peru, and Brazil. The Japanese, like the Chinese in Cuba, were brought to Brazil because of that country's gradual abolition of enslaved African labor and its inability to attract or retain European farmworkers. In Peru, they replaced rural Chinese coolies, who had been steadily moving to urban areas for better conditions. Like the Chinese before them, the Japanese would make major contributions to Mexico's economy, a fact evidenced during World War II, when some local economies became bankrupted after their forced displacement mostly to Mexico City and Guadalajara but also to Cuernavaca, Puebla, Celaya, and Querétaro.[20] And as the historian Sergio Hernández Galindo elaborates in his 2011 study *La guerra contra los japoneses en México durante la Segunda Guerra Mundial* (The War against the Japanese in Mexico during World War II), other Nikkeijin, included on a blacklist elaborated by the US government, were subject to espionage or imprisoned. In one case, that of Masao Imuro, he could easily have been deported, but "apparently, the Mexican and US governments held him hostage to exchange him for citizens of the allied countries trapped in Japan when the war broke out."[21]

Since colonial times, Asian populations in some Latin American countries, whether enslaved, paid servants, contract laborers, or free immigrants, have been vulnerable targets of racialization and economic envy. They shared and inherited the Orientalist "yellow peril" stereotype as well as a Sinicization process by which they were all considered *chinos* (Chinese). However, inter- and intranational heterogeneity should not be overlooked, particularly considering that the perception of different Asian ethnicities has varied across circumstances and periods. Regarding intranational differences, a good example is the rocky relationship between recent Chinese arrivals and the more integrated second- or third-generation ethnic Chinese in Panama, and how, according to the cultural anthropologist Lok Siu, the two groups have been perceived differently. Likewise, in Peru and Brazil, immigrants from mainland Japan originally regarded Okinawans as inferior. As Lok Siu contends, "Diasporic formations are in part produced in response to the exclusionary practices of nation-states. Yet, in practice, diasporas often generate their set of own exclusions" (2007, 73).

According to the literary scholar Ana Paulina Lee, "Throughout the latter half of the nineteenth century, Chinese migrants were increasingly recognized around the world as a coolie or yellow race" (2018, 8). Indeed, even though the Chinese in Mexico were mostly free workers, the worldwide stereotype of overseas Chinese as coerced, exploitable, and disposable labor of coolieism followed them throughout. Chinese coolies inherited stigmas and labor practices associated with black African enslaved labor that, according to Lee, still survive today: "The slave trade and the forms of immigration labor that occurred in reaction to the labor shortage anticipated by abolition produced a global idea of race that persists today, especially in postslavery societies and renders clear the idea that one's relation to racialized exploitative labor determines one's access to the rights of citizenship and recognition within the ethical boundaries of the state" (2018, 9).

Nevertheless, in Mexico, these different layers of racialization did not always clearly overlap. Although Nikkeijin in Mexico inherited some of these stigmas and prejudices, overall they were not "othered" at the same level as in the rest of Latin America. In fact, in part because they were symbolically associated with modernity, progress, and even "honorary" whiteness, Japanese communities were, for the most part, better treated than Chinese ones, which were marked by negative stereotypes, often imported from the United States. This double standard is apparent, for example, in *La raza cósmica* (*The Cosmic Race*, 1925), by the influential Mexican writer, secretary of education, and 1929 presidential candidate José Vasconcelos (1882–1959):

> It is not right for populations like the Chinese, who multiply like mice under the holy counsel of Confucian morality, to come and degrade the human condition, just at that time when we start to understand that intelligence serves to curb and regulate lowly animal instincts, contrary to a truly religious concept of life ... The young ladies of San Francisco have refused to dance with Japanese navy officers, who are such neat, intelligent men and, in their own way, as handsome as those of any fleet in the world. Nevertheless, they will never understand that a Japanese can be handsome.[22]

Chinese immigrants were initially welcome in the many Mexican regions in need of cheap labor that was willing to accept miserable living and working conditions. Years later, however, they were perceived as unfair competition and became racialized as agents of moral degeneration who were corrupting the nation's racial makeup and cultural fabric. It is also worthy to note that, although numerous studies present the import of Chinese workers as a remedy for "labor shortages," in Mexico and, in reality, throughout the Americas, they often arrived to fill a gap created by the capitalist system in which plantation and mine owners, along with railway companies, were unwilling to pay Mexican workers a living wage. As a result, Chinese immigrants working for low wages tended to create resentment among Mexicans.

Although Chinese, Filipinos, Koreans, and other Asian nationalities migrated to Mexico during the colonial and postcolonial periods, this study focuses mostly on cultural production by Mexican Nikkeijin. The earliest documented presence of Japanese in Mexico takes us back to the sixteenth century, when three enslaved men, purchased in Japan and renamed Gaspar Fernandes, Miguel, and Ventura, were first taken to Manila, and then Mexico, by their owner, a man named Pérez. As Lee reveals, slave traffic was common during the Manila galleon trade: "Portuguese traders working in the *Estado da Índia* [a reference to the more than fifty Portuguese colonial holdings and outposts in Asia] aided in supplying the Manila slave market and Manila galleon trade with enslaved people from Goa, Macau, and other parts of Asia" (2018, 28).[23] In addition, Japanese delegations under Jesuit guidance visited Mexico in 1610 and 1614 with the unfulfilled goal of establishing commercial agreements with the Spanish Empire (see Chapter 6).

Regarding this topic, the Pacific studies scholar Melba Falck Reyes and historian Héctor Palacios published the biography of Juan de Páez, a Japanese man who lived in seventeenth-century New Galicia (centered on modern-day Guadalajara). Born in Osaka in 1608, Páez likely arrived in Guadalajara around the age of ten, perhaps brought by Jesuit missionaries expelled from Japan. His cultural integration was eased by his Catholic education in Japan. As majordomo of Guadalajara's cathedral, Páez was in charge, along with another man, of the tithes and finances of the bishopric. He was also executor (*albacea*) of twenty-eight prominent men, including members of the clergy (Falck and Palacios 2009, 53). These responsibilities made him one of the wealthiest merchants in Guadalajara. He owned numerous enslaved women, made important connections with the local elite, and even became godfather to several local children (Falck and Palacios 2020, 49).

Páez met Luis de Encío, a Japanese merchant who had arrived in Guadalajara around 1634. He married Encío's only daughter, Margarita, probably in 1636, and together they had nine children. Before his death, the successful Páez left money for the celebration of masses for his soul and requested that he be buried in the cathedral, also leaving funds for it. He died in 1675 at the age of sixty-nine, leaving his wife, children, and seventeen enslaved women (Falck and Palacios 2020, 62). Falck and Palacios also mention a group of Japanese men in the area during the same period. Encío, born around 1595 and perhaps a *ronin* (a wandering samurai of feudal Japan with no lord or master), was among them. His Japanese name was Fukuchi Soemon (or Hyoemon), and he was originally from the town of Fukuchi, in Sendai Prefecture. Perhaps having arrived in Acapulco as a member of the Japanese embassy (from 1613 to 1620) led by Hasekura Tsunenaga Rokuyemon, Encío decided along with some of his peers to stay in Mexico. He probably first moved to Ahuacatlán and then to Guadalajara. As the leader of this Japanese group, Encío became wealthy in 1643 thanks to his coconut wine and mescal monopoly. His economic status allowed him and his wife to adopt nine orphan children (Falck and Palacios 2020, 46). He found misfortune, though, and ended his days mired in debt and poverty, supported by Páez, who had married Encío's daughter by Catalina de Silva, an indigenous woman from Ahuacatlán. Encío's daughters, incidentally, were not allowed to become nuns because of their *defecto de sangre* (defective blood). Encío died in 1666, around the age of seventy-one, and was buried in Guadalajara's cathedral.

Moving to the twentieth century, the Mexican historian María Elena Ota Mishima, in her pioneering work *Siete migraciones japonesas en México: 1890–1978* (Seven Japanese Migrations in Mexico: 1890–1978), reveals that between 1890 and 1901, Japanese arriving in Mexico were mostly agricultural laborers and free immigrants (nearly ten thousand Japanese arrived in Mexico during those years, the highest number ever). Between 1900 and 1910, workers came under contract; between 1907 and 1924, after the signing of the 1907 Gentlemen's Agreement between Japan and the United States, undocumented immigrants arrived; between 1917 and 1928, "qualified" immigrants; between 1921 and 1940 *yobiyose* ("called over") immigrants were requested to come from Japan to work in Mexico (in the *yobiyose* system, an established immigrant could apply to the Japanese consulate to "call over" a Japanese person for work); and from 1951 to 1978, technical workers came to labor in those specialized fields. According to Ota Mishima, most of these immigrants came from Fukuoka Prefecture, on the island of Kyūshū, the southwesternmost of Japan's main islands.

In 1888, President Porfirio Díaz's Mexico became the first country in the world to sign a treaty with Japan based on reciprocal treatment, which allowed citizens from both countries to travel to the other: it was known as the Tratado de Amistad, Comercio y Navegación (Friendship, Commerce, and Navigation Treaty).[24] After Mexico became the first Latin American country to accept Japanese immigrants, arrivals began in 1897, when twenty-eight *colonos* (settlers) along with six free immigrants, financially supported by their government, emigrated to the southern state of Chiapas to grow coffee there, as part of a mission aimed at helping the Japanese economy and imperialist projects.

In 1896, the Japanese government, represented by Viscount Enomoto Takeaki (1836–1908), foreign minister and minister of education, purchased over 160,000 acres in in Escuintla, Chiapas, and created the Sociedad Colonizadora Japón-México (Japan-Mexico Colonizing Company) with the intention of developing coffee plantations, such as the one at Colonia Enomoto, for the Japanese market.[25] Other Japanese immigrated on their own and purchased land without government support. Although a small Japanese community survives in Acacoyagua, Chiapas, this first Japanese settlement in Latin America failed due in part to poor funding, economic conditions in the area, tropical diseases, and the immigrants' lack of agricultural expertise and Spanish-language skills. Overall, as Falck Reyes explains, it has been estimated that between 1888 and 1910, "about 10,000 Japanese arrived in Mexico. . . . [T]he Japanese who had arrived in the United States were subject to discriminatory laws, which encouraged their flow to Mexico."[26]

Encouraged by three different Japanese immigration companies that recruited and transported immigrants, more Japanese soon arrived in Mexico to work in mining, sugarcane production in Minatitlán and Veracruz, construction and railroads between Manzanillo and Guadalajara, and fishing in Baja California (Ota Mishima 1985, 56–57). Many, however, refused the hard work and moved to other parts in Mexico and, mostly, the United States. Additional skilled laborers—both documented and undocumented—arrived later, settling in Baja California. Despite their small numbers, the Nikkeijin eventually came to dominate cotton farming and the fishing industry in Baja California Norte (Masterson and Funada-Classen 2004, 60). Others became small business owners or small farmers, or found work in the mines and fields of Sonora and Coahuila, often showing impressive upward mobility. Before World War II, the largest Nikkei communities were in Baja California, Mexico City, and Sonora, where they worked mostly in fishing and agriculture. Their economic success, however, would be cut short when they became racialized and demonized during World War II as a "fifth column" that needed to be uprooted and controlled. As had previously happened with the Chinese, it became apparent that the Nikkei did not enjoy the full rights of Mexican citizenship.

Also as the Chinese before them, many emigrated to northern Mexico in hopes of crossing the border to the United States. Others, expelled from the United States, stayed in northern Mexico in hopes of returning illegally. Although the Nikkeijin in Mexico, like other Nikkei communities throughout the Americas, suffered discrimination, racism, and displacement, they were generally better treated than the Chinese. According to the historian Jerry García, among the reasons for their more positive experiences were the high level of social integration and mixed marriages between Japanese men and Mexican women; the friendly relations between the Mexican and Japanese governments; and the relatively small size of the community, which, unlike the Chinese community, was not seen as an economic threat.

The historians Masterson and Funada-Classen note major differences between the Nikkei experiences in Mexico and those of other Nikkei communities throughout the Americas. Among them, cultural integration in Mexico took place at a much faster pace because of the high rate of intermarriage throughout the country, except for in Baja California, where the largest community of Issei (first-generation immigrants) resided (Mexicali alone had seven hundred Japanese immigrants): "The Japanese in Mexico did not confront the growing world military crisis after 1937 as a culturally unified community, as they did in the United States and most other Latin American nations. Rather, the children of many Mexican Issei who had married native Mexicans became quickly assimilated culturally and ethnically. The same process would not occur among other Japanese communities in Latin America until the Sansei or Yonsei, third or fourth generations" (Masterson and Funada-Classen 2004, 63). Among the reasons for the smaller number of Japanese in Mexico, Masterson and Funada-Classen list Washington's pressure on restricting Japanese immigration to Mexico, the Mexican Revolution (10 percent of Japanese left the country—Japanese, though, were not specifically targeted as the Chinese were), and further immigration restrictions during the Great Depression.

Japanese immigrants likely endured less oppression than Chinese immigrants because of the international prestige attained by the Empire of Japan after its 1905 military defeat of the Russian Empire. To many Mexicans, this military prowess made Japanese immigrants ideal soldiers: "Most of the revolutionary factions welcomed with open arms any Japanese male who wanted to fight within their ranks based on the belief that all Japanese had been trained as imperial soldiers" (García 2014, 187). Moreover, the symbolic capital provided by Japan's imperial possessions and armed victory over Russia "imbued [the Japanese] with elements of whiteness, due to a perception that Japan not only reached parity with Western military powers but also defeated them, thus placing them on par with the West" (García 2014, 186).

Consequently, many Nikkeijin participated as combatants, mercenaries, and spies, and many suffered casualties during the Mexican Revolution, including two who were allegedly hired by the United States to poison the revolutionary leader Francisco "Pancho" Villa but failed in their attempt. According to Masterson and Funada-Classen, 20 percent of the Issei in Coahuila reportedly became soldiers "because they had no other means of survival" (2004, 59). Yet today the descendants of these Nikkeijin, some twenty thousand in Mexico of the more than 3.6 million worldwide, strategically claim recognition for their heroic and patriotic efforts, just as Chinese Cubans do for their ancestors' participation in the War of Independence. For example, Fusaichi Otakara's grandson, Ricardo Pérez Otakara, states that the more than one hundred Japanese immigrants who took part in the revolution "enhanced the uprising with their anonymous bravery and heroism."[27]

According to the political scientist Satomi Miura, the Nikkei press appeared in Peru, Brazil, and Argentina about ten years after the first arrival of Japanese immigrants to those countries. By contrast, because of their smaller numbers, it took the Nikkei community in Mexico until 1925, twenty-eight years, to publish its first newspaper. Other newspapers appeared later: "In Mexico, a total of four Japanese newspapers were published between 1925 and 1941: the *Nichiboku Shimbum*, the *Mehiko Shimpō*, the *Mekishiko Shimpō*, and the *Mehiko Jihō*. It is possible that there was one more in Veracruz in 1935."[28]

Japanese immigration ceased during World War II. After the FBI spread rumors about a purported Japanese Imperial Navy landing and Japan's plan to take over several Latin American countries, Peru, for example, was happy to rid itself of its Japanese residents (of the 2,118 Japanese nationals deported from Latin America to the United States, 1,800 hailed from Peru). With the pretext of national security, the US government asked several Latin American nations to deport the leaders of their local Japanese communities to American internment camps. After breaking diplomatic ties with Japan in 1941, Mexico did not accommodate the American request to send Japanese residents to US internment camps. According to Hernández Galindo, then general Lázaro Cárdenas's opposition to deporting Nikkeijin influenced President Manuel Ávila Camacho (2011, 58). Instead, the Mexican government relocated them, including those who were naturalized citizens, from its Pacific coastal areas and the US border to Mexico City, Guadalajara, and other cities. Some were placed in designated areas or quasi-internment camps that had no barbed wires or soldiers, unlike internment camps in the United States.²⁹ The idea was to prevent the perceived threat of a potential fifth column that could carry out espionage, sabotage, and contraband within Mexico's national borders.

Indeed, from the inception of the immigration process, the Japanese Mexican experience was marked by the United States' proximity (a pull factor) and political influence. The Japanese government's self-imposed 1907 Gentlemen's Agreement, enacted to avoid the humiliation of a potential Japanese exclusion act similar to the one previously imposed on the Chinese in the United States, opened the door to Japanese emigration to Mexico (uninterrupted until the beginning of the Mexican Revolution in 1910, although Japan agreed to limit the number of passports to Mexico) and to other Latin American countries, like Peru and Brazil. The process was facilitated by cordial relations between Mexico and the Empire of Japan until after the attack on Pearl Harbor, when the Mexican government broke off diplomatic relations, despite the ostensible lack of support for doing so from the Mexican population. As is well known, most Japanese immigrants settled in the northern states of Mexico, not only attracted by jobs in mining, agriculture, commerce, and fishing, but also because of the proximity to the US border that enabled them to cross without authorization.

From the United States also came the "impact of hemispheric Orientalism" (García 2014, 28): Japanese immigrants inherited from Chinese immigrants a "yellow peril" prejudice that was disseminated in Latin America by US propaganda, and as a result, they began to be perceived as an inassimilable potential fifth column. Likewise, US antimiscegenation laws contributed to further damaging of the image of Mexico's Japanese community. Yet despite American political influence, the Mexican government initially challenged US hegemony by maintaining friendly diplomatic relations with Japan and refusing to send Japanese nationals in Mexico to US internment camps, as Peru and other countries did. In García's words, "Although Mexico denied any alliance with the Japanese empire, it nevertheless used the deteriorating Japanese-US relations as leverage to antagonize the United States as an early form of diplomatic weapons of the weak" (2014, 187). This attitude made the American government "question the position of Mexico in the event that Japan and the United States went to war" (García 2014, 39). Overall, despite the small number of Japanese immigrants in Mexico during World War II, US officials fomented generalized hysteria about "sleeper cells" and a potential fifth column of Japanese soldiers disguised as civilian immigrants in northern Mexico, and they exaggerated the number of Japanese who had illegally crossed into the United States. According to Hernández Galindo, their goal was to "justify discriminatory and repressive measures against migrants and to frighten the population into joining the fight against Japan."[30]

Although the Japanese were not deported to the United States, they were indeed displaced within Mexico. Aggravating the situation, the Mexican government never covered their transportation expenses for the forced removal or gave them any compensation after the war, although their frozen assets were returned. The Japanese community then purchased properties like the former Hacienda Temixco, near Cuernavaca, to house the nearly 3,500 displaced Japanese. In the end, many Japanese Mexicans were left displaced, separated from their families and businesses, homeless, unemployed, and without government protection.[31] Although later their houses and possessions were returned to them (some before 1945), many lost their properties or chose to stay in Mexico City or Guadalajara. As in other Latin American countries, including Peru and Brazil, the different treatment afforded in Mexico to citizens from the Axis powers during the presidency of the conservative Ávila Camacho from 1940 to 1946 reveals the level to which Nikkeijin were racialized. The borderlands historian Selfa A. Chew makes it known that "the relocation program was a racist project: it demanded the exclusive eviction of persons who were racially defined as Japanese, regardless of their nationality. While the Mexican government also evicted several German and Italian men from the borderlands, it did so considering each case on a personal basis, not to be uniformly handled based on membership in an ethnic or racialized group" (2015, 7–8). In her *Mudas las garzas* (*Silent Herons*, 2007), however, Chew offers a humorous case of Nikkei resistance to this forced relocation: "All these Japanese men had been ordered into confinement in Guadalajara, but disobeying the order, they fled toward the sierra . . . in San Rafael, Chihuahua, there is a sick Japanese man, who has lived there for twenty-five years, and he's willing to follow the relocations orders as soon as he gets well" (2012, 51). In keeping with this resistant attitude, some Nikkei communities, like the one in Chiapas, refused to participate in the exodus and managed to convince the state's government to support their extended stay. This was possible because, as Chew observes, the United States had no interest in the Mexico-Guatemala border (2015, 47).

Other Nikkei communities acquiesced to the Mexican government's demands. García reveals that because the government never provided economic or logistical support for the forced removal, the Nikkei community funded and organized it under the leadership of the Comité Japonés de Ayuda Mutua (Japanese Committee of Mutual Aid): "Minister Miura gave specific instructions to Matsumoto, Kato, and Tsuru that they were to protect the interests of the Japanese residing in Mexico. With the Mexican government's permission, assistance from the Japanese minister to Mexico, private Japanese donations, and the ex-members of the Mexico City, Mexicali, Tijuana, and Ensenada Japanese associations, the relief society CJAM was founded in January 1942" (168). According to García, the relocation experience ended up reinforcing Nikkei ethnic identity in Mexico. After the war, the leaders of the Japanese community who had coordinated the relocation process founded the Asociación México Japonesa (Japanese Mexican Association), which is still active today. The Nikkeijin, however, became divided between those who accepted Japan's defeat and those who refused to accept Japan's surrender (including Nakatani, the memoirist discussed in Chapter 2). Unlike in Brazil, however, the deniers, a small minority, never became violent.[32]

Across Latin America, after World War II, many of those Japanese who had planned to return to their homeland decided to stay, as Japan was devastated. Still, Mexico's official 1940 census recorded only 1,550 Japanese nationals in the country, although according to García, "nearly 6,000 Japanese nationals and 13,000 Mexicans of Japanese ancestry resided in Mexico on the eve of Pearl Harbor" (2014, 109). More recent Japanese immigration to Mexico has been associated with the presence of Japanese companies there. An estimated thirty thousand persons of Japanese ancestry currently live in Mexico, making it the fourth-largest Nikkei community in Latin America.

THE STUDY OF ASIANS IN MEXICO

The study of the Asian and Asian–Latin American presence, heritage, and cultural production in Latin America and the Caribbean, which may be included within broader transpacific studies, is an emerging academic field. Numerous books, articles, journal issues, dissertations, conferences, symposia, workshops, and new journals have been devoted to these topics in recent years. Several factors have contributed to the growing prominence of Asian and Asian-descended communities in Latin America and the Caribbean. Japan's international prestige first as a powerful Asian nation with an expanding empire and, after the postwar period, as an economic powerhouse, improved the image and self-esteem of Nikkei communities in Mexico and the Americas. Similarly, the emergence of the People's Republic of China as an economic and military superpower has brought renewed attention to the role and sociopolitical weight of Sino–Latin American communities as potentially strategic intermediaries in building links and trade relations with China. Globalization, therefore, has improved these

Asian communities' self-esteem and should also bring renewed attention to their cultural production.

While the significant Asian presence and heritage in Mexico was long understudied, this regrettable situation has dramatically changed in recent years with the publication of several books, in both Spanish and English, that have followed pioneering works by historians like María Elena Ota Mishima. In the history field alone, five English-language histories of the Chinese community in Mexico were published in seven years: Robert Chao Romero's *The Chinese in Mexico 1882–1940* (2010), Grace Peña Delgado's *Making the Chinese Mexican: Global Migration, Localism, and Exclusions in the US-Mexico Borderlands* (2012), Julia María Schiavone Camacho's *Chinese Mexicans: Transpacific Migration and the Search for a Homeland 1910–1960* (2012), Jason Oliver Chang's *Chino: Anti-Chinese Racism in Mexico, 1880–1940* (2017), and Fredy González's *Paisanos Chinos: Transpacific Politics among Chinese Immigrants in Mexico* (2017). During the same period, two more historical studies dedicated to the Nikkei community were published: Jerry García's *Looking like the Enemy: Japanese Mexicans, the Mexican State, and US Hegemony, 1897–1945* (2014) and Selfa A. Chew's *Uprooting Community: Japanese Americans, World War II, and the US-Mexico Borderlands* (2015). And one more focused on Asian slavery in New Spain: Tatiana Seijas's *Asian Slaves in Colonial Mexico: From Chinos to Indians* (2014).

Several other books have been recently published in Spanish, including José Luis Chong's *Historia general de los chinos en México, 1575–1975* (General History of the Chinese in Mexico; 2014); Gerardo Lara Cisneros's *¿Ignorancia invencible? Superstición e idolatría ante el provisorato de indios y chinos del arzobispado de México en el siglo XVII* (Invincible Ignorance? Superstition and Idolatry before the Provisorato of Indians and Chinese of the Archbishopric of Mexico in the Seventeenth Century; 2014); *Un episodio de la renovada relación México-China: Los primeros estudiantes chinos en México, 1974–1984* (An Episode of the Renewed Mexico-China Relationship: The First Chinese Students in Mexico, 1974–1984; 2014), edited by Omar Martínez Legorreta; *El japonés que conquistó Guadalajara* (The Japanese Man Who Conquered Guadalajara; 2009), edited by Omar Martínez Legorreta, Melba Falck Reyes and Héctor Palacios; *Presencia japonesa en Jalisco* (Japanese Presence in Jalisco; 2020), edited by Melba Falck Reyes; Sergio Hernández Galindo's *La guerra contra los japoneses en México durante la Segunda Guerra Mundial: Kiso Tsuru y Masao Imuro, migrantes vigilados*; and Daniel Salinas Basave's *El samurái de la Graflex: De enfermero de Villa a cronista fotográfico de Tijuana* (The Samurai of the Graflex: From Villa's Nurse to Tijuana's Photographic Chronicler; 2019).

Relatedly, the literary scholar Laura J. Torres-Rodríguez's *Orientaciones transpacíficas: La modernidad mexicana y el espectro de Asia* (Transpacific Orientations: Mexican Modernity and the Asian Spectrum; 2019) rewrites Mexican intellectual history. The book traces how, starting with *modernistas* like José Juan Tablada, twentieth- and twenty-first-century Mexican intelligentsia turned their gaze to colonial India and to Japan in a fruitful transpacific dialogue that came to replace the traditional transatlantic orientation in their search for new paths to a Mexican cultural modernity. Whereas *Orientaciones transpacíficas* explores how Mexican intellectuals and artists found in South and East Asia a mirror in which they saw themselves, this present book attempts to complement Torres-Rodríguez's research by focusing on how the same intelligentsia tended to erase the "Asia within" its own national borders. This erasure has improved in recent years thanks to the publication of a few works by Asian Mexicans and the abovementioned academic books, all of which focus on Asian Mexican communities. Indeed, the Mexican intelligentsia did not seek inspiration from local Asian communities, even though those communities presumably also possessed the ancestral knowledge that was so admired in Asian cultures from South and East Asia and often explored through the mediation of Western intellectuals. Therefore, this triangulation of "Asian" knowledge allowed for Europe to still display its capacity for mediation and remain the hegemonic center of cultural capital.[33]

The Mexican Transpacific mainly examines the contributions made by Nikkei immigrants and their descendants to Mexican culture, along with how they have been silenced, often through a discourse of *mestizaje* that is known to have been a veiled effort at imposing Eurocentric worldviews—José Vasconcelos's imagined *raza cósmica*, for example, left out people of Asian and African descent. This book also contrasts, through the study of Nikkei cultural production, the experiences of different Asian communities in Mexico, with particular emphasis on those living near the US border. At the same time, it takes a hemispheric approach by contrasting the experience of Asian communities in Mexico with those across Latin America and the Caribbean.

IMMIGRANT JAPANESE AND NIKKEI MEXICAN WRITING

Nikkei Mexican writing, which includes immigrant Japanese literature written in Spanish or Japanese either in Mexico or on the way to Mexico, is a literary corpus that responds to and reflects the specific ethnocultural experiences of Japanese immigrants and their descendants. Regarding Issei writing, I argue that, whether in Spanish or Japanese, it belongs simultaneously to two fields, Latin American literature and Japanese literature. More important, a transpacific, Asian–Latin American approach is most efficient for studying and understanding all these intricacies. Much like other Latin American ethnic literatures (indigenous, African, Chinese, Jewish, Arab), Nikkei Mexican literature, and by extension Nikkei Latin American literature, is part of Latin American writing. In fact, one of its main attributes is that it broadens our understanding of the Latin American sociocultural experience.

Nikkei Mexican writing has commonalities with other Nikkei Latin American literatures, but it also displays its own traits and symbols, such as the use of the Popocatépetl volcano as a metonymic extension of Mount Fuji. It is also important to recognize that Nikkei Mexican writing, in Spanish or Japanese, is an intrinsic part of Mexican and Latin American literatures because it contributes to the discourses of Mexican and Nikkei Mexican identity formation, as well as to definitions of Mexicanness and Latin Americanness. Moreover, as the next chapters make it clear, one cannot speak of a cohesive Nikkei Mexican identity; instead, there are different, heterogenous identities influenced by various factors, including gender and generation.

Nikkei writing in Mexico speaks to the specificities of a diasporic mentality: writers tend to share their memories of a distant or ancestral homeland that is real, idealized, or transformed by temporal and geographical distance, depending on level of contact with the sending communities back home. This same distance may lead overseas Japanese to keep loyalties to both homeland and receiving society, or even to switch loyalties when the sojourner mentality vanishes after it becomes apparent that return is unlikely. In this sense, Lok Siu, in referring to communities of Chinese descent in Panama, signals: "It is precisely this dual relationship, this tension between 'where you are at' versus 'where you are from' that constitutes the condition and the idea of diaspora and gives diasporic identification the potential to be empowering as well as disempowering" (2007, 76).

Along these lines, the cultural studies scholar Ien Ang argues that the diaspora "can be the site of both support or oppression, emancipation and confinement" (2001, 12). These different reactions to diasporic contexts are often reflected in immigrant writing. Ethnic enclaves, including residential and business areas such as Chinatowns and Little Tokyos, are often represented as a refuge from racialization and marginalization by mainstream society. However, even though in their fictional communities Asian languages and customs are welcome and encouraged, Asian characters may still see their own communities as sites of family self-exploitation (overworking and/or forcing relatives to overwork).³⁴ In other cases, ethnoburbs are considered a prison, as they prevent proper social integration into mainstream society. This is evident in Federico (Sekio) Imamura's (1910–) biography *Casi un siglo de recuerdos: Biografía de Federico Imamura* (Almost a Century of Memories: Biography of Federico Imamura, 1994), written by Antonio Murray, in which Imamura describes the exploitation that he and other immigrants suffered at the hands of a fellow immigrant: "Mr. Baba, our own countryman, took advantage of our helplessness and our need because, as I said, we could only enter the country if we had a permit and a job offer . . . exploiting several young Japanese who worked for him, he was undoubtedly making a good income, since he paid us neither salary nor benefits. We were trapped."³⁵ In this regard: "While being diasporic complicates the terms and practices of belonging, it also holds the promise of belonging to multiple communities. Similarly, while it facilitates the ability to identify with and draw on the cultural resources of several communities at once, it also means subjection to the multiple, overlapping, and sometimes opposing demands of these entities" (Siu 2007, 6).

Japanese Mexican cultural production reflects the evolution from an insular, sojourner mentality (before World War II most Nikkeijin in Latin America were convinced that they would be able to return to Japan) to a slow process of cultural integration into mainstream society. As one would expect, newer generations become less attached to Japanese customs and languages—including Japanese (*Nihongo*) and Okinawan (Uchināguchi)—increasingly negotiating national loyalties and cultural identities or simply identifying as Mexicans. This heterogeneity and fluidity of identity layers demonstrate that we must speak about multiple Asian and Nikkei identities in Mexico, rather than about a single one. In some cases, Nikkei persons or fictional characters may change their ethnocultural and national identification over time or simply have multiple public and private identities at one time. The identity-related processes of transculturation may be painful, as some Nikkei people and, as a reflection of their experience, also fictional characters endure nativism or Nipponophobia from mainstream society, in addition to family self-exploitation, xenophobia, and racism within their own ethnic communities.

As it happens in the rest of Latin America, the Nikkeijin in Mexico sometimes use their writing as a therapeutic tool for self-exploration or as a tactic not only to historicize their experience and cultural memory but also to inscribe their belonging to the national imaginary. Some of their texts reflect the processes of racial formation and racialization endured by

Japanese immigrants, whose different phenotype and strange customs (to Mexicans) have drawn the attention of mainstream society in different ways throughout the decades.

Remembering and re-membering—in the sense of regrouping, both metaphorically and physically—play a key role in Nikkei writing. Metaphorically, because the writing puts together again those consciousnesses disrupted or dispersed by migration and internal colonialism; physically, because of the forced displacement and internment of Nikkeijin living in border areas or on the Pacific coast during World War II and their eventual regrouping in Mexico City and Guadalajara. In this sense, Roshni Rustomji sees dismemberment as an effective colonization tool often used by the British in India: "I consider the attempts at dis-memberment and splintering of lands, cultures, races, ethnic groups, socio-economic classes, genders, and generations to be at the core of the processes of colonization. This dis-memberment is both literal and figurative and it exists not only within specific lands, communities, individuals, but also between different colonized lands, peoples, individuals" (2012, 24).

This is, however, as much a matter of spatial dismemberment (e.g., displacement, deportation) as it is a temporal matter: one finds traces of a disarticulated past in our present. For instance, during the 1990 presidential elections, most Japanese Peruvians refused to vote for Alberto Fujimori for fear that the Nipponophobia and looting of the 1940s would resurface. The fact that, unlike Asian communities in the United States, Asian communities in Latin America tend to hide (as is evident in their museums) episodes of racism and xenophobia, including deportation, looting, and massacres, may truly speak to these repressed anxieties emerging from haunting pasts. It is an emotional reaction to a perceived threat identifiable in the community's past. In the theorist Sara Ahmed's words, "The anxiety of the possibility of loss becomes displaced onto objects of fear, which seem to present themselves from the outside as dangers that could be avoided" (2015, 67). In Mexico's case, Japanese displacement, internment, and the hasty sale of their property (and, in a few cases, also imprisonment in Perote prison and deportation during World War II) are all scars of a punishing past. Thus, Rustomji reminds us of the paramount value of re-membering, among other things, to form alliances: "Re-membering— again without romanticism or sentimentalism—as a regaining not only a sense of who we were, but also as who we are and who we decide we need and want to be beyond being other-identified, constructed by others. Re-membering as also—and more importantly—the forming of alliances, creating communities between people who may not share similar geographies but definitely share histories and experiences of colonization and of resistance to colonization" (2012, 24).

Japanese Mexican writing is an essential component of this re-membering process. Narrating or poeticizing life experiences can heal immigrants and their descendants not only by drawing on memory but also by resorting to amnesia and denial, that is, "forgetting" in their writing those painful episodes that made cultural integration more difficult. The memories transcribed on paper do not always completely adhere to actual events but instead are refractive, selective, and partial, leaving aside, as is typical of first-person accounts, episodes susceptible to damaging the image of the authors or their communities. However, in rare cases, such as Issei Yoshigei (Carlos) Nakatani's memoirs (analyzed in Chapter 2), the author has no qualms about admitting his shortcomings and the suffering he brought to people close to him, even if there is also clear emphasis on his generosity toward others and the positive outcome of his lifelong efforts.

Forgetting is, indeed, an intrinsic part of remembering. While transforming or even inventing historical facts, forgetting still helps the coherence and interpretation of the narrative in process. This narrative of a memory, once articulated as story and shared, becomes the social memory of an ethnic community. Benedict Anderson, in the second edition of his seminal *Imagined Communities* (1983), discusses how nations consciously and unconsciously create a shared past through both memory and forgetting. Quoting the French Orientalist Ernest Renan's essay "Qu'est-ce que une nation?" (What Is a Nation?), Anderson reminds us that having a nation involves agreeing to "remember" certain legitimating events, such as victories and myths of origin, but also forgetting other events, like defeats, slavery, and the destruction of indigenous communities: "All profound changes in consciousness, by their very nature, bring with them characteristic amnesias" (2006, 204). Both collective memory and amnesia are therefore the core of the construction of nations and also the shared identities of ethnic communities.

The purpose of the present study is precisely to fill in those conscious or subconscious silences in Japanese Mexican narratives, as well as to expose the erasure of Asian Mexicans from official discourses and historical memories, including Mexican history books and textbooks. Undeniably, Asian communities continue to be viewed as outsiders, as not belonging to the country's makeup, and the COVID-19 pandemic contributed to reinforcing negative, racialized stereotypes about them. Yet although the Mexican census does not count the Asian population, it has been estimated that there are about twenty thousand Mexicans of Japanese ancestry, forty thousand of Chinese ancestry, and—in the Yucatán Peninsula alone—between thirty thousand and forty thousand of Korean ancestry. The denial of diversity among Mexican populations and these blanks in Mexican history have otherized Asian Mexicans, rendering invisible their important economic and cultural contributions.

Memoirists like Nakatani truly try to find meaning in or closure to their life experience through narrating real-life events in a way that appears coherent and believable. The critic interprets, therefore, what is always-already an interpretation of retrieved memories of experiences. In this sense:

> Forgetting is a necessary component in the construction of memory. Yet the forgetting of the past in a culture is often highly organized and strategic . . . cultures can also participate in a "strategic" forgetting of painful events that may be too dangerous to keep in active memory. At the same time, all cultural memory and all history are forged in a context in which details, voices, and impressions of the past are forgotten. The writing of a historical narrative necessarily involves the elimination of certain elements . . . A desire for coherence and continuity produces forgetting. (Sturken 1997, 7–8)

This "strategic forgetting" is consequently a major component of the forging and interpreting of collective cultural memories as recollected by ethnic groups such as Japanese Mexicans. Just like the cultural memory of the nation has often erased the presence of Asian communities, regardless of their impact on the economy and culture, so do individual authors select what must be remembered.

Literature is a type of representation that blocks certain memories, leaving readers without access to them; therefore, it simultaneously represents and hides life events. Regardless of how accurate or true the memories recollected in cultural production by Japanese Mexicans are, my interest here is the effect that these interpretations of the past produce on the reader or viewer, together with the sociopolitical implications they have or intend to have. Consequently, my focus is not on the historical events themselves, but on how Nikkei communities and mainstream Mexican society remember the past through writing, visual art, and performance. Thus, Nikkei narratives participate in the production of a historical memory that contributes to cultural integration and the creation of ethnocultural identities. What do these texts tell us about Japanese Mexican self-definition? What do texts written by Mexican authors who are not of Asian ancestry tell us about the changing perceptions of the Japanese and their descendants in the country? What do both tell us about Mexican national identity? How are past interpretations (by media, politicians, and popular culture) of the presence of Nikkei communities in Mexico related to current ones?

This book also explores whether Japanese Mexican writing exhibits particularities that differentiate it from the rest of Mexican cultural production. In spite of the numerous recent studies on the Asian presence in Mexico, Asians' cultural production, a main indicator of how these communities perceive themselves and want to be perceived, remains understudied. Its importance rests on the fact that it can work as an instrument for self-empowerment, thus providing agency and voice to traditionally silenced communities. It also veers the official discourse on mestizaje toward a more transnational, transpacific outlook. Asian Mexicans' cultural self-representations, including issues related to migration, diaspora, cultural integration, cultural nationalism, self-Orientalization, and hybridity, historicize their experience, which has been silenced and undertheorized until recently. They also provide a different historical understanding of modernity and nation building in Mexico, one from the perspective of a capitalist discourse on modernization that demanded cheap labor for plantations, mines, railroad construction, and US and British enterprises under the protection of then-dictator Porfirio Díaz. In addition, this corpus of works problematizes and redefines notions of race in Mexico and Latin America in general.

Japanese characters also appear in works by Mexican authors who are not of Asian ancestry. Together, the diasporic cultural production by Nikkei authors and artists on the one hand, and majority Mexicans about Japanese characters and issues on the other hand, complement historical, sociological, and anthropological studies on the topic, ultimately carrying out a collective retrieval of the social memory of Japanese Mexicans. These representational practices articulate a cultural history of the Nikkei diaspora in Mexico. They also shape the uninterrupted history of the cultural construction and circulation of ideas about Japaneseness and other discourses of Asianness in Mexico, as affected by historical events, state-sponsored cultural nationalism, and pseudoscientific racial theories such as late nineteenth-century social Darwinism (as applied to sociology, the wealth and power of the strong increase while those of the weak decrease) and 1920s eugenics, which contributed to preventing Asians from attaining full citizenship rights. In addition, this cultural production retrieves global circuits and transpacific accounts of how the resilient, diasporic, Nikkei populations in Mexico managed to maintain fruitful connections with their homeland and survive despite widespread oppression and internal colonialism.

The case studies in this book mostly employ a life-writing methodology that enables readers to move from the personal to the collective in understanding the impressive contributions of Japanese immigrants and their descendants to Mexican identity and society. Not only the trials and tribulations shared by the protagonists, but also the significant differences marked by gender, time period, and personal motivations for emigration, provide a framework to envision the richness and heterogeneity of Japanese Mexican cultural production and its significance, allowing us to fully understand the Nikkei experience in Mexico. Whereas the first two chapters explicitly deal with memoirs, much of the content in the remaining chapters, which explore poetry, manga, painting, and theater, draws from an (auto)biographical focus. For example, in the chapter analyzing the tanka poetry of Mitsuko Esperanza Kasuga, pen name "Akane," her biographical experiences as a picture bride (a term referring to the early twentieth-century practice among Japanese, Okinawan, and Korean migrant workers of obtaining brides living in the same region whence they came) and economic emigrant, provided by several relatives in the prefaces to her poetry collections, work with the historical context (forced displacement during World War II) to clarify the aspirations and frustrations suggested in her lyrical discourse. Collectively, this (auto)biographical discourse by and about a selected group of Japanese Mexicans offers, through literature and visual and performance arts, an eye-opening window to this transnational ethnic group's fascinating cultural history.

Beyond the subfield of Asian Latin American cultural production, this book adds a new dimension—the Asian–Latin American perspective—to previous life-writing studies, such as Silvia Molloy's *At Face Value: Autobiographical Writing in Spanish America* (1991) and Sergio R. Franco's *Autobiographical Writing in Latin America: Folds of the Self* (2017). As Franco explains, autobiographical expression includes different modalities besides autobiography, including "causeries, diaries, memoirs and reminiscences of various kinds" (2017, xi). In this context, the first two chapters of this book differ in the sense that, whereas the initial one treats Nonaka's memoir (focusing exclusively on his experiences during the Mexican Revolution), the other analyzes Nakatani's (plural) memoirs that cover his entire life. Most of Akane's production also deals with "writing the self" (to use the title of Peter Heeh's book) but through a lyrical approach. Another major difference between Akane's poetry and the aforementioned memoirs is that, in her case, the time elapsed between her real-life experiences and their lyrical rendering is typically much shorter, thereby making the types of distortions of referential truth that typically appear in autobiographies and memoirs less likely. Likewise, the life experiences of the group of Japanese pioneers who emigrated to Chiapas, re-created in the manga *Los samuráis de México* (see Chapter 4), were not written or illustrated by them; rather, their life story is mediated by two separate filters: the manga authors and the Nikkei descendants they interviewed. In Chapters 5 and 6, Nishizawa's visual art and Akiko's performance art are better understood in the context of their bicultural upbringing and transpacific experiences.

As is the case with most autobiographical expression, these works are necessarily selective and subjective reinterpretations of memories and recollections of a past that becomes resignified upon being filtered by the temporal perspective and, at times, by the suppression of painful or traumatic experiences. In this sense, narrative silences (e.g., Nonaka's refusal to write about his forced relocation from Tijuana after the Pearl Harbor attack even though he was a decorated veteran of the Mexican Revolution) may be as significant as the climactic point in a life story. Therefore, the sometimes contradictory writerly "I" represented in the text (e.g., Nakatani's sense of accomplishment toward the end of his memoirs and his ambiguous attempt to present himself as a model Japanese immigrant in striking contrast with his lifelong sporadic unethical behavior) may significantly vary from the real-life persons and the real-life experiences surrounding them.

Finally, the self-examination displayed in these life-writing examples suggests a certain individualism rarely attributed to Japanese identity and culture, one that is often (self-)described as a group-oriented society, perhaps as a result of the stereotypical assumptions propagated by Nihonjinron discourse (explained in Chapter 2).

THE BOOK AND ITS ORGANIZATION

Divided into three chapters, the first part, "Immigrant, Literary Negotiations of National Identity," focuses on the literary representation of processes of becoming Mexican in Japanese immigrant literature. Chapter 1, "Nonaka's Memoir: From Captain in the Mexican Revolution to Enemy of the State," is dedicated to the memoir by Kingo Nonaka, titled *Kingo Nonaka: Andanzas revolucionarias* (Kingo Nonaka: Revolutionary Adventures, 2014). Nonaka was an Issei who served as a nurse and captain under Francisco Madero and Pancho Villa during the Mexican Revolution but was later banished as the Nikkei community was under suspicion of potentially hiding spies. I call it a memoir with emphasis on the singular because it focuses on one aspect and time of his life: his participation in the Mexican Revolution. However, beyond that experience, in one of his many lives, Nonaka became Tijuana's first documentary photographer, leaving an invaluable pictorial legacy of the civil life of the fledging city. The analysis of Nonaka's memoir is complemented by the study of Shinpei Takeda's short documentary *El México más cercano a Japón* (*The Mexico Closest to Japan*, 2008) and Daniel Salinas Basave's *El samurái de la Graflex: De enfermero de Villa a cronista fotográfico de Tijuana*, both based on Nonaka's life.

The second chapter, "Challenges to Nihonjinron in Nakatani's Memoirs," studies the Issei Yoshigei (Carlos) Nakatani's unpublished autobiography "Novela escrita por Carlos Nakatani: Historia de su propia vida" (Novel Written by Carlos Nakatani. Story of His Own Life Story) that he began to write at age sixty-five. In it, he recalls his life experiences in Japan and Mexico. These memoirs, which show a turn from worse to better, are an important window to the social history of both Mexico and Japan during the twentieth century and a testimony to the (sometimes surprising) behavior of the small but visible Japanese community in Mexico. These memoirs, in plural, cover his entire life.

As the transpacific studies scholar Denise Cruz points out: "Given the centrality of a feminized, exotic East to the history of imperial expansion, gender has, for quite some time, been absolutely critical to the histories and cultures of the trans-Pacific. . . . Gendered examinations of the trans-Pacific world offer an opportunity to work against the binaried, heteronormative divisions of the East-West framework that have long been essential to the involvement of Europe and North America in Asia and the Pacific" (2017, 10–11). From this perspective, two chapters in this book focus on works by Nikkei women and on how they have contributed to feminizing a traditionally male discourse. Chapter 3, "Strategic Essentialism in Akane's Performative *Tanka*," is devoted to the eloquent tanka poetry of "Akane," the Issei Mitsuko Kasuga. Some of her poems were inspired by her family's forced relocation to Mexico City during World War II, the passing of her Japanese husband Tsutomu Kasuga, and her progressive identification with Mexico and its culture.

In part 2, "Japanese Mexican Visual and Performance Arts," Chapter 4, "Resignifying *Yamato-damashii* and Utopian Socialism in the Manga *Los samuráis de México*," centers on narration of the Enomoto colony's experience as delivered in this manga. It explores the rhetorical maneuver of resemanticizing the xenophobic, ultranationalist, Nihonjinron concept of *Yamato-damashii* (Japanese spirit or the soul of old Japan). Even though throughout Latin America the Nikkeijin tended not to present themselves as anticolonial or leftists, several of the pioneer Issei who went to Chiapas were socialist Christians trying to escape Japanese imperialism, just like those Japanese immigrants in Brazil portrayed in Karen Tei Yamashita's 1992 novel *Brazil Maru*.

Chapter 5, "Nishizawa's Bicultural Dialectics and the Critical Stereotyping of His Art," is devoted to the Japanese Mexican artist Luis Nishizawa Flores (1918–2014), known for his landscapes of volcanos, mountains, and the arid valleys of Central Mexico, along with his murals, including those made using ceramics, which often show Japanese and Mexican influences. It also examines critical overstatements of Japanese influences in his art as a common misconception when analyzing Nikkei-Latin American cultural production.

Chapter 6, "The Transpacific in Akiko's Theatrical Performance," returns to the feminization of the Japanese Mexican discourse. It analyzes, from the perspective of transpacific studies, how Irene Akiko Iida has contributed to a transpacific understanding between Mexican and Japanese cultures. The celebration of the first Japanese commercial delegation to colonial Mexico, the "return" of a Nikkeijin to Japan during World War II, the Mexicanization of Japanese cultural practices, including traditional theater, dance, and music—in all this the main common thread in her performance art is the search for transpacific cultural commonalities.

These six chapters, therefore, analyze case studies of Nikkei cultural production and the Nikkei presence and heritage in Mexico from 1906 until today. Some are complemented with sympathetic texts on the Nikkeijin published by Mexican authors who are not of Nikkei ancestry. Together, these works shed light on the arduous process of cultural integration into mainstream Mexican society and the heterogeneity of this social group.

Part I. Immigrant, Literary Negotiations of National Identity

CHAPTER 1

Nonaka's Memoir

From Captain in the Mexican Revolution to Enemy of the State

This chapter focuses on the experiences of the Issei José Genaro Kingo Nonaka (born Nonaka Kingo; 1889–1977), as detailed in three works: *Kingo Nonaka: Andanzas revolucionarias* (Kingo Nonaka: Revolutionary Adventures, 2014), his recollections of his revolutionary experience, edited by his son Genaro Nonaka García (1930–); the Japanese filmmaker Shinpei Takeda's documentary film *El México más cercano a Japón* (*The Mexico Closest to Japan*, 2008);[1] and the Mexican journalist Daniel Salinas Basave's (1974–) *El samurái de la Graflex: De enfermero de Villa a cronista fotográfico de Tijuana* (The Samurai of the Graflex: From Villa's Nurse to Tijuana's Photo Chronicler, 2019).[2]

One of the most famous visual icons of Mexico and its revolution is the photograph of Francisco "Pancho" Villa, the revolutionary general and leader of the legendary Northern Division, on horseback. The photo was taken after the ten days of fighting in April 1914 to take Torreón, Coahuila. Daniel Salinas Basave notes that, in the photo's background is discernible the twenty-four-year-old Japanese immigrant and self-taught nurse Nonaka, leading a mule-drawn ambulance (2019, 19). This army nurse would leave a mark not only in front of the camera but also, and equally important, behind it.

Other Japanese immigrants fought in the Mexican Revolution, including Fusaichi Otakara, Kisaburo Yamane, and the two Nikkeijin who reportedly tried to poison Pancho Villa.[3] Hernández Galindo (2011) also lists Tsuruo Nishino, who served as Pancho Villa's cook; Shinzo Harada, who taught martial arts to the soldiers of Venustiano Carranza, Emiliano Zapata, and Villa; Zenzo Tanaka, who inspired Cecilia Reyes Estrada's novel *La gallina*

41

FIGURE 1.1. Mexican Legion of Honor diploma offered by the Secretaría de la Defensa Nacional, Mexico City. September 6, 1967. Courtesy of Gloria Nonaka.

azul: Historia de una familia japonesa en México durante la Segunda Guerra Mundial (The Blue Hen: History of a Japanese Family in Mexico during the Second World War; 2016), fled La Oaxaqueña sugar plantation,[4] and became a cavalry lieutenant for the Ejército del Noroeste (Northwestern Army); Emilio Nakahara, who became second sergeant; and Antonio Yamane, who was promoted to first captain in Carranza's Constitutionalist Army. In addition, Selfa A. Chew, in *Mudas las garzas*, mentions that "there was a time when President Francisco Madero's most trusted man was Asahiro Tanaka" (2007, 13) and includes a photograph of him from around 1912 with the president and his family.

This is an impressive number of Issei revolutionaries, considering that in 1911 only 2,205 Japanese officially resided in Mexico (Salinas Basave 2019, 100); as stated, that number was up to 6,000 counting unofficial residents, according to García (2014, 109). Nonaka, whose participation in the Mexican Revolution was until recently unknown, authored his brief memoir *Kingo Nonaka*. Written in the first person, the memoir portion is only thirty-five pages long—the rest of the book consists of two lengthy prologues by his son Genaro Nonaka García and the historian Gabriel Rivera Delgado, as well as eighteen pages of photographs.

After Kingo Nonaka's old photographs and negatives resurfaced in a Tijuana market in 2001, Genaro began to look for his handwritten papers, scattered in his Mexico City house (Salinas Basave 2019, 233). Thanks to Rivera Delgado and editor Rafael Rodríguez, the memoir was published in 2014 by Artificios, a Mexicali publishing house. In his prologue, Genaro includes some family recollections and his father's 28 June 1973 interview by América Teresa Briseño, member of the Proyecto Oral del Instituto Nacional de Antropología e Historia (Oral Project of the National Anthropology and History Institute).

Rarely abandoning his modest, measured tone, Kingo Nonaka relates the important role he played under Madero, then under Villa. His experience may be typical of his countrymen's contributions to the Mexican Revolution, although he fails to mention any of his fellow Japanese corevolutionaries. *Kingo Nonaka* is also key for understanding the limitations of the notion of citizenship when individuals "look like the enemy," to quote the title of García's 2014 study. As Sergio Hernández Galindo elucidates in *La guerra contra los japoneses en México durante la Segunda Guerra Mundial*: "By losing its citizenship rights in this way, the Japanese population was subjected to processes of selective repression and mass accusations, from designating them *personae non gratae* to considering them spies of the Japanese Empire . . . was treated like an army of fifth columnists under the orders of the Japanese Empire, which planned a continental invasion."[5]

One of the main strategies immigrants have used to prove their loyalty to the host nation is active participation in wars of independence. The Chinese community in Cuba, for example, proffer its members' participation during the wars of independence against Spain (thousands are believed to have joined the insurgents in different capacities) as unquestionable evidence of their patriotism. In Nonaka's case, his selfless, tireless dedication to treating wounded soldiers (*federales* at first, then mostly revolutionaries) for five of the revolution's ten years, along with his serving as cavalry first captain in Villa's Batallón de Sanidad (Medical Corps) of the Northern Division were not enough to prevent him from being suspected of being a Japanese spy during World War II. Even though toward the end of his life he received the Condecoración al Mérito Revolucionario (Revolutionary Medal of Honor), the Mexican Legion of Honor, and other recognitions,[6] after the Japanese attack on Pearl Harbor in 1941, Mexican soldiers arrested Nonaka in his Tijuana home and forcibly relocated him to Guadalajara, an event similarly experienced by many other Nikkeijin in northeastern Mexico and other regions.

Although in his sparse work the memoirist concentrates exclusively on his adventures during the Mexican Revolution, leaving aside his early, humble beginnings as a pearl diver in Japan as well as his postwar life, it is plausible that this silence veiled his bitter disappointment, even if he held no resentment toward Mexico for his relocation: "Nonaka lives in peace and without grudges with Mexico although no one asked him for forgiveness or even apologized for having taken him out of his house and forced him to leave Tijuana."[7] It is also possible that Nonaka coped with this traumatic experience by burying it in his subconscious or that he purposely avoided reliving the ordeal through his life writing. Whatever the case, Nonaka here opts to forget (see the introduction on social memory and amnesia in nation building and shared pasts). Nonetheless, it is evident that he considered his participation in the Mexican Revolution the most intense and transformative period of his life, as he met and collaborated with the protagonists of one of the most transcendental events in Mexican history.

Along with Nonaka's memoir, I analyze two other supporting works on his life: Salinas Basave's *El samurái de la Graflex* and Shinpei Takeda's film *El México más cercano a Japón*. In *El samurái de la Graflex* the author creates a journalistic chronicle and fictionalized hybrid history based on Nonaka's memoir. For his research, Salinas Basave resorted to contemporary journals; memories that Tijuana residents still hold of the 1930s and 1940s; and interviews with Genaro, his only surviving son, who was eight-six at the time. This memoir resembles a historical novel in passages that contain dialogue or when Salinas Basave divines the protagonist's thoughts, as when Nonaka's uncle died of malaria in Chiapas or when Nonaka was diving in the Guzmán lagoon in search of a corpse. Also fictionalized is Nonaka's last Christmas Eve dinner with his grieving family in Tijuana in 1941, before he was arrested and relocated under suspicion of espionage.

The title, *El samurái de la Graflex*, adds a new dimension to Nonaka's memoir, which exclusively centers on his time under Madero and Villa, by including his tenure as a professional photographer. However, the term *samurái* (also found in some chapters, along with humorous references to "Zen"), aside from being somewhat Orientalist and stereotypical, is also misleading: in reality, Nonaka the soldier carried a weapon only at Ciudad Juárez, the first of the fourteen battles in which he took part. Salinas Basave points out that in the other battles, Nonaka served exclusively as a nurse. He clarifies that Nonaka did not remain behind in a hospital but instead was often treating wounded soldiers on the battlefield: "He usually risks his life like just another soldier and his ambulance wagon makes its way through a swarm of stray bullets."[8]

The cover of the 2020 edition of the memoir published by the Fondo de Cultura Económica evokes Nonaka's multifaceted life, with a red dot suggesting the Japanese flag and the famous image of Pancho Villa on horseback entering Torreón. Paradoxically, the iconic photograph is partially covered by an image of an old Graflex camera (like Nonaka's in Tijuana) that excludes the purported depiction of Nonaka in the background mule driving an ambulance. A small portrait of Nonaka, together with the images of a blue-and-white porcelain fish and a pearl, a reference to his days as a pearl diver in Fukuoka, Japan, complete the composition.[9]

Throughout the text, Salinas Basave includes epigraphs and compares certain episodes with those of other authors, including the Japanese writers Yukio Mishima, Yasunari Kawabata, and Haruki Murakami; the Mexicans Mariano Azuela and Julián Herbert; the American Susan Sontag; and the Spaniard Javier Cercas. The latter's depiction of Tijuana in his essay "La canción de Tijuana" (The Song of Tijuana) as both heaven and hell suggests Nonaka's full integration into that city's mainstream society and his later refusal to return upon learning that his house and shop had been looted.

El samurái de la Graflex moves well beyond Nonaka's biography to delve into the short histories of Tijuana and its Nikkei community,[10] as well as into the convoluted history of the Mexican Revolution, including when two Japanese immigrants failed to poison Villa and the massacre of 303 Cantonese in Torreón on 15 May 1911 by a local mob and Madero's soldiers. Even though Salinas Basave is not ethnically Japanese, his book's originality precisely resides in its rewriting of Mexico's official history from the perspective of the nonofficial (intra)history of one of its ethnic minorities. Thus, it coincides with Julián Herbert's (1971–) *La casa del dolor ajeno: Crónica de un pequeño genocidio en La Laguna* (*The House of the Pain of Others: Chronicle of a Small Genocide*, 2015), a chronicle, journalistic report, essay, and historical study that exudes empathy for an Asian ethnic group in Mexico (here, the Chinese community), providing, along the way, a new perspective on the revolution and on race relations in Mexico.[11]

El samurái de la Graflex offers a nuanced, panoramic context to the revolutionary adventures that Nonaka so succinctly narrated in his memoir. For example, it locates the inducement of twentieth-century Japanese emigration to Mexico in the 1888 Tratado de Amistad, Comercio y Navegación (Friendship, Commerce, and Navigation Treaty) signed by the governments of Mexico and Japan in Washington, DC. The treaty, the first that Japan signed on equal terms with another nation, opened the door to the emigration of Japanese workers to Mexico. Throughout the narration, Salinas Basave emphasizes Nonaka's impressive ability to overcome all obstacles and to adapt to new circumstances. *El samurái de la Graflex* also celebrates his unquenchable, lifelong thirst for learning new skills and for adopting different types of work: pearl diver, water carrier, seed and feed shopkeeper, janitor, nurse, soldier, barber, photographer, detective, toy manufacturer, and co-founder of an automotive mechanics school and a cardiology institute.

The other work that complements analysis of Nonaka's memoir is Shinpei Takeda's *El México más cercano a Japón*, a documentary film that explores the history of Tijuana's Nikkei community from the 1920s through Nonaka's photography and biography. Blending Nonaka's photography with recollections of friends and relatives from Mexico and Japan, this short film sheds light on the plight of this small community during World War II. In addition to providing the memories of Nonaka's son Genaro, Genaro is also the film's narrator and interviewer of current and former members of Tijuana's Nikkei community. Since most are elderly Issei and Nisei, it is clear that this is a rapidly disappearing community, although, in the closing scenes, some express hope that, through the Japanese Association of Tijuana, newer generations of Nikkeijin will become interested in Japanese language and culture.

The short film opens with scenes of daily life in Fukuoka, Japan (e.g., a Buddhist temple, shops, a koi pond), which are blended with images of a crucified Christ and graffiti in Tijuana, suggesting the complex process of cultural hybridization for Nikkei immigrants in Mexico. We then hear Shinpei Takeda tell the 104-year-old Iku Nonaka, who lives in Fukuoka, that her brother Kingo did many important things and worked as a photographer in a Mexican city on the US border during the 1920s, where her nephew still lives. Iku remembers only that when her siblings fought, Kingo would threaten to tie them up if they did not behave. She also recalls how she cried after all of her brothers emigrated and her mother said they would not return soon.

After these opening scenes, Shinpei gives center stage to Genaro Nonaka García, who, in Baja California Norte and Oaxaca, interviews his late father's friends and representative members of the local Nikkei community. The first interviewee is an elderly Nisei man called Samejina, owner of a store in Salina Cruz and son of one of the three hundred Issei who, like Kingo Nonaka, walked for more than three months from Santa Lucrecia, Oaxaca, to Ciudad Juárez in hopes of crossing into the United States. Interestingly, according to Samejina, although his father had originally secured a visa for Peru, he jumped ship in Mexico in hopes of reaching the United States by land, as he had planned before leaving his native country.

Next, Genaro interviews a Nisei shop owner named Alberto Iwao Yashuarama, born in Tijuana in 1934. His parents, Iwao explains, first emigrated to Los Angeles, California, but during Prohibition in the United States, opened a bar and a nightclub for American tourists in Tijuana. He also boasts about how, from 1938 to 1940, his father owned a baseball team called México-Nipón that won the Mexican national championship.

The documentary then moves to Ensenada, where Genaro interviews a nonagenarian Issei, Shinohara Chiyoka, who was his father's friend when she owned a restaurant across from his photo shop. Shinohara describes Nonaka as a sort of detective, because "he knew a lot of things." In 1929, she had moved to Tijuana, where, she admits, one could make a lot of money from all the American soldiers who crossed the border to drink and gamble. She recalls how, because US consular functionaries would often eat at her parents' restaurant, she heard about the Pearl Harbor attack before anyone else in town. To her surprise, Mexicans cheered for Japan after learning of this. Yet the Nikkeijin soon afterward were given a month to leave border and coastal cities. These memories evidence the rift between the Mexican government's decision to comply with the US government's wartime demands and Mexican popular sentiment: "The Mexican government would warn of a supposed Japanese invasion to convince the population to support US policy and accept a strategic alliance with that country; an alliance that was not well received by the majority of the population."[12]

Shinohara sold her restaurant and took a bus with her mother and sister to Mexico City, where they survived until they managed to open a restaurant thanks to her sister's sale of doughnuts. Had it not been for World War II, Shinohara assures, she would have never left Tijuana. Although originally planning to return to Tijuana after the war, she changed her mind because of the proliferation of prostitution rings that made that city increasingly unsafe for raising her daughter. In fact, Shinohara remembers how scared she became when a young boy, pretending that she was his sister and a prostitute, asked some American soldiers if they liked her. Despite these negative experiences, Shinohara states that she would not return to Japan because Mexicans are currently much nicer than Japanese.

Finally, Genaro talks to three former presidents of the Japanese Association of Tijuana who bemoan that, after the Pearl Harbor attack, the Mexican government gave wealthy Japanese men only seventy-two hours to leave Tijuana in order to keep their property. Nikkeijin like Yasuhara and Ishino, they expose, owned three blocks of businesses that were confiscated by the police, who, according to them, subsequently made a fortune selling those properties to friends. The three elderly Nikkeijin bemoan the fact that, after all was stolen from them, local authorities even built a market at the location of the old Japanese baseball field. "¡Puros sinvergüenzas!" (Pure scoundrels!) one of them exclaims indignantly. Although the US government provided $500 to each Japanese family to move away from the border and coastal areas, the governor of Baja California state kept all the money for himself; as a result, the Nikkeijin had to pay to relocate to Guadalajara or Mexico City. Showing photographs in sumo wrestlers' attire, the interviewed former association presidents share their pleasant recollections of founding the association and a sumo team in 1927. The interview ends with their detailing how they purchased the association's building with donations and how they hoped to preserve Japanese culture for future generations.

BEFORE THE REVOLUTION

One of seven children, Nonaka was born in 1889 to the peasants Bunsishi and Tasuyo Nonaka in Fukuoka Prefecture, on the island of Kyūshū. According to Genaro's introduction to *Kingo Nonaka*, Nonaka narrated his decision to migrate thus: "With great sadness for leaving the land and, more than anything, for leaving my parents and siblings behind, I left Japan in the company of Yinkuro, my older brother, and my uncle Shiotaro M. Nonaka, my father's brother, on a ship bound for Panama, with a stopover in Hawaii and Salina Cruz, Mexico. The reason for this trip was not a desire for adventure, but economic necessity, due to the excessive population growth. During the trip we almost did not feel tired, because of all the excitement and projects that we were planning."[13]

This passage suggests that Nonaka had internalized the government's questionable official argument that it was encouraging emigration because of overpopulation. During the voyage, his brother Yenkuro was forced to remain in Hawaii due to a gastric illness; after recovering, he settled there, where he had sixteen children and led a prosperous life (Kingo would see him again fifty years later). Nonaka and his uncle arrived in San Benito (today Puerto Madero) in Salina Cruz, Oaxaca, on 30 December 1906. Five days later, they traveled to Santa Lucrecia, Oaxaca, where more than a thousand Japanese who had been unable to find work as planned on a coffee plantation were working on a sugar plantation with five hundred Mexicans. Nonaka worked as a water carrier for a while, but on 15 February 1907, his uncle died of malaria and, according to Salinas Basave, was buried in a mass grave (2019, 59). Alone in an unknown land, not knowing Spanish, and with only five hundred pesos to his name, Nonaka decided to migrate to the United States, walking north for three months along railroad tracks with a group of his countrymen until they reached Ciudad Juárez, Chihuahua, where a Japanese immigrant community existed.

In *El México más cercano a Japón*, Genaro clarifies that his father, along with approximately one hundred other Japanese immigrants who were unable to find work in Oaxaca in the summer of 1907, headed north after learning that there was plenty of work in the United States. To survive the three-month journey of nearly 1,600 miles, the unfortunate Issei had to forage along the way. Some were imprisoned and sentenced to forced labor in Mexicali, and a few others died in route. Once he reached Ciudad Juárez in 1908, Nonaka spent some time sleeping on a bench at the Plaza de Armas while waiting for an opportunity to cross into the United States. Perhaps because he looked younger than he was, his son explains, a local nurse named Bibiana Cardón (his "godmother," as Nonaka called her) adopted him, paid for his education, taught him Mexican customs and the Spanish language, and had him baptized with the name of José Genaro. After Nonaka learned the Cardón family trade at a seed-and-feed warehouse, he established his own business, which later was vandalized. His adoptive mother later asked the hospital where she worked, Hospital Civil y Militar in Ciudad Juarez, to allow him to come with her. One day, he voluntarily began to pick up the patients' trash and was then offered a janitor job ("a sort of zen sweeper,"[14] in Salinas Basave's comical words).

A year later, Nonaka was licensed to work in the infirmary and, with his on-the-job knowledge, was promoted to nurse's aide. On his twenty-first birthday, he became a nurse, assisting doctors in surgery. He proudly describes himself as a quick learner and a hard worker: "In the absence of medical personnel and after observing how surgeons worked, I learned how to use the scalpel and to suture wounds, or to heal recently operated patients, without rest, without sleeping or sleeping for a few hours, without rest days, without national holidays, end-of-year, or Easter breaks."[15] Indeed, "the careful assistance and cordial demeanor Nonaka gave to his patients became well known in Chihuahua, and his services were constantly requested" (García 2014, 58). In *El samurái de la Graflex*, the sympathetic Salinas Basave contextualizes Nonaka's professional success by pointing out that, between 1900 and 1910, when Mexico's population was fifteen million, the ten thousand Japanese who entered the country legally "often turn[ed] out to be more efficient and hard-working than Mexicans."[16]

A NURSE AT THE FRONT LINE OF THE REVOLUTION

The most interesting episodes in Nonaka's life took place between 1911, when he reluctantly became a participant in the Mexican Revolution, and 1915, when Villa's famous Northern Division was dissolved. The conversations recounted in his memoir provide valuable information about historical events and Madero's and Villa's behavior. Nonaka provides insightful

FIGURE 1.2. Kingo Nonaka working as a nurse at the Hospital Civil y Militar in Ciudad Juárez, July 3, 1911. Courtesy of Gloria Nonaka.

information but appears to refrain from harsh criticism, opting instead for a more objective narration. For instance, in what may seem a criticism of the American government, he mentions in passing that "the US government did not hinder the flow of arms to a great extent."[17]

During that convulsive period of Mexico's history, Nonaka met an injured Madero in Casas Grandes, Chihuahua, and then Villa, who would eventually promote him to first captain in Zacatecas. Jerry García confirms these dates: "According to government records José Kingo Nonaka entered the revolution on April 15, 1910 and fought with the Constitutionalist Forces of the Northern Division under the command of General Francisco Villa and remained under his command until November 15, 1915. The citation indicates that Nonaka participated in military campaigns in Chihuahua, Durango, Coahuila, and Zacatecas from 1913–1914 as part of the medical corps" (2014, 58–59).

In his memoir, Nonaka recalls how one day he decided to take a much-needed break from work at the Hospital Civil y Militar of Ciudad Juárez to pay a visit to his countryman Ricardo Nakamura in Viejo Casas Grandes, Chihuahua. Upon arrival he found, to his surprise, two thousand federal soldiers.

FIGURE 1.3. Nonaka holding a rifle near city hall. Taking of Ciudad Juárez, May 1911. Courtesy of Gloria Nonaka.

On 4 March 1911, Madero had arrived in Galeana, Chihuahua, whence he attacked Casas Grandes two days later. The federal colonel Agustín Valdés repelled the attack and a hand grenade wounded Madero. When Madero's men knocked on Nakamura's door asking for alcohol for the wound, Nonaka, unaware of who the injured man was, offered to treat him. Subsequently, the grateful future president of Mexico offered Nonaka money (he declined) and entreated him to join his army's medical team: "Take the money, and besides, you, doctor, are coming with us, and you will be our doctor, so put on your coat and hat, and let's go" (Nonaka 2014, 31).[18] Although Nonaka argued that he had to return to the Hospital Civil y Militar of Ciudad Juárez, Madero insisted: "Come on, the country needs people like you, doctor."[19] Nonaka adds that Madero's troops already had a competent Italian doctor, but unfortunately he was always inebriated.

Nonaka proceeds to recount the substandard medical conditions in which he treated wounded soldiers, working long hours and with limited staff. As mentioned, he was eventually forced to fight with the combined forces of Villa and Pascual Orozco during the first taking of Ciudad Juárez in May 1911: "The day after we arrived, the month of May was about to begin and the Maderistas, led by Pascual Orozco and Francisco Villa, were preparing to attack the stronghold. On the morning of May 8, the shooting began (this was the only time I acted as a soldier, in subsequent actions I was incorporated into the medical service)."[20] Characteristically, he provides no further details. (There is a photograph of Nonaka holding a rifle after the battle, near the city hall, which Salinas Basave mentions.)

Other memoir passages provide fascinating details about the composition of Madero's troops: "I remember that when [Madero] wanted to take the town square in Casas Grandes, besides the revolutionary troops, he brought along about a hundred peasant types, armed with shotguns, 22-caliber rifles, 30-30 carbines, some with machetes. But when the Maderistas crossed the Rio Grande to take the Ciudad Juárez's town square, there were more than a thousand fully armed men, they were of different nationalities, such as Italians, Germans, Mexicans, White Americans, African Americans, and Texans."[21] We also learn about the character, motivations, and modus operandi of some of the protagonists of the Mexican Revolution. For instance, when Nonaka asked Madero the day they met why Mexicans kept killing one another, the future president gave this forthright and lucid response: "I head a group that is killing others, though we are all the same people. Those others belong to the federal army, to dictator Porfirio Díaz's followers. For Díaz, we Mexicans have no rights, justice, or equality. We are slaves of rich foreigners and among us Mexicans, we have very competent people who can do any job, however subtle it may be. But for President Díaz, who only supports wealthy foreigners, Mexicans do not exist. This is why we are killing his supporters and his folks. Did you get that, Doctor Nonaka?"[22] Likewise, when Nonaka tells Madero that his wounded soldiers keep dying unattended at the hospital because of a dearth of staff, the revolutionary leader threatens doctors and nurses with revoking their licenses unless they immediately return to the hospital at Ciudad Juárez (later named after Madero himself): "Each doctor who has been or is working in an office, if he does not show up within an hour, his office will be closed and he will also lose his professional license, so send troops you trust to carry out the order."[23] Later, always proud of how much Madero trusted him, Nonaka recalls how he was promoted to nursing staff chief. According to Salinas Basave, the future president told him with a pat on his back: "I trust you, Mr. Nonaka. Ever since you treated my wounds in Casas Grandes, I knew that you would not fail me. I fully know that the hospital will be in good hands."[24]

Although this was the last time that Nonaka saw Madero, he continued to help the general's family. In his prologue to the memoir, Genaro quotes a note published by Sergio González in *Revista Mexicana de Política Exterior* (Mexican Journal of Foreign Policy) explaining how, thanks to Nonaka's mediation, Kumaichi Horiguchi, a brave man in charge of the Japanese government's business section in Mexico, saved the lives of Madero's family. By placing the Japanese flag in front of the general's home, Horiguchi prevented José Victoriano Huerta's henchmen from murdering them (Nonaka García 2014, 22). This episode is also included in Salinas Basave's *El samurái de la Graflex*.

A similar relationship of trust and respect later formed between Villa and Nonaka, who, in his memoir, expresses his gratefulness and affection for the general. Under Villa's leadership, Nonaka was part of what Rivera Delgado considers the best medical corps of the Mexican Revolution. Salinas Basave also points out that Nonaka was part of the first professional medical corps in the country's military history. Indeed, between 1913 and 1914, Nonaka participated with seventeen other of Villa's doctors and nurses in various battles, including in Chihuahua, Ojinaga, Bermejillo, San Pedro de las Colonias, Paredón, Torreón, and Zacatecas. Often calling him *muchachito* (little boy), as apparently was his style, and exhibiting the same trust in Nonaka that Madero had displayed, Villa named Nonaka first cavalry captain of the Medical Battalion and, according to Nonaka, chief of the two hospital trains that transported two thousand wounded soldiers to Ciudad Juárez and their three hundred workers: "And now, my captain Nonaka . . . *muchachito*, I want General Máximo García to give you a letter here where he appoints you as the Main Chief of the two trains, for the knowledge of all the workers who travel on the trains, so that they obey and respect you, I recommend you to be very careful with the injured. See you in Ciudad Juárez . . . my doctor Nonaka."[25] Salinas Basave questions the veracity of this claim, arguing that the person responsible for the trains was actually the doctor Andrés Villarreal, a surgeon from Monterrey: "Nonaka is commissioned to the Madero Brigade as head of nurses. He has eighteen people under his authority and his hierarchical superior is Máximo García, director of the hospital in Ciudad Juárez."[26] In any case, Nonaka played a central role in Villa's medical corps, which were treating two thousand injured soldiers.

In October 1915, Nonaka's countryman Ricardo Nakamura informed him that Villa had urgently requested his assistance in finding the corpse of General Rodolfo Fierro, who had drowned a few days earlier in the Laguna Guzmán, in Nuevo Casas Grandes. Fierro, Villa's executioner, was known as "El Carnicero" (The Butcher), and he also goes by that nickname in Martín Luis Guzmán's 1928 novel about the Mexican Revolution *El águila y la serpiente* (*The Eagle and the Serpent*) about the Mexican Revolution. Since Nonaka had practiced underwater diving in Japan, after searching four days, he was able to locate and retrieve the general's corpse. Before five hundred witnesses, the Nikkei bitterly recalls, Colonel Buenaventura Herrán, Fierro's father-in-law, removed the rings, bracelets, watch, and a bag from the corpse before leaving on horseback. He did not remunerate Nonaka even though he had offered two thousand pesos to whoever managed to retrieve the corpse.

This diving episode is briefly mentioned in Rafael F. Muñoz's novel *Vámonos con Pancho Villa* (Let's Go with Pancho Villa; 2008), which mentions that "a Japanese diver" rescued Fierro's body. Salinas Basave also turns this anecdote into the opening chapter of his *El samurái de la Graflex*, which describes the general as a ruthless murderer and his death as stupid, avoidable, and inglorious: his horse became bogged in the mud at the lagoon's bottom, supposedly weighed down by all the stolen gold he was carrying. Salinas Basave re-creates the scene with Villa's soldiers mocking the short Japanese man they see meditating in the lotus position in order to slow his heart rate before diving. We also learn that Nonaka, who had not dived for nine years, had passed a diving test in Fukuoka by holding his breath for at least three minutes.

In one of the most interesting anecdotes about their relationship, after his 9 March 1916 attack on Columbus, New Mexico, Villa asked Nonaka for a favor: to travel at once to San Buenaventura to treat sixty-four wounded soldiers hidden in a church basement. The general asked Nonaka and his wife, Petra García de Nonaka, not to dress like nurses to maintain secrecy: "Before finishing, General Villa told us: 'I'm not going back to Columbus with the gringos, because General Pershing is after me. He is a gringo and is coming with many soldiers. Please don't hand the wounded over to the Americans. The priest already knows everything, I explained it to him just like I did with you; I trust you, because only you are strong, little boy. Goodbye.' And he left with his people" (Nonaka 2014, 47).[27] This was the last time he saw Villa. As in other passages, Nonaka takes pride in the complete trust that Madero and Villa had in him.

But Nonaka also provides an insider's view of the Columbus incident. The American government had previously allowed federal forces led by the generals Plutarco Elías Calles (1877–1945; president, 1924–1928) and Álvaro Obregón (1880–1928; president, 1920–1924) to enter US territory to attack General Villa's army from the rear. Their assault in Agua Prieta caused many casualties and forced Villa to flee. This violation of the nonintervention treaty, along with American sales of defective weapons, infuriated Villa, who, with six hundred soldiers, attacked Columbus—still the only time a Latin American army has attacked US national territory. In retaliation, President Woodrow Wilson sent General John J. Pershing and ten thousand soldiers to capture Villa, but the Mexican revolutionary managed to successfully evade the expeditionary force.

According to Nonaka, after, responding to Villa's request, he and his new wife, Petra, clandestinely treated wounded men in the San Buenaventura church, the priest betrayed Villa by handing over the soldiers to Pershing,

FIGURE 1.4. Kingo Nonaka and his wife Petra García de Nonaka. Courtesy of Gloria Nonaka.

fleeing to the United States, and keeping the ten thousand pesos Villa had given him to shield his men. Nonaka and his wife, in peasant attire and pretending to sell sweets and cigarettes, looked, to no avail, for the wounded men near the American encampment. Nonaka suggests that they were probably executed, because people reported hearing many shots coming from where the Americans had gathered. Salinas Basave underscores how the loyal and grateful Nonaka did not hesitate to comply with Villa's request, risking his own life and that of his wife, even after the general went into hiding: "Doing the most wanted fugitive a favor could cost the newlywed his life."[28]

A third important historical figure in Nonaka's memoir is General Álvaro Obregón. When Obregón, Villa's nemesis, requested Nonaka's help to treat his 160 wounded soldiers, the Nikkei nurse too complied without hesitation (and openly admitting that he had served under Villa), even though the hospital's personnel had not been paid for months. Salinas Basave clarifies that, although Nonaka was still loyal to Villa, "in the Mexico of 1917 what matters is to be on good terms with Obregón and Carranza."[29] This episode bespeaks a talent for keeping lines open to both sides that probably served him well, years later, in concealing his real feelings about Pearl Harbor and the Pacific War.

Indeed, Nonaka was informed that a train carrying Obregón's wounded soldiers would be arriving from the United States. When Obregón arrived, Nonaka informed the general that the hospital staff had not been paid for seven months. The future president promised to provide the salaries: "'We do not have enough money, but as soon as I get to the city of Chihuahua, I'll send it to you, and I'll also solve your problem, I promise you.' After eight days the money arrived, two hundred dollars for each doctor. He sent me a letter congratulating me on my good service and five hundred dollars in a canvas bag."[30]

Obregón would not be the last to recognize Nonaka's tireless efforts and service. Nonaka informs his readers that in 1919, tired of much work little pay, he decided to resign from the Hospital Civil y Militar Francisco I. Madero. Colonel Algudín, his boss, gave him a thousand pesos as a token of his appreciation. Nonaka then proudly told Captain Jesús Negrete that he saved the lives of more than two thousand Mexicans: "I saved the lives of officers, soldiers and civilians, a little more than two thousand people. I worked in hospitals or on battlefields as a Red Cross nurse, without taking weekends or holidays off. . . . Each nurse oversaw more than forty wounded, but I was assigned many more, because it was said that my approach was more thorough and kind."[31] Corroborating Nonaka's memories, Salinas Basave evinces sympathy for this man who all know as "El Japonés" (though he doesn't mention this moniker in his memoir) (2019, 122) when he describes him consoling dying soldiers, as either confessor or recorder of their last wills: "That thin nurse with slanted eyes and a boyish face is a kind of redeeming angel who looks at the wounded in the eyes, whether he seeks their trust and strength or just firmly holds their hands to comfort them."[32]

Nonaka was not just proud of his own achievements and heroism during the revolution; in his memoir, he generously praised the leaders he followed and admired. In the end, although he joined the revolution only reluctantly and accidently, it is apparent that he came to truly admire Villa and Madero, their ideals, and their aspirations. He tells of fond memories of participating in several battles, first with Madero's troops, then with Villa's Northern Division. By the memoir's end, Nonaka celebrates Madero's 1911 presidential inauguration and refutes the accusation that Villa was just a *bandolero* (bandit): "Belonging to the underdogs, those who work much for little money, he is against the brutal exploitation of man by his fellow man. He continues aspiring to become the leader of a cause that redeems the class to which he belongs, the poor, those forgotten by society and, if anyone who will fight for a more just country arises, he is to be followed. Thus, Villa closely follows Francisco I. Madero, the man and his ideas, and joins him" (Nonaka 2014, 63).³³

As is often the case in first-person life narratives, we cannot assume that everything is true, because writers tend to provide the best possible image of themselves and their social group. For example, the Mexican historian Jesús Vargas Valdés questions some of Nonaka's claims, arguing that there is no historical evidence that a Nikkeijin treated Madero's wounded hand or arm after the failed attack on Casas Grandes.³⁴ He contends that in the memoir by Madero's bodyguard Máximo Castillo, *La simple historia de mi vida* (My Life's Simple Story), written between 1914 and 1915,³⁵ Castillo narrates how a Mexican doctor treated Madero several days after the battle. He likewise maintains that Nonaka could not have simultaneously been working with the Red Cross and acting as chief of Villa's medical team on the two trains carrying wounded soldiers that Nonaka mentions—in reality, he was merely the chief nurse in a nursing brigade, working under Máximo Castillo. According to Vargas Valdés, the medical corps of the Northern Division was the largest, best equipped of the revolutionary forces, and it is doubtful that a nurse could have been in its charge. Finally, the historian also belies Nonaka's claim that Fierro's body, when retrieved from the Laguna Guzmán, was laden with gold jewelry. He insists that, according to other historical narrations of the time, it was devoid of any article of value.

Nonetheless, besides Nonaka's unquestionable resilience, adaptability, and thirst for knowledge, another factor in his success during the revolution was perhaps positive stereotypes about Nikkeijin in Mexico, resulting from Japan's defeat of Russia: "Mexicans believed that all Japanese were imbued with special military skills or knowledge that might contribute to their cause, and as a result, they were not only given a wide berth but also conscripted" (García 2014, 58). Incidentally, the Japanese defeat of Russia also led the United States to perceive Japan as a threat to its own hegemony in the Pacific region: "From then on, the United States considered Japan a military rival and Japanese migration to the Americas as a serious problem, 'a new yellow menace' much more dangerous than that posed by Chinese immigrants."³⁶

TIJUANA'S FIRST DOCUMENTARY PHOTOGRAPHER

The resourceful Nonaka is also known for having left a valuable testimony of the city's short history, thanks to his photographs of an emergent Tijuana. After resigning from his nursing job at the hospital in Ciudad Juárez, he moved with his wife and two children to Baja California. He tried his luck at farming in Mexicali and mining in Ensenada until, according to Genaro, he fell in love in 1921 with the then peaceful town of Tijuana and decided to settle there. He worked as a barber, then as a merchant and later as a self-taught photographer.

In *El samurái de la Graflex* Salinas Basave reveals that during a photography session at a Ciudad Juárez surgery room, as he was about to leave behind his military and nursing life, Nonaka became impressed with a photographer's Graflex camera and resolved to eventually purchase one. According to Genaro in the documentary *El México más cercano a Japón*, his father, while working at a barber shop in Tijuana, posed for a picture with his coworkers and, upon seeing the outcome, became fond of photography. He purchased a camera and began to take pictures of daily life in Tijuana. He took the rolls of film to be developed in a San Diego photo shop until one day the manager suggested that he open his own photography laboratory in Tijuana. Following his advice, the self-taught Nonaka opened, in Calle Segunda, a photo studio that he named La Moderna. It was the first processing laboratory in Tijuana. When the lab burned down, he opened another one in Calle Sexta, which he named Estudio Nonaka. Since much was lost in the fire, Genaro tells us, in *El México más cercano a Japón*, that his father, a restless and creative man, invented a glass negative that would withstand the heat.

Later, on account of his reputation as a portrait photographer, the Delegación de Gobierno (Government Deputy's Office), following the recommendation of Joaquín Aguilar Robles, a fellow Freemason (no additional information is provided in the three works studied about Nonaka being a Freemason), hired him to photograph American fugitives arrested by the Tijuana police. Rivera Delgado points out that Nonaka, always thirsty for new knowledge, completed in 1923 a correspondence course on photography, dactylography, criminology, and graphology offered by Chicago's Institute of Applied Science (2004, 6–7). (A photograph exists of a balding Nonaka dressed in suit and tie, wearing dark eyeglasses and a gray moustache, showing off the institute's certificate). With time, he founded the Departamento de Identificación de la Comandancia de Policía de Tijuana (Tijuana Police Identification Department). A photograph, shown by Genaro in *El México más cercano a Japón*, shows his father dressed in a police uniform, alongside his wife, two daughters, and three sons. All in all, Nonaka is the father of Tijuana's documentary photography and also its dactylography; as a member of Tijuana's police department, he introduced that study of finger printing.

For two decades, Nonaka's documentary photography covered the daily life of residents in the fledgling border town that would grow into a large city—in 1921 Tijuana had 1,021 inhabitants; today it has more than 1.5 million). Yet until 2002, this important photographical archive was lost. In 2001, Fernando Aguilar Robles Maldonado, a retired schoolteacher and son of the Tijuana policeman who had recommended Nonaka to the department, discovered a cardboard box with two rolls of negatives inside at a local flea market. Labeled "Foto Nonaka," the box turned out to contain photographs of the city when its population was around five thousand. He contacted Genaro to ask permission to publish and disseminate the pictures. Unbeknownst to the son, when his family moved to Mexico City, Nonaka left some photographic materials, including seven hundred Tijuana negatives, with a friend in Tijuana.

Aguilar Robles Maldonado developed more than two hundred of the photographs in San Diego and archived them with the aid of the historian Gabriel Rivera, director of Tijuana's Archivo Histórico. Aguilar Robles Maldonado later donated more than three hundred of the photographs to the archive. At the same time, Genaro discovered his father's memoir and other photographs in his parents' house in Mexico City. The outcome of this find was the memoir *Kingo Nonaka*. A collection of his photographs, titled *Nonaka en Tijuana: Retrospectiva de la Tijuana de antaño* (Nonaka in Tijuana: An Exhibition of Yesteryear Tijuana), was exhibited in 2002 at the Centro Cultural Tijuana and the Archivo Histórico, as well as in San Diego and San Ysidro, California. Salinas Basave adds that Aguilar Robles also created a calendar, posters, and postcards from Nonaka's photographs.

Rivera Delgado declares that Nonaka's photos, taken with his Graflex camera and focusing on the town's commercial, social, and political life, offset the negative stereotypes associated with tourism, vice, and crime:

> It is a very important legacy. It provides a new perspective on the city of Tijuana, which has historically been linked to the Black Legend. Nonaka's photos, taken from 1923 to 1942, show us a different Tijuana. He focused on cultural, civic, and sports events, as well as on how it grew from town to city.... Before 1923, when he opened his first studio, all Tijuana photography was touristy, shot by tourists and reporters. But, thanks to Nonaka's photos, we can now rewrite Tijuana's story from a different viewpoint: he captured a socially and culturally restless Tijuana.[37]

Salinas Basave also lauds Nonaka for salvaging the past of a city often blemished by its reputation as Sin City and for focusing on the civic, day-to-day lives of Calle Segunda residents. For instance, one of the first photographs that Genaro shows in the documentary is an enlarged panoramic shot of Tijuana—allegedly the first ever taken—that his father took in 1924. He shows where in the sparsely populated town his father's photography studio and home were located.

In his free time, whenever he was not taking portraits of individuals, Nonaka took hundreds of photographs of the city, and "his classical images reveal the Tijuana of the period."[38] During the 2019 presentation of Salinas Basave's *El samurái de la Graflex* at the Centro Cultural Tijuana, Genaro celebrated the achievements of his self-taught and self-made father: "He knew nothing of photography, but learned as he went along. It is incredible what he did with his first photos. He once told me that he wanted Tijuana to be seen as one looks through a window so that tourists would quit badmouthing it."[39] From these comments, it is evident that, before being relocated to Guadalajara, his father had put down roots in Tijuana and was striving, in his own way, to improve its reputation; the city's negative image as a gambling getaway for American tourists made him uneasy.

As further evidence of his sociocultural integration, Nonaka became a naturalized citizen in 1924 and, ten years later, a member of a Masonic lodge and the Asociación Japonesa de Tijuana (Japanese Association of Tijuana). As if his professional achievements were not enough, in 1934 Nonaka founded an auto mechanic school in Tijuana. Genaro recalls his father as a great man, a dedicated father, and an altruistic person who suffered upon seeing local teenagers, without access to postsecondary education, sweeping the streets or getting drunk on weekends. To change this situation, Nonaka cofounded the Escuela Industrial de Mecánica Automotriz (Industrial School of Auto Mechanics), sponsored by the local government and industry, wealthy individuals, and himself. When President Pascual Ortiz Rubio visited Tijuana, Nonaka, seizing the moment, convinced him to partially fund the school. As a result, the school opened successfully. Later, when Nonaka met future president Lázaro Cárdenas (1895–1970; president, 1934–1940) during a visit to Tijuana, he also beseeched him to support the trade school.

Discretely but effectively, Nonaka devoted himself to the betterment of his beloved city. Salinas Basave goes as far as to conceive of Nonaka as a man who "embodies the myth of Tijuana's founding,"[40] to the point that both the city and Nonaka officially came into existence in the same year, 1889.

FROM PATRIOTIC HERO TO PERSONA NON GRATA

In Tijuana, the proud and hardworking Nonaka had finally found economic stability and happiness. However, international events in the Pacific region led to his fall from grace in Tijuana and his ensuing stigmatization as an enemy of the state. Hernández Galindo expounds on how Nikkeijin across the Americas lost their rights as citizens and were repressed and suspected of spying for Japan: "To all national governments in this continent, this population, regardless of age or gender, became a fifth column under the orders of a Japanese Empire that was planning to invade this part of the world. It is important to note that a large part of this population had been born in the host countries and did not speak Japanese fluently."[41] Several events led to the US government's increasing fear of a Japanese invasion from Mexican territory. In 1910, a Japanese naval training squadron visited the port of Salina Cruz, Oaxaca, and was cordially received by a Mexican delegation. During the visit, Japanese officers took part in a ceremony celebrating "the courage of the young Mexican soldiers who died in Chapultepec castle during the American invasion of Mexico in 1847."[42] At the time, different US intelligence reports alleged that Japan was trying to instigate a war between Mexico and the United States, and was even trying to purchase the supposedly strategic Caribbean Mexican island of Isla Mujeres. Furthermore, American intelligence had managed to decode messages sent by the Japanese Foreign Ministry to its different diplomatic delegations throughout Latin America that "revealed the imperial interests of Japan in the area and accelerated the breakdown of relations between the two powers."[43]

Then again, Japanese embassies in Latin America regularly involved local Nikkei communities in Japan's imperial designs. They would ask them, for example, for financial donations to support the invasion of China and viewed them as "natural bridges to develop the commercial contacts, needed by Japan, in their countries of residency."[44] Consequently, US propaganda began to exaggerate the dangers of a Japanese invasion coming from Mexican territory and to discredit and stigmatize, often with racist overtones, the local Nikkei community; it did likewise in Peru and in other Latin American countries. This type of World War II, anti-Japanese American propaganda is shown in a scene in *El México más cercano a Japón* in which the Japanese are described as primitive, murderous, and fanatical: "Their weapons are modern, but their thinking is outdated by two thousand years," says a man in an American propaganda film.

As stated, after the surprise attack on Pearl Harbor, Nonaka, like many other Nikkeijin in the northern states, was forcibly relocated to Guadalajara. The day after the Pearl Harbor attack, Mexican president Ávila Camacho broke off diplomatic relations with Japan and took new measures to limit the freedoms of the resident populations from the Axis powers: bank transactions were limited to withdrawals of five hundred pesos a month, gathering centers in Mexico City were closed down, and naturalization cards dated before 1939 were canceled. The national press began to publish anti-Japanese propaganda, claiming, for instance, that Japan was planning an invasion of Baja California to set up a base to attack the United States. According to Salinas Basave, although Nonaka initially feared for his Japanese countrymen in Mexico, he still felt safe as a naturalized Mexican citizen. Yet he was soon surprised that no clients visited his shop and even his coworkers at the police station had become aloof: "Suddenly, his slanted eyes have transformed him into a villain, a secret agent, a suspect, a spy at the service of Emperor Hirohito, a person to be distrusted."[45] On 6 January 1942, following the Mexican president's order to remove all Nikkeijin from the US border area, soldiers arrested Nonaka at his home and informed him that he had forty-eight hours to relocate to Guadalajara. As a revolutionary war veteran, he pleaded his innocence to Lázaro Cárdenas, then a member of the government. Nonetheless, he was relocated to Guadalajara along with more than fifty Japanese—the trip took three days in an uncovered military truck. Not allowed to carry much luggage, adds Salinas Basave, Nonaka brought only his Graflex camera, a medal Villa gave him at his promotion to first captain, and some clothing. His family followed him a week later.

Salinas Basave argues for use of the term *concentration camp* when referring to the Guadalajara location: "The government does not want to call the situation in Guadalajara a concentration camp, but the truth is that it cannot be called otherwise."[46] Indeed, although they were not considered prisoners, the Nikkeijin were not allowed to leave the city. These movement restrictions are vividly re-created in Cecilia Reyes's novel *La gallina azul*, based on interviews with the Issei Zenzo (José) Tanaka, who fled the terrible working conditions of La Oaxaqueña sugar plantation, and his son, the doctor René Tanaka: "There were only two limitations: not breaching the perimeter that the government had designated for each of the concentration houses [in Mexico City], and not traveling at night. And he [a government official] gave every family a map with the marked area outside of which, he warned us, we could not go. If we trespassed, we would be handed over to the authorities or taken straight to prison."[47] A character in the novel, Zenzo Yamada, was temporarily arrested for leaving the perimeter in search of a physician for a seriously ill child.

Soon after his arrival, Nonaka requested to be transferred from Guadalajara to Mexico City. Salinas Basave describes those first months in Mexico City as the saddest and most depressing for Nonaka: "Kingo is broken inside, emotionally devastated. He never imagined that the Mexican army would repay him thus and that Cárdenas would not answer to his calls."[48] Adding to his frustration, after finding out that his house and studio had been looted, Nonaka, feeling betrayed by friends who failed to defend him from accusations of espionage, swore never to return to Tijuana. Once in Mexico City, he treated other relocated Nikkeijin, whose main health problem was depression, according to Salinas Basave. In fact, Genaro recalls that, having lost all they owned, some Nikkeijin from Tijuana died from sadness.

Salinas Basave openly denounces this dark episode of Mexican history, which he describes as shameful. Even though the Mexican government had not, at the time, declared war on the Axis powers, it complied with Washington's directive to remove Nikkei communities from the northern border states first, and then from Veracruz, Sinaloa, and Chiapas. These people were also relocated to Guadalajara and Mexico City.

The government refused, however, to send them to internment camps in the United States, as Peru and other Latin American countries had done. Salinas Basave denounces this measure as sheer anti-Japanese racism: "That anti-Japanese purge is a vilely racist and unconstitutional act because the constitutional guarantees of Mexican citizens are being trampled on."[49] The author bemoans that, after residing in Mexico for almost four decades, having heroically saved thousands of lives during the revolution, having been a naturalized Mexican, and having established a Mexican family, the Mexican military unfairly removed Nonaka from Tijuana: "Kingo Nonaka is a fully-fledged Mexican who has lived two-thirds of his life in Mexico and has a Mexican wife and five children. He left Japan thirty-five years ago, speaks perfect Spanish, and thinks and writes in that language. True, he has never renounced his birthplace or his ancestors, but Kingo Nonaka has nothing to do with that imperialist war and does not rejoice in the attack on Pearl Harbor."[50] Likewise, Hernández Galindo denounces the injustice and the fact that, to this day, there has been no official apology from the Mexican government: "In the United States, decades after the war, the government recognized the legal and moral errors caused by the concentration and dispossession of immigrants, offered them a public apology, and awarded them compensation. Nothing similar has happened in Mexico to date."[51]

None of these three texts dealing with Nonaka reveals whether he ever expressed his opinion on Japanese imperialism or the Pearl Harbor attack. Moreover, we cannot make assumptions, because the stances of the different Nikkei communities in the Americas, and of individuals within each community, were far from uniform, depending on factors such as level of cultural integration and social class. As Hernández Galindo observes, "The attitude of Japanese immigrants toward their country of origin and toward the war itself is a very complex phenomenon that must be carefully studied, since there was an enormous diversity of positions and feelings that strongly divided the Japanese communities in this part of the world."[52] *El samurái*

FIGURE 1.5. Nonaka being congratulated by Mexican president Gustavo Díaz Ordaz and decorated by the secretary of national defense General Marcelino García Barragán, Mexico City, September 6, 1967. Courtesy of Gloria Nonaka.

de la Graflex, however, describes Nonaka's predictable dismay after learning of the atomic bombs dropped on Hiroshima and Nagasaki: "At last, the samurai sword falls to the ground and the Emperor signs the unconditional surrender. Kingo Nonaka immerses himself in absolute silence and remains mute for several days."[53]

In spite of these disheartening events, Nonaka's noble, philanthropic spirit did not change: he decided to open a toy factory and hired twelve

FIGURE 1.6. Unificación Nacional de Veteranos de la Revolución (National Unification of Veterans of the Revolution) diploma for his service to the Revolution, Mexico City, June 4, 1968. Courtesy of Gloria Nonaka.

Japanese employees from among those in the community who most needed a job. Later, he left the toy factory to his children and, a master at reinventing himself, began to work with Ignacio Chávez, a cardiologist, after twenty-five years of being away from hospitals. Together, they opened the charitable Instituto Nacional de Cardiología (National Institute of Cardiology), devoted to serving low-income patients.

Some years later, Nonaka accepted a job at the Hospital Muguerza de Monterrey (Muguerza Hospital of Monterrey), in Nuevo León. Fifty-five years after leaving Japan, he returned to his homeland, with a layover in Hawaii to visit his brother Yinkuro, who had become a prosperous pineapple exporter. Salinas Basave discloses that, after more than two months of travel in a Japan that had changed dramatically since his departure, Nonaka began to miss Mexico, a country that he did not resent even if no one apologized for his relocation from Tijuana.

After a decade in Monterrey, Nonaka returned to Mexico City. In 1967, at a ceremony for veterans he was awarded a medal and a lifelong pension from President Gustavo Díaz Ordaz (1911–1979; president, 1964–1970). He was also presented with a document from the Secretaría de la Defensa Nacional

FIGURE 1.7. Former soldiers of Francisco Villa's Northern Division (Nonaka is third from left) in the inauguration of the Monument to Pancho Villa, in Avenida Universidad, Mexico City, June 1970. Courtesy of Gloria Nonaka.

(National Defense Secretariat) that certified his participation in fourteen battles during the revolution and his officer's rank.

Nonaka later received other awards for his *mérito revolucionario*, including the Revolutionary Medal of Honor, from the Mexican government. In Salinas Basave's words, "In his old age, he will now receive recognition and an homage from the same government that once persecuted him."[54] In *El México más cercano a Japón*, Genaro proudly displays a photograph of his father wearing the four medals he received for his service in the armies of Madero and Villa.

After working for some time as a dietitian toward the end of his life, Nonaka retired. His wife's death affected him so profoundly that he died soon thereafter. Genaro recalls how peculiar it was to witness such a dynamic, entrepreneurial man lying motionless in bed. At the advanced age of eighty-seven, Nonaka became ill with kidney complications. He passed away in 1977 and was buried in Mexico City's Panteón Jardín cemetery.

This memoir by an Issei is a case study on how some Japanese immigrants became absorbed, for different reasons, by the vortex that was the Mexican Revolution. Despite their valuable and even heroic contributions to their adopted country, World War II would later turn them into enemies of the state.

CHAPTER 2

Challenges to Nihonjiron in Nakatani's Memoirs

Focusing on the pioneering Japanese settlers—teachers, journalists, merchants, prostitutes—in the Korean Peninsula between 1910 and 1930, the historian Jun Uchida (2014) demonstrates that, even if their primary motive was personal interest, these "empire brokers" became de facto tools of imperial domination. In Uchida's view, their mundane, daily lives became inseparable from the Japanese empire's expansionist aims. Japanese Brazilian literature occasionally exposes the fact that Japanese immigrants in Latin America also served a secondary role, not as tools for domination as in Korea, but as international commerce brokers, senders of remittances, and improvers of Japan's political influence and worldwide image.[1]

This chapter, by contrast, explores a text that reflects no intention to improve that image. If anything, it perhaps unintentionally challenges the positive yet self-essentializing stereotypes associated with Nihonjinron (theories or discussions about the Japanese), a sort of "strategic essentialism" (to use Spivak's term) through which the Japanese have derived advantage from positive stereotypes propagated by Westerners. For many Japanese intellectuals, Nihonjinron, a sort of knowing exaggeration, represented a "regime of truth." A new knowledge associated with power, its effectiveness is supposed to be more important than its actual truth. They decided that it was true for different reasons, including repairing a damaged Japanese national identity, instilling nationalism during imperialist expansion, and gaining goodwill during times of anti-Japanese hysteria in the United States.

Nihonjiron is a genre of texts that responds to a somewhat contrived "ideology" (in Harumy Befu's terms) about Japaneseness and Japanese national and cultural identity. As the cultural anthropologist Blai Guarné points out, "Defined in the essential contrast between the no-less essential notions of 'the West' and 'Japan,' the *Nihonjinron* is a discourse on Japanese identity with the aim of ascertaining the ontological principles of 'Japaneseness'" (Guarné 2009, 323). Expounding an essentialist national psychology of the Japanese, or *Nihonjin*, books like Nitobe Inazō's *Bushido: The Soul of Japan* (1900), explains Guarné, recovered nineteenth-century, Western stereotypes about an exotic Japan in an attempt to create a new international image of the country, which had been damaged by its imperialist adventures in East Asia. After World War II, this nationalistic rhetoric was recycled to repair a severely marred Japanese identity. These books about the Japanese written by foreigners "were read by the Japanese themselves, who became convinced that they could present themselves to the West in such a way."[2] The self-exoticizing stereotypes of the Nihonjinron visual imaginary, created toward the end of the nineteenth century and recovered as a reaction to the country's post–World War II zeitgeist, were constructed mostly to prove how different Japan was from a West that had replaced China as cultural Other during the second half of the nineteenth century).

From this perspective, this chapter analyzes the memoirs of the Japanese immigrant Yoshigei (Carlos) Nakatani (1910–1992), who invented "Japanese peanuts" in Mexico City in 1945. Nakatani's memoirs go against the grain of much of Latin American Nikkei literary and cultural discourses. To be sure, I am not implying that all Japanese–Latin American authors have bought into Nihonjinron discourse, but it is not uncommon for Japanese–Latin American writing to follow its assumptions; Nakatani's autobiography is therefore a notable exception. This chapter examines Nakatani's unpublished memoirs "Novela escrita por Carlos Nakatani: Historia de su propia vida" (A Novel by Carlos Nakatani: His Own Life's Story). This *novela*, incidentally, is not a novel, but his memoirs or autobiography, seemingly written with few literary or aesthetic aspirations: the memoirist uses a colloquial, often unemotional, matter-of-fact language and at times switches topics without much transition; the memoir's sociocultural value, however, is undeniable. "Novela escrita" is also one of the few available testimonies of the at times surprising behavior and vicissitudes of the small, but visible Nikkei community in Mexico (another is Akane's lyrical rendering of her family's daily life, analyzed in the next chapter). The work describes twentieth-century episodes that are seminal to the social histories of Mexico and Japan.

"Novela escrita" was rediscovered by Emma Chishuru Nakatani Sánchez, Nakatani's granddaughter, and became the object of her undergraduate thesis. It is important to remember again here that memoirs do not necessarily always portray the past as it happened; they are, instead, a selective narrative of that past, mediated by the effects of time in Nakatani's memory and by his own choice of relevant episodes to narrate while keeping others to himself. Regardless, it is not so much the historical truth of the narrated events that interests me but rather how Nakatani remembers them, and also their effect on the reader. I am particularly attentive to the memoirist's choice of recalled situations, such as his community's racism toward his mixed-race children. I then ask myself, why did he include those memories and not others? Are there sociopolitical or cultural implications that induce him to omit those others? What motivated him to write his memoirs and at that stage of his life? What type of reader does he have in mind? What is the objective of his writing? Is he thinking about articulating his community's historical memory or just relating a personal account for his relatives? Is Nakatani trying to prove or establish his own Japaneseness, Mexicanness, Japanese Mexicanness, or all of these? Perhaps delving into his biography will help us answer some of these questions.

Nakatani departed from the port of Yokohama in 1932 aboard the Japanese ship *Gueiya-Maru* and arrived in Manzanillo, Colima. Thanks to the *yobiyose* (or "called over") system, allowed under the 1924 Treaty of Commerce and Navigation between Japan and Mexico, he immigrated to work for El Nuevo Japón owned by the Japanese entrepreneur Heiji Kato, which made buttons out of mother-of-pearl shells. It was in 1975 that Nakatani decided to write his memoirs. Although he began to write them in Japanese, he later opted to dictate them in Spanish to his wife, Emma. According to his granddaughter, also named Emma, he made that decision because only a few people in the community could read Japanese (Nakatani Sánchez 2002, 11). Therefore, Nakatani's original text went through two different filters: his wife's transcription and his granddaughter's proofreading.

"Novela escrita" opens with the story of a small-town peasant family in Japan around 1918. We learn about Nakatani's adventures in his native Japan, and especially about two young women who left their mark on his life. He proceeds to narrate his daily life as an immigrant in Mexico City. Like many of his countrymen, Nakatani had planned to work in Mexico for only a few years, but he later changed his mind and stayed. Unlike other Latin American Nikkei narratives, his memoirs do not stress adaptation and cultural integration; tellingly, he did not seek Mexican citizenship, although he claimed to have felt more Mexican than Japanese.³ He reveals, however, that he converted to Catholicism in 1933, forsaking his Shinto religion. He adopted the Christian name Carlos to marry the Mexican Emma Ávila Espinoza. He also downplays racism; he does mention, however, a fight he had with an indigenous man who called him *chale*, a racial epithet directed at Asians in Mexico.

In the first pages, we find the recollections by Nakatani—"Yoshio" to friends and relatives—of his humble origins. When he was five years old, he sadly recalls, his parents owned the poorest house, with dirt floors, in the town of Sumoto-cho, on the southeastern part of the island of Awaji. Lacking the money to lease land for agriculture, his parents worked at a paper factory, but their combined salaries barely fed their eight children. Nakatani's brothers chopped wood in the forest and, along with the rest of the family, made and sold tatami mats to make ends meet. Often cold and hungry, Nakatani noticed his parents' worries. From early childhood, he not only felt empathy for human suffering—his most positive trait throughout the narrative—but also was keenly aware of class differences. This awareness instilled in him a desire to succeed financially. Although his father, Kigey, eventually made a fortune selling cattle, his family did not benefit from that wealth until several years later.

CONTRADICTING NIHONJINRON'S TENETS

As part of the Japanese Empire's emigration-based expansionist designs, Japanese arrivals in Latin America were expected to comport themselves exemplarily in host countries. The idea was to create an international image of Japan as a modern, philanthropic nation that supported local, rural economies with its technological expertise and diligent émigrés. This type of model immigrant behavior and success story can be found, for example, in Cecilia Reyes Estrada's novel *La gallina azul*, in which Zenzo Yamada, the protagonist's immigrant father, is given the keys to the town of Ures: "Your father deserves that recognition. The *jamoncillo* [candy made of ground pumpkin seeds] that he and your mother brought to the area has fed many people; businesses were established that flourished with jamoncillo, now recognized as a town symbol."⁴ Inheriting his father's virtues, the Nikkei protagonist, André (Haruki) Yamada, becomes a prestigious oncologist after enduring many challenges and identity-related uncertainties.

The same type of success story and upward mobility appears in Federico Imamura's memoirs *Casi un siglo de recuerdos*. Arriving in Mexico in 1932, Imamura began a life of sacrifice, hard work, and resilience as an immigrant when he first suffered exploitation by a compatriot. He then experienced several business failures before succeeding, eighteen years after his arrival, with his innovative bakeries in Monterrey. His success is more in line with the usual life narratives of Nikkeijin in Latin America. For example, in one of the many passages in which Imamura's worldview aligns with Nihonjin-ron tenets, he describes the day of his departure from Japan: "We Japanese are made to suffer, to face trials stoically. We cannot cry or groan. We must face the trials that life imposes on us with serenity and patience. I could not cry then and my mother even less . . . With that same serenity, Japanese mothers gave up their sons by the thousands to go to the battlefront to die in Japan's armed conflicts."[5]

Masterson and Funada-Classen, in their case writing about Japanese emigration to Brazil, described the official pressure to which emigrants were subjected: "Before leaving the port of Kobe, these Brazil-bound Japanese and Okinawan immigrants were addressed by a representative of the Japanese government, who warned them that they should 'not disgrace Japan' and that if they did not succeed they should not return to Japan, even in death" (2004, 44). Imamura seems to take these precepts quite seriously: "I also knew that if my plans failed, I would seek, to respect my ancestors' honor, a way to die by my own hand and with dignity, in which case I would not return either. A return in defeat to Japan was not possible either. I would be singled out, considered unworthy, and rejected forever by my people."[6] In keeping with this dictum, Nakatani also emigrates to Mexico wishing to become successful and wealthy. In fact, he vows that he will not return to his homeland unless his goals are achieved: "I wanted to strike it rich because I could not die without returning to my homeland."[7] Yet, as will be seen, the intention of improving Japan's image seems not to have guided his life in Mexico.

Nakatani's memoirs adopt a different positionality from that of most first-person accounts by Nikkeijin in Latin America (see also the next chapter on Akane). In Peru and Brazil, for example, Nikkei writing tends to denounce past racism, xenophobia, oppression, and disenfranchisement; to exalt Nikkei culture and achievements, and to claim belonging to the host nation while stressing their cultural differences. Nakatani's "Novela escrita," by contrast, goes in a different direction. For example, he does not emphasize the evolving nature of identities in the diaspora or how those constantly become transformed and reproduced by new experiences. Whereas Akane renews her Japanese bonds through childhood memories to then celebrate her affiliation to the host country's mainstream culture and identification as a culturally hybrid Japanese Mexican, in Nakatani's diasporic discourse, identity formation is not a central issue.

More importantly, by openly defying, consciously or not, the official expectations of exemplary behavior and, by extension, the self-essentializing stereotypes of Nihonjinron, his narrative is unique in Japanese–Latin American literature. For instance, staples of Nihonjinron discourse, such as mystical communion with nature for Japanese people, so prevalent in Akane's poetry, are absent in Nakatani's prose. Likewise, in only a few passages is Nakatani concerned with preserving social harmony. Nihonjinron's nationalistic, mythical self-image, influenced by Western stereotypes about Japanese temperament and culture, has evaporated from Nakatani's pages. His unmasking of the self-stereotyping fallacy of an unchanging Japanese worldview represents a challenge to the essentialist fantasies of national homogeneity, purity, and exceptionalism. In Nakatani's counternarrative, Japan ceases to be the non-West, and despite all the autoethnographic cultural translations, Japanese temperament and culture are no longer so unique. The self-examination carried out in "Novela escrita" eschews these national and nationalistic mythologies as it presents a more individualistic way of being Japanese. Nakatani represents all those Issei like him who were excluded from a Nikkei discourse marked by teleological, salvational, and heroic self-definitions influenced by Nihonjinron ideology and the Japanese government's geopolitical strategies. He has no qualms about depicting himself and some of his fellow countrymen as they truly were, in all their defects, even if deviating from essentializing ideological discourses about the purported ontological traits of the Japanese or the equally mythical idea of a timeless, static Japanese identity.

Nakatani's sui generis choice of representation of self and community makes his memoir an intriguing text. His granddaughter Emma highlights, in her insightful thesis, how the text presents the memoirist "as a good man; that is, as a man who managed to adhere to values taught during his childhood, despite having left his native country at age twenty-two."[8] By contrast, even if this is the text's ultimate message, it is much more compelling to explore how he arrives at that point: the autoethnographic recollections of his life experiences, first in Japan, then in Mexico, offer a divergent image from that of the exemplary Japanese subject who strives abroad to improve his country's image, as it is with most first-person accounts of Japanese immigrants in Latin America.

From a different perspective, it is also critical to keep in mind the relationship between migration-driven expansionism and Japanese imperialism. Whether they were aware of it or not, pre–World War II Japanese immigrants were pawns of the imperial project and their government's capitalist social engineering. In the case of Brazil, for example, some of these immigrants were veterans of the Russo-Japanese War who achieved leadership positions, including in the terrorist organization Shindō Renmei (Subject Path League).⁹ Their purported official duty was to ensure that the Nikkei community remained loyal to the Empire of Japan, creating pockets of resistance against Western cultural and political domination.

Many of the remaining Japanese immigrants in Latin America were part of social groups that the Japanese government deemed undesirable, an excess population of impoverished, landless peasants in southwestern Japan who had begun to create unrest and political problems. The political scientist Toake Endoh exposes this governmental ruse: "Others call the emigration program nothing but *kimin* (dumping people) for having abandoned the migrants in the hostile and difficult natural or socioeconomic climates of foreign countries over ten thousand miles away. Some former emigrants have filed suit against the Japanese migration authorities, who the plaintiffs believe were responsible for their plight and affliction" (2009, 2). The government targeted the southwestern region to alleviate political tensions: "Class relations that developed uniquely in the southwestern region were fomenting social antagonism against the economic and political establishment. The dispossessed or marginalized population was radicalizing their ideology and actions against their class enemy and the state" (Endoh 2009, 2). By encouraging emigration, the Japanese government hoped to rid itself of potential social problems, create new markets for Japanese products, and acquire additional, badly needed food sources and raw materials.

Along with the economic benefits of international trade, the Japanese imperial government was counting on these emigrants' future remittances. Although it voiced the excuse of reducing overpopulation through emigration, its real goal was to expand its sphere of political influence. In this context, although the Japanese government declared the need to settle its excess population abroad, it truly believed that continued population growth was beneficial for the empire's expansion: "It rationalizes migration-driven expansion, [or] 'Malthusian expansion,' as both a solution to domestic social tensions supposedly caused by overpopulation and a means to leave the much-needed room and resources in the homeland so that the total population of the nation could continue to increase. In other words, Malthusian expansionism is centered on the claim of overpopulation, not the actual fear of it, and by the desire for population growth, not the actual anxiety over it" (Lu 2019, 4). Overpopulation was therefore a mere pretext to settle citizens abroad, where they would increase Japan's sphere of political influence.

As mentioned, Japanese immigrants in Latin America were manipulated and exploited by their own government for imperial expansionism.

Prewar Japanese foreign policy, imperialism, biopower, and territorial aims included the encouragement of state-guided migration, which plausibly influenced Nakatani. Indoctrinated by imperialist propaganda, many Japanese immigrants in Latin America saw themselves as heroic imperial subjects fulfilling a patriotic mission explicitly detailed by Emperor Hirohito (emperor, 1926–1989).

Nakatani's behavior throughout most of his working life, however, does not reflect a concern for Japanese imperialist, expansionist ideology; instead, he exhibits an individualist subjectivity that ignores group-oriented outlooks. Among some of the outlandish actions in Japan described in his memoirs, Nakatani steals the ashes of a recently cremated child and ingests some of them, believing they would cure an ongoing illness, and then flushes the rest down a toilet. Likewise, while drinking and gambling, Nakatani spends the money that Zuyako, his prostitute partner, gives him from her earnings. And although he invites another woman out on a date, he becomes jealous that Zuyako buys clothing and limits their weekly encounters on account of increased clientele. At one point, Nakatani considers killing her. In his own words, it is his awareness of what happens to men who kill their partners that leads him instead to emigrate. When they later live together, Nakatani promises Zuyako he will stop gambling, but unable to do so, he loses money she had planned to send to her family. He admits his guilt but tries to come across as a victim after a gambling outing with friends: "I had made up my mind not to go because Zuyako was becoming fed up, but they came for me and I could not resist the temptation."[10] Nakatani becomes increasingly frustrated with Zuyako, not only because of her sex work but also because she has him taking care of her ill father, in her village, for several weeks. After his return, they have an argument, and Nakatani knocks her down onto a muddy street.

Resettlement in Mexico does not bring an end to his questionable behavior. Two years after arriving, Nakatani asks for the hand of Emma Ávila Espinosa. Because she is underaged, her parents ask for a five-year wait for the nuptials. He nonetheless elopes with her and impregnates her. Later, they marry in a civil ceremony, against the racist policy of his employer that forbids marriage between Japanese employees and Mexicans. Worse yet for Nakatani, his vices continue; gambling was illegal in Mexico, and as a consequence, he spends some nights in jail. He calculates that, after working for twenty-five years in Mexico, he gambled no less than 90 percent of his earnings. At one point, his artist son, Carlos, tired of his gambling, decides to move in with a friend's family. For his children, it was at times a relief when he did not return from a gambling outing because, in his absence, they did not feel obligated to work as hard in the family business, which might bespeak of a potential case of family (self-)exploitation.

Nakatani's behavior is not exceptional. Many Nihonjin (Japanese in their native land) and Mexican Nikkeijin behaved in ways that contradicted the values celebrated by Nihonjinron. For instance, when Nakatani opens a restaurant with Zuyako in Japan, many clients who were granted credit failed to pay their debts, which caused the business to close. Likewise, in Mexico, Nakatani blames some of his coworkers for his nightly outings and gambling habit. Their heavy drinking and gambling keeps them from going to work. In fact, at year's end, their angry boss, Kato, does not give them a promised bonus because of their poor performance. Nakatani also recalls that the immigrants' gambling habits meant that their Mexican colleagues did most of the work at the factory: "We continued to gamble. Sometimes we stopped working for three days; we felt confident because Mexican workers were already doing the work. We had trained them and, while gambling, we occasionally made sure that the young guys were doing a good job."[11] The Spanish original, with the use of the condescending *muchachos* (boys) and the verb *inspeccionar* (to inspect, to make sure), reveals a thinly veiled sense of superiority over "lesser" native coworkers; the Nikkei, however, admit that the Mexicans work hard and that they trust them to complete the work.

As if imitating José Joaquín Fernández de Lizardi's picaresque protagonist in *El periquillo sarniento* (*The Mangy Parrot*, 1816–1831), a Japanese coworker of Nakatani's, Fukuyama, shamelessly confesses to his friends that he has purchased a counterfeit license to practice dentistry and opens a dental office. Later, we learn that another Japanese immigrant, Ojara, likewise purchases a phony license and becomes a successful dentist. Again, regarding the dubious work ethic of some Nikkei in Mexico, which stands counter to those claimed in most Latin American–Nikkei life stories, two cousins, Isibasi and Jasimoto, tell Nakatani that, tired of American racism, they moved to Mexico City, where Mutaguchi, Nakatani's godfather, lent them five thousand pesos to open an ice cream shop—unfortunately, they declared bankruptcy six months later on account of mismanagement. In another example, several other Issei coworkers at the button factory "betray" (in Nakatani's words) the boss, Kato, by returning to Japan before their five-year contracts expired (Kato later pays Nakatani to leave the factory and find another job). Nakatani also mentions Mitsuma, a Japanese immigrant who moves from Guadalajara to Mexico City to avoid paying his debts. Unethical work and life behaviors, therefore, were a serious problem for Nakatani as well as for many other Nikkeijin in Mexico. Nikkei self-criticism continues, as is characteristic of these memoirs, even in scenes depicting the unjust, forced displacement of Nakatani's compatriots during World War II. At one point, for instance, he laments that "nobody wanted to work" in the community because they thought the war would soon be over.¹² A few lines later, Nakatani adds that "while some relocated [to Mexico City] Japanese struggled to make a living, others gambled away what little they owned."¹³

Without explicitly stating it, Nakatani criticizes the racism of the Nikkei community in Mexico City toward mixed-race descendants like his own children: "There was a Japanese school in Calle Cinco de Febrero. To fundraise, they always held parties where children danced and parents gave envelopes with money. . . . My wife and children also participated. They gifted them envelopes with money, but I donated them to the school. That's how I cooperated with that primary school. But they never invited my children to attend it."¹⁴ While his ethnic community's racist attitudes hurt Nakatani's feelings, he chooses to ignore them and does not mention them again in the memoirs. Yet before World War II, some Issei throughout the Americas deemed Nisei as inferior, in part because of their inability to speak Japanese, their ignorance of the cultural norms of the so-called Japanese spirit (another Nihonjinron concept), and their intermingling with local populations. As to mixed-race Nisei, racism was the major reason for their rejection.

Besides a record of his inspiring generosity toward his countrymen, including many whom he did not know personally, Nakatani uses his memoirs to disparage men (by name and surname) who betrayed him or did not repay their loans. One was his former partner Jayasaka, who plagiarized the "ranchero," a type of food invented by Nakatani, and sold it for lower prices, thus stealing Nakatani's clients away. This was particularly egregious because Emma, Nakatani's wife, had been selling Jayasaka's product, as a favor to him, for two years. Fortunately for Nakatani, who had opened a candy workshop in his house in 1943, this dispiriting episode induced the motivation he needed to come up with his popular Japanese peanut.

NEGATIVE ROLE MODELS

In perhaps an attempt to justify his past behavior, Nakatani incorporates a number of negative role models throughout his work. He begins with his father, Kigey, who had children with several lovers and abandoned the family when Nakatani was five years old. Kigey boasts about his wealth around town while his legal wife and children suffer cold and hunger. When Nakatani's oldest brother asks his father for money, Kigey throws him out of his new, luxurious house. Later, when Nakatani's two younger sisters die of disease, their father does not pay for or attend the funerals. As Nakatani describes his father's behavior, withholding explicit judgment, one can only surmise his disappointment early in life. At one point, however, he describes himself wondering: "Why did my father have such a criminal heart?"[15] Young Nakatani nonetheless acknowledges a positive trait in his father: a work ethic that made him wealthy.

Kigey is the first among several Japanese negative role models mentioned in the memoirs. We then learn, for instance, that two of his older brothers, following in their father's footsteps, would spend their mother's restaurant earnings in alcohol and geishas. One eloped with a young woman and later would father a daughter with his cousin who, becoming bedridden after the delivery, was neglected by his brother (adding insult to injury, he brought a lover to the house).

In his youth, Nakatani becomes an apprentice at a candy shop, working around fifteen hours a day for little wages (apprentices typically worked for free). There, he learns to make different types of candy, a training that would change his life once in Mexico. After working at the candy shop for over two years, he, mistreated by his mentor, resigns and is then hired at a factory that makes mother-of-pearl buttons on the island of Awaji. It is there that he first learns the dangers of ludopathy: "People who worked in those factories, because they earned good wages, developed vices. Most of these workers were grown-ups and came from Osaka. That's why my mother asked me to return to the restaurant. She knew that those who worked in those factories always ended up badly."[16] Others, like his relative Kisimoto, also mention the button workers' penchant for gambling and frequenting prostitutes, a possible cause for the high rate of suicide among them.

Ethical shortcomings cross gender barriers too. Throughout the memoirs, Nakatani recalls the poor behavior of several women, including his abusive paternal grandmother. After his father hires two young prostitutes to work at the bar that he opened behind the restaurant (Nakatani calls Japanese bars *pulquerías*, although there was no pulque then in Japan), Nakatani sleeps with them but portrays himself as victimized by the two women. Eventually, Nakatani meets Chioko Hirata, a girl who wants to run away with him because her rich father has sex with the servants, brings geishas home, and has sexually abused and impregnated his underage niece. The father even goes to the restaurant with the intention of purchasing Zumiko, Kigey's fourteen-year-old daughter, whom he wishes to make his lover. A wealthy man thereby feels entitled to procure a minor in exchange for money to add to his harem of lovers. Chioko's older brother, she laments, is equally depraved: "I'm a minor and for this reason, I don't like to intervene, but I always see the face of immorality in my father and brother!"[17] In the end, after Chioko convinces Nakatani, he makes every effort to reunite with her in Osaka, where her parents had sent her after her plans to run away were discovered, but she is already engaged to another man. It is, at least in part, because of his disappointment with Chioko that Nakatani emigrates to Mexico: full of spite, he promises that one day he will return triumphantly from abroad to show Chioko who he is. These passages portray an unflattering picture of Japan at the time, one far from the idealized Nihonjinron perception. By including these episodes, Nakatani seems indifferent to official mandates of improving Japan's reputation abroad.

Nakatani goes on to find a job at a glass factory in Osaka (the owner prefers to hire honest workers from Awaji Island because Osaka workers keep robbing him), where his mean coworkers force him to gamble. It is then, as a teenager, that he meets his tragic flaw: "One night, the oldest [worker] woke me up with a kick and said, 'I've lost all my money and I want you to play [cards] in my place. I think you'll have beginner's luck.' I told him, 'I don't know how.' 'I'll teach you,' he answered. This was the first time that I picked up a deck of cards. This was to cause my misfortune, all the bitterness in my life, and all my family's suffering for many years."[18] Without entirely avoiding responsibility, the contextualization of his gambling problem is undoubtedly presented here as the victimization of a naive, young man.

Once in Mexico, Nakatani continues to come across corrupt and unethical Nikkei men.[19] Interestingly, during a business trip to Mazatlán during Carnival, Nakatani realizes that he is not well received there and that a Japanese employee at his hotel refuses to speak to him. It turns out that the local Japanese community fears that he and his godfather, with their gambling habit, may end up damaging their impeccable local reputation. Thus, they are told, "Many Japanese have begun saying that they have been living in Mazatlán for a long time, have worked earnestly, and thus have earned everyone's respect; now, people of their same race have come to damage their good reputation and they will not allow it."[20] Ultimately, the local Nikkei's intuition was accurate because Nakatani and his godfather were jailed for illegal gambling. During that time, Nakatani incidentally receives a letter from his wife informing him that she has just given birth to their fourth son.

While acknowledging his own shortcomings, Nakatani at times tries to deflect responsibility by blaming others for his gambling addiction. For example, he once states: "One day he [Nakagaki] came and told me: 'I want to go gambling.' He showed me $500 cash . . . 'Mr. Nakatani, you know where those places are, so take me.' I didn't want to, but he insisted."[21] Nakatani next admits to spending five continuous days gambling and drinking.

LOOKING FOR REDEMPTION

Nakatani provides multiple episodes in his memoirs that show his boundless generosity. Thus, when he meets a starving boy or the stranded former owner of the button factory, he gives them enough money to improve their situations. Elsewhere, Nakatani appears too gullible, trusting, even naïve. For instance, in Japan, he gives a coworker a check to cash on his behalf, and having done so, the coworker disappears with the money. Later, on his way to Mexico, Nakatani allows his future Nikkei coworkers to borrow money in his name. But his largest act of kindness takes place when he risks his life to free six women from forced prostitution. While working at the button factory in Kyoto, Nakatani reluctantly joins two coworkers on a trip to an island with dozens of brothels. In one of them, he meets a young Zuyako, who reveals her sad story to him: because of her family's financial difficulties (her father is an alcoholic and her mother, a gambler), she is sold for fifteen thousand yen to a brothel whose male keeper, it turns out, is raping the six women working there. Because armed thugs protect this pimp, no one dares to rescue the desperate victims.

In the end, Nakatani turns his brothel visit into an act of heroism: "I couldn't sing that day. My thoughts were on these women's situation and I thought 'if I don't help them, they'll never be able to escape from that hell.' That's why I was ready to do so, but I was afraid. Back then, there were some bad people around."[22] When the three coworkers again visit the brothel, Nakatani astutely proposes to use the women's three-meter-long obis (kimono belts) to climb down the building. The next day, the brothel's goons go to question Nakatani at the factory, but he feigns no knowledge of the escape. This story, in the end, takes on fairy tales overtones: the heroic prince charming comes to the rescue of the damsel in distress and makes it his quest to free the young woman from an evil master and to make her his partner. Indeed, to show their gratitude (*on*) and pay their debt (*giri*) to their saviors, the women offer to marry them, but only Nakatani stays with Zuyako. Surprisingly, Nakatani often confesses that when the news of the rescue of these women appeared in the newspaper, he felt guilty for having caused the pimp's bankruptcy. Again, it is clear in these passages that Nakatani is not presenting a pristine image of his native country, but in fact, he has no qualms about revealing the darkest side of Japanese society during this time.

In other scenes, Nakatani teaches his trade to others, lends them money, and even fights Mexican men who have affronted his countrymen. During World War II, he and other Nikkeijin in Mexico City try to alleviate the hardships endured by the displaced Nikkeijin arriving from border states. It is noteworthy that, when he helps Istani, a Nikkei, Nakatani seems to be influenced by Mexican social customs; he has internalized those social obligations associated with a relationship known as *compadrazgo*: "I felt an obligation to help him because he was my fourth daughter's godfather."[23] However, he feels disappointed after Istani returns to Japan without even bidding him farewell.

Istani was not the only countryman who let him down. Because Nikkeijin were not allowed to open businesses or purchase property during World War II, Nakatani let his friend Sakaguchi register his car under in the name of his wife, Emma. This favor backfired when, after Sakaguchi failed to fully pay for the car and ran over a pedestrian, the police came to arrest Nakatani's wife. He also allowed Sato, also a Nikkeijin, to open a button factory in Emma's name, thereby providing an example of how Nikkeijin eased the discrimination against them.

Nakatani's final redemption comes in 1970, when he at last visits his native Awaji. The decision was made after three of his gambling cohorts suddenly died and Nakatani's children, fearing for his life, convinced him to visit Japan with Emma. Upon his return, he proudly shows his friends and relatives that, as he had promised, his life goals were met. In grateful recognition, Nakatani confesses that his success is owing to the owner of the candy factory where he learned the trade while working as an apprentice. He pays a visit to the owner's gravesite, burns incense, and gives his widow money in an envelope, in accordance with local customs. Much to his delight, Nakatani's brothers mention that his return, after having become successful abroad, improved the family's reputation, which had been severely marred by Isambo and Ichiro, two of the brothers: "Now that you and your wife, having accomplished such good deeds, are here, things have changed, you have restored our surname."[24] Nakatani also feels deeply honored when the town's mayor invites him to ring the new bell brought from Kyoto (the previous one was melted during the war to make weapons); he then is interviewed by local journalists. Toward the end of his visit, Nakatani gives a talk at the grammar school that he attended and, on his departure, is given a warm farewell by many of the islanders.

The good news continues once he arrives back in Mexico City: the factory's performance has improved under his son Armando's watch. Months later, encouraged by Armando's proposed solution to his gambling addiction,

Nakatani again visits Japan, where he indeed relinquishes his vice. He makes two additional trips to Japan to take his daughter Graciela to a hospital. Here, the memoirs abruptly end because, as his granddaughter Emma points out in her study, the final pages are missing.

In these memoirs, Nakatani tries to make sense of his life experiences in two different countries. Despite all the suffering caused by his gambling addiction, his eventual success due to his work ethic and a triumphant return to Japan, ultimately validate his life journey. He seems particularly proud of having paid for his children's education and his generosity with his compatriots. In this sense, the memoirs are a moral tale, a didactic narrative in which, as in Lizardi's *El periquillo sarniento*, he warns his children and readers not to deviate from the right path and to avoid vices at all costs. Somehow, Nakatani did learn a lesson from his father: regardless of one's educational attainment, through hard work and resilience, economic success is attainable. Despite all adversities, including a brother's death, his disappointment with two women in Japan, his drinking and gambling habits, and the disenfranchisement of the Nikkei community during World War II, Nakatani's resilience allowed him to reach the "promised land." At the end of a turbulent life, he felt accomplished and proud of his achievements. He passed away from cancer in 1992, at the age of eighty-two.

MEMOIRS AS AUTOETHNOGRAPHY

In *Imperial Eyes: Travel Writing and Transculturation*, the literary scholar Mary Louise Pratt argues that "if ethnographic texts are a means by which Europeans represent to themselves their (usually subjugated) others, autoethnographic texts are those the others construct in response to or in dialogue with those metropolitan representations" (1992, 7). Pratt emphasizes the "transnational" nature of autoethnographic texts as opposed to simplistically considering them "authentic" or "autochthonous" representations of a culture's essence. Yet she also maintains that, through autoethnography, the former object of ethnographic representation "talks back" to the Western Others; that is, they contest the biased representation carried out by exogenous, metropolitan ethnographers with a supposedly more accurate and authentic self-representation based on the author's insider status. These insider autoethnographers are then supposed to correct the notion that their culture is "lacking" or "backward" and, consequently, ripe for colonization.

The literary scholar James Buzard questions Pratt's approach because, in his view, she leaves no room to investigate "how an individual member of a culture goes about *securing* the authority to represent or 'speak on behalf of' the culture to which he or she belongs" (2005, 13–14). He reminds us, quoting James Clifford, that no inherent authority should be given to the autoethnographer for the simple fact of being an insider to the "traditional" culture, peripheral community, or ethnic group. From this perspective, one must be cautious when analyzing how insiders like Nakatani, Nonaka, and Akane choose to represent their own culture in their native Japan or the hybrid culture of Mexican Nikkeijin.

Rather than clearly demarcating the space of the researcher from that of the researched, autoethnography embraces personal involvement and subjectivity, allowing writers to express their feelings and emotions in their research. There is, as a result, no intention to give the impression of objectivity, detachment, or neutrality in knowledge production, which brings autoethnography closer to ethnic memoirs like Nakatani's. In this sense, the communication scholars Laura. L. Ellingson and Carolyn Ellis see autoethnography as a critical "response to the alienating effects on both researchers and audiences of impersonal, passionless, abstract claims of truth generated by such research practices and clothed in exclusionary scientific discourse" (2008, 450). While Nakatani's "Novela escrita" belongs in the literary realm rather than the social sciences, it does deploy autoethnographic techniques.

As does autoethnography, Nakatani's memoirs link his autobiography and personal experiences with the wider sociopolitical, cultural, and economic ramifications that affected his ethnic group of the era. Autobiography and ethnic identity go hand in hand in this confessional text, as the memoirist selects significant episodes of his own life to be recalled, some affected by historical events with repercussions for his entire ethnic group. His personal narrative and storytelling include passages with interpretations of his own culture and assessments of the Japanese Mexican community, which give his writing ethnographic overtones. In certain passages, the memoirs become a sort of textual *Wunderkammer*, or cabinet of curiosities, in which the author seems to be trying to pique his readers' curiosity and inspire wonder by explaining idiosyncratic behaviors and describing objects that Westerners would consider strange or exotic.

Nakatani's autoethnographical memoirs are moved by conflict-driven drama that evinces emotional responses from the reader. His erratic behavior and inability to control his ludopathy, together with his penchant for drinking and gambling with fellow Japanese immigrants, are self-consciously presented as addictions that almost ruined his life and brought suffering to his close relatives. Some passages seem to seek the reader's empathy for this imperfect man who struggles with addiction. Despite all his mistakes and flaws, Nakatani's confessional tone does elicit compassion from the reader and allows for redemption at the end of the narrative. By re-creating the circumstances that gave rise to such behavior, he offers a justification in search of forgiveness, perhaps from the very relatives he hurt in the past.

His personal story invites criticism, even cultural criticism, which makes it more credible than the more common hagiographic accounts about flawlessly patriotic and abnegated Japanese immigrants. Moreover, although his peculiar behavior cannot be generalized to his ethnic group, the memoirs certainly make it clear that he is not the only Nikkeijin to behave improperly, indecorously, or unethically. A merit of these memoirs is precisely that it provides a more human, realistic face to Japanese immigration in Latin America.

Nakatani provides much ethnographic information about the Japan of his formative years: explaining how a man would adopt his wife's surname upon marriage; considering the neighbors in the seven closest houses to yours part of the family; and treating the ill with baths of sulfuric water, by consuming water with the patient's excrement in it, or eating ashes from a dead person on an empty stomach. Several passages reveal other Japanese folk notions, such as considering leprosy a divine punishment, or customs of different types of suicide like *seppuku* (hara-kiri) or *jigai* (slitting the aorta artery). Likewise, after he runs away with Chioko and her family searches for her all night, Nakatani explains her relatives' fear: youngsters would often commit suicide out of *sentimentalismo*, or sentimentalism (2002, 142). Similarly, when Zuyako is showing Nakatani the beautiful hometown lake, she reveals, "Here, in this lake, many youngsters commit suicide from heartbreak."[25]

Some anecdotes included in the opening chapter are indicative of why first-person accounts cannot always be taken at face value. For instance, we learn that while trying to fish one day, Nakatani falls into the river and later becomes sick. It is then decided that it was the *tanuki* who had brought on the illness. Nakatani proceeds to explain, through a legend, what he truly believes: "There is in Japan a legend about this animal. It is invisible but, when someone urinates where its young are, it takes revenge by taking over that person's body. Doctors are unable to cure this illness. My fever continued to be elevated. I told my mother that I wanted to eat rice and beans, but the one really asking was the tanuki because, in my moments of lucidity, I could not remember a thing."[26] The *tanuki* is a real nocturnal animal, also known as the Japanese racoon dog. In Japanese folklore, however, there is a supernatural being based on the *tanuki* called *bake-danuki*. The mischievous *bake-danuki* is considered a master of disguise and of shape-shifting.

Some believe that it can transform itself into any object or person to possess its victims.

In his cultural translation, Nakatani proceeds to explain that, after three months of illness, his family sought the help of someone who, in Mexico, would be considered a medium (possibly referring to an *itako* or Japanese spiritual medium).[27] The medium asked the sick boy to take rice balls and sweet-potato candy to a small convent while asking the *tanuki* for forgiveness. One day, the *tanuki* finally leaves his body, telling him: "For so long I ate rice and I enjoyed it so much; now I'm leaving."[28] After that, Nakatani fully recovers. He, therefore, interprets this magical occurrence as just another mundane event in his life. Other folktales are scattered throughout the text. Later in the memoirs, Nakatani is convinced that a lamp that fell on his bed meant that his mother had passed away in Japan. Likewise, toward the memoirs' end, Nakatani sees the ghost of Yukugama, a deceased friend, by his bed one night and recalls that he had forgotten to meet his friend's wish: to send his family one of his possessions after death.

Other passages resemble *costumbrista* scenes,[29] like the one describing his wooden *geta* footwear (Nakatani Sánchez 2002, 154) or street fighting between youth gangs: "In Japan, every neighborhood had groups of rebellious boys that liked to fight each other. Only two boys, one from each group, fought one on one and whoever won became the leader."[30] In another passage, Nakatani describes an object that does not exist in the West: "Next to him, there was a vase with ashes that was burning. This was a Japanese custom. An iron was placed among the ashes so that it would remain hot. It was used to iron the wrinkles of kimono lapels."[31]

There are also passages that go beyond the description of cultural peculiarities. Early in the memoirs, for example, Nakatani displays his sense of social justice by condemning the discrimination against the Korean ethnic minority in Japan, known as Zainichi-Kankoku-jin or just Zainichi (Japan resident), the country's second-largest ethnic minority after the Chinese:

> About 150 students with Korean blood came from two towns. Centuries before, the empire sent a delegation to Korea to hire some twenty persons to perform demeaning jobs in Japan. Over time, this ethnic group increased in numbers to approximately half a million, all trying to eke out an existence. Because their children could not be registered at birth as ethnically Japanese, they were labeled Shingemin. When they argued with the Japanese, these called them the epithet Shingemin to their faces. Having befriended them, I wondered why the Japanese saw them as different and offended them like that. It hurt me to witness this.[32]

Nakatani mentions further on that Koreans (and at times Okinawans) worked in railroad construction or mining. Zuyako explains to him that they sing "to see if they manage to free themselves from that hell," and that they purchase their groceries with cardboard pieces issued by the company because they receive no monetary wages.[33] Nakatani observes that, while the water in the Japanese employees' public restroom was clean, that in the Korean workers' was extremely dirty. These episodes open his eyes to the unjust treatment of Koreans in Japan: "It saddened me to see how they daily beat Koreans because they missed work and, I asked myself, 'Why do the Japanese treat these poor people like that?'"[34] Similarly, on the voyage to Mexico, the ship stopped at the port of Los Angeles, where Nakatani becomes upset upon witnessing how African American workers were being treated: "I was surprised because, though they were big, strong black men, they were treated so badly; I asked myself how was that much discrimination possible and my heart ached."[35]

As a member of an ethnic minority in Mexico, Nakatani identified even more with the plight of this discriminated-against group who could trace their roots to a Korea under Japanese occupation (1910–1945). He proudly remembers how he befriended several ethnic Korean children and how he would eat their food out of respect because he did not much like it. Although he criticizes his countrymen for discriminating against ethnic Koreans, Nakatani also recalls having a fight with an ethnic Korean friend and calling him the xenophobic epithet for Koreans in Japan "Shingemin." Soon thereafter, fifty members of his ethnic group showed up at Nakatani's restaurant demanding an apology. He and his brother hence stopped going to school because their new enemies would impede their entry.

PATRIARCHAL RECOLLECTIONS OF WIVES IN MEXICO

A major component of the ethnographic value of Nakatani's memoirs resides in the fact that it provides an insider's window to the daily life of the Nikkei community in Mexico City, which he describes as "small but very united."[36] The following passage, for instance, reveals interesting information about Japanese picture brides who traveled to Latin America: "At times, these women do not reach their destination. On the voyage, they fall in love with another passenger; for this reason, they never come alone, be they married or single. They also commit suicide by throwing themselves into the sea."[37] One wonders, then, as to how voluntary these voyages were for certain picture brides. Nakatani also offers the example of a frustrated picture bride who, after seeing in a Japanese newspaper an advertisement about a millionaire immigrant in Mexico looking for a wife, married the "jealous and miserable" Istani. The woman vents to Nakatani about how she has come to understand why Istani's previous wife committed suicide.

Nakatani's notion of an ideal Japanese wife is apparent in a passage in which he expresses his admiration for the spouse of a man named Mutaguchi: "Mutaguchi made a lot of money and every day there were large dinners at his home. His wife was named Victoria and I admired her. She was a very prudent woman. When her husband was at the table with guests, she was always in the kitchen at her husband's call. Though he not always needed her, Mutaguchi still, out of habit, constantly called out Toya, her nickname."[38] Following a sexist, patriarchal logic insinuated in the earlier description of his relationship with Zuyako in Japan, Nakatani's admiration for the presumably Japanese Victoria was based on her submissiveness to her husband. This masculinized memory of a Japanese wife in Mexico stands in sharp contrast to the female agency emphasized by Akane in her tanka (see the following chapter) and to that of Zuyako, who refused to give up her job despite Nakatani's jealousy. Moreover, in Nakatani's memoirs, gambling, drinking, and partying seem to be associated with a type of toxic masculinity that prioritizes male bonding and diversion over the family's well-being: "We had already been married three years. My son was two years old when we had a girl who we named Alicia. I couldn't stop gambling and I would get together with some of my countrymen. The habit was so ingrained that, on weekends, which was when I played, I would not return home to sleep. My worried wife would call my godparents thinking I was there but, having told her no, they would worry as well."[39] Nakatani admits that sometimes he would entirely forget about his wife and children.[40] He also laments missing investment opportunities because he had squandered his savings by gambling.

Nakatani's wife is an abnegated, distressed background figure throughout the memoirs but gains more protagonism in the description of their trip to Japan. Nakatani often praises her patience with him throughout the years and is obviously proud of her diligence and resilience at work. Yet we rarely hear her voice or even name, although it was she who transcribed her husband's narrated biography. Tellingly, only toward the end of the story does Nakatani acknowledge her: "Emma, *which is my wife's name*, likes to have her hair done."[41] He credits her several times for having the foresight to save to invest in their business or for offering excellent advice (e.g., not traveling to Sonora to borrow money). She nevertheless features mostly as an afterthought in many of his personal decisions, including registering his Nikkei friends' possessions (Sato's factory and another Nikkeijin's car) under her name during the war, a decision that almost ended in her arrest. From his granddaughter Emma, we learn that, besides having seven children, her grandmother also had six miscarriages, a result of her excessive working (Nakatani Sánchez 2002, 24). It is astonishing that this recurrent family tragedy is not even mentioned in the memoirs.

JAPANESE IMPERIALISM

From the information gathered so far from Nakatani's memoirs, particularly keeping in mind his disinterest in improving Japan's image in Latin America, one would assume that he was one among many Japanese men who never felt interpellated as an imperial subject.[42] Still, a close interpretation of his stance vis-à-vis Japanese imperialism provides a different outlook. As is characteristic of Nikkei literature in Latin America, Nakatani conveniently avoids addressing Japanese aggressive imperialism and colonialism in his writing. Despite this collective imperial amnesia, some of his passages provide interesting hints about his viewpoints. For instance, referring to compulsory military service in Japan, he alludes to the "fanaticism" of the young, characterized by its nationalistic, militaristic nature: "In Japan, there was much fanaticism and when it was time to be drafted into the military, youngsters saw themselves as responsible men and felt immense joy."[43] Nakatani admits to failing the draft's physical because he does not meet the minimum-height requirement. Ashamed, he bemoans his inability to serve his country and fears his father's disappointment.

When Nakatani returns to Awaji to obtain an official good-conduct certificate to emigrate to Mexico and "clean his life," the functionary initially refuses for this reason: "Why are you moving abroad? Don't you know that the fatherland needs soldiers?"[44] Only after Nakatani starts to weep as he kneels and reminds him that men can also serve the homeland abroad does the delegate give in. He reminds them: "You are going abroad and must succeed."[45] Then, another man interpellates Nakatani as an imperial subject by reminding him about his duty to return triumphantly. His economic success is therefore presented as an imperative for a government determined to improve its international image. As in other Latin American–Nikkei narratives, the emigrant—Nakatani here—confesses that it would be humiliating to return before becoming successful: "Mom, I'm leaving. I hope to succeed and return. And if I don't make it, I can't return!"[46] Therefore, at least initially, his move to Mexico must be conceived of at the intersection of self-interest and his country's imperialism.

Nakatani provides his version of Japan's annexation of the Ryukyu Islands, one that is in line with Nihonjinron discourse. On the voyage to Mexico, he meets several Okinawan picture brides and narrates to them the origins of karate, as he learned it at a judo club, as well as the story of the Ryukyu Kingdom, their homeland: "Eventually, Japan won [defeated de Russian Empire] and took Formosa, Korea, and Manchuria. With this triumph, Japan's territory grew fifty times over. Okinawa joined Japan and you asked to adopt our flag and began to learn our language. Your kimonos used to be a bit different but, since the war, they are now like ours."[47] To Nakatani, it was not an imposed annexation; Okinawa requested it. The truth of the matter is that the Ryukyu Kingdom was first invaded and made a vassal state by the Satsuma Domain of Japan in 1609, then transformed into the Ryukyu Domain by the Empire of Japan in 1872. Seven years later, it was formally annexed as the Okinawa Prefecture.

Two years after his departure, Nakatani met Emma, made Mexico his home, and no longer wished to return to Japan; however, he still worried about his country's wars. He mentions, for example, that the yen's worth was lower because of "the war between China and Japan. On the one hand, we were happy, we earned good money, yet we were concerned about the situation Japan was undergoing."[48] Nakatani, proceeding to mention the second Sino-Japanese War (1937–1945), does not acknowledge Japan's imperialist motives that led to millions of casualties, an outcome known as "The Asian Holocaust." It is unclear whether he had bought into his country's militaristic propaganda or whether he simply was unaware of how problematic Japan's aggressive foreign policy was at the time. Nakatani also recalls celebrating with the rest of the Japanese community the Japanese emperor's birthday at the consulate in Mexico City.

Other passages more directly reveal that Mexico's Nikkei community was aware of political developments back home. For instance, we learn that Oku, a Nikkei gambler, was robbed by two Mexican policemen and left nude on the street, until a kind American couple helped the scared immigrant. Retelling the story to Nakatani, Oku states: "That couple was American, Nakatani. I don't understand how I managed to find such humane people who helped me, despite the fact that the political relationship between Japan and the United States is very tense."[49] Incidentally, as an example of active resistance and a reluctant trust in the Mexican police and legal system, Nakatani, ignoring the advice of his Mexican friends, later accompanied Oku to the police station. There, Oku identified the two corrupt policemen, who were eventually sentenced to fifteen years in prison. Oku, fearing for his life, returned to Japan.

Nakatani recalls the origin of his country's differences with the United States after the latter prevented further sales of Mexican oil to Japan: "We the Japanese who lived in Mexico were concerned. We knew that there was a lot of oil here, but that it would not be sold to Japan, and without it, Japan would be in trouble."[50] Of particular interest is his description of the Nikkei community's reaction to the Japanese surprise attack on Pearl Harbor on 7 December 1941, which decimated the US Pacific Fleet: "Ojara turned on the radio and we heard on the news that Japan had bombed Hawaii. Hearing the news, we felt immense joy. . . . Forty of us met, some already aware, others not. Ojara said, 'I called you because this is a serious situation and we must think carefully. We are US neighbors, but Mexico is on Japan's side; here, we face no danger, but this country is America's neighbor. Why did Japan attack before declaring war?'"[51] The Nikkei community's initial sense of security turned into worry: Would Mexico side with Japan? Interestingly, a pro-Japanese Mexican army colonel asked Nakatani to translate Japanese radio war dispatches to pass on to his superiors. The above excerpt, however, subtly conveys a sense of shame stemming from Japan's attack without a previous declaration of war. Nakatani added that they spent the entire night talking and wondering why Japan would start a war nine years after its hostilities with China.

Even though he remains confident that President Ávila Camacho is on the side of Japan, the consul Coshida warns Mexico City's Nikkei community of a possible emergency situation. Eventually, Ávila Camacho had no alternative but to declare war on the Axis powers in May 1942, after German U-boats torpedoed and sunk two Mexican ships. At a climactic point in the narration, Nakatani recalls the order to relocate the Nikkei community: "A month passed and, with sadness, we learned that Japan was withdrawing. A Japanese submarine near Los Angeles had fired a couple of cannon volleys but they fell into the sea. Many people saw this. The United States, angered, ordered Mexico to break diplomatic relations with Japan and to relocate us. That was the order."[52] The memoirist does not comment on the fact that, according to his own words, Mexico, a sovereign nation, took orders from the United States. In this context, the international migration expert Francis Peddie suggests that the Mexican government adopted this measure in pursuit of three interrelated goals: "To assure domestic stability through the elimination of a 'fifth column' from within; to appease the United States' fear that Japan, directly or through its subjects residing in Mexico, would use Mexican territory to attack America; and to comply with the obligations set forth in the 1930s and 1940s Pan-American agreements for the defense of the

Western Hemisphere as well as to promote political and economic cooperation within it."53

Nakatani also recalls Japanese diplomats' send-off after their official expulsion (the Portuguese embassy represented Japan in Mexico) and how the consul reminded the 140 Nikkeijin at the ceremony that the Japanese government expected proper behavior from them. Although this is not mentioned in Nakatani's memoirs, according to Peddie, one of the repatriated men was Heiji Kato, from El Nuevo Japón, who had hired Nakatani. Kato, had also been one of the three businessmen chosen by the Japanese legation in Mexico City, before it was expelled from the country in February 1942, to organize the Comité de Ayuda Mutua (Committee of Mutual Assistance), in charge of helping displaced Nikkeijin who arrived in the capital city.

According to Nakatani, the consul yelled "Long live the emperor!" three times, and several Nikkeijin fainted. Subsequently, Nakatani, in the passage in which he most expresses his anguish and suffering in the memoirs, worries about his family's welfare once he is interned with the other Nikkeijin, destitute as he was on account of his gambling. Relieved after learning that they are to be interned in Mexico City, he continues to express his compassion for the many Nikkeijin arriving from other states who lost their jobs and properties: "Five days later, the Japanese from the provinces began to arrive, but those who suffered the most were from Ciudad Juárez, Mexicali, and Tijuana. They did not have time to sell their belongings. Many were millionaires, but they had their fortunes invested and only brought a little cash. Afterward, their friends, benefitting from the business temporarily under their trust, turned their backs on them. It was January, it was cold, and they suffered hardship."54 Traveling under substandard conditions, some Nikkeijin lost their lives. As Peddie points out, "Under these conditions, not everyone held out: a baby and two elderly individuals died on the way. Besides being tired, hungry, and destitute, those relocated arrived at their destinations without food, shelter, or work."55

Nakatani reveals an uglier side of Mexicans' response to these measures: some took advantage of the displaced Nikkeijin.56 We also learn that destitute Nikkeijin found refuge in the Hacienda Batán, owned by a certain Matsumoto. Here, Nakatani is referring to the flower shop owner Tasuguro Matsumoto, responsible for the jacaranda trees found across Mexico. Peddie explains:

> To solve this problem, Sanshiro Matsumoto "made available to them his property, the Hacienda Batán" . . . Nearly one hundred displaced Nikkeijin, lack-

ing shelter, went there. However, with the continuous arrival of more Japanese from the border and coastal states, Batán was no longer large enough to accommodate them all. According to an undated list from the Interior Ministry, Batán became temporary housing to 569 individuals . . . who slept on mattresses supplied by Heiji Kato. This situation [needing additional housing] forced the *kyoeikai* members to seek a permanent solution: relocation to an agricultural field in the former Hacienda de Temixco in the state of Morelos.[57]

In the end, some 3,500 Nikkeijin, mostly middle class, were displaced. This is a significant number considering that Mexico's Nikkei community was estimated at 6,000 (Peddie 2006, 79). Others ended up in prison for traveling outside Mexico City, like Nakatani's godfather, who had gone to Acapulco to gamble and was arrested under suspicion of espionage; he remained incommunicado for two months.

Confirming Nakatani's denunciation, Peddie provides additional information about the many cases of exploitation and abuse against relocated Nikkeijin, including extortion, blackmail, and bribery at customs and immigration offices, and even forced labor, as was the case for fifty-six Japanese immigrants in Villa Aldama, Chihuahua (2006, 88). Likewise, Selfa Chew, in *Mudas las garzas*, records the extorsion suffered by Nikkeijin from Ciudad Juárez at the hands of the immigration director (2007, 111). Adding to these affronts, Nakatani explains, the Mexican government froze the bank accounts of Nikkei residents, allowing them only to withdraw a maximum of five hundred pesos a month. Henceforth, nationals hailing from Axis powers could not become naturalized citizens; those who naturalized in the prior two years lost their citizenship. But it was not only Mexicans who took advantage of the chaotic situation; according to Nakatani, Matusina, a Nikkeijin who owned a watch store, stole the funds the Japanese embassy had set aside for providing housing to the displaced Nikkeijin and refused to help those who arrived in the capital city. Another Nikkeijin was surprised smuggling weapons out of the Japanese embassy. And although Nakatani mentions this strange episode only in passing, the reader is left to wonder why the Japanese embassy kept so many weapons. Was the link between state-sponsored emigration to Mexico and Japanese imperialism stronger than we were led to believe? In any case, in the midst of this chaos, desperate Nikkeijin arriving to Mexico City would ask Nakatani for guidance because he had resided in the city for many years.

Unsurprisingly, Nakatani tells a very different story from the official accounts about the Hacienda Temixco, where many displaced Nikkeijin were housed: "Near Cuernavaca, in a town called Temixco, there was a refinery, but it had been closed. Seven Japanese capitalists rented it out and brought the poor relocated immigrants there. Because its surrounding land was extensive, they turned it into a rice plantation to take advantage of the available labor; however, they paid them starving wages. . . . Many people suffered but, because of their extreme situation, they allowed themselves to be exploited."[58] He recalls seeing small children sleeping on dirt floors and many dying there of different causes. Nakatani therefore challenges the historical discourse that presents these capitalists as generous heroes who saved the displaced Nikkeijin by providing them with a place to stay; rather, he exposes their opportunism and unscrupulous exploitation of their compatriots' dire situation.

At one point, nonviolently echoing on a much smaller scale what happened in Brazil with the terrorist group Shindō Renmei after World War II, Nakatani and some friends founded a patriotic club in response to the anti-Japanese animosity they felt in the streets: "When I went out on the streets, I would hear comments about my country, good and bad. Four of us jointly created a Patriots Club. With time, membership reached three thousand, including women and children."[59] Suddenly, a diasporic nationalist discourse appears in the memoirs. As happened throughout Latin America, certain gullible Issei, alienated by discrimination and upheaval during the war—and isolation to boot for Brazilian Nikkeijin—believed rumors about Japan's victory. Tokyo radio's announcements of bogus Japanese battle victories significantly contributed to the propagation of this falsehood. In addition, many Nikkeijin, with limited knowledge of Spanish (or Portuguese), did not have access to local information sources. Furthermore, having lost representation after the expulsion of all members of the Japanese embassy and being without access to the remains of the ancestors for worship, many turned to the emperor as their paternal figure and sole icon of leadership—emperor worship, therefore, became a transnational form of Shintoism. Some Issei, still convinced of Japan's invincibility and slowly losing respect for the older generation, formed underground *kachigumi* (victory groups) and refused to acknowledge the emperor's unconditional surrender after the US bombing of Hiroshima and Nagasaki. These groups strived to keep their ethnic community's pride and loyalty to Japan intact, and in Brazil and Hawaii, where the first Japanese immigrants hired to work on sugar plantations had arrived in 1870, they were even certain that a Japanese fleet would come to take them to Japan-held territories. The same rumors about a fast-approaching Japanese fleet reappear in Reyes Estrada's novel *La gallina azul* and in Federico Imamura's memoirs *Casi un siglo de recuerdos*.

Whereas a large majority of Brazilian Nikkeijin initially supported Shindō Renmei, only about half of Mexican Nikkeijin supported the Patriots Club (the Japanese Mexican version of the Japanese Brazilian Kachigumi or "Victorists"), according to Nakatani. Again, this assertion significantly differs from historical claims that they were but a small minority in Mexico. It seems safe to assume that the nationalist education received in Japan prevented Nakatani from believing that Japan could be defeated in war. Eventually, his blind patriotism led him to distance himself from his beloved godfather, Mutaguchi, soon before his death, given that the latter knew that Japan had no chance of winning the war. At war's end, Nakatani, revealed as a staunch nationalist, refuses to believe that the Japanese emperor has surrendered. In fact, on the emperor's birthday, he participates in a demonstration, along with Patriots Club members, on Calle de los Niños Héroes, protesting the "fake news" of Japan's defeat. Although mainstream Mexicans mocked them, Nakatani sensed the respect of the police. He went as far as to collect funds, as did his friends Sakaguchi and Nishikawa, to travel to Japan to verify whether his country lost the war. The two friends made the voyage; incredibly, Nishikawa refused to accept defeat, even after his visit. Sakaguchi, by contrast, met his son and brother who assured him. Only after losing all his money and deciding to make a new type of candy, *ranchero*, did Nakatani begin to forget about his patriotic club. In the end, Nakatani and Sakaguchi were expelled from the club for acknowledging Japan's defeat.

History books often affirm that after World War II, with Japan in ruins, Latin American Nikkeijin realized that their dream of going home was over; they would have to continue to reside in Latin America and adjust to the new circumstances. Nakatani mentions that, after the war, five hundred Nikkeijin in Mexico did return to Japan. Those who could afford the fare, like his friend Istani, waited anxiously for more than three months for the ship to dock. Some resold their tickets for a tidy profit without difficulty. Many made the voyage and left their businesses behind. According to Nakatani, this was a terrible mistake: "The Japanese who returned to Japan failed; those who stayed in Mexico made a fortune."[60] For instance, his deported former boss Kato lost his investments in Mexico because they were stolen by three employees to whom he had entrusted their oversight.

Likewise, although it is known that most relocated Nikkeijin stayed in Mexico City after the war, Nakatani mentions families that returned to Sonora, Mexicali, and other places where they owned property. He also emphasizes cases of interethnic solidarity: certain wealthy Arabs, for example, loaned money to someone who, forty years later, became the wealthiest man in the Nikkei community. By contrast, this passage suggests that relations between Nikkei and Chinese immigrants in Mexico City were a bit more problematic: "Unfortunately, I found a Chinese gambling house on a street in Dolores. No Japanese went there, except for me. Those there were heartless people who took drugs. I don't know where they got the money to gamble."[61] Even though Nakatani overcame Japanese prejudice toward the Chinese and visited the gambling house, he could not help but mistrust and deride them.

Nakatani proceeds to describe the American military presence in Sonora during the war. After a long trip there to borrow money from a friend named Kadama, someone he helped in Mexico City, he notices that his friend's house is quite luxurious. His friend explains: "When they relocated my family in Mexico, the US government sent soldiers here for surveillance. This house was built for them. After the war, they gave the property to my father before leaving; my father then worked the land and earned much money."[62] Incidentally, despite his boundless generosity with Nikkeijin in Mexico City during the war, Nakatani not only did not obtain the loan but also had to endure the insults of Tanaka, an inebriated compatriot who had made his fortune there: "Tanaka had the biggest ranch there and plenty of money. That's why he felt so important and wanted to boss everybody around."[63]

Nakatani observes a change in Nikkei work ethic caused by the war's outcome: "Vice increased with Japan's defeat. Many countrymen began to drink and gamble. When Japan was an empire, all worked hard for the fatherland. Now, some still work, own profitable businesses, but they work to increase their own capital."[64] The same idea is later melancholically restated: "Now that Japan lost, they have forgotten their homeland."[65] Nakatani, however, makes no mention of his own hard work in Mexico in the context of supporting the Japanese Empire.

Finally, regarding the memoirist's views on Japanese imperialism, his granddaughter Emma reveals what is not entirely apparent in her grandfather's memoirs. Her uncle, the painter Carlos Nakatani Ávila, recalls his father teaching him an aggressive war song: "I learned that song that you've heard me sing when I got together with your father . . . 'Aishinkoku.' It entailed forty odd stanzas, and it was a war song that encourages the Japanese to fight on, to kill whoever gets . . . I learned all fortysomething stanzas, each stanza has four lines. . . He taught it to me. For what? I do remember that sometimes they met, those who approved of a militaristic Japan."[66] The word *Shinkoku* included in the song's title refers to Japan as a divine land, founded and protected by the power of the *kami* (divine Shinto beings) and the holy imperial lineage. With the expansion of Japanese militarism and colonialism, this concept, stressed in times of war by state-supported Shintoism, became associated with nationalism, hegemonism, and xenophobia. It seems clear that the patriotic, nationalist education that young Nakatani received influenced him throughout his life. And although he married a Mexican woman and spent most of his life in Mexico, it is hard not to notice, throughout a narrative that constantly emphasizes the importance of friendship and loyalty, a peculiarity in these "affective economies": most of his friends were Nikkeijin. Tellingly, he asked his children to look for Japanese visitors during the 1968 Mexico City Olympic Games to invite them over to the house. When he mentions non-Nikkei men, they are often framed within the context of confrontation.

As stated, Nakatani's self-reflective musings and regrets for past mistakes also have a didactic, moralizing role, as exempla of the path to follow. Although humbly acknowledging his wrongdoings and the harm he caused his loved ones, he highlights his eventual economic success via ingenuity and a strong work ethic. He likewise showcases his own generosity with other Nikkei immigrants, even though several never repaid him their debts and some even turned their back on him.

Whether intentionally or not, Nakatani's counternarrative questions the monolithic cultural script about Japanese immigrants in Latin America, all the while disrupting the ideological discourse and representational practices of Nihonjinron as a regime of truth. This (perhaps accidentally) oppositional discourse produces a counterknowledge that adds eye-opening nuance to the Japanese Mexican cultural imaginary. Beyond discourse formation and ideology, his memoirs disclose, apparently without much censure or concern for the making of a Japanese Mexican social identity, the true daily lives of Nihonjin and Nikkeijin. His outlook represents a counternarrative to official discourses of the Japanese nation. In this sense, it is an important historical document, one that contradicts some of the received knowledge about the history of Nikkei immigration in Mexico, including episodes about the motivations of the capitalists who rented the Hacienda Temixco and the Mexican Nikkeijin who refused to believe Japan had been defeated in World War II. The traditionally heroic protagonist of an epic overseas adventure, above all in first-person narratives, becomes a sort of antihero who is unashamed to showcase his virtues and his flaws, even within the story's moralizing and didactic ultimate message. "Novela escrita" is also a good example of the need to use an Asia–Latin America epistemological lens and heuristic focus, which turns Asian–Latin Americans from passive objects into active subjects of knowledge as opposed to taking the region and its people as mere passive objects of study.

CHAPTER 3

Strategic Essentialism in Akane's Performative *Tanka*

This chapter focuses on the tanka, a classical Japanese poetic genre, written in Japanese by the Issei Mitsuko Esperanza Kasuga (pen name "Akane"; 1914–2002) throughout her life. Akane's verses belong to that interstitial stratum mentioned in the introduction: the author, an immigrant writing in Japanese, feels nostalgic about her homeland but increasingly (and later deeply) rooted in Mexican culture and with a sense of belonging to the host country. Are we to assume that this is Japanese, Mexican, Nikkei/Japanese Mexican, immigrant literature (*imin bungaku*), or all the above? Perhaps more important is the awareness that, with all those symbolic edges blurred, a transpacific epistemological position or critical lens is in order for its analysis.

After Akane self-published her poetry in two volumes, *Tanka by Akane* and *Haiku by Akane*, 113 of her tanka were compiled and thematically arranged in the trilingual English, Spanish, and Japanese edition *Akane, Immigrant Poet: The Tanka of Mitsuko Kasuga*, edited by Aiko Chikaba and translated by the poet Naoko Shin. The poems were also published in a bilingual Japanese and Spanish edition (often with significant and interesting interpretative discrepancies, as will be seen) under the Spanish-language title *Akane: Los tankas de Mitsuko Kasuga, migrante japonesa en México* (Akane: The Tanka of Mitsuko Kasuga, a Japanese Migrant in Mexico), also edited by Aiko Chikaba, but translated by Miwa Teresa Pierre-Audain Kasuga and versified by Mara Pastor. The Spanish edition—with varying levels of aesthetic success in the translations' lyricism—includes a brief interpretation of each poem. Both editions include a detailed biography of this exceptional poet, based on the epilogues written by Akane herself in both works, her essay "Suberihiyu" (Purslane), and the text *Ojiichan* by Hermelinda Kasuga Osaka. The editions have similar covers, including the black-and-white photograph of a serious, young poet dressed in traditional Japanese attire, taken just before her emigrating to Mexico in 1930. (The Spanish edition's back cover includes a photograph of an elderly Akane.) Several other tanka and haiku by Akane are yet to be translated and published. Her family in Mexico is in possession of the two self-published collections on which the two published translations were based.

Akane chose two classical Japanese genres for her poetry: haiku and tanka. A *waka*, today known as tanka (literally "short song"), is a thirty-one-syllable poem, known in the West for its five unrhymed lines, with a 5-7-5-7-7 syllable count (in Japanese, the five units appear on a single line). Originating in the eighth century, during the Heian-kyō era (794–1185), tanka became popular as a way for lovers to express their romantic feelings for each other. It was also the form par excellence in poetry contests at the Japanese Imperial Court. In an effect often compared to the Western sonnet, a pivotal image or turn in the third or central line of the tanka often connects the first three lines or tercet (5-7-5, *kami-no-ku* or "upper lines"; the ancestor of the haiku) with the closing couplet (7-7, *shimo-no-ku* or "lower lines"). This image or turn indicates a harmonious transition or shift from the description of a sensory experience or exploration of an image in the *kami-no-ku* to the expression of the personal response or emotion induced by that image in the *shimo-no-ku*. Traditionally, a range of words or *engo* (verbal associations) bridges the two sections. As Janick Belleau explains: "Nowadays, what characterizes a tanka is how it juxtaposes emotion and sensory experience. An image, a scent or a sound can bring on an emotion that relates to impermanence–of things and of beings in this world. The resulting outcome would be a feeling of sadness mixed with hope: nothing lasts, but seasons, aren't they regularly reborn? The parallels between life and cycles of nature are therefore constant" (2012, 2).

Tanka do not usually include a *kigo*, or seasonal term often present in haiku. Yet it is common for images of nature to trigger fleeting emotions, intuitions, and thoughts, which may be either gratifying or upsetting (reminiscent of the death of a loved one, for example). Many of the greatest tanka poets were women, including Lady Murasaki Shikubi, author of the early eleventh-century classic *Genji monogatari* (*The Tale of Genji*), which includes nearly eight-hundred tanka. Akane undoubtedly mastered the main virtue of this poetic form, smoothly uniting an intense physical sensation with deeply intimate emotion.

Akane's tanka provide a valuable insight into the intimate, daily life of a "picture bride" (*shashin hanayome*) in Mexico, as well as into the collective and relatively unknown history of Japanese picture brides in Latin America.[1] Often failing to earn enough money to purchase a return ticket to Japan, Japanese immigrants began to consider the picture bride system as an alternative. They resorted to a local matchmaker (*nakodo* in Japanese) who provided photographs along with recommendations by the women's families. Considered an abbreviated version of the traditional custom of *miai kekkon*, or arranged marriage, in which a man and a woman were introduced to consider the opportunity of courtship and marriage, the go-between provided information about the prospective bride's age, health, wealth, and family background.

Some Japanese women from impoverished families, like Akane, became picture brides for economic reasons, in hopes of being able to support their families back home. Others were simply obeying their parents' wishes or escaping familial responsibilities such as filial piety, thus gaining additional freedom. The marriage was considered official in Japan once the bride's name was entered in her husband's family registry. Occasionally, picture brides were disappointed to meet a husband who was considerably different from the person in a photograph or living in unacceptable conditions. Like Akane, many picture brides tried to teach Japanese culture and traditions to their children and stayed in touch with other picture brides they met during the voyage. Some risked their reputation by eloping with men (*kakeochi*) they met during the voyage or at the destination.

According to the biographical information included in the poetry collection, twenty-two-year-old Akane, impoverished and feeling rejected by her own society, decides to emigrate to an unknown country. There she will manage, through hard work and resilience, to empower herself, her family, and her community despite of multiple misfortunes and tragedies. Her nostalgic poetry traces the brave path taken by a powerless, young picture bride who, against all odds, eventually recovers her agency and carves her own destiny. Akane's poetry is a major contribution to Japanese immigrant and, by extension, Nikkei literature in Latin America. Along with the works of the Peruvian Doris Moromisato and the Brazilians Tizuka Yamasaki, Mirian Lie Hatanaka and Maria Cecília Missako Ikeoka, her work challenges the relative invisibility of Nikkei women's discourse in the region.

AKANE'S "SPIRIT OF *GANBARE*"

Latin American Nikkei discourse often includes the "spirit of *ganbare*" (roughly meaning "hang in there," "try/do your best," "do not give up," frequently voiced in Japan to encourage people to succeed or to wish them good luck), as a national trait that is essentially Japanese.² In reality, there is nothing exclusively Japanese about being resilient and succeeding abroad. Akane's description of her and her husband's unrelenting struggle to prosper perhaps falls within this Japanese–Latin American discourse that suggests an exceptional Japanese essence. Born in 1914 in the small town of Ina, Nagano Prefecture, to a well-to-do family of silkworm and rice farmers, Akane benefited from educational reforms implemented during the Taisho period (1912–1926), which allowed her to attend, at the age of twelve, the progressive Ina School of Secondary Education for Girls. As a benefit, for instance, she visited the ports of Yokohama and Kobe on a graduation trip, an event that perhaps opened her eyes to the outside world.

Her decision to emigrate to Mexico was influenced by several personal and historical circumstances. First, after an employee of the local silkworm farmers' cooperative stole money in 1926, Akane's father, who served as treasurer, felt compelled to cover the losses with his own money. With her family bankrupted, young Akane began to notice that her neighbors were treating her contemptuously. A year after the devastating event, her mother's untimely death forced Akane to leave school to take over household and business responsibilities, thus forfeiting her dream of attending college. According to Chikaba, editor of *Akane, Immigrant Poet* and spouse of Akane's grandson, the poet used to say that she probably would not have made the risky decision of emigrating to Mexico had her mother not passed away.

Akane's reason for emigrating was to marry Tsutomu Carlos Kasuga, a Japanese immigrant who had moved to Mexico five years earlier. In 1930, at the age of twenty, he left for Mexico to join other Nagano immigrants, because the United States, his first choice (he dreamed of working in Hawaii), had passed laws preventing Japanese immigration. Akane had never met Kasuga; she had seen only the one photograph that the matchmaker brought her and had heard about his filial piety and reputation as a hard worker. Since their respective fathers had formalized their marriage in Japan, Akane was already a married woman who had adopted her husband's surname when she left for Mexico. At the age of twenty-two, she traveled by herself at a time when Japanese society frowned on such a journey, departing from the port of Yokohama (like Nakatani, in the previous chapter) in the cargo vessel *Rakuyo-Maru*, with the Chilean port of Valparaíso as its final destination. Foretelling her future devotion to literature, all she carried in her only suitcase were twelve books, a Japanese flag, and two changes of clothes (Chikaba 2016, 143). In Yokohama, she met two other Japanese picture brides headed for Mexico with whom she would stay in touch for the rest of her life. Their ship arrived in San Francisco, California, thirty days later, in June 1936, before again departing for Manzanillo, Mexico, where Akane disembarked. A train took her to her final destination, Cerritos, in San Luis Potosí, 370 miles inland, where she met Tsutomu Carlos Kasuga, four years her senior. No welcoming or wedding ceremony awaited Akane; instead, the morning after her arrival, she worked in the same local store as her apprentice husband, assisting clients even though she did not know a word of Spanish.

With time, she would overcome poverty, the deaths of relatives, and other adversities, working tirelessly to raise six children, becoming the teacher of many other Nikkei children, and helping her husband succeed in his numerous businesses. More importantly, she found time to write and, on occasions, published original tanka and haiku. According to Chikaba, although Akane had sporadically written poetry throughout her life, she began to take her vocation more seriously in 1955, thanks to the promotion of Nikkei poetry societies by the Japanese ambassador to Mexico. Joining these groups allowed Akane to share her writing with others and to receive valuable feedback.

As to Kasuga's motivation to emigrate, the Great Depression complicated the economic situation for Nagano Prefecture's farmers, as it stopped exports of silk textiles to the US. Kasuga's family, like Akane's, had incurred a large debt in Japan. After repaying the debt, Kasuga saw immigration to Mexico as a way out of a complicated life. Since most Japanese immigrants in Mexico were single men who lacked the funds to pay for a return trip, they saw the picture bride system (asking relatives to be matchmakers) as the most fitting manner to find suitable spouses. Chikaba clarifies that, although Akane was seventeen years old, an ideal age for marriage, in Japan then, "marriage was unlikely for a young woman from a family without assets. Akane knew that without the ability to provide the bridal furniture and dowry, she would have a low status in the family she married into" (Chikaba 2016, 134). Considering her limited marriage options, she decided to accept Tsutomu's matchmaker's offer.

Chikaba's biographical section includes other interesting episodes, such as the unexpected reaction of Mexican neighbors after the Pearl Harbor attack on December 7, 1941: whereas the local Japanese community in Cárdenas became concerned and Akane even feared that their store would be closed, the following day their Mexican customers congratulated them effusively and celebrated the attack. Still, popular support for the Japanese Empire did not prevent the Mexican government—or those of Peru and other Latin American countries—from meeting the US government's demand to forcibly relocate Japanese nationals and their descendants. Consequently, in mid-1942 the Kasuga family was given seventy-two hours to resettle by train with their three young children to Mexico City. According to Chikaba, though devastated, the Kasugas were moved by the support of their Mexican neighbors and local authorities. Both not only paid what they owned to their store but also wrote to the Mexican government asking that the Japanese be allowed to stay in Cárdenas. Earlier in the biographical section, we learned that local Mexican farmers trusted the Kasugas from the day of their arrival, thanks to the reputation of the Japanese for honesty. On the day of departure, neighbors went to the railway station to bid them farewell: "Normally stoic, Mitsuko could not stop the tears from rolling down her cheeks" (Chikaba 2016, 163).

At first, although life in the capital was harsh, the Kasugas survived owing to Tsutomu's precarious job selling fruit and vegetables. Chikaba points out that, although Akane and Tsutomu soon realized that Japan was about to be defeated, they refrained from sharing that information for fear of being considered traitors; part of the Nikkei community (among them, Nakatani; see Chapter 2) still believed in their country's invincibility (Chikaba 2016, 166). Adding to the adversities, a year after arriving in Mexico City, Akane suffered a miscarriage. It is quite plausible that the stress brought on by the forced relocation adversely affected the pregnancy.

Akane and Tsutomu, as most of their compatriots, decided to stay in the capital at war's end, since Mexico City offered better educational opportunities for their six children. After selling their house in Cárdenas, they opened a candy shop in partnership with another Nikkei family. Eventually, in search of better integration and investment opportunities, the couple became naturalized Mexican citizens, and Akane converted to Catholicism. They later opened a second candy store that sold chamoy (Mexican-style *umeboshi*) and then founded a toy and fountain pen factory. Tsutomu also exported Mexican opals to Japan and imported Japanese bracelets and accessories. Although his opal business was lucrative, Tsutomu decided to transfer its title to one of his brothers living in Japan who was facing economic difficulties. Instead of simply willing a successful export business to his children, Tsutomu wished them to make their own way, as he was convinced that hard work and diligence strengthen moral character. From a different perspective, this business transfer evinces that immigrant Japanese in Mexico kept binational networks, with the sending communities at times significantly contributing to the economic life of their hometowns. Thus, a transpacific examination of diasporic populations reveals the economic and cultural connections that these persons often create with their (ethnic) homelands.

AKANE'S INTIMATE POETIZATION OF FAMILY LIFE

Akane composed eloquent tanka that memorialize the beauty, joy, and hardship in daily life, including her family's suffering during World War II and the passing of relatives. They also serve as the site where she performs her diasporic idea of Japaneseness, which incorporates elements from Nihonjinron. With the passage of time, her poetry also came to enact her adopted Mexicanness or subtly reposition the author in between the national spaces of Mexico and Japan, in the third space (to use Bhabha's term) of Mexican Nikkeijin. Other poems fluctuate between the celebration of Japanese or Mexican cultures and the critique of certain customs, but rather than openly rebelling, Akane found in her poetry a refuge from unpleasant circumstances.

The opening poem in *Akane, Immigrant Poet* was written in Japan (the only one in the collection) in 1936, soon before she left for Mexico. It reflects young Akane's innocent titillation about the prospect of finally meeting her husband in person:

> my maiden form
> cinched in this obi
> I long for you to see me—
> I think about it
> and I blush. (Kasuga 2016, 16)

It follows the traditional structure of the thirty-one-syllable (5-7-5-7-7) tanka. We first find the physical sensation, an opening image being explored (the young poet looks at her body), followed by an intimate emotion (the anticipation of meeting her husband for the first time), which are effortlessly united by the pivotal central line.

Other melancholy tanka record feelings of personal, irreparable loss. Thus, when Akane finally returns to Japan, it pains her to see how much her father has aged. Another poem reveals how Akane accepted her destiny and took full responsibility for her bold decision to accept a marriage proposal from an unknown Japanese immigrant in Mexico:

> I defied everyone
> when I crossed that ocean,

so it can't be helped.
when I am in pain,
I accept my circumstances. (Kasuga 2016, 51)

The poem's Spanish translation discloses that, by moving to Mexico, the poetic voice went against her family's advice: "When I crossed the sea / against what my people / told me there."[3] Likewise, instead of the closing line "I accept my circumstances," which suggests passive serenity and resilience, the Spanish translation ends quite differently, with an emphatic directive to herself, a call to action of sorts: "Do what you have to do!"[4] In any case, in both translations Akane deploys her agency by depicting herself as a resolute woman who followed her calling, as it is also evident in the second poem of the collection:

across
distant seas,
paving my own way—
a great duty
to fulfill. (Kasuga 2016, 17)

Early on, Akane appears as a woman with a clear vision for her life and with the resolve to achieve it. The sense of duty mentioned in the penultimate line, however, leaves the reader wondering whether it is to herself, her family, her country, or all these. Her assertive nature permeates other poems in which she declares her pride in only walking the path she has drawn for herself, away from dishonest people.

Akane's poetry, so often illustrating fleeting moments of awe before the beauty of nature or family life, occasionally embraces even deeper, more spiritual, or philosophical overtones:

I have nothing
to embellish my appearance
but this frame of mind,
to collect inner truths
and live on. (Kasuga 2016, 52)

The poetic voice found harmony despite of all the turbulence in her life. Instead of worrying about her physical appearance, a societal imposition on women, she focuses on her mind, her knowledge. However, the Spanish translation provides a slightly different interpretation, as "collecting inner truths" is changed to "living without lies," which may hint at potential regrets about past personal attitudes rather than her peace of mind.[5] Another tanka reflecting self-knowledge suggests that the poetic voice has learned to accept herself for who she is, with her own limitations:

> from here,
> how should I live?
> by discovering
> my own limitations
> I can see myself (Kasuga 2016, 58)

Even though by then the Kasuga family was affluent because of its "work ethic," in her verses Akane distances herself from materialist outlooks:

> they talk as if
> possessions
> are proof of success.
> I avoid such folks
> and drink my tea. (Kasuga 2016, 54)

Instead of flaunting her wealth or material possessions, Akane declares her preference for leisurely drinking tea. The *sadō*, or traditional Japanese tea ceremony, popular on the islands since the ninth century, represents purity, tranquility, respect, and harmony, not material accumulation and ostentation. In this context, true success in Akane's poetry is associated with the joy of being surrounded by her children and grandchildren, who, while kissing her, call her *obaachan* (grandmother).

Yet one could easily contrast this spiritual, idealistic rhetoric in her poetry with Akane and her husband's real-life self-exploitation through constant overwork. After all, as we learn in the biography, her husband worked all day, had almost no time for his children, and ended up suffering from chronic fatigue; Akane, for her part, remembered childbirth as her only leisure time. Tsutomu's obsession with looking for new business opportunities to increment the family's income—decisions that lead to his physical exhaustion—contradicts Akane's lyrical disinterest in money and material accumulation, even if the new income was mostly used for their children's travel and education. As seen in Tsutomu's decision not to let his children inherit his opal export business so as to strengthen their moral character, the Kasugas believed in the virtues and benefits of what they perceived as a strong "work ethic." To them, hard work was a source of fulfillment and self-respect.

In Akane's tanka, though, the values associated with material accumulation and greed give way to an entirely different axiology: the joys of motherhood and family life. Some poems reflect her drive to instill in her children a strong pride in being Japanese Mexican. And in times of struggle, motherhood is what keeps her optimism:

> ten years ago,
> I married this man.
> we are poor,
> yet my five children
> fill my heart. (Kasuga 2016, 19)

Her children, who embody her hope and pride, fill the poetic voice with serenity. When any one of them is absent, Akane describes how much she misses them:

> under the garden sun
> plums dry as I reminisce
> about my distant child.
> the parrot squawks
> his name. (Kasuga 2016, 34)

Akane's husband, Tsutomu, is her other anchor in life, even after his passing. Consequently, Chikaba reveals that Akane always traveled with a small pouch containing some of her husband's ashes. Tellingly, while at the Popocatépetl volcano in 1975, on the second anniversary of her husband's death, a sixty-year-old Akane gripped his ashes while pondering, in a more metaphysical and dramatic tanka, about the insurmountable barrier between life and death:

> feeling
> this vast distance
> between life and death
> my hand grips
> a piece of my husband's bone. (Kasuga 2016, 112)

In the poem's Spanish translation, while the "vast" distance turns into a more penetrating "infinite" one, the graphic scene of Akane's hand gripping a piece of bone becomes a fist grasping her beloved husband's ashes. A year later, another poem portrays the poetic voice still patiently waiting for Tsutomu's return, as his clothes and shoes remain where they were left on the day of his passing. She bemoans that not even in her dreams does her late husband visit her; still, Akane looks forward to joining him in the afterlife to inform him about their children's deep roots in Mexico. As readers, we witness the documentation of the poetic voice's healing process throughout her poems, a process that is never fully completed.

Akane, Immigrant Poet also includes self-referential poems about the writing experience, which at times becomes frustrating:

> I have spent days
> with this tanka,
> scattered and unformed,
> it rains
> without a hint of clearing. (Kasuga 2016, 68)

Common to romantic poetry, the pathetic fallacy (the reflection of the poet's feelings before nature or the attribution of human emotion to it) in the closing couplet or *shimo-no-ku* links Akane's feelings to natural elements. But even in these metapoetic and self-reflective poems, family life takes center stage. Thus, another similar tanka laments the fact that her inability to complete it has led the poetic voice to speak harshly to her grandchildren.

PERFORMING MEXICANNESS

Concomitant with the celebration of family life, we find in Akane's poetry a performance of what she conceived to be essential elements of Mexicanness that contribute to the creation of new forms of cultural citizenship. Rather than being an echo of her progressive affiliation to a Mexican national identity, however, her poetry becomes an active agent of this conscious, performative process, thereby demonstrating the role of culture in the formation of social identities in contact zones. These social identities fluctuate and negotiate their positionality vis-à-vis the different Japanese and Mexican nation-building narratives.

The philosopher of language J. L. Austin was first to elaborate on the capacity of performative speech acts to consummate an action (nominating, sentencing, promising), as seen, for example, in promises, betting, the language of referees and judges, or the pronouncement of a priest at a wedding. In these cases, the action described by the sentence is actually performed by the very utterance of such sentence. Similarly, the gender theorist Judith Butler, building on Austin's linguistic theories, claims that gender is socially constructed through performative speech acts and nonverbal communication that define and maintain identities. Therefore, instead of identity being a source of actions such as speech or behaviors and gestures, it is the illocutionary speech acts (i.e., they actually *do* rather than just *represent* something), along with symbolic communications and social signs, that contribute to the formation of an individual's identity. This type of gender performance, which Butler compares to theatrical performance, ends up creating gender identities. Under constraint, prohibition and taboo, individuals act out their gender according to the ritualized and stylized repetition of internalized gender norms. This repetition, argues Butler, is not performed by the subject but instead enables the very condition of the subject. In Butler's words, "the act that one does, the act that one performs is, in a sense, an act that's been going on before one arrived on the scene" (1988, 526).

Just as gender, according to Butler, is a performative act that has been rehearsed like a script written by hegemonic, heteronormative social conventions, it can be argued that national filiation and affiliation are performative acts as well. In the case of Akane's performativity of national allegiance, however, it is not so much an imposed or instinctive filiation to the Mexican nation and culture (bound to birthplace or nationality) as a voluntary and deliberate social affiliation. As Edward Said claims in referring to secular critics in *The World, the Text, and the Critic*, this social affiliation responds to "social and political conviction, economic and historical circumstances, voluntary effort and willed deliberation" (1983, 24–25). Whether Akane's adopted Mexicanness responds to a strategic desire for cultural integration, a sincere national identification, or both, this is not as critical in this chapter as is considering how her affiliation to her adopted country's dominant culture is performed—whether instinctively, consciously, or strategically—in and through her poetry. It is also equally relevant to examine how this performance of sociocultural affiliation, a self-making process, is then negotiated with her own proud Japaneseness or with an interstitial performance of Japanese Mexicanness in those tanka where the poetic voice symbolically situates herself within the liminal position of Mexican Nikkeijin. In this sense, Akane's repeated declarations of national allegiance to Mexico in her poetry are in themselves performative speech acts of reality making and self-Mexicanization. In other words, Akane's discursive practice enacts the Mexicanness it names.

In her poetry collection, Akane also tries to make sense of own trajectory, personal growth, and controversial, life-changing decisions: whereas the *kami-no-ku* or opening tercets of her tanka describe landscapes, people, and objects that evince certain emotions, the *shimo-no-ku* or closing couplets interpret her ideas and feelings aroused in response to the opening three lines. These tanka also narrate a personal account of Akane's lived experience in Mexico and try to persuade both the reader and the poet herself of her own alternating or coalesced Japaneseness, Mexicanness, and Japanese Mexicanness. Her written words enact the new reality of what she perceives as her adopted Mexicanness.

Throughout the process of uprooting herself from Japan and rerooting in Mexico, one finds several symbolic material culture replacements in Akane's poetry. For instance, in her lyrical imaginary, the Popocatépetl volcano (her original book in Japanese includes a photo of Popocatépetl along with photos of her with her family) metonymically displaces the symbolic role of Mount Fuji, which had previously condensed Japaneseness in the form of a metaphor.[6] Japan's Mount Fuji is considered a national treasure and a unifying national symbol. As such, it inspired haiku by Matsuo Bashō (1644–1694) and paintings by Hokusai (1760–1849), the most famous (at least in the West) poet, *ukiyo-e* painter and a printmaker of the Edo period, respectively.[7] Tellingly, *El Heraldo de Nisei*, a Spanish-language newspaper of the Nikkei community, published in Mexico City and subtitled *Órgano Informativo de la Segunda Generación* (Second Generation Information Source), includes a photograph of Mount Fuji on the first page of its 28 February 1948 issue, with the heading in capital letters "El símbolo de una raza" (A People's Symbol).

That El Popo—as Akane, following the popular nickname, affectionately refers to it in her poetry—is known among Japanese Mexicans as Mexico's Mount Fuji suggests that Akane was not alone in reimagining it as an identity reference. Anyhow, the case can be made that a coded Japaneseness is included in her poetry's Mexican patriotism.

Akane was buried in her adopted country, as she had announced in this tanka:

directly facing
the peak of Mount Popo,
cosmos
cover this hill.
I've chosen my burial place. (Kasuga 2016, 121)

Here, typical of tanka, the poet's senses react to a natural landscape, a hill covered with cosmos flowers near Mount Popo, which stirs mixed emotions: pleasant memories of Japan and painful ones of her late husband. Unlike Tsutomu, she did not choose to have part of her remains buried in her native Japan. Nonetheless, Akane's choice of burial on a hill full of flowers (like one from her place of birth) facing a volcano that for Mexican Nikkeijin recalls the iconic Mount Fuji, suggests that, along with her proud Mexicanness, her native land remained close to her heart. Another reason to be buried facing the Popocatépetl volcano was that half of Tsutomu's ashes lay there, as this tanka reminds us:

> a cold wave is coming
> the weather forecast
> reports.
> snow will blanket Mount Popo
> where my husband sleeps. (Kasuga 2016, 111)

This volcano's special place in Akane's lyrical imaginary is further evidenced by its inclusion in other poems, like one that hails the 1977 construction of the Liceo Mexicano-Japonés (Japanese Mexican High School; commonly known as "Liceo Japonés"), a bilingual school for Nikkeijin and non-Nikkei Mexican children, originally planned by her husband:

> preparing this land
> let the sound of the
> bulldozer's engine
> reach the peaks of Mount Popo
> to announce the construction. (Kasuga 2016, 116)

Akane wishes her late husband, whose partial ashes lie atop the volcano, to know that she never gave up on his dream.

Just like Mount Popo stands as a Mexican trope for Mount Fuji in her poetry, the ephemeral beauty of the by then quintessentially Mexican jacaranda (though imported from South America) blossoms smoothly replaces or translates *sakura* (cherry tree), a renowned symbol of Japan. Thus, in a tanka about impermanence and the passage of time, we read:

> time passes
> like the flow of water;
> it slips quietly by,
> on those who remain
> jacaranda blossoms fall. (Kasuga 2016, 118)

Reversing the characteristic sequence of tanka, the sensory experience of admiring the bright-colored jacaranda blossoms falling on people is juxtaposed in the closing couplet, and the mixed feelings it evokes open the poem in the tercet: *tempus fugit* melancholy but also the hope conjured by the passing of the seasons that gives rise to the thought of rebirth. In this tanka, therefore, Akane enjoys a Mexican cityscape from a traditionally Japanese perspective: she perceives the cherry blossoms of her earlier years in Japan as transformed into jacaranda blossoms, a positive but melancholic symbol of mortality and life's transience. These are often associated with the concept of *mono no aware* (literally, "pathos of things," or a sensitivity of ephemera), a sense of sadness or nostalgia evinced by contemplating an object. Again, although in reality this is not an exclusively Japanese concept of beauty (it is also found in Western poetry), it has often been associated with Japanese cultural exceptionalism in Nihonjinron discourse. The falling leaves elicit a spiritual longing that reminds the serenely nostalgic Japanese immigrant of the need to acknowledge that all is finite and imperfect.

Elsewhere, yucca flowers take the symbolic place of edible *yurine*, or lily bulbs (wrongly translated as "roots" in the poem), which have medicinal properties and are often used in dishes for Kyoto-style tea ceremonies and Japanese New Year:

> yucca flower
> similar in taste to
> lily root
> simmering in an iron pot
> on this rainy day. (Kasuga 2016, 231)

The rain evokes nostalgia (pathetic fallacy) for the tastes of her formative years in Japan.

With time and owing to an acquired taste for local food, Akane begins to identify as a Mexican and enjoy a sense of belonging in her host country, as the following tanka shows:

> quesadillas of
> squash blossom and
> huitlacoche
> are my special favorite.
> I am becoming Mexican. (Kasuga 2016, 69)

The Spanish translation assigns the squash blossom and corn smut quesadillas a more active role, as if they were turning the poet "more and more

Mexican."[8] Her early appreciation for Mexican food denotes that the anticipated process of cultural integration is coming to fruition. Within the same lyrical performance of diasporic belonging, other poems present the purchase of Mexican vegetables like *nopales* (Akane loved cacti in general) in the market or the cooking of typically Mexican food like the stew *pozole* in the context of a cozy, homey atmosphere:

> a rainy night—
> I wait for my tired daughter
> to return home,
> a pot of *pozole* soup
> simmering over the fire. (Kasuga 2016, 36)

As is somewhat common in haiku and tanka, Akane introduces nature elements in the poem. Here, the rainy night again raises Akane's concern while waiting for her exhausted daughter to return home from work. Incidentally, according to the editor of her poetry collection, locals were impressed by her mastery of local cuisine: "Mitsuko's take on *mole poblano* . . . had a reputation for tasting more authentic than the version made by Mexico City locals" (Chikaba 2016, 202).

Switching from Mexican food to Mexican dances, later tanka depict Akane, at the age of seventy, dancing with locals during Carnival or packing shrimp, as another Mexican, among local women at her daughter's factory in Mazatlán. Akane also enjoyed her morning exchanges at the local market and visiting markets wherever she traveled, as she considered them the best windows to local culture (Chikaba 2016, 235). Even the use of popular, affectionate, Spanish expressions there, like "marchantita, tenga usted!" (here you go, dear customer!), bring her happiness. Akane's pronouncements of sincere love for her host country manifest and help her perform her Mexican patriotism time and again:

> my grandchild
> attends kindergarten
> and learns by heart
> the national anthem of Mexico.
> I want to sing with you. (Kasuga 2016, 92)

Again, the closing line is quite different in the Spanish translation, in which it is the child, rather than the grandmother, who asks "we're going to sing together / let's sing granny!,"[9] making the poem slightly less patriotic.

By the time of the 1968 Olympic Games in Mexico City, Akane felt proud of her new country's achievement:

> viva México!
> our president
> and the crowd
> shouted in unison.
> my tears welled up. (Kasuga 2016, 218–19)

It is noteworthy, incidentally, that Akane never mentions the Tlatelolco massacre at the hands of the Mexican Armed Forces of unarmed civilians protesting the Olympics on 2 October 1968. Likewise, by celebrating in another tanka how her granddaughter was listed in the Civil Registry office as just any Mexican, she chronicles her own belonging, even though some bystanders still reject her alterity.

By contrast, the poetic voice declares in other tanka a hardly veiled split with local mores, thus implying that the cultural clash is perhaps not quite over. Accordingly, the following poem reacts against a type of behavior that could have been considered inappropriate in the traditional Japan where Akane grew up:

> those who can
> crudely express
> their feelings;
> I feel envy,
> I feel pity. (Kasuga 2016, 53)

This thought can be associated with *honne* and *tatemae*, concepts that, in Nihonjinron discourse, are often introduced as exclusively Japanese, even though it is not uncommon in other cultures to avoid social conflict through a more reserved behavior, saying at certain times what one really thinks and at others what is expected of you. Whereas *honne* refers to a person's true inner feelings, intentions, or thoughts, which are supposed to be privately kept or revealed only to close friends, *tatemae* brings us close to "political correctness" because it is a diplomatic, public position rendered in accordance with what is expected socially, a stance associated with maturity. This is plausibly the reason Akane pities those who openly reveal their deepest feelings. Yet she also feels certain envy, perhaps because, unlike her, they have an escape valve to vent their sorrow or anger.

Paradoxically, the Mexican Nobel laureate Octavio Paz, in the chapter "Máscaras mexicanas" (Mexican Masks) of his classic *El laberinto de la soledad* (*The Labyrinth of Solitude*), sees avoiding the expression one's feelings, *rajarse* (cracking) in his own words, as a quintessentially Mexican behavior: "Every time a Mexican confides in a friend or acquaintance, every time he opens himself up, it is an abdication. He dreads that the person in whom he has confided will scorn him. Therefore confidences result in dishonor, and they are as dangerous for the person to whom they are made as they are for the person who makes them . . . when we have confided in someone who is not worthy of it, we say, 'I sold myself to So-and-so.' That is, we have 'cracked,' have let someone into our fortress" (1985, 30–31).[10]

Other tanka become sites of resistance where Akane denounces the latent xenophobia she has suffered in Mexico. The following one focuses on the hateful gaze of onlookers:

"you immigrant!"
though they scorn us,
we carry
with pride a spirit
that is pure. (Kasuga 2016, 60)

The Spanish translation uses stronger, more confrontational language and adds an important nuance: the words "you immigrant!" are not actually spoken by bystanders but implied through their Othering glares. We then read: "eyes that scream: / damned immigrants! Don't stare / say it instead."[11] The dignified poetic voice, therefore, challenges this symbolic violence, daring bystanders to say aloud what they are thinking, because she well "knows" deep inside that Japanese immigrants' spirit is pure and noble. Akane proudly defies, through her writing, the public contempt endured by Nikkeijin throughout and shows that dignity in the face of adversity is an asset for her and her community. Rather than victimization, there is resistance here.

PERFORMING JAPANESENESS

Akane's poetry at times performs her newly acquired Mexicanness to confirm her belonging to the host country. Yet it also focuses on the lyrical representation of her understanding of Japanese and Nikkei cultures. These poems bring her discourse closer to Nihonjinron views. If Nihonjinron constructs the idea of Japaneseness in contrast with Western cultures, in Akane's writing that cultural Other is Mexico. Her discourse on Japaneseness and, in particular, her view of Japanese culture as unique are in binary opposition to the discourse on Mexicanness: comparisons and contrasts between the two cultures, along with conflations of facts, constructs, myths, fantasies, and ideals, help to imagine and define cultural differences.

In one poem, Akane switches to an alternative identification as a Japanese or Nikkeijin, admitting her nostalgia for her birthplace and culture, sixty years after immigrating:

> over sixty years
> I have lived
> in Mexico,
> the flavors of ginger flower *miso* soup
> move me to tears. (Kasuga 2016, 72)

Foodways are a key node of cultural transmission. Whereas some of the tanka here celebrated quintessentially Mexican food like *huitlacoche*, nopales, quesadillas, and *pozole*, others are odes to traditional Japanese dishes like sushi and *misoshiru* (miso soup) or the vegetables and plants important to Japanese cuisine, like bamboo, *karashina* (leaf mustard), and *yae-zakura* (pickled flower buds).[12]

In other poems that contribute to her lyrical performance of Japaneseness, Akane exhibits behaviors that are commonly admired in Japan and that, perhaps in response to Western essentialization, Japanese have adopted as (purportedly) key elements of their national psychology. The idiosyncrasies distinguish them from non-Japanese, especially Westerners. For instance, in a 1954 tanka, Akane displays what, in the West, would be perceived as "self-restraint":

> I shall swallow
> my unspoken words,
> though I am
> deliberately slandered
> in this article before me. (Kasuga 2016, 55)

As part of the stereotypical Nihonjinron discourse, Japanese traditional society expected stoic behavior, that is, the concealment of emotions to maintain social harmony. Therefore, Akane refrains from reacting after reading a slanderous article on the opening of a Japanese school in her home. She dealt with the accusations in a dignified manner by writing the tanka rebuke.

This type of self-control is associated with the concept of *enryo*, often considered characteristically Japanese, and particularly after World War II. According to the *Kōjien* (Authoritative Japanese Dictionary), it refers to the withholding of self-expression or actions toward people in consideration for another person, thus avoiding conflict. It can also refer to declining an invitation or petition, or to refraining from celebrating events in order to maintain public order.[13]

A similar response reappears after her husband's demise, when the poetic voice does not allow herself to cry, even though she is aware that it could alleviate her deep pain:

> if I cried
> out loud, my heart
> would ease.
> I know this yet I cannot cry
> as a spring day passes. (Kasuga 2016, 101)

Here, perhaps again falling into the trap of Nihonjinron discourse, the socially expected Japanese reaction to a deeply painful event may be detrimental to her mental health; however, she declares herself incapable of escaping embedded social norms. More importantly, she records such behavior in her writing as if to provide additional evidence of what she perceives as her deep-seated Japaneseness.

Although establishing parallels between one's life and Mother Nature's seasons is common in tanka writing, here the mysterious last line has a double meaning: a note explains that it refers to the fact that her husband's surname, Kasuga, means "spring day." Likewise, in a 1974 tanka, Akane laments how she constantly holds back her tears:

> someday,
> a day to cry
> to my heart's content.
> will it come true?
> I've endured without tears. (Kasuga 2016, 110)

In the Spanish translation's very different ending, Akane wonders whether one day she will at last weep until she has shed her last tear. She presents her typically Japanese behavior as an obstacle rather than an asset: *enryo* prevents her from overcoming her grief and also provides valuable rhetorical proof of her own Japaneseness.

After Tsutomu died at a hospital, Akane's family found her stoic behavior shocking: "To everyone's surprise, Mitsuko did not cry. She politely thanked doctors and nurses, and calmly went about gathering their belongings in the hospital room. This image of the unbreakable, dry-eyed mother was branded in Ermelinda Michiko's memory. 'She was like a female *samurai*,' Mitsuko's oldest daughter would recall" (Chikaba 2016, 222). Her own family explains her odd behavior by identifying her with one of the main archetypes of Japaneseness in the West (later adopted by the Japanese themselves in Nihonjinron discourse): the fearless, stoic samurai. In switching gendered roles, the archetype of abnegated and submissive geisha gives way to the demeanor of the traditionally male warrior. Apparently, Tsutomu behaved similarly. A tanka included in the collection recalls:

> several times
> played for a fool,
> my husband's sorrow
> was never spoken.
> he took this to his grave. (Kasuga 2016, 11)

As his wife did, he too resorted to self-control during difficult times by trying to keep his concerns to himself.

Akane returned to Japan in 1962, twenty-seven years after her departure. Yet her hometown and homeland were never far from her heart, as homesickness permeates her entire oeuvre. Even her pen name "Akane" evokes nostalgia for her *furusato* (native place; literally, "old village"), as it refers to "the auburn tinge of Ina's evening sky" (Chikaba 2016, 188). Recollections of the past, of her childhood and adolescence in Japan, are key to the identity construction that takes place in and through Akane's poetry. Incidentally, this nostalgic evocation of the *furusato*, which reflected the collective sentiment of cultural loss after the swift emergence of modernity, has also been identified with Nihonjinron discourse: "The imagery of the *furusato* appealed to the most essential Japaneseness, nostalgically evoking a traditional past that was disappearing, one subjected to the centrifugal forces of economic, cultural, and political internationalization."[14] In this context, some of Akane's first tanka recall her childhood joy in Nagano as she watched her parents' sericulture and played with stilts in the garden:

the aroma of mulberry
permeates the cocoonery.
my mother, feeding new leaf,
was so youthful,
so beautiful. (Kasuga 2016, 81)

Akane resorts to a rhetorical device typical of tanka, in which a scent, sound, or image evokes a memory or emotion. Through her yearning for these smells, landscapes, and soundscapes, she builds her own notion of self. Simultaneously, this poem, like several others in the volume, performs her Japaneseness through a perceived mystical communion with nature that, in Nihonjinron discourse, is also supposed to be another Japanese national trait or element of the national psychology. In Funabiki's words, it is "a—unequivocally essentialist—discourse according to which the Japanese have developed an extremely sensitive to nature character and an attitude of non-opposition, of non-resistance to it."[15] Guarné likewise defines it as a type of cultural essentialism: "The influence of *Nihonjinron* thought is particularly deep in the production of knowledge on contemporary Japan, in and out of its frontiers. In its narrative, the systematic reproduction of stereotypical images on the mystical communion with nature, linguistic uniqueness, racial and cultural homogeneity of a group-oriented society operates as a persistent scheme in the normative prescription of what the 'Japanese culture' is" (2009, 323).

Like the mulberry scents, certain sounds, such as ice cracking under her feet in the central Mexican town of Tacubaya (surprising considering the local climate), also trigger reminiscences and longing for those early days in her native town:

the sounds
of my steps on ice,
so crisp.
feeling nostalgic,
I continued walking all the way. (Kasuga 2016, 74)

As discussed earlier in the introduction, social memory, and specifically collective amnesia, is a key factor in national identity formation. From this perspective, the poet's selective memory filters out negative reminiscences of what made her leave Japan, keeping only the positive ones. In another tanka, even though the poetic voice unconvincingly claims that she is not homesick, she admits her compulsion to buying cosmos from a florist.

Likewise, her poem about digging *takenoko* (bamboo shoots, the tough outer skin of which is used in sushi) in the spring echoes her nostalgia for Japan. Even at the age of sixty-nine, her conversations while making miso with her daughter-in-law about the Sanaburi festival, celebrating the completion of rice planting and prayers for a good harvest, recall pleasant memories of Ina, their Japanese hometown. Her sensitivity to the seasons, attraction to certain flowers, appreciation of certain smells and sounds in nature, and communion with nature generally define for Akane her own Japaneseness.

Interestingly, whereas in Japan spring cherry blossoms symbolize a time of renewal and life's fleeting nature (their peak beauty lasts about two weeks), a cherry tree that Akane brought from Japan and planted in Mexico embodies, in the following poem, quite the opposite: permanence and perpetuation. It becomes a symbol of her ethnic identity and continuation of her lineage in Mexico, hence the "infinite clusters":

> this yae-zakura,
> transplanted
> from Japan,
> now blooming in Mexico,
> filled with infinite clusters. (Kasuga 2016, 83)

The poet's communion with nature is so intense that, in the ensuing poem in the collection, as she picks *yae-zakura* buds, she feels possessed by her mother. This sort of metempsychosis—a transmigration of a soul that, after biological death, is reincarnated in a different physical body—evokes Akane's pride in her family and ethnic origin.

The two previous poems may also be contextualized within the frame of the Japanese custom of *hanami*, which consists of enjoying the transient beauty of spring flowers, especially cherry (*sakura*) or Japanese apricot (*ume*) trees. This flower-viewing tradition is related to the Buddhist concept of *mono no aware*: the amazement at and sensitivity toward beauty's ephemeral nature that reminds viewers of life's fleetingness and impermanence. This same tradition contextualizes Akane's delight at witnessing her grandson's reaction to noticing the first blooming Japanese apricot flowers:

> "grandma
> come quick, look!
> ume pickle flowers
> are blooming!"
> my young grandchild exults. (Kasuga 2016, 94)

FIGURE 3.1. Akane with her family in Mexico. Courtesy of Aiko Chikaba.

For Akane, her grandson's outburst is proof that Japanese cultural traditions live on in the new Kasuga generation. Paradoxically, this fruit will also be used to make *chamoy* sauce, a Japanese Mexican invention, and not traditional Japanese food. As her family's cultural mediator, Akane also relishes singing her grandchildren the same lullabies that she sang to her children. Hence, through her voice, Japanese culture lives on in the family.

Her son Carlos Tsuyoshi Kasuga Osaka recalls, in his preface to *Akane, Immigrant Poet*, that his mother would often say: "I will not be defeated." Reminiscent of Nihonjinron discourse, this statement reflects the typical *ganbare* spirit of a resilient and hardworking Japanese woman determined to achieve her goals despite life's challenges. A tanka echo this mentality:

"do not give in!"
reflecting on the good and the bad
of these words
I feel regret,
yet I utter them once more. (Kasuga 2016, 23)

This tanka's Spanish translation adds a final reflection to the English version: "I reflect and decide / to repeat it to my children."[16] She chooses, therefore, to instill in her children the same resilience that has guided her life. "The bad" in the second line and her regret for teaching it warns that a willful mindset may lead to a life of hardship similar to her own. Like *enryo* in other poems, this supposedly Japanese cultural trait, the *ganbare* spirit, may ultimately have negative consequences if it ends up preventing the attainment of happiness.[17]

Other tanka by Akane focus on parts of her own body. When looking at her aged hands (*acabadas*, or "finished" hands in the Spanish translation), she finds beauty in them because, as a homemaker, they managed to raise no fewer than six children:

> with these
> gnarled hands
> our six
> children were nurtured.
> I admire my hands. (Kasuga 2016, 24)

Instead of "I admire my hands," the Spanish version concludes powerfully, with the poet finding beauty in the traces left by hard work: "I can see them, they are beautiful."[18] This tanka can be read in the context of *wabi-sabi*, a Japanese aesthetic concept that describes finding beauty and serenity in simple, imperfect, and/or impermanent objects or landscapes. It emphasizes accepting transience, the fact that nothing lasts, is complete, or perfect. According to the cultural anthropologist Harumi Befu, *wabi-sabi* is also considered uniquely Japanese in essentialist Nihonjinron discourses: "Aesthetic concepts such as *ki* (élan), *iki* (elegance), *sabi* (rustic simplicity), *wabi* (melancholic rusticity) and *mono no aware* (empathic unity) are considered exclusive to Japan and, therefore, unique exponents of its culture."[19] Such a concept celebrates imperfection and transience, finding beauty in asymmetrical pottery. As Emma Taggart observes, "items exhibiting *wabi-sabi* are seen to be more beautiful with age. And the more fragile, broken, or individual a humble object is, the more it can be appreciated" (2018, n.p.). Adhering to this line of thought, Akane's humble hands are damaged by hard work and aging, but this is precisely what makes them beautiful and admirable to her.[20] This tanka is best associated with the *sabi* part of the expression *wabi-sabi*, which refers specifically to the beauty of aging, celebrating the passage of time, and the impermanence of life (*wabi* describes the beauty of asymmetric, unbalanced items).[21] In a similar tanka, Akane thanks her feet for bringing her to Mexico and allowing her to stand at the time of the composition.

Other poems by Akane memorialize the importance of her husband Tsutomu's presence in her life after thirty-six years together. He died of pancreatitis in March 1973, at the age of sixty-two. Following his request and reflecting his dual national affiliation, half of his ashes were placed around a pine tree at Popocatépetl; the other half was buried two months later in his native Ina, Japan. Bemoaning her loneliness, she hears his laughter in the sound of waves, misses holding his warm hand while walking together on moonlit nights, and remembers him as a tirelessly working man. She teaches her grandchildren, to their delight, that their *ojiichan* (grandfather) will return during the Obon festival, a Japanese Buddhist-Confucian custom honoring the spirits of ancestors, which typically involves cleansing their graves before they visit the *butsudan*, or household altar. Perhaps rhetorically, in several poems Akane recriminates her husband's spirit for not returning during the Obon festival while she waited patiently.

Akane's poetry also addresses her feeling of belonging or lack thereof. Language, for example, is an occasional reminder of her outsider status. While her Mexico-born children and grandchildren give her a sense of acceptance in the host country, they also make her feel foreign, as the following lighthearted poem suggests:

"wrong again, Mamá!"
my children correct me
as I rehearse my "L."
in the end I get lost
between "L" and "R." (Kasuga 2016, 25)

After many years in Mexico, Akane's inability to pronounce the sounds of certain letters brings out her conspicuous Otherness, turning her into a *gaijin* (foreigner or outsider) in her children's eyes.

Interestingly, unlike Yoshigei (Carlos) Nakatani, subject of the previous chapter, who began to write in Japanese only to realize that almost no one would understand him, Akane wrote her poetry in that language, even though she had learned Spanish by interacting with her customers. In fact, she also taught her children and those of her immigrant neighbors Japanese at her school. In 1977, fulfilling her husband's dream, she opened the Liceo Mexicano-Japonés, which would go on to become quite prestigious. She proudly memorialized its construction in a tanka:

my late husband
must be watching from the peak of Popo
as today is the day
our President
laid the foundation stone. (Kasuga 2016, 227)

Incidentally, the use of the possessive *our* before *President* again underscores her sense of belonging in her host country.

Along with the possibly negative references to *enryo* and the *ganbare* spirit in some poems, other tanka continue to distance Akane from her native culture, which she comes to view more critically. She expresses in one poem her opposition to certain unwritten societal rules regarding the approach to love and romance in Japan:

> love is
> a sin, they say
> in my mountain country.
> I can't help but
> carry this regret. (Kasuga 2016, 57)

Her poetry becomes a site of cultural contestation where she openly questions her compatriots' approach to human love. The poem's Spanish translation offers a different conclusion, signaling perhaps that her love for her husband is still alive: "I still carry one / within me."[22]

After Akane's parents passed away in the early 1970s, her poems began to reflect her pain and nostalgia for her homeland, which came to be seen as increasingly distant because no one was there awaiting her letters:

> I stare
> at the single point where
> the sun sets in the sea.
> father and mother are gone,
> my hometown ever distant. (Kasuga 2016, 79)

The loss of her loved ones weakens her link to the motherland, as do perhaps her stronger ties to Mexico.

A JAPANESE MEXICAN THIRD SPACE

Like the *chamoy* sauce she likes to prepare for her children, Akane has a hybrid identity, Japanese and Mexican, without a manifest conflict between the two identities. At the age of sixty-one, Akane unapologetically places the two national flags with which she identifies on her factory's roof to convey that Nikkeijin are at work:

flags of
Mexico and Japan
placed proudly
atop the factory roof:
"Here are *Nikkei*" (Kasuga 2016, 59)

These flags trace the last stop in her multiple, at times simultaneous, identities: a native Japanese filiation coupled with a Mexican affiliation that occasionally gives way to a Japanese Mexican or Nikkei hybridity. These identities, in fruitful dialogue with one another, correspond to different places of enunciation and epistemological positions reflected in her poems. Together, all three contribute to the formation of a new cultural citizen. Yet the factory flags boldly map the interstitial spaces of Japanese Mexicanness in the country's capital and subtly destabilize the rigidity of national borders. Along these lines, Akane's home showcased a Buddhist altar next to an image of Our Lady of Guadalupe, the patroness of Mexico and a unifying national symbol for its citizens—a religious syncretism that acknowledged her Japanese and Mexican bonds.

A ROOM OF HER OWN

As Catherine Ceniza Choy and Judy Tzu-Chun Wu clarify, "the analytical category of gender is constitutive of trans-Pacific world-making. Trans-Pacific migration is a gendered process that raises critical questions" (2017, 4). Regarding Japanese immigration in Mexico, for example, this is evident in its uneven gender ratios. Initially, mostly men migrated. Later, "picture brides" were brought over from Japan, though in smaller numbers (see Chapter 6). Immigration inducements for women were different: whereas marriage was the objective for their ocean crossing, men were mostly guided by financial motivations or patriotic duty.

Transpacific emigration may have also brought new outlooks on gender issues. In the stories of Nakatani and Akane, we find out about Japanese "picture brides" who, even before the culture shock of becoming familiar with the mores of the host society, were taking advantage of the transoceanic passage to subvert gendered norms and escape the destiny that others had presaged for them. In Akane's poetry we not only find her excitement about meeting her future husband but also her later reconsiderations of Japanese expectations regarding love and romance. We also observe her pride in acknowledging the many advances made by women worldwide and her own defiance of feminine beauty criteria through lyrical descriptions of her body.

These intersectional analyses of gender and race provide a more nuanced perspective of Japanese immigration in Mexico and its cultural production. In Akane's case, writing represented a refuge from gendered roles in society. As Chikaba perceptively concludes, "tanka provided a space in which she could be completely free. In her tanka, she was neither a 'mother' nor 'wife.' In poetry, Mitsuko found a way to engage with the world as an individual" (2016, 189). Poetry writing offered Akane a space where she could be autonomous and could afford being vulnerable. As her older son Carlos states in his preface to the Spanish translation, she "never showed her weaknesses" to her children.[23] Some of Akane's poems also mention different personal affronts she endured. In reaction to those situations, poetry becomes again her refuge, a therapeutic exercise that provides emotional support and helps her recover serenity.

Akane initially writes from the perspective of an impoverished person and an immigrant but also, in an intersectional framework, as a woman. One of her tanka feminizes Japanese immigrant discourse in Mexico by celebrating women's achievements and progress. She dreams about a better life for future generations of women:

> even women
> fly to space.
> such an era has arrived.
> I dream the world
> of those born hereafter. (Kasuga 2016, 67)

She also reserves her right, as a woman, to withhold some of her lyrical work:

> a handful
> of tanka I have never shared,
> held in secret,
> living my forties fervently,
> I am a woman! (Kasuga 2016, 56)

To return to the problems with the translation of her poetry, while the English version closes the tanka by celebrating womanhood, the Spanish translation is more self-effacing, radically changing the message by taking away her agency: "I am just a woman!"[24] Her situated knowledge addresses different women's issues, including motherhood, marriage, childbirth, and physical appearance, from the perspective of an immigrant woman. Against societal expectations of women's beauty, for instance, she prioritizes her inner beauty, contained in her mind and in her search for truth.

Akane's Nikkei poetry, full of personal anecdotes and memories, at times reads like an impressionistic personal diary resulting from a dialogue with the nature surrounding her in Mexico and in her native Ina. It then develops into a device for the ongoing construction of multiple identities (Japanese, Mexican, Nikkei) in dialogue with one another. The inflexibility of national borders is disrupted by her entry into a hybrid, third space of Japanese Mexicanness, as well as by her performance, through writing, of a diasporic, dual national affiliation. Her writing exhibits an unapologetic cultural mobility, a harmonious marriage between Japanese and Mexican epistemologies and worldviews that fuse into a Nikkei one. While her representational practices (symbolically exchanging iconic national mountains and flowers, or poeticizing the inscription of her newborn Japanese Mexican grandchildren in the Mexican Civil Registry, for instance) also historicize the collective experience of Japanese immigrants and their descendants in Mexico (particularly that of women), she indirectly redefines what it is to be a Mexican woman. In addition, Akane's poetry offers a fascinating glimpse into how national cultures are transmitted and reshaped in the diaspora. More specifically, in this process of identity formation, the poet selects and decides which cultural practices, national symbols, and behaviors are quintessentially Japanese and should therefore be transmitted to or imposed on new Nikkei generations.

The poet was seventy years old by the time her tanka collection was finally published. Eventually, though, her tanka became known both in Mexico and in Japan, where the newspaper *Asahi* published fifty of her haiku and tanka. One tanka was selected for its excellence at a poetry contest devoted to the theme of "the journey" and held at Japan's Imperial Palace:

spent one day
of my trip to Bali
in the furrows of a field
catching river snails
with children from the village. (Kasuga 2016, 229)

In 1987, Emperor Hirohito awarded Akane with the Order of the Secret Treasure, Sixth Class, in recognition of her impressive contributions to the

Japanese Mexican community. She died in 2002 at the age of eighty-eight, leaving behind more than forty descendants and a literary legacy that merits consideration for both its aesthetic and its sociocultural contributions. Akane's legacy transcended her early history as vulnerable picture bride or passive victim of World War II internal colonialism to restore the agency of Japanese immigrant women in Mexico, and particularly picture brides, to cultural memory. Having become increasingly assertive with age, she also gendered the discourse of Japanese immigration in Mexico and provided a script about the evolving cultural citizenship of Japanese immigrants, from Japanese filiation, to Mexican affiliation, and finally to the hybrid third space of Japanese Mexicans.

Part II. Japanese Mexican Visual and Performance Arts

CHAPTER 4

Resignifying *Yamato-damashii* and Utopian Socialism in the Manga *Los samuráis de México*

Analysis of the manga in this chapter serves as a link between the first and second parts of this study. Originating during the mid-1900s, modern-day manga may be defined as Japanese-style comics or graphic novels typically printed in black-and-white, serialized in large manga magazines, and published in Japan. Manga exist for a variety of genres—including history, romance, sports, science fiction, fantasy, horror, and erotica. Manga are not comic books but rather graphic novels. As the cultural studies scholar David W. Foster explains:

> It has been well established that one fundamental difference between comic book art (with its rather ad hoc graphic exuberance and an accompanying thinness of narrative profundity) and graphic narrative as it has established itself as a contemporary cultural genre has been a set of underlying principles of narrative coherence that promote reader introspection and the sustained contemplation of a complex and ambiguous aesthetic object. Over-the-top WHAM! BANG! KERPOW!, often tied to fanciful action images of raw physical experience, yield to the often highly nuanced and multiple ambiguous sequencing of lived human events, often with no conclusive sense of THE END. (2016, 83–84)

This chapter analyzes the historical manga *Los samuráis de México: La verdadera historia de los primeros japoneses en Latinoamérica* (The Samurai of Mexico: The True Story of the First Japanese in Latin America, 2008), originally written in Japanese by Hisashi Ueno, with illustrations by the artist Konohana Sakuya. It was published in 1994 by the Japanese publisher

Chuokoron Sha as *La historia de la Colonia Enomoto en México* (The History of the Enomoto Community in Mexico). On the one hand, it is immigrant literature, because Ueno was an Issei staff member at the Japanese embassy in Mexico. On the other hand, it is a graphic narrative belonging to visual culture. The Spanish publication resulted from the collaboration of Kunio Nanbu, president of Nabel Enterprise; Koji Hashimoto, former president of the Japanese Mexican Association; Shozo Ogino, former president of *Nichiboku Shinbun*; and Kenichiro Kawaji, JICA's representative in Mexico. It was translated by Koji Hashimoto, Héctor Kawakami, Alfonso Muray, Akihiro Nakaune, Rafael Shimizu, and Isawo Toda, all members of the Japanese Mexican Association.

The manga mostly recounts the Meiji-era adventures of the first Nikkeijin in Chiapas, a state deemed ideal for growing coffee. Following the Japanese original, *Los samuráis de México* must be read, in its Spanish-language translation, from right to left, beginning with the last page. The manga's cover features three Nikkei men, foreshadowing the absence of women among this first group of Nikkei in Mexico. The "true story," as the subtitle notes, recalls the 1576 *Historia verdadera de la conquista de la Nueva España* (*The True History of the Conquest of New Spain*), by the Spanish conquistador Bernal Díaz del Castillo (1492–1581), itself meant to correct Francisco López de Gómara's previous account of Hernán Cortés's 1519 victory over the Aztecs. Díaz del Castillo though López de Gómara minimized his own soldiers' participation, giving all the credit to Cortés. In this example of intertextuality, we might wonder which narrative of Japanese immigration in Mexico this manga is correcting.

Los samuráis de México displays some traits of testimonies, not least of which is that the subtitles tend to claim a historical truth. In Chiapas, Ueno meets an elderly Nikkei immigrant, Seiichi Niimi, known as Don Santiago and the last surviving member of the Enomoto group. Niimi was an eyewitness to the historical events recounted in the manga. As in Latin American *testimonios*, he relates to Ueno the Enomoto group's travails, not just his own; his testimony represents his community's collective voice.[1] *Los samuráis* delivers a veiled sociopolitical denunciation of the Japanese government's injustice and corruption. There is a pragmatic impetus to disclose how the Japanese government turned its back on these Issei, who ended up suffering hardship, illness, and untimely death. Like *testimonios*, this manga deviates from the impersonality of historical discourse: the author, who is also the first character introduced in the story, openly expresses his admiration for the brave men whose mission was to help their fatherland by providing resources and improving its image abroad. Unlike *testimonios*, however, there is no sense of polemical urgency in *Los samuráis de México*, as the related events transpired a century earlier. Instead, the aim is didactic: in the acknowledgments the author expresses his interest in ensuring both that Chiapas's Nikkeijin are aware of their ancestors' heroism and that other Mexicans discover the friendly historical relations between Mexico and Japan.

According to the cultural theorist Stuart Hall, "identities are the names we give to the different ways we are positioned by, and position ourselves within, the narratives of the past" (1999, 225). Therefore, knowing the history of Japan's first state-sponsored immigration to Latin America has the potential to shape not only Japanese Mexican identities but also Mexican identities in general, as both are in constant negotiation. Ueno and the manga artist Sakuya thereby lend their voice to this group of compatriots and to their descendants who, for the most part, were forgotten by history and also mediate the direct testimony of Niimi, the Colonia Enomoto's last survivor.

SAMURAI-LIKE HEROISM AND "THE JAPANESE SPIRIT"

The main character of *Los samuráis de México*, Ueno, discovers a Nikkei community in Acacoyagua, Chiapas, while traveling to Guatemala. His car breaks down there and a Nikkeijin helps him out. Sakuya, the manga's illustrator, goes to great lengths to convey that this Japanese descendant no longer has the typical Japanese phenotype: his physical characteristics and behaviors are more Western; for example, he hugs Ueno, a stranger, breaking Japanese protocol. Ueno becomes visibly uncomfortable with the unexpected embrace.

In one panoramic illustration, the Nikkeijin takes Ueno to a park in the town's outskirts. There, an obelisk with the etched names of the first thirty-six Japanese to arrive in Acacoyagua was erected in 1968, on the seventieth anniversary of Japanese immigration to Chiapas. Stressing the monument's importance to the story, Sakuya draws it no fewer than six times, four in the opening pages and two at the end. The Spanish phrase "homenaje y gratitud del pueblo de Acacoyagua" (tribute and gratitude of the people of Acacoyagua) is visible at the base of the monument. Also engraved is a Spanish translation of this seventeenth-century haiku by Matsuo Bashō (1644–1694), the most famous poet of the Edo period:[2]

> summer grass
> of warrior's dreams
> the aftermath[3]

As evoked by Bashō's haiku, all that remains of the early arrivals' efforts, sacrifice, and heroic deeds are the ruins or aftermath of their dreams in the form of summer grass. While the Spanish version opts for "heroes" instead of "warrior," both choices convey admiration for the epic achievements of these immigrants. Standing before the obelisk, Ueno suddenly turns emotional, feeling those "ancestors' breaths whose lives ended in Mexico."[4] This haiku appears twice (the original version and then the Enomoto leader Ryojiro Terui's interpretation) in the manga's last pages to again underscore its important symbolism and the protagonists' samurai-like heroism.[5]

In contrast with the previous chapter on Nakatani's memoirs, and more in keeping with Nikkei-American narratives, *Los samuráis de México* features real-life heroes of an epic overseas adventure.[6] On arriving at their destination, the Enomoto immigrants are reminded that they must try to improve Japan's international reputation: "You are the representatives of Japan. Show your strength and courage to Mexicans."[7] Tellingly, in an ensuing vignette, Terui senses the historic importance of their adventure and declares: "I feel like we are like characters in a novel."[8]

In his undergraduate thesis, Charles Joseph MacRobie Fliss studied the Orientalization of what he calls a "Pure-Japan" among American manga fans:

> Pure-Japan is an Orientalist narrative created by American anime and manga fans to represent Japan, but the narrative also serves to provide collective identity for the fan community. . . . Through their interpretations of anime and manga, the elite of the fan community developed an idyllic view of Japan . . . [that] is thoroughly Orientalist. The narrative textualizes and essentializes the people of Japan and their nation. . . . Fans appropriate the right to speak from the Japanese, silencing Japanese narratives of self and nation. (2012, 85–87)

A similar essentializing operation takes place in *Los samuráis de México* but with nationalistic overtones. It unproblematically privileges a key concept in Nihonjinron discourse: the existence of an unchanging, static, and unique "Japanese spirit" (*yamato-damashii*; literally, "the great spirit of harmony") that guides the Nikkei immigrants' resilience. Kusakado, the group's supervisor, states: "We are going to sow the *Yamato* Japanese spirit in this great Mexican land!"[9] Likewise, another character, faced with the grueling task of clearing the jungle for farming, promises: "Here we will show our Yamato Japanese spirit."[10] This approach is also emphasized in the title by the term *samuráis*, a central archetype of Japaneseness in the West later adopted by Nihonjinron discourse. These modern Nikkei immigrants in Mexico consequently come to metonymically symbolize the survival of the values associated with those idealized warriors of medieval and early modern Japan.

Although the idea of Japanese spirit (*yamato-damashii*) can be broadly interpreted as the cultural values and characteristics of the Japanese people, it is important to keep in mind that, during the first half of the twentieth century, Japanese nationalists turned this idea into a key message of imperialist propaganda, which is invoked several times in the manga. Originally coined during the Heian period (794–1185) to counter Japanese cultural values with values of those arriving from Tang-dynasty China (then Japan's cultural Other), it was later encouraged by the Meiji government as a central aspect of Japan's imperial military doctrines. According to the linguist Roy Andrew Miller, after the First Sino-Japanese War and the Russo-Japanese War, nationalists turned *yamato-damashii* into "the official rallying cry for the Japanese armed forces in World War II" (1982, 13). The term is thereby discussed in Nihonjinron discourse and is historically associated with Japanese nationalism.

Relatedly, in 1958 the sociologist Tetsundo Tsukamoto pointed out the obsession with the Japanese spirit in Japanese Brazilian schools: "The Japanese school is where the Japanese spirit is acquired through the teaching of the Japanese language. Moreover, its acquisition must primarily result . . . in maintaining the Japanese concept of family, one imbued with great respect for both parents and the paterfamilias's authority."[11] Similarly, and still in Brazil, the social psychologist Daniela de Carvalho reveals: "In the 1930s, the nationalistic orientation of education toward the promotion of yamato-damashii (the Japanese spirit) was strengthened. The *Nisei* were taught how to be 'good Japanese,' and the *Kyōiku Chokugo* (Imperial Rescript on Education), retained as a 'relic,' guided the education system" (2003, 14). The *yamato-damashii*, with its emphasis on emperor worship and Japan's military invincibility, has also been associated with ultranationalist groups like the Japanese Brazilian Shindō Renmei, whose leader, the former Japanese army colonel Junji Kikawa, was a fanatic believer in this concept. It is therefore somewhat surprising that the same Japanese spirit is repeatedly invoked and celebrated in *Los samuráis de México* without caveat, even if it did guide the young protagonists' actions and ideals.

Interestingly, the use of the term *Japanese spirit* in *Los samuráis de México* differs from its original nationalistic and xenophobic meaning. Yet it is unclear who is responsible for this maneuver: perhaps Ueno, the author; Seiichi Niimi, the last surviving member of the Enomoto group; or the mediating descendants of this group. This move is particularly noticeable when we learn about Tsuchihiko Kishimoto and Tokichi Kohashi, two Japanese immigrants contemporary to the Enomoto group. Because of prevalent anti-Japanese sentiment, they left their university studies in the United States and moved to Mexico in 1897—Kohashi's long hair in the illustrations is likely anachronistic and more in tune with today's manga characters. Two years later, they formed the Kohashi-Kishimoto Society in Escuintla, Chiapas, the first Nikkei-owned coffee production company in Mexico. Their goal, to create a business that would yield enough profit to then help the local population, is denoted in the manga as "the Japanese spirit:" "Here too the Japanese spirit was rooted in the Mexican land."[12] With branches in Acapetahua, San Isidro, and other towns, the Kohashi-Kishimoto Society provided more than one hundred jobs and became one of the richest companies in Chiapas. Having maintained their ownership during the Mexican Revolution, the two immigrants' dream was cut short when the Mexican government expropriated coffee plantations and forcibly displaced the men to Mexico City during World War II. Afterward, Kohashi remained in Mexico City, but Kishimoto returned to Escuintla, where he worked as a physician (even though he was a veterinarian) and built a school named after Benito Juárez to educate local children.

Incidentally, *Los samuráis de México* features another Nikkei immigrant who worked as a doctor without a medical degree. After Dr. Nihei Tamiya passed away, the people of Escuintla asked Renji Otta, a farmer who had served as the doctor's assistant, to become the new physician. Otta agreed. Much beloved by all, he died from malaria at age forty-two, in 1917. A former patient exemplified the locals' gratitude by giving Otta's family his cows so that they could sell them and return to Japan with the proceeds. *Los samuráis de México* references that a street and a monument in town are dedicated to him.

Along with "Japanese spirit," other colonial and imperialistic vocabulary uncritically permeates the manga. For instance, early in the narrative we learn that Viscount Enomoto—drawn realistically as a distinguished military man with moustache and sideburns, based on a well-known photograph—purchased "virgin" forests in Chiapas to clear them for agriculture and "colonization." The virgin concept is later reintroduced, when we learn that Dr. Eiji Matsuda, a Nikkei botanist, fashioned a taxonomy of "the then virgin" flora of southwestern Mexico.[13] This vocabulary is reminiscent of the time-honored stereotypes of colonialism, characteristic of imperialist projects that conceived of places in Africa and the Americas as an exotic tabula rasa awaiting population and exploitation by imperial subjects. Yet we later learn that when the Enomoto immigrants reach their purchased lands, they come into contact with the "natives." Perhaps, then, the reason for the term *virgin* was to avoid speculation that Nikkei immigrants were displacing the local population, referred to in colonial terms as "natives." (Notably, the manga makes no allusion to indigeneity.)

Los samuráis de México also buys into the Meiji government's use of overpopulation as an excuse for state-guided emigration; the real motivations were quite different. We are reminded that the first thirty-six Enomoto immigrants who arrived in 1897, all men in their twenties, were trailblazers of Nikkei immigration in Latin America, having arrived in Mexico before later mass immigrations to Peru (1899) and Brazil (1908). They were part of the nearly one million Nikkei who moved to the Americas as *dekasegi* (temporary workers), fleeing poverty and, according to the manga, overpopulation. In yet another wink to colonial imagery, the botanical scientist Eiji Matsuda is illustrated oddly with a British colonial safari helmet.

Like Nakatani's memoirs, *Los samuráis de México* deviates from the more common narratives of cultural adaptation and progressive integration into Mexican mainstream society. Instead, consistent with this colonial-minded viewpoint, this manga's teleological argument mobilizes a paternalistic mentality in which the Nikkeijin appear to play a salvational role (a sort of Japanese version of white saviorism) in the region: they provide charitable assistance by building three schools, treating the sick, and evangelizing the locals, thus lessening the dire poverty of the "natives." In fact, this peculiar use of the noun *native* perhaps reveals not only a settler colonial mentality but also a sense of racial superiority. Although acknowledging deficiencies in the immigrants' agricultural skills, overall there are condescending overtones in the description of their activities.[14] Thus, on the very first page of the manga, where "the Enomoto spirit" had not yet become "the Japanese spirit," we read: "These young Japanese were imbued with the Enomoto spirit, which was based on a new migratory idea consisting not only of amassing a fortune, but also of living with and devoutly serving the natives of the place, in order to establish a permanent settlement for the benefit of the people."[15] While these Japanese immigrants may well have contributed to economic development in Chiapas, the text misses the context of imperial propaganda that frames these power dynamics. Tellingly, in the Brazilian context, the political scientist Philip Staniford argues that, at one time, there was a superiority complex among the Nikkeijin in relation to the local population:

> Immigrants shared a solidly developed and positive self-image with their countrymen in Japan. Such a feeling was explicitly or implicitly manifested in the so-called "Japanese spirit" (*yamato-damashii*) and in their conviction

that the Japanese are capable of facing and overcoming adversity. They consider themselves hard, intelligent workers, able to control any situation and to find adequate solutions. This positive self-image is more intense overseas when they compare what they consider their "civilized" politeness and finesse with the "rude" characteristics they find in other cultures. We, as a "people," are different from "them," foreigners they considered "primitive" (*geshijin*) and savage (*yabanjin*).[16]

Yet this Nikkei altruism emphasized in the manga does echo historical events. It is corroborated by the fact that during World War II, Nikkeijin in Chiapas were allowed to stay in their homes longer than those elsewhere before being relocated, because of demands made by local citizens and politicians who were grateful for all the Nikkeijin had done and viewed them as vital contributors to their community's welfare. Therefore, the manga strategically introduces the main message: from the outset of immigration, the Enomoto Nikkeijin's altruistic and virtuous spirit forever left its mark on Japan-Mexico relations, as it fomented reciprocal friendship and respect for Nikkeijin in Mexico.

UNCONDITIONAL PATRIOTISM DESPITE DECEPTION AND BETRAYAL

In *Los samuráis de México*, the Japanese government does not receive the same praise as the Nikkei immigrants do. The manga openly denounces the false promises made to the immigrants ("success is guaranteed," affirms a sponsor) by Viscount Enomoto and the government he represented.[17] Exaggerations and lies consequently led the unwary immigrants to suffer such hardship that some went to Mexico City to beg the Japanese ambassador to send them home. In addition, the manga has no fear of declaring the Enomoto project a failure—in fact, the second chapter is titled "The Failure." However, it does celebrate how some members of the original group eventually managed to reinvent themselves: in September 1904 at the Tajuko ranch, Ryojiro Terui, Kumataro Takahashi, Rokutaro Arima, Asajiro Yamamoto, Saburo Kiyono, and Waka Suzuki—all survivors of the Enomoto group—created the San-Ou cooperative, which later became the Sociedad Cooperativa Mexicano-Japonesa (Japanese-Mexican Cooperative Society). Among the numerous obstacles they faced were two major historical events that curtailed their aspirations: the Mexican Revolution and World War II.

Los samuráis de México celebrates the Enomoto group as patriots who devoted their lives to supporting their homeland from abroad. Indeed, distinguishing them from most Nikkei immigrants in Latin America, they do not see themselves as temporary immigrants; from the start, they permanently settle in Mexico. One of the thirty-six immigrants, Shintaro Yamada, makes the ultimate sacrifice, as he becomes ill during the forty-eight-day voyage to Mexico and dies near Acapulco. Even though there are some clashes at first between students and employees, as well as between workers under contract and the six free, independent immigrants, they all share the common goal of glorifying and helping Japan by improving its international reputation and providing needed resources.[18] This is repeatedly emphasized throughout the manga, with drawings of the men holding a Japanese flag and the inclusion of kanji (characters used in the Japanese writing system) to evoke cultural authenticity. Thus, celebrating their patriotism and echoing the hardly veiled diasporic nationalist discourse that runs through the manga, a large vignette shows one of the remaining thirty-five immigrants holding a large Japanese flag. After an arduous walk to their destination, during which four men become sunstruck, a man shouts, "We'll make history here! Let's start!"[19] After arriving on 19 May 1897, the men are shocked to find a jungle near the town of Escuintla, but they are still in high spirits. Although disillusionment and even desperation soon sink in, another immigrant proclaims his patriotism and national pride: "We are top-rate people who have come to colonize this land for the glory of Japan!"[20]

Feeling abandoned by their government, they still invoke Japanese pride to achieve their goals and resort to their own motivation: Terui draws energy from his Christian faith, while Otta treats his sick countrymen with no other physician nearby. At one point, their supervisor Kusakado feels compelled to admit that Viscount Enomoto has not provided new funding, so they will not receive their salaries. In a vignette, he expresses his sincere apology to the group in *dogeza* posture, kneeling on the ground and bowing, prostrating himself and touching his head to the floor, following traditional Japanese etiquette. We learn that although Viscount Enomoto and his Nichiboku Takushoku immigrant association managed to collect only half of the projected budget, they sent the emigrants to Mexico anyway. As the manga bemoans several times, the men were abandoned, almost sacrificed, by the Japanese government. After a year in Chiapas, the Enomoto group had to admit their inevitable failure, caused by the flawed initial research—Kusakado, though an agronomist, had purchased arabica coffee plants, which grow only at higher altitudes; their arrival in Chiapas during the rainy season; and a dearth of government funding.

In July 1897, ten members of the Enomoto group deserted and walked nearly 750 miles for thirty-six days, with little food, to the Japanese

Empire's diplomatic mission in Mexico City. A vignette shows them weeping, in rags, and with overgrown hair and beards, begging to be sent back to Japan. The consul, Murota, takes them in for a month, but after consulting with the Japanese government, he makes them return to Chiapas—the government indolently accuses them of desertion for having breached their labor contracts. Although another coordinator and other immigrants arrive in Chiapas, the Enomoto group is dissolved a year after its creation.

Six of the original Enomoto immigrants, however, decide to stay in Chiapas and persevere. In 1901, they founded the successful Cooperativa Mexicano Japonesa (Japanese Mexican Cooperative) at the Tajuko ranch. In another exaltedly patriotic vignette with kanji, an immigrant, holding a large Japanese flag, encourages his peers "to build our colony and to be useful to Japan."[21] They fear that if they abandon the project under a Mexican government that trusts and supports Japan, it will be detrimental for future Japanese immigration to Mexico. Therefore, despite feeling betrayed and abandoned by Japan, their patriotism remains as strong as ever.

FROM UTOPIAN SOCIALIST TO CHRISTIAN UTOPIAS

Several of the pioneers in Chiapas were Christian and seemingly socialist. In his *El samurái de la Graflex*, Salinas Basave explores the sources of Viscount Enomoto Takeaki's fascination with Mexico and socialist affiliation: "Viscount Enomoto, who belonged to a noble shogunate lineage, resided in France between 1862 and 1867, where he studied naval technology with the French Navy. During those years, he had time to chat with many officers who had participated in France's occupation of Mexico, especially with Captain Jules Brunet, who instilled in him the idea that Mexico was a magical, rich, and mysterious country. Besides hearing fanciful testimonies about Mexico, Enomoto became familiar with Charles Fourier's theories about utopian socialism."[22] After returning to Japan, he tried to establish an independent community on the island of Hokkaido, the Republic of Ezo, which was based on samurai ethics and the collectivist views on the French philosopher Charles Fourier. He was, however, defeated by the Emperor's army and imprisoned for three years. According to Salinas Basave, after Enomoto is rehabilitated and, surprisingly, named foreign minister by the emperor, "he does not abandon his socialist ideas and, deep in his heart, continues to dream of founding a commune governed by the principles of egalitarian labor and samurai ethics."[23] He then tried to create in Mexico a version of the Hokkaido community.

In *Brazil Maru*, a novel by Karen Tei Yamashita based on immigrants in Brazil, the Nikkei families who emigrate to Brazil are pacifists fleeing the Meiji government's growing militarism. Feeling alienated in their own country, these prosperous, educated, and Westernized expatriates (they follow Jean-Jacques Rousseau's philosophy and listen to Antonín Dvořák's music) dream of creating a new, utopian society based on Japanese values, a little Japan in the hinterlands of the state of São Paulo. In fact, the protagonist Kantaro Uno seems alienated from his native Japan, indifferent to geopolitical issues and impartial during the conflict in Brazil between the Kachigumi, those refusing to accept Japan's defeat in World War II, and the Makegumi, those accepting it. Given this example, a different rationale to the one offered in the manga is possible: one might wonder whether the real-life Enomoto pioneers, also Christian socialists, were likewise fleeing Meiji militaristic and imperialist politics as opposed to being guided by patriotic and nationalistic ideals.

Following the rationale in the manga, a vignette in *Los samuráis de México* depicts all six immigrants of the Cooperativa Mexicano Japonesa holding a Japanese flag while promising to be the foundation for future generations of Nikkei immigrants. To overcome the Enomoto project's failure, they create, under Terui's leadership, the San-Ou cooperative, which prohibits private property: participants must surrender their personal interests, expect no salary, and accept that all property is shared; in return, the cooperative will cover their food, clothing, and lodging expenses. Besides working at their Tajuko ranch, where they distilled spirits, made bamboo baskets, and opened a convenience store, the members of the cooperative had other jobs, such as pharmacist and store clerk, and they shared their income among themselves. Within five years, the cooperative's wealth grew fourfold, which allowed it to expand into Acacoyagua, Escuintla, and Tapachula.[24] In time, the cooperative, which had one of the two telephone lines in Escuintla, was able to purchase additional land around Acacoyagua for cattle raising and vegetable farming.

The narrative of *Los samuráis de México* points out that their cooperative idea is reminiscent of a socialist state. Indeed, the organization of the cooperative is reminiscent of utopian socialism and Fourier's ideas. In the 1840s, following Fourier, numerous communes (known as *phalanxes*) were established in different countries, including in the United States (Ohio's Utopia is among the most famous). Fourier conceived of harmonious collaboration as the key to social success and increased productivity. In his secular socialist utopia, work, freed from exploitation and alienation, was to be transformed into play and pleasure, into an "attractive labor" stemming from liberated passion. Unlike most Marxists and anarchists, utopian socialists did not believe in class struggle or social revolution; instead, their exemplary small communities were supposed to demonstrate the efficiency of cooperative socialism to society. Perhaps the San-Ou cooperative as described in *Los samuráis de México* must be understood within the framework of these efforts to reshape society through exemplary socialist communities.

Although the manga never mentions it, this type of organization is also reminiscent of French socialist Pierre-Joseph Proudhon's (1809–1865) *mutualisme* (mutualism), a type of economic system that opposed land and capital entitlement, because, according to him, the derived profit inevitably led to debt, social instability, and war. He likewise believed that land property and capital possession created wage workers who, in turn, were subjected to the despotism of a boss. Opposed to wage labor, profit, worker exploitation, and large concentrations of wealth and property, Proudhon encouraged peasants' and artisans' small-scale property, like the one described in *Los samuráis de México*.

The failed capitalist Enomoto venture, then, transforms into the San-Ou cooperative's successful socialist planning: "The cooperative was the most important Japanese enterprise abroad," declares *Los samuráis de México*.[25] Once economic stability is achieved, the six cooperative associates begin to plan their children's future, ensuring their proper education and financial welfare. This emphasis on education—underscored throughout the manga—is materialized in the 1906 founding of La Aurora Primary School. *Los samuráis de México* depicts this school, the outcome of Nikkei philanthropy, as the foundation of Nisei and non-Nikkei children's education in this region of Mexico. Terui also funded a trust that made it possible for cooperativists' Nisei children to live with Japanese teachers at the school to learn Japanese, since their Mexican mothers—all Enomoto immigrants were men—were unable to teach them the language at home.

Moving on from utopian socialist to Christian utopias, a fact that may surprise the manga's reader is that some of the immigrants, including Tsunematsu Fuse and Eiji Matsuda, were devout Christians. According to *Los samuráis de México*, both belonged to and propagated "la religión cristiana sin iglesia" (Christian religion without church; Ueno and Sakuya 2008, 4), that is, nondenominational Christianity, or churches not formally aligned with any specific Christian denomination. Later, an illustration depicts a building façade in Acacoyagua that reads "Iglesia Evangélica Cristiana Independiente El Buen Pastor" (The Good Shepherd Independent Christian Evangelical Church).

Chapter 5 in *Los samuráis de México* focuses on a different group of Nikkei immigrants in Chiapas. We learn that, in 1900, Tatsujiro Fujino, a congressman from Shiga Prefecture, decides to revive the Enomoto Immigrant Association's failed project. Indeed, even after Viscount Enomoto dissolves his immigrant association, its contract remains with the Mexican government assuring annual payments for its purchased land. A man named Tatsujiro Fujino, who, like Enomoto, was enthusiastic about the benefits of emigration to Mexico, decides to assume the old project, changing its name to Fujino Emigrant Association. He then convinces his countryman Tsunematsu Fuse, a fervent believer of the type of Christianity preached by Pastor Uchimura, to emigrate to Chiapas. Here, the manga seems to refer to Uchimura Kanzō (1861–1930), a Christian evangelist and pacifist who fervently opposed the Russo-Japanese War in his newspaper columns.[26] In 1901, Uchimura founded the Mukyoaki (Nonchurch Movement), the first Japanese independent Christian "church" movement, whose main message was complete reliance on God and independence from human "wrappings" or forces. Uchimura considered an organized religion an obstacle to the true practice of the faith and did not consider Christian sacraments indispensable for salvation.

An expert agronomist, Fuse manages to avoid his predecessors' mistakes. He emigrates with his wife in 1900, becomes a Mexican citizen, improves "native" education, and diversifies agriculture and cattle raising by introducing Holstein cattle to the Hacienda Xalapa. Whereas he introduces electricity and the telephony to the area, his devout Christian wife also evangelizes "the natives" and improves their diet, along with teaching Japanese to Nisei children. Fuse becomes deeply involved in the local community, often attending town-hall meetings. Like his predecessors, he too is attacked by bandits who hang him; fortunately, he is saved at the last minute by other Nikkeijin. Being a good forgiving Christian, Fuse prevents the Nikkeijin from retaliating: he instead chooses to build what he called "the country of hope."[27]

In 1922, Eiji Matsuda (wearing a British colonial safari helmet in the vignette), with money earned through a research project on the mass production of eucalyptus trees funded by the Japanese army, is able to continue Fuse's utopian Christian venture at La Esperanza ranch. Like Fuse, Matsuda is also attacked by bandits, but he manages to convince them to spare him by explaining that, in the future, they will have no one else to rob. Also like Fuse, Matsuda is sure that the bandits do not hate the Nikkeijin. After La Esperanza prospers, Matsuda provides employment for many locals, who are amazed when paid the promised wages; other employers always underpay them. When Matsuda explains to them that God sees all and that it makes no sense to cheat, they become disappointed with the local Catholic priest who has not taught that doctrine and begin to follow Matsuda's preaching. He then offers to teach them the Bible, all the while teaching "the natives" to read and write and taking care of orphans. Eventually, he attracts more than two thousand to build a temple that still stands in today's Acacoyagua.[28] An illustration in the manga shows that there is now a monument to Matsuda and closes the section by celebrating the survival of Fuse's and Matsuda's Christian ideals.

STRATEGICALLY LIMINAL POSITIONING

It is no surprise that a diplomat like Ueno wrote a text celebrating the longstanding friendly, mutually beneficial relations between Mexico and Japan. But the manga also includes a somewhat veiled message to today's Mexican Nikkeijin: it is a cross-cultural conduit between the two countries, working to do so just as their ancestors did. Thus, early in the first chapter, we find a representative of the Mexican delegation in Japan addressing the soon-to-be emigrants: "I trust that you who are going to live in our country will contribute to strengthening the ties of friendship between the two countries."[29] Later, in a key vignette, the leader Terui reiterates the idea: "I think that after one hundred years our descendants should speak Spanish and Japanese in order to serve as a bridge between Mexico and Japan."[30] It is thus implied that, following their ancestors, that Mexican Nikkeijin must strategically establish themselves as a link for the improvement of economic, political, and cultural relations between both countries. This stance has been commonly adopted by Nikkei communities throughout the region.[31]

The cooperativists, faithful to their original objectives at the time of their emigration to Mexico, demonstrate their altruism by creating three schools in the towns of Acapetahua, Acacoyagua, and Escuintla. These important social contributions later led the local population to resist the government's forced displacement of the Nikkeijin during World War II. The cooperative's next major project, the creation of a much-needed Spanish-Japanese dictionary, symbolizes this liminal role between both cultures.[32] In one vignette, the elderly Seiichi Niimi, the last surviving Enomoto immigrant, shows Ueno a copy of the worn-out Spanish-Japanese dictionary, the first published, according to Niimi. The need for a bilingual dictionary is illustrated in the one instance of humor in this intense and often melodramatic manga: a Nikkei immigrant, angry at local children for saying the Spanish word *vaca* (cow), believes that they are insulting him with the Japanese word *baka* (stupid).

The destruction of the railway system during the Mexican Revolution prevented needed products from reaching the Sociedad Cooperativa Mexicano-Japonesa, which was forced to shut down in 1920, after twenty successful years. In the manga, a realistic vignette includes General Pancho Villa in Ojinaga; in another, his soldiers take over the railways; and in a third, six cooperativists weep. After the end of the revolution in 1920, President Álvaro Obregón, sketched realistically in another vignette, decided to compensate foreign companies for their losses during the conflict to show goodwill to foreign investment. In contrast to the strong compensations demanded by the United States, France, and England, the Nikkeijin in Chiapas sent a letter written by Terui and the Japanese consul to the Mexican president in which they renounced their corresponding compensation in spite of their major economic losses: "We, though foreigners residing on Mexican soil, must also share the Mexican grief."[33] This represents the key exemplum in the manga.

The manga includes a summary of the letter illustrated with the Mexican and Japanese flags representing the fraternity between the two nations. The summary conveys the Nikkeijin's gratitude to Mexico, a country they have come to consider their new homeland. A vignette depicts an emotional President Obregón in tears (there is much crying in this manga) after reading their letter. A vignette follows that returns us to the manga's title by including this phrase: "The country of the samurai . . . Japan."[34] Another patriotic vignette that includes the Japanese flag reveals that, following the example of Terui and his cooperative, the entire Nikkei community in Mexico is renouncing government compensation. Emphasizing the manga's main idea, the author reminds us that this exemplary generosity strengthened the goodwill between both countries. Terui's motto is then repeated: "We will be the bridge between Mexico and Japan."[35]

This same strategic, liminal Nikkei positioning continues by exemplifying Fuse's Mexican patriotism. In 1911, while delivering a lecture in Japan, an audience member notices the scars on his neck. After Fuse explains that Mexican bandits, after robbing him, proceeded to hang him and would have killed him had fellow Nikkeijin not saved him, another audience member argues that the bandits should have been machine-gunned. To everyone's surprise, Fuse defends the bandits, who, in his view, did not hate Nikkeijin but were marginal groups fighting for survival. In a revelatory moment, he then exclaims, "I will not allow you to offend the citizens of my country, Mexico!"[36] Proud of his cross-cultural identity, he unashamedly calls Mexico his country, even before a Japanese audience in Japan.

The closing chapter, focusing on the World War II period, again emphasizes the altruism of Nikkei immigrants in Chiapas and the gratitude of the local population. It praises the Mexican government's "benevolent" treatment of the Nikkeijin, as, unlike in Peru, Mexico refused to send its Japanese residents to US internment camps. Instead, they were allowed to live freely in Mexico City and Guadalajara (the manga does not mention the implemented movement restrictions). *Los samuráis de México* then speculates that it was perhaps the Nikkei community's unwillingness to accept compensation after the Mexican Revolution that influenced the government's apparent magnanimity during World War II.

The chapter also reveals that, although a few Mexicans mocked the Nikkeijin during the war, most treated them well. For example, in a speech the Escuintla mayor calls Japan a country of savages, and an elderly lady throws a rock at him, accusing him of being ungrateful and asking rhetorically: "Who helped deliver your daughter? Who built the school? Who brought electricity? Who built the bridge at the town's entrance? All thanks to the Japanese!"[37] In the ensuing vignettes, an angry mob takes the mayor away on their shoulders. We are then informed that, despite having lost all their possessions, the Nikkeijin behaved exemplarily.

Next, a Nikkeijin named Tadasu Tsuji writes the Mexican president offering to help in a new literacy campaign and reminding him that his community founded schools in Chiapas. In response, the president acknowledges through an emissary their contributions and allows Nikkei families from Chiapas to return home to continue their literacy efforts. When the emissary expresses his hope that this decision would partially offset their suffering, Tsuji reminds him that, in Mexico, they have experienced more joy than suffering. He then explains how Nikkeijin and non-Nikkeijin had lived in harmony and how a process of transculturation has taken place: locals play sumo, cook *mochi* (sweet rice dough) and *onigiri* (rice balls) and beans, and make fireworks. Finally, Tsuji states that Chiapas Nikkeijin love Mexico and will remain there always because it is a land of eternal hope. An emotional vignette shows the emissary weeping. Thus, the Nikkeijin fulfill the original teleology of attaining economic success, living in harmony with the locals and contributing to the country's prosperity. In the final double-page vignettes, we see the Nikkeijin welcomed back to Chiapas by locals, the army, and a music band. They hug and greet one another effusively. The last of the manga's illustrations, before the bilingual farewell ("Gracias, México. Arigatou"; Ueno and Sakuya 2008, 218), depicts a road with a mountain in the background that is reminiscent, again, of Mount Fuji.

In the acknowledgments, Ueno emphasizes the traditionally excellent relations between the governments of Japan and Mexico. After all, Mexico was the first country to sign a treaty with Japan on equal terms and the first

Latin American country to open a Japanese consulate, in 1891. Thanks to the Enomoto cooperative, Ueno reminds us, the first Japanese-Spanish dictionary was published and the Convenio de Libre Ejercicio del Médico, Dentista y Farmacéutico (The Free Practice of Physicians, Dentists, and Pharmacists Agreement) was signed by the two countries. After World War II, the Mexican ambassador to the United Nations was the first to request Japan's admission into that world body. In 1955, Mexico was also the first country with which Japan signed a cultural agreement, and in 2005, both countries signed an economic cooperation agreement. Hoping that his manga might help the Nikkeijin learn about their ancestors' achievements, Ueno closes by wishing that the story of the Enomoto group will one day be turned into a film (in Japan, when a manga series becomes very popular, it is sometimes made into an *anime*, a Japanese-style animation).

Los samuráis de México, written by a diplomat after his interview with an Enomoto pioneer and many of the group's descendants, celebrates the history of reciprocal benefit between Mexico and Japan (the Japanese term *otagaisama*, meaning "each one looks after the other" comes to mind). Its meaning is found in the Enomoto group's sustained and disinterested altruism. *Los samuráis de México* is also intended to educate today's Mexican Nikkeijin, who, despite being proud of their ethnic origin, are often unaware of their ancestors' heroism. The reader is left to wonder whether this ignorance of ancestors' past is the outcome of the decision to suppress their suffering and not talk about their experience. The manga, though, encourages them to take advantage of their ethnocultural background and strategically liminal position to advance binational exchanges between their country and the ancestral homeland.

The manga recycles colonialist or imperialist imagery (safari helmet) and concepts (Japanese spirit, virgin lands, natives, colonization), even providing new nuance to known words and phrases, like "Japanese spirit," to disguise a case of state-guided emigration policy that was intimately linked to Japanese imperialism. It is unclear, however, whether this resignification of "the Japanese spirit" was made by Niimi, the survivor of the first Enomoto group who was interviewed; by the group's descendants; or by Ueno, who articulated their stories into a coherent narration. In any case, as a sort of *captatio benevolentiae*, the author and illustrator of the manga, along with several of the its pioneering protagonists, express their gratitude to Mexico, "the land of eternal hope." Regardless of its apparent sincerity, this gratefulness works as a rhetorical device to capture Mexican readers' empathy.

Again, despite the manga's testimonial traits and its re-creation of the immigrants' relentless patriotism vis-à-vis their government's deception and betrayal, it is tempting to consider the possibility that the Enomoto pioneers, as well as their contemporary peers in *Los samuráis de México*, may actually have been fleeing Meiji militarism and/or experimenting with utopian socialism, just as the real-life socialist and Christian Nikkeijin portrayed in the novel *Brazil Maru*. Paradoxically, in a sort of Japanese Orientalism directed at Mexico, this manga describes Chiapas as a Japan-Mexico contact zone from the perspective of Nikkei immigrants, but mediated by a Japanese national, living in Mexico, who works for the Japanese embassy and is thus invested in (re)enhancing the international image of his country. This hero-producing narrative effectively mobilizes colonial vocabulary to praise the alleged selfless altruism of a group of exemplary Japanese turned Mexican ("gone native") who learned to respect and love their host country.

CHAPTER 5

Nishizawa's Bicultural Dialectics and the Critical Stereotyping of His Art

Although there are numerous Nikkei visual artists in Mexico, none has reached the fame and influence of the Nisei Luis Nishizawa Flores (1918–2014).[1] This chapter focuses on the blend of two artistic national traditions in Nishizawa's art and on the stereotyped critical reception of his art in Mexico. As will be shown, while traces of traditional East Asian aesthetics are found in his work, Mexican critics tend to overstate them because of his Japanese surname, a common prejudice in scholarship about Japanese–Latin American cultural production.

Kenji Nishizawa, Luis's father, immigrated from Nagano Prefecture to Mexico in 1908. His mother, María de Jesús Flores, hailed from Tenopalco, Mexico. Born at San Mateo Ixtacalco Hacienda in Cuauhtitlán, Luis Nishizawa was a lonely and introverted child who spent much of his time tending to his family's cattle. This time spent in a bucolic setting, coupled with a proneness to solitude, is reflected in the serenity evoked by many of his landscapes, which often include cows and other farm animals. In a 1953 interview with the Mexican journalist and writer Elena Poniatowska, then working for the newspaper *Excélsior*, Nishizawa reminisced: "During those long days in the countryside, I would pay attention to the most intimate detail of every tree leaf, of every grass blade, of every small cornfield. I paid attention to the color shifts caused by the sun's rays on treetops, to the shadows, flowers and fruits, and to the animals that I so absentmindedly led to graze . . . Painting was in all of nature's shapes, in the air's breath, in the essence of the Hacienda de San Mateo's black sand."[2]

In 1925, after his family moved to the working-class Tepito neighborhood in Mexico City, Nishizawa began to study jewelry making and music. It was not until 1942 that he enrolled at the Escuela Nacional de Artes Plásticas (National School of Fine Arts; former Academia de San Carlos) to formally study art. Although this timing coincided with the height of the 1940s Mexican muralist movement, one distinguished by its nationalist ideology, Nishizawa also studied other painting styles, including expressionism, abstraction, and Japanese artistic traditions. He began to receive international recognition after being selected as one of the five most outstanding artists at the 1958 Tokyo International Biennial. In 1963, he studied engraving with Yukio Fukazawa and Ichikawa, renowned Japanese intaglio printmakers. He traveled the following year to Tokyo, where he took a brief course in woodblock printing at the Center for Japanese Artists—in 1975, Nishizawa took more art courses in Japan.

Nishizawa received his master of arts degree in fine arts in 1947; eight years later, he started teaching at the Escuela Nacional de Artes Plásticas (National School of Fine Arts) of the Universidad Nacional Autónoma de México (UNAM), where he eventually became an influential professor. (The university bestowed him with the title of *maestro emérito* and an honorary doctorate in 1996). In 1964, he married Eva Zepeda, a painter with whom he had four children. Nishizawa continued his craft until his 2014 death, at the age of ninety-six, in Toluca, Mexico. His funeral was attended by then president Enrique Peña Nieto.

Although Nishizawa expressed himself through multiple artistic media, including sketching, engraving, sculpture, ceramics, and stained glass, he is singularly recognized for his oil or tempera easel paintings and murals. A most accomplished Mexican landscape artist, he derived his inspiration from the arid and desertic orography of central Mexico—much of his art depicts wide horizons, typically large meadows or rocky reliefs with mountains or volcanoes in the background, such as the Valley of Mexico's Popocatépetl and Iztaccíhuatl, as well as the Nevado de Toluca. Nishizawa is also known for his watercolor paintings, like *María*, his 1971 profile of a girl, and his black ink drawings reminiscent of *sumi-e* (traditional Japanese ink-wash painting), such as the somber and expressionistic pieces included in his 1970–1972 series *Las vacas flacas, los sueños rotos* (Lean cows, broken dreams).

In that series, one finds strange, black-and-white human figures, some naked and in distorted or obscene positions. Some of these works present a more playful, burlesque side of Nishizawa, leaning at times toward surrealism. Indeed, besides natural sceneries, the human figure is important motif in his oeuvre, especially in his murals and early paintings. The peaceful calm of his landscapes often turns into a expressionistic angst in his human figures, closer to the aesthetics of Mexican muralism, as evident in his 1959 acrylic *Figura* (Figure) and in his 1980 lithography *Caín* (Cain).

FIGURE 5.1. Luis Nishizawa, "Oxidación," from the series *Las vacas flacas y los sueños rotos* (Lean Cows and Broken Dreams), 1971. Courtesy of Adriana Nishizawa.

FIGURE 5.2. Luis Nishizawa, "Caín," 1958, charcoal, 62.5 × 88.5 cm. Courtesy of Adriana Nishizawa.

Nishizawa's first individual exhibition took place in 1951 at the Salón de la Plástica Mexicana (Mexican Fine Arts Salon).[3] Today, his works are exhibited in private and permanent collections of prominent museums in Mexico, Japan, the United States, Panama, and Bulgaria.[4] In 1990, Nishizawa was inducted as a full member of Mexico's Academia de Artes. Three years later, he became artistic creator (*creador artístico*) and honorary member of the Consejo Nacional para la Cultura y las Artes (National Committee for Culture and the Arts). In addition, acknowledging his artistic achievements, the Mexican Post Office created a commemorative stamp in his honor.

In 1992, in recognition of his valuable work as an artist and art professor for almost fifty years, the government of the State of Mexico opened the Museo Taller Luis Nishizawa (Luis Nishizawa Museum Workshop), located in Toluca. There, besides the inclusion of his personal archives and approximately eight hundred of his works, including oil paintings, watercolors, prints, stained glass, mixed media, and a mural, Nishizawa and other instructors taught art.[5] As Margarita García Luna, the director of the museum, explains: "The stained-glass in the first patio depicts the Nishizawa clan *mon*, a heraldic symbol given to Japanese clans that distinguished themselves through their contributions in battle or to culture. The symbol depicts two sparrows nesting in the bamboo they chose because of this plant's strength and flexibility. Bamboo bends with storms and hurricanes, later straightening up and moving in the wind. This symbol associates the human with the intelligence of a sparrow and flexibility in times of adversity" (n.d., 36–37).

This interesting detail perhaps evinces Nishizawa's pride in his ethnic heritage and his interest in Japanese perspectives. As to his international recognitions, the Japanese government presented him with the Sacred Treasure of the Dragon Award in 1987—he is the only artist to have received this award and Mexico's National Prize for Arts and Sciences (in 1996). Nishizawa also received the Premio Estado de México en Artes José María Velasco in 1984, and Mexico's CONACULTA named him a creator emeritus.

BLENDING MEXICAN AND JAPANESE ARTISTIC INFLUENCES

Several critics have pointed out the importance of Japanese heritage and training in Nishizawa's art production. He himself acknowledged how his art reflected his Japanese and Mexican ethnic heritages: "I inherited sensitivity from one grandfather, discipline from another, so my plastic art production has been the dialectic between my two roots."[6] Although

FIGURE 5.3. Stained-glass in the patio of the Nishizawa Museum Workshop. Courtesy of Adriana Berenice Ávila Caballero.

the motives and themes of his art are mostly Mexican, his Japanese cultural background and training are evident in the styles and techniques he employed. This is acutely noticeable in his drawings, as the art critic Crespo de la Serna indicates: "It also seems to me that he does not betray his Japanese origins in those same landscapes because, in some more than in others, especially in his drawings, one notices Hokusai's and Hiroshige's synthetic style and supreme line elegance."[7] Guadalupe Villa Guerrero likewise affirms: "Japanese art holds no secrets for Nishizawa; it is precisely in landscape painting where this knowledge is ostensibly manifested.... One of Nishizawa's greatest contributions to Mexican landscape painting is found in works derived from the Japanese, especially in those of tones achieved with the resources offered by black and white."[8]

Despite the influence of the Japanese art that he so admired, the main subjects of his art are for the most part the lands and people of his native Mexico. Tellingly, when the Mexican journalist, novelist, and politician María Luisa Mendoza (also known as La China Mendoza) visited Nishizawa's workshop as he worked—in her own stereotypical words—with "Oriental impassivity,"[9] and asked if he wanted to visit Japan, he answered: "Yes, I do. In fact I earnestly wish to go, but now, more than anything else, I wish to know my country, understand it, and be able to convey it in every one of my brushstrokes."[10] The source of inspiration for the motives of his paintings' and murals' motifs is thus quite clear.

Many of Nishizawa's works depict deep, panoramic, barren landscapes of the central Mexican highlands, including the Valley of Mexico, Morelos, Guanajuato, Puebla, and the State of Mexico. I earlier explored in this study the metonymical association between the Popocatépetl volcano and Mount Fuji in Akane's poetry. This is also evident in Nishizawa's numerous paintings of volcanoes. For instance, *Popocatépetl*, a 1970 mixed-technique painting on canvas, is strongly reminiscent of traditional depictions of Mount Fuji. According to Xavier Moyssén:

> Luis Nishizawa's greatest contribution to landscape painting in Mexico is found in works derived from the Japanese tradition, especially in those with tones achieved with one or two colors, particularly with those options that black and white offer, as primary colors. They are magnificent works mostly painted on large sheets of paper. This contribution is wholly manifested in innumerable works, particularly in paintings such as the one devoted to "Popocatépetl" (1970), which could well be the famous Mount Fuji due to how, in his depiction, it rises majestically, with a reddish hue, in the midst of a transparent blue background like the air that surrounds it. (1981)[11]

The bluish fog on the mountainside and the insinuation of the top of the mountain, rather than its detailed depiction, do recall Japanese paintings' inclusion of volcanos like Mount Fuji.

According to the filmmaker and literary theorist Trinh T. Minh-Ha, in East Asian paintings "horizontal and vertical fogs constitute a disturbance of the unfolding of the narrative, a transition in time, a passage to the supernatural, a transitory period between two states of things and a prelude to manifestation" (2011, 74). Just like a *torii*—the traditional Japanese gate found in Shinto shrines—symbolically marks the transition from the physical world to the divine, so does this type of fog in East Asian paintings. The fog also seems to separate the sacred from the profane in Nishizawa's *Popocatépetl*, a painting with an almost mystical atmosphere, as well as in *Los volcanes vistos desde el valle de Tlayacapan* (The Volcanoes Seen from the Tlayacapan Valley) and in his 1981 ink drawing *Las calderas* (The Craters), from the series *Paisajes para mi padre* (Landscapes for my father). Whereas in Nishizawa's paintings this type of fog is either white or simply suggested by the blank paper, in *Juchitepec*, a work in India ink on paper, it turns sky blue.

The Popocatépetl volcano reappears, along with other mountains, in one of Nishizawa's incursions into surrealism, the Mixografia (engraving technique) *El sueño de mi madre* (My mother's dream, 1960). With the bluish volcano as the background, on the center-left of the canvas is a strange circle with a young woman's head, presumably his mother, lying down and with open eyes. It is unclear whether the head is floating on the warm-colored rocky land or peeping out from a hole on the land. Nonetheless, the imagery seems to imply that her mother dreamt about the Popocatépetl. The influence of surrealism resurfaces in several of his still lifes, in which there are small ears, birds, insects, shrimp, and different objects hanging from threads against a mostly empty background, as in his acrylics *Homenaje* (Homage, 1978), *Mis modelos* (My models, 1979), and *Langostino* (Prawn, 1988).

In others of his volcano depictions, Japanese connotations have less to do with Mount Fuji similarities than with the Japanese-influenced techniques. This is so with several of his ink drawings—such as *Tepoztlán, Cerro del Tesoro, al fondo el Popocatépetl (Tepoztlán)*, and *El Popocatépetl desde el Cerro del Tesoro (Tepoztlán)*—in which the different white and brown tones in the volcanos' snowcaps, along with fine lines and strokes, recall landscapes by the Japanese painters Hokusai and Andō Hiroshige (1797–1858), the latter of whom is considered the last great master of the *ukiyo-e* tradition and is best known for his landscape series *The Fifty-Three Stations of the Tōkaidō* and *One Hundred Famous Views of Edo*.

In addition to the Popocatépetl, Nishizawa also painted the volcano Iztaccíhuatl, a 17,160-feet dormant volcanic mountain.[12] In his 1998 ink-on-paper *Iztaccíhuatl*, currently in the Nishizawa Museum Workshop, he painted, with the characteristic simplicity of his compositions, the four snowcapped peaks of Iztaccíhuatl in white and yellow tones. The hillside is painted in deep marine blue, instead of the green trees of real life, giving the impression that the ethereal volcano is floating in the sky over yellowish-green fields with sparce trees. He painted this dormant volcano numerous other times, in engravings and ink, at times with the fog beneath the sky-blue snowcapped peaks, making the floating, uncanny impression even more intense. In other renderings, Nishizawa changed the coloring and added new elements: piles of straw, a cow, a moon.

Another example of the influence of traditional East Asian landscapes is in the ink-on-paper work *El valle de Tlayacapan al atardecer* (The Tlayacapan Valley at sunset, 1981). Using only the white of the paper and different tones from ocher to brown, the artist depicts a wide, sober horizon with rocks and trees in the front, an arid valley in the middle, and mountains in the background. *El valle de Tlayacapan al atardecer* is a sort of Mexicanized, less colorful version of Hiroshige's *ukiyo-e* landscapes, but more like traditional Chinese painting. In these panoramic depictions of idealized, ink-on-paper landscapes with few objects, traditional Chinese artists tried to capture the scene's essence or spirit, a reflection on the painter's mind rather than its actual form. This type of East Asian introspective contemplation in which the painting reflects not necessarily the actual scene but its reflection on the artist's mind seems to have influenced some of Nishizawa's ink landscapes. By searching for the essence of what is being depicted, he aims to achieve a fusion of painting with thought.

With delicate, thin brushstrokes reminiscent of traditional East Asian landscape painting, Nishizawa depicts the arid, lonely orography of central Mexico. These same techniques and approach may also be appreciated in other ink works, such as his 1980 *El nevado* (The snowcapped mountain). By contrast, other similar ink paintings, such as the 1980 *Rocas de Chalco* (Rocks of Chalco), evidence his mastery of realistic, detailed ink drawing and painting that differ from traditional Japanese and Chinese influences.

In other works, Nishizawa's art does not aim for otherworldly introspection but recalls the traditional Japanese aesthetic concept of *yūgen*, a term used to refer to how poems or visual art can vaguely suggest the depth of things, the unfathomable, or the ineffable. *Yūgen*, however, does not refer to another world but to a deeper plane in this world. This approach can be perceived in some of Nishizawa's ink-on-paper works, such as his 1980 *San Blas*, a beautiful painting of five cows (perhaps reminiscent of the family's cattle he tended as a child) grazing in a foggy background, with two chickens in the front of the scene. *Yūgen* is achieved in this piece through the oneiric depiction of serene and graceful nature, which suggests subtly, almost effortlessly, the gateway to something more profound and inaccessible. Rather than representing everyday reality, then, the artist, with a refined elegance attained through a minimum number of brushstrokes, insinuates the shape of the animals, some of which blend into the natural background. Without focusing on detail and with profound reserve—like the minimalistic approach of the haiku—a simple, rural scene is elevated to the evocative, suggesting nature's deeply lyrical and mysterious beauty. In other words, the dreamlike, frozen-in-time atmosphere of the scene awakens moods, feelings, and thoughts.

Nishizawa's Japanese ethnicity is evident in this piece, not only because of his artistic style but, more explicitly, also because a Japanese emblem made with a *hanko* (personal seal) appears, as in many of his works, in red above signature. In an interview with Juan Baights, Nishizawa justified—perhaps unconvincingly—the seal's use not so much to stress his Japanese ancestry but to add color to the painting: "When I put a seal on my paintings, in the Japanese style, I do it so that it gives them a touch of color. The seal balances the monochrome drawing. That red seal is part of the picture."[13] One might convincingly argue that, in reality, the use of the *hanko* responds to a conscious or unconscious desire to be inscribed in the artistic tradition of his Japanese ancestors. He is creating his own precursors.

Among Nishizawa's most important paintings are *Paisaje: Valle de México* (Landscape: Valley of Mexico, 1947), *Paisaje de Yagul* (Landscape of Yagul, 1976), and *Pátzcuaro* (1960), in which the blend of his Mexican and Japanese heritage and training is evident. In *Pátzcuaro*, a painting of Michoacán's Lake Pátzcuaro and its surrounding volcanic mountains, Japanese-influenced techniques and style are distinct. While at the front of the scene is a house surrounded by fishing nets and plants rising from the water, in the foggy background there is a small boat with three persons and a nearby mountain. As with *yūgen*, this atmospheric lakescape invites the viewer to consider the existence of deeper meaning in nature.

Japanese painting influenced Nishizawa even before he studied in Japan. The art critic Elisa García Barragán highlights, in particular, his admiration for Hiroshige: "Luis Nishizawa tells us about the impact that the exhibition of Japanese painter Andō Hiroshige's prints, held at the Palace of Fine Arts, had on him.... Hiroshigue fascinated him and, like [Mexican poet José Juan] Tablada, Nishizawa has mystically and devotedly followed the Japanese master's trajectory. Aware of his admiration for Hiroshigue's superior art, Alfredo Zalce shared some Japanese 'dry inks' with Luis Nishizawa, who began to experiment in his works with Japanese inks and techniques, an activity that little by little permeated his production with paintings that were full of light and synthesis."[14] The influence of Hiroshige's subtle use of color gradation (*bokashi*) in his prints is noticeable in Nishizawa's ink works like *Tepoztlán* (1960), in which the mountain's light ocher becomes progressively darker as the viewer's sight slides to the trees below, eventually reaching orange tones at the bottom right.

A more contrasted color gradation, from dark at the mountaintop to light in the valley, is noticeable in the striking ink-on-paper drawing *Serranía de la villa* (Mountain range of the village, 1965), where, perhaps accidentally, the sharp brushstrokes that configure the plants in the first plane resemble, at first glance, kanji. The art critic Raquel Tibol has noticed an "Eastern calligraphic synthesis in his landscapes."[15] *Serranía de la villa* and a similar painting from the same year, *Serranía de Santa*

Catalina, also display distant traces of East Asian traditional landscape painting, of *sumi-e* in particular. This type of monochromatic brush painting is carried out with the same ink used in East Asian calligraphy, which is toned down in gradations from black to the lightest shades possible of ink and water. With virtuoso brushwork that evokes simplicity and spontaneity, the *sumi-e* artist, as in traditional Chinese painting, is supposed to sense the spirit or essence of the scene (instead of simply imitating nature) to raise the viewers' sensibility. *Sumi-e* landscape painting is typically imaginary or loosely based on reality. It purposefully leaves out unnecessary detail and, influenced by Zen practice, reduces reality to its purest and barest form: a few brushstrokes, and a brushstroke per mark, on white paper convey the complexity and essence of reality. Although Nishizawa's *Serranía de la villa* and *Serranía de Santa Catalina* are reminiscent of *sumi-e* painting, they deviate from it in that there is often more than one brushstroke per mark.

Other ink drawings, like *Tepoztlán*, are instead reminiscent of the traditional Chinese *shan shui* style, known for its brush-and-ink depictions of mountain landscapes, often including rivers and waterfalls. Again, regardless of how the actual subject appeared, the aim is to transmit how the *shan shui* artist perceived that natural scene. Although no river or waterfall is depicted in *Tepoztlán*, the disposition of the mountains and their shape—more reminiscent of Vietnamese jade mountains than Nishizawa's usual Mexican arid landscapes—evoke the idealized, impossible Chinese landscapes of vertical foggy mountains, found, for example, in paintings by the Yuan-dynasty artist Gao Kegong (1248–1310) and the Northern Song-dynasty artist Guo Xi (c. 1020–c. 1090). In the case of *Tepoztlán*, there is the impression that Nishizawa was more interested in transmitting his feelings about those mountains and trees, or what they inspired in him, rather than providing a faithful description of what he saw. Tellingly, Nishizawa explicitly expressed this same artistic disposition in a 1976 interview with the art critic Juan Baigts for *Diorama de la Cultura: Excélsior*: "Now I have chosen a type of semi-figurative painting in which space has a central role. I like suggested atmospheres that engage the viewer. I try to draw the viewer into my world. Landscape is generally linked to poetry. For me at least, the shape that a volcano or a countryside provides is not important, but rather the elements in play with through which one seeks a plastic, emotional, and poetic solution."[16]

In some of Nishizawa's paintings, the coloring of some of the etchings (the five 1992 landscapes, all titled *Paisaje*, or "Landscape," posted at the Academia de Artes website), deviates from the more frequent realism of his work: some are entirely red or yellow; others display unrealistic deep blue or orange; in others the sky's blue blends with that of the mountain.

BEYOND MEXICAN MURALISM: GLAZED CERAMICS AND CULTURAL HYBRIDITY

Another important facet of Nishizawa's career is his mural painting—he completed his first mural between 1958 and 1959. Except for the collective mural *Canto a Martí* (Song to Martí, 1976), displayed in Mexico City's Centro Cultural Martí, Nishizawa's mural art tends to be devoid of political connotations.

Still, one finds traces of Mexican muralism's expressionism as well as its frequent use of pre-Hispanic symbolism. For example, the Aztec gods Tláloc, Quetzalcóatl, and Ehécatl are depicted in Nishizawa's first major mural, the ecologically themed mural in acrylic on white cement *El aire es vida y la salud es la mayor riqueza* (Air is life and health its greatest wealth, 1959).[17] Tibol has noted the increasingly allegorical nature of his paintings during the 1950s and particularly in *El aire es vida*, which she considers the artist's last piece of contemporary Mexican realism (1984a, 7–10). Other large murals with similar characteristics are *La justicia* (Justice) and the 1988 acrylic on canvas *El hombre y la libertad* (Man and freedom).[18]

In *El hombre y la libertad*, Nishizawa avoids making specific historical references, presenting instead a group of dynamic, naked male figures that seem to be airborne after an explosion, with the largest, most prominent figure at the mural's center. The entire background displays a Mexican flag. Like the great masters of Mexican muralism, Nishizawa expressed in his murals and his easel paintings an interest for the masses.[19]

Nishizawa is also known for being the first Mexican artist to create a ceramic mural. According to Tibol, it was his Japanese friend, the print artist Toneyama Kōjin (1921–1994), who convinced Nishizawa to use ceramics in his 1969 mural *Un canto a la vida* (A song to life), located in Celaya, Guanajuato (Tibol n.d., 116). Made with high-temperature-fired color ceramics, it portrays a pre-Hispanic snail whence the Aztec gods Tláloc (water) and Tonatiuh (sun) emerge. They feed on the corn from which an indigenous figure is born.

Nishizawa's interest in Mexico's pre-Hispanic world is also evident in his 1987 ceramic mural *Códice prehispánico* (Pre-Hispanic codex), displayed in the library of the Centro Cultural Mexiquense in Toluca. Another important glazed ceramic mural is the monumental *La imagen del hombre* (Man's image, 1991), which includes, at the bottom left, a Daoist yin-yang symbol.[20]

One of his most inspiring murals is *El espíritu creador siempre se renueva* (The creative spirit is forever renewed, 1981), whose composition recalls *Un canto a la vida*. In it, we find the shaven head of a Japanese boy with hands coming out of the mouth of a mythological fish.[21] The boy is illuminated by a solar disc as he advances toward an atomic science symbol with a red and yellow pinwheel. Created in collaboration with his assistant, the young Japanese painter Sotshi, this work is found in a Keisei subway station in Narita, Japan. Nishizawa's friend, Toneyama, finds a synthesis of Japanese and Mexican elements in the colorful work: "Here, his loving view of the Japanese tradition and the sturdy concept of the Mexican mural coexist peacefully. A phrase he uttered while remembering his father on its inauguration day resounds in my ears: 'His blood still has a voice.'"[22] Nishizawa himself acknowledges Japanese influences in his mural. Homma Masayoshi, the director of the National Art Museum of Urawa, concurs: "An Asian heart immersed in Mexican humanism that touches the aesthetics of sacrifice."[23]

His gray and rusted stone mural *El lecho del universo* (The bed of the universe, 1987), located in Museo de Arte Moderno at the State of Mexico's Cultural Center, resembles a Japanese rock garden or Zen garden, as indicated by Tibol (n.d., 125). Nishizawa uses gray ceramic tiles to create a large representation of the quintessentially Mexican *petate* (reed mat), which is decorated with rocks. Yet perhaps unintentionally, the rocks resemble the floating rocks that symbolize mountains and the reed mat evokes the typical ripples traced by raked gravel or sand, repeated in miniature stylized landscape in dry gardens. In Nishizawa's bicultural dialectics, the Mexican *petate* and the Japanese dry garden become fused into a fruitful cultural hybridity.[24]

In his admission speech to the Academia de Artes on 5 June 1990, "Consideraciones de la técnica como libertad de expresión" (Considerations of technique as freedom of expression), Nishizawa underscores how important it is for artists to master technique and be knowledgeable of artistic materials as tools for self-expression. He then reveals the main motivation behind his use of ceramic tiles in his murals: "Taking into account the great conservation problems raised by some Mexican muralists' works, I have made my mural work with permanent materials, materials that can be indoors or outdoors of any venue. I have created two ceramic murals: one, now twenty years old, has undergone no changes; the other, in Japan, is composed with the same material."[25] Durability, therefore, was his concern when choosing materials for his murals. Avowedly, Nishizawa shared the same concern when painting on canvas. According to García Luna, among

Nishizawa's durable materials feature ceramics, *recinto* (black sedimentary rock), and distemper (a scenery or mural painting process whereby pigments are mixed with an emulsion of egg yolk or white) (n.d., 37).

BLENDING ANCIENT ARTISTIC TRADITIONS: *TAKU-HON* AND MAYAN ART

In a clear example of how he combined the artistic traditions of both countries, Nishizawa, along with the Japanese artist Toneyama Kōjin, applied *taku-hon* (ink rubbing) to reliefs in Mayan tombstones, lintels, and jambs.[26] One of these *taku-hon* pieces is the 1973 *Lápida de los esclavos* (Slave headstone), created in Palenque. *Taku-hon* stone rubbing is considered one of the oldest printing methods. It was invented in sixth-century China and Japan to create prints of texts and textured surfaces. It is done by pressing a dampened, thin *washi* paper onto a surface, allowing it to almost dry, and then pressing a *tampo* pad with ink onto the object.[27] Through this printmaking technique, the scripts of sutras engraved on stone or other surfaces were transcribed onto paper and preserved in books. Nishizawa and Toneyama blended Japanese and pre-Columbian artistic traditions by applying *taku-hon* stone-rubbing techniques to the surfaces and reliefs of Mayan art. They exhibited these prints on three occasions,[28] and a book titled *Taku Hon: Calcas por Kojin Toneyama y Luis Nishizawa* (Taku Hon: Traces by Kojin Toneyama and Luis Nishizawa) was published by the Instituto Nacional de Bellas Artes in 1965.

CRITICAL OVERSTATEMENT OF ASIAN INFLUENCES IN NISHIZAWA'S ART

A Mexican artist considered a role model to Nishizawa is José María Velasco (1840–1912), whose panoramic Mexican landscapes greatly influenced him, according to critics like Tibol, Arturo Rico Bovio, and Enrique Cortázar. Although Velasco's works, like the seven renditions of his 1875 masterpiece *El valle de México* (The Valley of Mexico), show similar depth and faraway mountains, they were more classically realistic and detailed than Nishizawa's. According to the art critic Villa Guerrero, Nishizawa also acknowledged his admiration for Francisco Goitia (1882–1960): "The main influence I have on my landscape painting is from Francisco Goitia, who was not a landscaper, but his painting 'La Hacienda de Santa María' is one of the works that has most impressed me."[29] Goitia was, in fact, the artist who encouraged Nishizawa to study Japanese engraving techniques (Tibol

1984a, 89). Tibol has also underscored Julio Castellanos's (1905–1947) sway on Nishizawa: "Nishizawa initially chose to paint like a Mexican[n]ist realist, greatly influenced by Julio Castellanos's refinement in his execution."[30] Other role models were the nationalist José Chávez Morado (1909–2002), known for his paintings, murals, and lithography, and Alfredo Zalce (1098–2003), renowned for his paintings of Michoacán's indigenous people and for introducing Nishizawa to Japanese "dry inks."

Nishizawa's art also echoes Mexican muralism, particularly José Clemente Orozco's (1883–1949) socially engaged expressionism and Diego Rivera's (1986–1957) portraits. In his mixed-technique *Niña desgranando maíz* (Girl husking corn, 1950), for example, one finds traces of Rivera's portrayal of girls, as Moyssén points out (n.d., 16). In this portrait and others, such as his tempera on paper *Doña Luz* (1946), one finds the same interest exhibited by the great Mexican muralists in the dignified representation of the daily, rural life of indigenous and humble Mexican social classes. Nishizawa's drawings of the customs and daily life of indigenous people from Chiapas and Yucatán, in ink, Conté crayon, or color pencil, undoubtedly belong to this Mexican tradition.

Doctor Atl, pseudonym of Gerardo Murillo (1875–1964), one of the pioneers of the Mexican movement for artistic nationalism and a painter fascinated by volcanos (especially the Paricutín) and the orography of central Mexico in general, also influenced Nishizawa's art through his use of curved, asymmetrical horizons and the depth and width of his landscapes (García Barragán n.d., 60; Rico Bovio 2000, 5). These curved horizons appear, for example, in Nishizawa's work in ink on *torinoko* paper *Barranca del Cobre* (1984); the *suiboku* ink-on-paper drawings *El Ajusco* (1994) and *Cajetes* (Bowls), a wide, arid landscape with a large bowl-shaped hole at front and snowcapped mountains in the background; and the 2002 etching *Paisaje con vacas* (Landscape with cows).

Nishizawa claimed that Orozco and Rembrandt were the two artists who had impressed him the most. Elaborating on his main artistic influences in the aforementioned 1990 admission speech to the Academia de Artes, he mentions them, along with other well-known European, Mexican, and American artists. He likewise acknowledges his debt to his teachers, particularly regarding his technical ability.[31] Tellingly, the only Japanese artist he mentions in the speech is an unnamed contemporary ceramist who told him: "All my life I have longed to be just an artisan who can mix his feelings with clay for the kiln fire to do its miracle."[32] However, as it is often the case with the critical reception of Latin American Nikkei writers, critics have tended to overemphasize Asian influences in Nishizawa's art.

Along with the East Asian artistic influences in his paintings and drawings, additional traces of his Japanese ethnicity appear in realistic self-portraits and in those of his relatives. Thus, in his mixed-technique *Mi padre en su larga agonía* (My father in his long anguish, 1965), there is an elderly Japanese man sporting a white beard, dressed in a blue robe, sitting in an armchair, with eyebrows arched as if in pain. Two years later, he portrayed his Mexican mother wearing a black jacket in the oil painting *Mi madre* (My mother), and in the mixed-technique work on canvas and wood of the same title, also sitting in an armchair and with a sad countenance. In both compositions, his parents' aged hands are prominent. He also painted one of his daughters in a rather strange 1988 watercolor portrait titled *Miwako*, in which the girl's Asian facial features are merely suggested, as if the painting were partially erased or left incomplete. According to Moyssén, the spirit of Japanese art is contained in this portrait, but he provides no further explanation (León Portilla de Diener n.d., 16). In reality, other than the fact that the subject is a Nikkei girl, there are no evident traces of Japanese influence in the technique or colors used in *Miwako*.

The artist's own Japanese phenotype is evident in most of his self-portraits, including his 1959 *Autorretrato* (Self-portrait), a 1988 watercolor self-portrait, and a 1997 tempera-on-canvas self-portrait that is part of the Academia de Artes' collection. By contrast, no evident Asian phenotype appears in his 1985 red, surrealist etching *Autorretrato* (Self-portrait), in which a hand holds a small, circular mirror that partially shows part of the artist's face. It is surrounded by two fish looking in opposite directions, which Antonio Rodríguez interprets as the Chinese symbol representing the yin-yang duality (n.d., 148). In 1981, he also painted *sumi-e* and color portraits of Japanese ceramists in Shigaraki, Japan, titled *Hirao, ceramista japonés* (Hirao, Japanese ceramist) and *Yumiko, ceramista japonés*, respectively. Other than the fact that the models are Japanese, however, there is, in my view, no evidence of artistic Japanese influences in the techniques or colors used.

Perhaps Nishiwaza's own stated admiration for his father has affected these critical assessments. Consequently, Villa Guerrero quotes the artist's memories about his beloved immigrant father:

> We would listen to him with real delight. He would talk about the heroic deeds of ancient samurais, stories that enriched my imagination and my knowledge of the world. . . . He also sang very old samurai songs to us. . . . They reminded him of his childhood and, though he came to Mexico at a very young age, he was always educated and lived within the samurai

spirit. All that I have achieved as a painter and as a man, I have done to honor my father . . . I believe that in life we all have a person who gives meaning to it and who is the reason for what we do. For some, it is a woman; for others, an ideal; for me, it is my father.[33]

Consistent with this viewpoint, the social anthropologist Mónica Del Arenal Martínez del Campo argues, somewhat stereotypically, that Nishizawa inherited from his father "Zen discipline and philosophy (a sense of honor, personal integrity, loyalty, and a deep sense of respect for the individual)."[34] She then lists critics who have pointed out—at times unfoundedly, in my opinion—Japanese artistic traces in his landscapes.

Regarding the critical overstatement of Asian influences in Nishizawa's art, consider the following examples. Writing in 1961 for *Artes de México*, Rafael Anzures celebrated the fact that, in his view, Nishizawa had at last found an original style precisely because he accepted his Japanese origins: "Nishizawa's painting begins to be authentic because it flows fluently from its internal source—Asian and Latin American—just like the blood of the two races runs through the painter's veins."[35] It seems, therefore, as if the only path for Latin American artists of Japanese descent to be considered "authentic" by critics were that they somehow reflect East Asian cultural traits in their works.

Of particular interest are also the comments made by Anzures during the Second Interamerican Biennial of Mexico of 1961, when he described Nishizawa's "really remarkable pictorial metamorphosis" during the previous year.[36] He commended the artist for finally abandoning what he considered a contrived fixation with "trying to be Mexican" and instead welcoming his "authentic Japaneseness":

> For many years, Nishizawa showed in his work a strong concern for presenting himself as "Mexican," like this, in quotation marks. This obsession, truly pernicious, kept him stagnant. . . . What has given his current painting a breath of originality, a freshness, a true pictorial-artistic hygiene, its own brilliance and singularity has been, as I was saying, Nishizawa's decision to at last express in his work his Asian emotions and soul. This time, however, he does so in a natural and authentic way, that is to say, as a true Japanese, without quotation marks. Now he himself must feel that he breathes in a clean atmosphere, without previous commitments. Because by being naturally original when one is thus, rather than trying to be contrivedly "original," the tensions of the soul are loosened; anguish, a negative component, vanishes and it is then possible to reach fullness of expression more easily.[37]

There is much to unpack in this passage. First, although Anzures maintains it is a common tendency among artists of Nishizawa's generation, he still considers his interest in Mexican motives a sort of inauthentic mania that must be overcome. Then, even though the artist was born and raised in Mexico, the real, authentic Nishizawa, according to this critic, is to be found in his supposedly repressed Asianness. Only through the unleashing of his silenced, genuine Asian nature, "as a true Japanese," will he ever achieve not only originality and freshness but also "artistic hygiene" and a "clean atmosphere." In other words, the purportedly affected Mexicanness in his art was making Nishizawa unclean, ersatz. The critic-*cum*-psychoanalyst reaches the conclusion that, thanks to his newly released "Asian soul," Nishizawa at long last managed to attain artistic originality; the angst was gone so he could breathe. One could easily argue, however, that we are reading Anzures's psychological projection of his own anxieties: because Nishizawa, a painter with a Japanese phenotype and surname, has finally met Anzures's artistic assumptions and expectations, the latter can finally put his apprehensions aside. In the remainder of his critique, Anzures insists that in reengaging his Japanese side, Nishizawa has found his true self; that is, by "acting naturally," he has eventually attained not only artistic authenticity and originality but also spiritual liberation.

Many Mexican critics fall into the same trap. Tibol, for instance, also overstated the presence of Japanese art in Nishizawa's works: "The identification with his Japanese roots brought him back to the nurturing of the beautiful image as a reaffirmation of dignity, and to the practice of painting landscapes with its implicit monumentality and splendor."[38] The critic finds a combination of expressionism and what she terms "Orientalism" in the series *Las vacas flacas*, *Los sueños rotos*, and *Recuerdos y presencias* (Memories and Presence), first exhibited in 1972.

Instead of using the term *Orientalism* in the sense famously articulated by the postcolonial theorist Edward W. Said, when she mentions "very refined, almost cryptographic lines,"[39] she seems to be referring to the imitation of East Asian arts by Nishizawa. Tibol likewise connects, without further explanation, his still lifes with his Asian background: "These still lives are meditations, poems, mythologies in homage to their ancestors."[40]

Antonio Rodríguez is another Mexican critic who overemphasizes the traces of East Asian art in Nishizawa: "It is almost mandatory, when talking about Luis Nishizawa, to mention Japanese art and Zen philosophy. It is known that the artist, because of his background, his own sensitivity and his readings, travels and contacts with other artists, has shifted his gaze toward his father's homeland, whence he has received influences that are in no way opposed to his eminently Mexican cultural background."[41] Rodríguez also finds East Asian influences in Nishizawa's 1978 *La naturaleza muerta* (Still life), from the series *La vida en el silencio de las cosas* (Life in the silence of things), arguing that it is closer to Asian than European abstract painting. He says of the 1979 *Langosta* (Lobster): "Like the Japanese masters, he dared to treat a humble crustacean with the same dignity that past European painters treated, in their portraits, the then glorious monarchs."[42]

Again, the connection between Japanese art and the inclusion of seafood in a still life does not seem self-evident. Perhaps the fact that in paintings like the 1978 mixed-technique still life *Langosta plateada* (Silver lobster) one finds a lobster in front of a white background with a red circle may have reminded Rodríguez of the Japanese flag. However, in a related painting simply titled *Langosta* (1979), the large circle in the middle is whitish against a reddish background; an analogous circle appears in a previous work, the lithography *Pez dorado en otoño* (Golden fish in autumn, 1977), in which the blue and red over a golden background recall a view of planet Earth from outer space, not that Japanese flag.

Rodríguez further notices the imprint of Japanese landscapes in Nishizawa's oil paintings and the drawings exhibited in 1989 at the Centro Cultural Mexicano-Japonés.[43] In a piece for the magazine *Política* in 1961, he associates, without elaborating, Nishizawa's art with classic Chinese painting (Tibol 1984a, 84). More shocking, Rodríguez sees traces of the tendency to abstraction in Japanese figurative art in *El aire es vida*: "always fluctuating between Mexico's dramatic passion and the tendency toward the great abstractions of Japanese art."[44]

There is a tendency to overstate Asian cultural and artistic debt, and this is seen also with the Peruvian poet José Watanabe and other Nikkei Latin American writers and artists.[45] Wrong identity expectations are also common when dealing with Asian–Latin American writers and artists. Unsurprisingly, just as a Peruvian critic took for granted that the name of the Peruvian writer Siu Kam Wen was simply the pen name of a writer with no Chinese ancestry (given the author's command of the Spanish language), Elisa García Barragán reminds us that a local critic, in his review for *El Tiempo* on 19 July 1946, assumed that Nishizawa was a Japanese national: "The Japanese Nishizawa exhibits a landscape that, within the traditional modality, is well achieved. You can see in him the marked influence of Velasco."[46]

At least another two Mexican art critics conceived of the possibility that Nishizawa did not necessarily have to inherit his father's cultural traits. P. Fernández Márquez, writing for the magazine *Revista Mexicana de Cultura* in 1951, states: "Although Mexican because of his mother and birthplace, he comes from an Asian father, as his name indicates. However, he could have not inherited that detailed and careful nature that he exhibits in his paintings. But he did, and he uses it to interpret, with very Mexican compositional and colorful effects, landscapes, traditional scenes, and beings."[47] Likewise, Pablo Fernández Márquez acknowledges: "All this is very natural if we consider that the artist, although Mexican through his mother and birthplace, descends from an Asian father. He could, however, not have inherited that detailed and careful nature."[48] Though acknowledging that Nishizawa could easily have not inherited what he considers a typically Japanese detailed and careful disposition, Fernández Márquez still assumes that Nishizawa's attention to detail must be an outcome of his Japanese roots. Interestingly, Nishizawa's landscapes are much less realistic and detailed than, for example, those of Velasco.

Again espousing a one-sided criticism, Teresa del Conde has argued that some of Nishizawa's still lifes "are characteristic examples of the introduction of typical codes from his paternal Japanese culture."[49] She adds, however, that she is not addressing Japanese iconography,

> but rather how he places the elements in space, simultaneously experienced in a macrocosm and a microcosm, a duality evident in Eastern philosophies. In such cases, the painting contains few elements, two or three figures, while the space where they are arranged is an abstract background that plays a central role. The relation of proximity or distance among the figures are measured in the same way as in Japanese gardens, for instance, where trees, plants, and stones are carefully arranged in such a way that they integrate asymmetric environments; thus, the importance of each thing is stressed as well as their closeness in terms of distance and form.[50]

Once more, the assumption that the mentioned pictorial traits are Japanese in origin seems somewhat contrived.[51]

Overall, Nishizawa's elegant blend of Mexican and Japanese technical influences and artistic traditions to create a personal style, together with the exaggerated perception of his art's Japaneseness by Mexican critics, are representative of the prejudice, contradictions, and stereotyping that continue to have an impact on Asian–Latin American cultural production in general.

CHAPTER 6

The Transpacific in Akiko's Theatrical Performance

This chapter focuses on the performing art of Irene Akiko Iida Naito (1963–; stage name "Akiko"), a Mexican of Japanese ancestry. Her art further contributes to opening a space for Nikkei female subjectivity and gendering the Japanese Mexican transpacific imaginary. Founder and director of the Akikompania theatrical company, Akiko is a dancer, singer, actor, and director of Japanese theater.[1] She offers new approaches to Mexico's scenic work by reframing it in relation to her transpacific worldview and the country's own transpacific history. By looking beyond the nation and across the Pacific Ocean, she has achieved a unique impact on the Mexican cultural landscape. In fact, she is plausibly the only person in Mexican theater devoted to this Japanese-Mexican cultural exchange.[2] Akiko has also contributed to the reframing and reconfiguration of Mexico as part of the Pacific Rim.

Along with her theatrical work, Akiko has performed in the fifteen-minute Mexican short film *Espero que estés bien* (I hope you are well, 2016), directed by Lucía Díaz Álvarez. In this drama, a Japanese immigrant (played by Roberto Kameta) tries to build a life in Mexico City, away from his family, but his project is interrupted by his mother's (played by Akiko) unexpected visit. After living several years in Mexico, their relationship is virtually nonexistent, and unresolved family issues prevent him from moving on with his life. Moreover, Akiko played the role of an interpreter in two episodes of the 2017 Mexican black-comedy web series *Las trece esposas de Wilson Fernández* (Wilson Fernández's Thirteen Wives, 2017), based on the 2014 Argentine television series of the same name. She also appears as an actor in some episodes of the television series *Madre solo hay dos* (Mother there are only two), directed by Lucía Díaz Álvarez.

Akiko learned Japanese from her parents and grew up seeing herself as both Mexican and Japanese. Her father, Toshiaki Iida, emigrated to Mexico in 1945; her mother, Chiyoko, arrived as an already-married picture bride in 1962. Both were Buddhists. Akiko studied at the Tacubaya Gakuen grade school from 1969 to 1975 and at the Escuela Secundaria y Preparatoria de la Ciudad de México from 1969 to 1975. She recalls how in school other children would tease her with racial epithets and would sing ditties like "China, china, japonés, come caca y no me des" (Chinese, Chinese, Japanese, eat poop and don't give me any). This early harassment led her to question her ethnic and national identification. As the anthropologist Takeyuki Tsuda points out in his study of Japanese Brazilian "return" emigration to Japan, "Ethnic consciousness usually remains dormant until individuals experience some external event or change that destabilizes or 'decenters' their identities, causing them to actively question and reconsider their ethnicity as they confront new experiences and incorporate and integrate new forms of identification. It is this type of occasional identity decentering that enables the self to change and develop (as it is eventually 'recentered')" (2003, 156). When her Mexican ethnic identity was denied by other children, young Akiko was pushed to reexamine her social identity. Consequently, she decided to proudly own her Nikkeiness—or perceived Japaneseness—the very source of peer rejection. This strengthened self-perception became essential to her professional life because it enabled her to create culturally hybrid works. The derision she suffered reinforced her Japanese and Nikkei identification, but after an eighteen-year stay in Japan, she returned to Mexico City, her birthplace, wishing to learn more about her country. She particularly feels attracted to Mexico's pre-Hispanic heritage.

Eventually, her ethnic performance of Japaneseness (beyond the notion of the nation-state) was carried out via theatrical performance. This may be considered a figurative "return" to the ancestral homeland through the adoption of shared cultural markers. This metaphorical return would later become physical, once she moved in 1979 to Japan—a country previously visited twice with her family—to study theater at the Takarazuka Music School in Osaka. Having traveled with her mother to Japan, Akiko remained in that country alone. Once in Osaka, she also studied at the Hanayagui Academy of Traditional Japanese Dance. In 1991, she received her bachelor and master degrees in Japanese dance from Shihan-Natori School in Osaka. She also took an intensive course of Noh theater in Tokyo. From 1981 until 1993, she was a member of the Takarazuka Kagueki theater company, performing under the stage name "Irene Sachikaze" in more than sixty shows throughout Japan. Akiko returned to Mexico City in 1993.

Symbolic exclusion from one world (Mexican mainstream society) meant first an incorporation into another (Japanese society) and then, through fluctuations and negotiations of national allegiances, the adoption of a hybrid, binational identity. Ultimately, her adopted cultural identity and claim to membership in the Mexican community became apparent in her desire to turn ethnic and national boundaries into transnational cultural bridges. As she mentioned in our interview, "My wish is to communicate to Japan that which is Mexican and to Mexico that which is Japanese."[3]

As Akiko recalls, it was while living in Japan in 1978 that she began to love her native Mexico and decided to learn more about it. Today, Akiko has strategically adopted a diasporic, transnational identity that is at the core of her artistic creations. The first Latin American to graduate from the Takarazuka School of Arts in Osaka, the most prestigious and rigorous theater company for women in Japan, she has become an example of what it is to live and work transpacifically, as if following the movement of a pendulum that swings, back and forth, from West to East.[4] Although while living in Japan, Akiko performed in commercial theater, her company, Akikompania, produces cultural, noncommercial theater. She admitted in our interview that an advantage of working in Mexico is that its government is supportive of these types of cultural activities.

Akiko's theater company focuses on productions that highlight cross-cultural relations between East and West, and particularly the artistic fusion between Mexican and Japanese arts and cultures.[5] This is a sort of transpacific approach from below, because rather than following governmental dicta, often associated with commerce, conflict, or imperial aspirations, we find a single woman determined to establish, from the perspective of friendship and collaboration, a fruitful dialogue between Mexicanness and Japaneseness. Akiko's transpacific imaginary therefore challenges the traditional regional divisions conceptualized by area studies and the hegemonic desires of countries like the United States, China, and Japan, conceiving instead the Pacific Ocean as a bridge for the encounter of cultures rather than as a separating, divisive geographical barrier.

Akikompania's first production, the children's musical *Juan, el Momotaro* (Juan, the Momotaro), debuted in 1997. The company's other shows are *Crepúsculo de la cigüeña* (Twilight of the stork); *KAI-ON, sonidos del mar* (KAI-ON, Sea Sounds); the musical theater performance *Contramarea, el regreso del samurái* (Countertide, the return of the samurai, 2010), which toured Mexico and Japan; the award-winning *Mai-Sho-Gaku, trazos de fuego* (Mai-Sho-Gaku, fire strokes, 2013); *Nikkei... Correo de Hiroshima* (Nikkei... Letters from Hiroshima, 2018); and *KANAWA, corona de hierro:*

abismo astral (KANAWA, iron crown, astral abyss).[6] Moreover, Akiko has acted in *El gallo* (The Rooster); *Ópera para actores* (Opera for Actors; Teatro de Ciertos Habitantes Company, directed by Claudio Valdez Kuri); *Humboldt: México para los mexicanos* (Humboldt: Mexico for Mexicans); *El automóvil gris al estilo benshi japonés* (The Gray Automobile à la Japanese Benshi, 2019); and *Babel, reconstruyendo comunidad* (Babel, Community Rebuilding). Akiko was also a founding member of Edén, Expresión de Gracia (Eden, Expression of Grace), a traditional Japanese dance and musical group focused on cross-cultural exchange.

JUAN, EL MOMOTARO: THE MEXICANIZATION OF A ONETIME XENOPHOBIC, WARTIME, JAPANESE PROPAGANDA ICON

Akiko was the coauthor, director, choreographer, and producer of the children's musical play *Juan, el Momotaro* (1997–1999), staged during the centennial celebration of Japanese immigration in Mexico.[7] It was based on the children's book *Juan, el Momotaro: Obra de teatro infantil inspirada en una leyenda japonesa* (Juan, el Momotaro: A Children's Play Based on a Japanese Legend, 1997), which she cowrote with the Mexican writer and theater director Susana Wein.[8] In this piece, Akiko Mexicanizes a well-known, traditional Japanese folktale by turning its popular hero, Momotarō, into a Japanese Mexican boy, "Juan, el Momotaro."[9] She choreographed the play with Mari Asahi and was also responsible for the theatrical adaptation; Japan-born artist Miho Hagino, who resides in Mexico City, was the stage designer. The plot deals with an elderly Japanese immigrant who, calming his Sansei grandson after a nightmare, tells him the Japanese story of Momotarō, a boy who was born from a peach tree and who saved his people by fighting the Lord of Evil and his malevolent *onis*.[10] Through Juan's adventures, the young audience discovers Japanese martial arts (kendo, sumo, and karate), traditional axioms contained in sayings and riddles, and Kabuki theater details (makeup, costumes, and movements) mixed with Mexican cultural elements.

The folktale, whose oral version may have originated as early as the fourteenth century, was transcribed during the early Edo period (1603–1868) and popularized, with a few changes, through grammar school textbooks during the Meiji era (1868–1912). According to the Meiji version, an old, childless woman, while washing clothes in a river, finds a giant floating peach. As they try to eat it at home, she and her husband discover that it has a boy inside. The child, whom they named Momotarō, explains to the couple that the gods wished him as their son. As an adolescent, Momotarō decides to fight a band of *onis* who are ravaging the land. While heading for Onigashima (Demon Island), where they live, he is joined by a talking dog, a monkey, and a pheasant, all enticed by his millet dumplings. Together, they raid the ogres' fort, defeat them, and return home with the *onis*' treasure and their captured chief.

According to the Asian studies scholar Nahoko Kahara (2010), the novelist Yamamoto Yūzō revealed that in certain versions, Momotarō attacks the *onis* because they are devouring his people and plundering the land, while in other versions the ogres seem to be tantamount to foreigners who are unjustifiably punished. On the whole, Momotarō's story, besides being a tool for patriotic didacticism, was also used as propaganda during the Sino-Japanese War, the Russo-Japanese War, and World War II. In contemporary Japan, however, Momotarō stands for compassion, courage, power, and filial piety.

Perhaps inserting autobiographical traits, Akiko turns the story into the identity crisis of a Sansei boy in Mexico, which is ultimately resolved once he learns to appreciate the commonalities between the Mexican and Japanese cultures. In the end, following her transpacific instincts, Akiko transforms an old Japanese fairy tale into a contemporary Mexicanized children's story. More important, the young Japanese protagonist, often portrayed as wartime xenophobic icon, has become a Mexican Nikkeijin—perhaps Akiko's alter-ego—who fights his own nightmare-causing demons: his identity uncertainty caused by his two names and by being both Mexican and Japanese. Keeping in mind that Akiko considers theater an artistic expression that tends to heal the soul, theater—and this play in particular—is perhaps how she fights her own personal demons.

The children's book *Juan, el Momotaro* tells the story of a Nikkei boy who is spending a few days at his Issei grandfather's home. It unravels in contemporary Mexico City. The list of characters introduces Maoo as a Japanese mythological character with his face painted in Kabuki style and walking on stilts. Maoo's *onis*, dressed in red and blue and with painted faces, are small, horned mythological demons, with large mouths that open to their ears and sharp fangs. They are covered with coarse body hair and carry heavy spiked clubs.

In the dark opening of one of the several versions of the one-hour play, we hear Japanese music and sinister Maoo, the Lord of Evil, laughing maliciously. The audience can see his image on a screen. Throughout this version of the play, traditional drawings of Japanese landscapes appear at the backdrop. Declaring that peace, tranquility, and happiness bring him only anguish, he decides that it is time to let loose his lackeys, the *onis*, to spread

FIGURE 6.1. Part of the cast of *Juan el Momotaro*. Courtesy of Irene Akiko Iida.

death, pain, envy, and mistrust everywhere. Next, we hear Juan, dressed in blue pajamas, crying because of a nightmare. His *ojiichan* (grandfather), wearing a kimono, enters the room and asks Taro (as he calls the boy), in Spanish, what is wrong. The scared boy unaware of his whereabouts, calls out for his mother who, as his grandfather reminds him, is traveling. He calms his grandson by telling him it was only a nightmare. He proceeds to philosophize that it is better for the boy to suffer while he is young because it will better prepare him for life.

The boy complains about his grandfather calling him "Taro," as he insists that his name is Juan and that no one is called Taro in Mexico. Smiling, the grandfather explains that he is Juan and Taro: "Fruit, important, but without root there is no fruit. You, Mexican. I, *ojiichan*, Japanese. You fruit, not root, how good two things you are: Mexican and Japanese. Double advantage, if you take opportunity, put a lot of effort into it, it will be very lucky for you and everyone."[11] Delving into the identity uncertainties at the core of the play, he stresses that Juan must learn to be both Mexican and Japanese.

In the second scene's opening, the grandfather begins to tell the boy Momotarō's story. His voice begins to fade away and the audience discerns the shadows of the four sensei (teachers) singing "The Song of Momotaro" while dancing around a giant peach to traditional Japanese music. They carefully knock on the peach, and Juan, wearing pajamas, steps out asking about his whereabouts and the identities of the sensei. They tell him that he is Momotaro, celebrate his arrival as a defender of good, and advise him to be prepared to fight evil. Because his name is Juan, the boy argues that they are confusing him with someone else; the sensei explain that he is truly Momotaro, he who came out of a peach to do battle against Maoo and his onis.

Baffled, Juan allows them to dress him for battle in a vest and a *hachimaki*, a Japanese headband with a kanji typically at the front, worn as a symbol of effort or courage. In a humorous nod to Japanese Mexican transculturation, when the protagonist asks to substitute the *hachimaki* with a Mexican sombrero, they remind him that this is a Japanese folktale and that the *hachimaki* will keep bad spirits from taking him over, since the soul resides in one's forehead. Likewise, when they give him two katanas, he asks for a revolver instead. Addressing the mestizaje question guiding the play, when Juan reminds the sensei that he is Mexican, they tell him that because his grandfather is Japanese, tradition has it that he came from a peach. Perhaps as another metaphor for Japanese Mexican transculturation, the sensei, after some deliberation, agree to provide him with a revolver as long as he uses it only in case the katana fail him. Then, a sensei teaches him kendo (Japanese bamboo swordsmanship) to ready him for battle against Maoo, as he reminds him to fight with loyalty, honor, courage, and sincerity. Before leaving the stage, Juan and the sensei sing and dance to "The Song of Momotaro."

The third scene opens at the end of a storm with a big dog dressed in a loincloth like a *yokosuna* (sumo wrestler champion). When he urinates on Momotaro's peach, an indignant Juan emerges from it and scolds him. The dog, named Dog, representing loyalty and strength, apologizes and explains that he is to teach him sumo wrestling and ensure that Juan will fight for only virtuous causes. He then sings a song about sumo wrestling. During the lessons, two *onis* spy on them and mock their movements. Later, the *onis* cause Dog to fall down and tease Juan by taking off his vest and bursting balloons.[12] After becoming inebriated, the *onis* sing "Onis, los demonios" (Onis, the Devils) and threaten the young audience with floods, earthquakes, disease, death, and universal matricide.

Juan and Dog then return to an empty stage in the fourth scene and ask the audience whether they have seen the *onis*. Continuing with their

FIGURE 6.2. *Onis* enclose Juan, Monkey, and Dog in glass cage. Courtesy of Irene Akiko Iida.

quest, both try to open a door they have come upon when the sly and skillful Monkey (representing wisdom), sent by the sensei, appears on stage to assist them. Monkey succeeds in opening the door and all enter a dark corridor where they are spooked by the *onis*. The three advance until the *onis* lock them up in a glass cage.[13] With the *ukiyo-e* painter Hokusai's painting *The Great Wave off Kanagawa* projected on the screen, the *onis* cause a storm, tossing the three characters from the ship into the ocean.

At the sixth scene's opening, the sensei send the curious and just Swallow, which represents bravery and leadership (and replaces the pheasant from the original story), flying over the sea to find Juan and ask him a riddle. To relieve hunger while imprisoned, Juan gives his companions *kibi dango*, a small, magical rice ball that he carries in his vest.[14] The *onis* begin to reduce the size of the cage imprisoning them, but Dog inadvertently solves Swallow's riddle (in a different version the *onis* tie them up). In scene 7, Maoo is angered by Juan and his friends' escape from the cage and orders the *onis* to recapture them so he can eat them. In the eighth scene, Juan, Dog, Monkey, and Swallow discuss how to defeat the Lord of Evil while he is watching on tragedies throughout the world on television, like fires, earthquakes, car accidents, and death.[15]

FIGURE 6.3. Juan el Momotaro's friends in a small ship. Courtesy of Irene Akiko Iida.

After the brave Swallow, showing leadership skills, suddenly flies toward Maoo and throws a liquid at him, Juan and the animals join her in the fight. Maoo realizes that the *onis* are losing the battle and pauses it, claiming that the chaos counters tradition. He believes they should fight only by means of traditional martial arts and weaponry—only Juan bears a traditional weapon. After Juan manages to defeat the *onis*, one at a time, with his katana, he challenges Maoo to fight him with his club, but the latter betrays tradition and pulls out the revolver Juan had dropped. Then, Monkey aims his flashlight at Maoo's face, blinding him. The other companions open the door to allow in sunlight, which melts him. Maoo suffers punishment for breaking tradition, and they all then sing the song about the court case. In the tenth scene, having put the *onis* on trial, Juan and the animals decide to forgive them, giving them a chance to redeem themselves. Again, they all sing and dance "The Song of Momotaro" together.

In the closing scene, when Juan's grandfather wakes him up and greets him *ohayō* (good morning), the boy realizes that it had all been just a dream. He tells his grandfather how, in his dream, he had defeated Maoo and the lesson he learned by experiencing the old Japanese Momotarō legend: "To succeed you have to fight with virtue; if you only have power, sooner or later things will go wrong."[16] Juan/Taro realizes that the

FIGURE 6.4. Scene from *Juan el Momotaro*. Courtesy of Irene Akiko Iida.

FIGURE 6.5.
Another scene from
Juan el Momotaro.
Courtesy of
Irene Akiko Iida.

story's ethical values are shared by both Japanese and Mexican cultures and that this commonality helps him to feel comfortable in his double cultural heritage.

CONTRAMAREA, EL REGRESO DEL SAMURÁI: HONORING A PRELUDE TO JAPANESE-MEXICAN DIPLOMATIC RELATIONS

Akiko's theatrical interests veer away from the static nature of the nation-state—whether Mexican or Japanese—focusing instead on the transnational movement of people, materials, cultural practices, ideas, and languages. This time, the transpacific and transatlantic (Japan, Mexico, Europe) event explored coincided with the fourth centennial celebration of friendship between Mexico and Japan. Akiko, in the play *Contramarea, el regreso del samurái* (2010), takes on Hasekura Tsunenaga Rokuemon's (1571–1622) historic visit to New Spain (present-day Mexico and the US state of California) in 1614, which in Mexico has been considered the fourth centennial of the opening of diplomatic and commercial relations between Mexico and Japan, even though, not being an independent country yet, the viceroyalty of New Spain could not have had "diplomatic relations" with Japan. Even so, there were other, not well known or as important Japanese missions to New Spain (the 1581 Tenshō embassy, another one in 1610, and a failed one in 1612), but Hasekura is considered the first Japanese ambassador to the Americas and Spain. The play, written, coproduced, and codirected by Akiko, was performed in Acapulco, Veracruz, and Mexico City, cities visited by Hasekura, as well as in Tokyo, Nagoya, Fukuoka, Kagoshima, and in Hasekura's hometown of Sendai, where a replica of the San Juan Bautista galleon in which the samurai sailed was used as the stage.

Akiko revealed to me that the word *contramarea* (countertide) in the title evokes all the adversities faced by a man who does not give up. It also alerts the viewer to the fact that the Japan-Mexico Pacific sea route ran opposite to the usual navigation routes of the time. As to "The Return of the Samurai" in the title, it refers to how Hasekura recalls his adventures during his return voyage to Japan.

Referred to as the Keichō embassy (1613–1620), it was led by Hasekura, a *kirishitan* (sixteen- and seventeen-century Japanese Catholic) samurai of Japanese imperial ancestry who was baptized as Felipe Francisco Faxicura in Madrid. Hasekura and his delegation traveled for three months from Japan to Cape Mendocino, California, and from there to Acapulco, New Spain, where they stayed for two months and left a group of Japanese merchants awaiting their return from Europe. After visiting Mexico City, they sailed from Veracruz to Havana, where they stopped for six days. From Cuba, the Japanese mission departed for San Lúcar de Barrameda, Spain. In 1615, after eight months visiting Seville and Madrid, the group departed for Rome, with a brief stop in the French harbor of Saint-Tropez, due to bad weather. By the time Hasekura returned home, he found a dramatically changed political and religious climate. As the Pacific studies scholar Melba Falck Reyes explains, "The samurai Hasekura led the trip accompanied by about 180 Japanese, arriving in Acapulco in 1614. It is known that some Japanese remained in Mexico. It took Hasekura seven years to carry out this undertaking. When he returned to Japan in 1620, Christians were severely persecuted."[17]

This historic diplomatic expedition promoted by Date Masamune (1567–1636), a Sendai *daimyō* (feudal lord), had two objectives: to request that King Phillip III of Spain allow Japanese commercial relations with New Spain and to encourage Pope Paul V to send a Catholic bishop and as many Franciscan missionaries as possible to Sendai. The Peruvian writer and researcher Fernando Iwasaki stresses, in particular, the influence of Father Luis Sotelo, Hasekura's Spanish interpreter: "The *daimyo* Date Masamune, lord of Aizu, induced by the ambitious Franciscan friar Luis Sotelo, named the samurai Hasekura as ambassador to the Spanish Crown. The expedition left Tsukinoura in 1613 and traveled to Mexico, Seville, Madrid, Roma, Genoa, Seville, Mexico, and Manila; it returned to Japan in 1620."[18]

Upon their return to Spain from Italy, Phillip III refused to sign the trade agreement on grounds that the delegation did not represent Japan's true ruler, Tokugawa Ieyasu, who had been deporting Christian missionaries and persecuting Christians since January 1614. Indeed, on 5 February 1597, the shogun Toyotomi Hideyoshi sentenced twenty-six Christians to death in Nagasaki: a Franciscan missionary born in New Spain in 1572, San Felipe de Jesús (the first Mexican saint and Mexico City's patron saint), five Europeans, and seventeen Japanese, three of them children. The persecution of Christians was renewed in 1613, the same year the Keichō delegation set out from Japan, and 1637. In June 1616, the mission left Seville for New Spain, leaving behind some who decided to stay (today, some seven hundred people in Coria del Río have the surname Japón). On his return to Japan, the frustrated Hasekura stayed in New Spain for five months, and in April 1618, he arrived in the Philippines. He arrived in Nagasaki in August 1620 and died of an illness two years later, having failed to produce significant results. Although Hasekura was baptized, Hasekura's gravesite is located in Miyagi's Enfukuji Buddhist temple. After the Keichō delegation, the shogun Tokugawa Hidetada broke commercial relations with Spain in 1623 and diplomatic ones in 1624; the Tokugawa shogunate would follow an isolationist policy known as Sakoku (closed country), which interrupted commerce and diplomatic relations with most foreign countries from 1639 until 1853.

Contramarea, el regreso del samurái, directed by Victoria Gutiérrez and Akiko, focuses on Hasekura's return trip to Japan, during which he first sailed in 1619 to Acapulco, before arriving in Manila and then Japan the following year. During the voyage, Hasekura recalls episodes of his adventure. As he reflects on the clash of cultures and religions he has witnessed, he undergoes an inner identity struggle (Akiko, as a Japanese Mexican, identifies with him). Even though he failed to achieve his diplomatic objectives, the play does not present the delegation as a failure because it managed to establish groundbreaking contacts with other countries. Throughout the play, musicians Alejandro Néstor Méndez Rojas and David Méndez Rojas, who belong to the Mexican band La Tribu, interpret Hasekura's feelings and emotions by means of their drums and other instruments.

A minimalist stage design with mooring lines and a large rope ladder hanging from the ceiling evokes the presence of the San Juan Bautista, the galleon in which Hasekura's delegation traveled. With traditional Japanese flute playing in the background, Hasekura (played by Akiko) appears on stage formally attired, wearing a white headband and holding a white fan in his right hand.[19] He slowly "slide walks," as in traditional Noh theater. He opens his hand fan and sings.

In another scene, holding a lantern and speaking in a dramatic tone, Hasekura struggles to walk aboard the ship on account of a strong wind, which the audience can hear. His solitude and desperation are represented by his struggles against the elements during the long voyage. Once he reaches the rope ladder, he straddles it like a horse, falls to the floor, and laughs as if he lost his mind. In a happier scene, Hasekura, with two katanas hanging from his belt, celebrates his arrival to New Spain. Although the historical aim of this Japanese delegation was to meet with representatives of King Phillip III on behalf of the *daimyō* Date Masamune, in the play he joins an Aztec warrior dressed in a colorful feather outfit, perhaps representing the essence of Mexicanness (Akiko admits a fascination with Mexican pre-Columbian culture). At one point, the Aztec warrior performs a spiritual cleansing on the Japanese emissary by burning ceremonial copal (tree resin) and shaking a rattle.

Hasekura likes finding similarities between his own culture and that of the Aztecs. To celebrate his identification with the cultures he finds in colonial Mexico, he dances to pre-Hispanic tunes that, because of the similarities that he perceives, progressively become the "Suzume Odori," a fan-displaying folkloric dance that is typical of the festivals in Hasekura's Sendai. The audience notices a transition from Mexican to Japanese rhythms that suggests a transoceanic commonality between the two cultures: the Japanese flute music at one point blends with the sounds of Aztec ankle rattles. Likewise, the Aztec warrior's colorful shield is split to create the impression of two Japanese hand fans, which Hasekura uses, one in each hand, as he performs the Aztec dances. It is in this scene that one finds the exact moment of transpacific fusion between Mexican and Japanese cultural practices that is so central to Akiko's artistic imaginary. Japanese language, dance, and music blend with Aztec music and dances to induce, in Hasekura, joyful recollections of his seven-year mission. In a subsequent scene, he sings in Spanish and has an alcoholic beverage with a drunken Spanish sailor whom he meets on the ship heading to Spain.[20]

Another scene re-creates Hasekura's visit to the Vatican. Shadows of large Christian crosses on stage, together with the sound of bells and Gregorian chants, remind us that he and several of his companions were Christian. On stage, he works on his calligraphy and hones his katana-fighting skills. In a scene, Hasekura, singing a Catholic song in Latin and asking the Virgin Mary to pray for him, takes the frame of a painting from the floor and places it before his face, an act that is meant to remind the audience of his visit with Pope Paul V. A known painting of the period depicted this encounter, when Paul V gave him the keys to the city. For the occasion, Hasekura wore a white *haori hakama*, a Japanese kimono that Akiko also wears in the play.

In the last scene, an exhausted Hasekura struggles to climb the rope ladder. The play ends with him up atop the rope ladder, turning into a shadow before fading away. Finally, he performs a *dogeza* (traditional Japanese etiquette gesture used to apologize or express deference or the desire for a favor from a person of higher status in which one kneels on the ground and bows until one's head touches the floor). The fade reflects real-life events: as some of Hasekura's relatives and servants were being executed in Japan for their Christian beliefs, Friar Sotelo was captured in Japan and burnt at the stake in 1624. Eventually, the Keichō delegation was forgotten, until the 1873 Iwakura mission to Europe, led by Iwakura Tomomi, when participants read related documents in Venice. Today, however, this diplomatic group is honored through statues of Hasekura in Acapulco (Mexico), Havana (Cuba), Coria del Río (Spain), Civitavecchia (Italy), and

FIGURE 6.6. "Hasekura Tsunenaga in Rome." Painting of Hasekura wearing a white haori hakama during his visit to the Pope. Archita Ricci, formerly attributed to Claude Déruet Claude Deruet. 1615. Public domain.

Tsukinoura and Osato (Japan). In a way, this play is another "monument" to celebrate their historical feat.

Contramarea, el regreso del samurai is based on the Japanese, Catholic author Shūsaku Endō's (1923–1996) novel *Samurai* (*The Samurai*, 1980), a fictional account of Hasekura's voyage that emphasizes the cultural and political difficulties that he encountered in the West. As Akiko explained in our interview, like Hasekura in New Spain, she went through a similar cultural shock after moving to Japan to study theater: "Having to accept things you don't understand because of the language, customs, and ideology. Not being able to express what one feels or thinks."[21] During the long voyage, Hasekura depended on his interpreter and felt overwhelmed by responsibility and obstacles.

Unsurprisingly, Akiko is moved by Endō, because the novelist is known, like her, for comparing Japanese experiences and perspectives with those of the West, albeit in his case from an ambivalently Christian perspective.[22] Akiko's performance re-creates some of the novel's episodes, often revealing Hasekura's shock upon encountering Western culture. In her review of the play, the Mexican playwright and theater director Lucía Leonor Enríquez criticizes this fragmentary nature: "Its impact is limited because it remains a series of mere impressions at certain moments that, although attractive, do not end up showing the samurai's incision or wound.... [O]ne cannot help but wonder what would have happened if the playwright had delved into the depths of Hasekura's life so as to not superficially address his life."[23] In Akiko's defense, however, a Kabuki performance typically shows only the most important aspect of a story; the play does remain faithful to the key elements of Endō's novel. In it, as the literary scholar José I. Suárez suggests, it is the interaction between Hasekura and Father Sotelo (Father Velasco in the novel) "that allows readers to grasp the mindsets of a Japanese samurai and a Catholic missionary of the period. Through a Socratic approach, Endo lays bare not only the *pro et contra* of two opposite perspectives of life and death, but also presents us with what must have been his life-long conundrum: to simultaneously be Japanese and Christian (2019, n.p.).

Connecting Christianity with conquest, the novel does not portray the ambitious Father Velasco positively. In Japan, he covets a bishopric, despises Jesuit hegemony, refers to the Japanese disparagingly, and tries to convert the delegation's merchants by unscrupulously assuring them that their baptism will be good for business. Once in New Spain, the delegation, after witnessing how indigenous societies are ruined by Christian civilization, fears that the same thing could happen to their own. In this sense, Suárez argues that Endō "seems to have grappled his entire life with his 'Japaneseness' and his inherited religion.... Endo, like Hasekura, became Catholic to achieve the expectations of others and, though he never renounced the imposed religion, he saw in his own ethnicity a moral superiority that atoned for the longstanding, US-inflicted, imperial wound" (2019, n.p.). In the end, both protagonist and his author struggle to balance their Japanese worldview with the adopted foreign Catholicism.

As in Endō's novel, in *Contramarea* the East meets and clashes with the West in yet another transpacific, cultural tour de force. Hasekura's adventure was, in fact, a prelude to those twentieth-century Japanese emigrants who dreamed of a brighter future. Akiko herself is a product of that dream.

MAI-SHO-GAKU, TRAZOS DE FUEGO: INTRODUCING MEXICAN AUDIENCES TO TRADITIONAL, JAPANESE ART FORMS AND MYSTICISM

Akiko wrote, produced, directed, and performed the visually stunning *Mai-Sho-Gaku, trazos de fuego* (2013), again coinciding with what has been wrongly considered the fourth centennial of the opening of diplomatic and commercial relations between Mexico and Japan. She was also responsible for the actors' makeup and stage design, and along with the Mexican *Butoh* (a type of Japanese dance theater created in 1959) dancer Arturo Tames, choreographed the play.

In her performances, Akiko tries to remain faithful to Japanese classic theatrical forms while innovating and introducing a contemporaneous art form. *Mai-Sho-Gaku*, for example, resorts to Kabuki and *Butoh* theater techniques. The classical Kabuki dance-drama, one of Japan's three major traditional theater forms, along with *Noh* and *Bunraku*, was created as a female dance troupe by Izumo no Okuni, a woman who worked as an attendant at Kyoto's Grand Shrine of Izumo in 1603, during the Edo Period. In 1629, it became a male troupe after many Kabuki female actors were accused of prostitution; to this day, Kabuki is performed and danced by men only.

Created to entertain the working classes, Kabuki theater is known for its stylization: actors wear extravagant costumes, wigs, and *kumadori* makeup, characterized by its brightly colored stripes or patterns over white base, which suggests the character's personality traits. The actors' exaggerated, stylized, dancelike movements help in defining the characters and moving the story for an audience that often has difficulty understanding the archaic Japanese language typically used in these performances. Kabuki theater, which mixes mime, acting, and vocal performance, often uses revolving platforms, trapdoors, and footbridges to allow for dramatic entry or exit in the audience's midst. As may be heard in *Mai-Sho-Gaku, trazos de fuego*, live music is performed with traditional instruments.

However, rather than traditional Kabuki theater, Akiko practices a type of Nihon Buyō called *Kabuki buyō*. After the Japanese government banned female actors from playing Kabuki, Nijon Buyō became its own traditional dance, independent from Kabuki.[24] In our interview, Akiko elaborated on this rich tradition:

> Kabuki origins date back to the year 1600, when Okuni, a priestess, performed an invocation dance in the Izumo Kingdom. Then, Kabuki was performed by women, which is why it was called Onna or Yujyō Kabuki (Kabuki for night ladies). Then came the Wakasyu Kabuki (Kabuki for young people) and later the Yarō Kabuki (Kabuki for rogues), in which only men participated, as is the case today. However, since the beginning of the twentieth century, with the movement of Shinbuyō (contemporary dance), Japanese dance underwent a transformation in 1924, when it ceased to be called Kabukibuyō to gain independence and took on the broader name of Nihonbuyō, in which men and women participate indiscriminately, in contrast with Kabuki theater.[25]

As for *Butoh* dance theatre, it was created in 1959 through the collaboration of its founders, the dancers Tatsumi Hijikata and Kazuo Ohno, who were feeling overwhelmed by the tragedy of the US atomic bombing of Hiroshima and Nagasaki. Looking for a less Westernized expression of Japanese tradition, Hijikata and Ohno began to explore new dance forms in which primal, raw emotions could be openly expressed. They sought primitive forms of beauty and experimented with grotesque and disfiguring dance movements. *Butoh* is characterized by avant-garde, playful, and grotesque imagery; extreme or absurd environments; and taboo topics—Hijikata shocked Japanese society with his 1959 performance of *Kinjiki*, a poem alluding to homosexuality and bestiality. *Butoh* is usually performed with slow, controlled movements by actors whose bodies are daubed in white paint, as in several scenes in *Mai-Sho-Gaku, trazos de fuego*.

Mai-Sho-Gaku explores the ephemeral nature of life. Again, pre-Columbian, indigenous musical instruments and other cultural practices are blended with Japanese traditional arts, creating a transpacific fusion. Its multidisciplinary nature is reflected in the title: *Mai* means "dance" (a Kabuki, Butoh, and gymnastics blend here); *Sho* (*shodō*) signifies calligraphy, the art of writing ideograms; and the ideogram *Gaku* refers to music (ethnic music). *Mai-Sho-Gaku, trazos de fuego* is the story of a young *bonzo* (Buddhist monk; played by Yolox Medina, a *shōdōka*, or calligrapher, in Mexico, and later by Berenice Contreras, a Japanese calligraphy student and Hindu dance performer). For the third season, Akiko decided to replace the bonzo with Miko, a priestess caretaker of Buddhist temples performed by Yukari Hirazawa, a *shōdō* teacher and *koto* performer.

Surrounded by positive and negative forces, the *bonzo* seeks transcendence and liberation of his consciousness through meditation and calligraphy. Akiko resorts to abstraction and rich visual aesthetics based on Japanese mysticism. The mise-en-scène includes philosophical references to the *bonzo*'s inner struggle to liberate his captive consciousness. By invoking the Shinto deities of the "elemental forces" through calligraphy (tracing different kanji on large canvases and the characters' bodies), his fears are embodied. This materialization of his fears is suggested in an advertising poster announcing the play that contained the line "Because knowledge alone was not enough, he forged his mind with words."[26]

The two elemental forces related to the play's mystic symbolism are water and fire. Whereas water represents passive, negative subconscious energy, fire symbolizes active, positive conscious energy. The water deity (Akiko) and the fire deity (Tames) undergo a metamorphosis: fire becomes the *fude* (paintbrush) and water, the *sumi* (India ink). Both embodied deities meet, dance, and fuse. Having overcome these obstacles, the monk transforms from a mere calligrapher or scribe monk (*shodoka*) into an artist who paints a colorful phoenix, symbol of rebirth. In the end, his longed awakening arrives: the *bonzo* finds his identity and achieves a state of awareness associated with living the moment as unique. He is reborn with a higher consciousness level.

In a scene, Akiko's character (water), dressed in a black kimono, bends backward along with fire, Tames, dressed in a red kimono. The audience can hear traditional Japanese music played with a *koto* (Japanese harp) and *taiko* drums. Two thin bamboo walls stand to the side as well as a Shinto *torii*. The guardians of the *torii* are Fujin, the wind deity (played by Alejandro Méndez), and Rajin, the deity of lightning (Tenoch Méndez). Akiko's character paints with thick, black, brush lines the seminude body of Tames. As if the ideograms were alive, the two dancers' painted, moving bodies represent elegant strokes of calligraphic writing. As a woman plays *taiko* drums, Akiko, resorting to Kabuki theater techniques, appears as Shishi, the lion. The undulations of Shishi's long mane recall the strokes of a paintbrush (*fude*) used to record the *bonzo*'s thoughts and emotions. In certain scenes, Akiko and Tames appear scantily clad on stage, an aspect of *Butoh*. Tames dances while carrying Akiko on his back.

The play, therefore, evokes life's brevity, as stated in an advertising poster: "Even a flower's flagrance withers."[27] While less obviously than in *Juan, el Momotaro* or *Contramarea, el regreso del samurái*, in this play Akiko addresses the transpacific dialogue and fusion between Japanese and Mexican cultures by innovating classic Japanese theatrical forms through the incorporation of pre-Columbian music. Along the way, *Mai-Sho-Gaku* teaches Mexican audiences about Japanese traditional theatrical forms, dances, philosophies, and calligraphy, celebrating Japanese culture in commemoration of a historic prelude to the diplomatic relations between Mexico and Japan.

NIKKEI... CORREO DE HIROSHIMA: AKIKO'S THEATRICAL INTERPRETATION OF A NOVEL ABOUT MEXICAN NIKKEIJIN DURING WORLD WAR II

The ninety-minute play *Nikkei... Correo de Hiroshima* (2018) is based on the novel *Correo de Hiroshima* (Letters from Hiroshima, 1995) by the Chiapas author Víctor Manuel Camposeco (1943–), which incorporates testimonials about Hiroshima's bombing and links the Nikkeijin experience with that of the Nihonjin.

In this partially epistolary novel, the Nikkeijin Angelina Toyomoto, a medical student in Japan, describes Japan's mood during its invasion of China. She also recounts her experience as a Hiroshima survivor.[28] In the first transpacific letter included in *Correo de Hiroshima*, Oliva writes to her daughter Angelina from Tapachula, Chiapas, in 1940, expressing her misgivings about the Japanese invasion of China but feeling relieved that she is far from the war zone. Besides telling Angelina about her brother Teiko's alcoholism, the mother reveals to Angelina what motivated her father, Hara Toyomoto, to emigrate to Mexico (he originally wished to go to Hawaii or the United States) and recalls how they met: "When your father arrived in Tapachula from Japan, with Furukawa, Yamazaki, Exal and all the others, he did not speak a word of Spanish and was penniless, almost starving. He only had the uncultivated land that the government of Japan had purchased for them, the pioneers as I call them, here in Soconusco. But hey, what they did bring was a huge will to work, which surprised us, along with the tenaciousness that you know so well."[29] Toward the novel's end, we learn that Hara moved to Mexico, together with two hundred other Japanese, in search of a better life and agriculture work. In the Soconusco region, the Japanese government had purchased half a million acres of agricultural land of which Hara received a plot in Tapachula. There, he settled, raised a family, and eventually became a plantation owner.

While in Japan, Mexico-born Angelina becomes increasingly attached to her ancestral country, both culturally and politically, to the point of becoming a fervent nationalist and supporter of Japan's invasion of Manchuria: "In short, may all be for Japan's integrity and destiny, which are above all other interests . . . Japan will prevail, its fate is sacred, like our Emperor."[30] This scene connects with the diasporic nationalist discourse included in certain passages of Nakatani's memoirs, Akane's verses, and the manga analyzed in previous chapters.

Angelina's letters also express her indignation about the US diplomatic and commercial pressure on Japan: "The United States is trying to lead Japan down a dead end, to destroy our potential and humiliate us. They will not prevail. Japanese strength and willpower is well above this infamy."[31] She even establishes a parallel between these events and the US landgrab after the Mexican-American War (1846–1848). Later, Angelina celebrates "the victory at Pearl Harbor" and "the great victory at Bataan, a year ago, where the arrogant British and the Americans got what they deserved."[32] Incidentally, there were no British soldiers in the Battle of Bataan (7 January–9 April 1942), which was fought by the United States and the Philippine Commonwealth, led by General Douglas MacArthur, against the Imperial Japanese Army and Navy.

In keeping with her bicultural background, Angelina plans to marry Yoshi Nomura first in a Shinto ceremony and, once in Mexico, in a Catholic one as well. In her first letters, she explains her double loyalty to Mexico and Japan: "I'm sorry to talk to you about the current situation in Japan as a Japanese, which I actually am, while not denying my Mexican origins. I face life with one foot in Japan and the other in Mexico, in Tapachula to be precise, well rooted in those people, in you guys; I too am from there."[33] Her subsequent letters record her increasing identification with Japan and her unconditional support for Japanese imperialism. Indeed, in contrast with other Mexican novels, such as Cecilia Reyes Estrada's *La gallina azul*, whose Mexican-born Nikkei characters identify as Mexican rather than as Japanese, in Manuel Camposeco's *Correo de Hiroshima*, Angelina, at the beginning, identifies as both Mexican and Japanese but, as the plot unfolds, increasingly becomes Japanese. By the time her son Genji is born in Japan, she declares that they are a Japanese family. Also, after she and her husband graduate from the Imperial University of Tokyo and become physicians, Angelina feels that she owes it to Japan to stay to treat the war wounded and not leave the country as her parents were begging her to do, particularly after the Pearl Harbor attack.

While some chapters narrate the secret planning and eventual dropping of atomic bombs in Hiroshima and Nagasaki, the novel, speaking through an omniscient narrator critical of the entire action, mainly re-creates the war horrors in Japan. Angelina describes the bombing of Tokyo by more than three hundred B-29 American airplanes and strongly condemns the dropping of more than two hundred thousand tons of napalm on the city—most buildings, made of wood and paper, were destroyed by the immense fires. She goes on to lament that, in less than four hours, one hundred thousand citizens died and twenty thousand more were injured: "'The streets were rivers of fire, people were struck on fire like matches. At dawn, long lines of burnt, ash-covered, stunned individuals, walked aimlessly like of ants columns,' says the *Asahi* journalist."[34] Although Angelina confesses to her mother that they are expecting a similar bombing attack in Hiroshima, she is convinced that Japan's "superior destiny" will not allow it to be defeated. She is confident that the United States will sign a peace treaty, that is, until she witnesses the atomic mushroom and its horrendous consequences: "What I saw seemed like a hallucination, the city became a hell! People came out of the rubble, from among the flames and the ashes, monstrously burnt. They instinctively went to the Hospital. For each one standing, ten were thrown to the ground, dead or dying."[35] She then details the horrors at a Hiroshima hospital, where she tries to treat those who arrive with their bodies completely burnt. Despite thinking that she has lost her husband and her son (the latter survived), Angelina has not a moment to stop and cry; she must devote all her energy to treating, with scant resources, the injured.

Meanwhile, on the other side of the Pacific, optimistic at first because of war news received through short-wave radio, her parents become unsure that Hiroshima will be spared from the air bombings. News of the atomic bomb leads them to believe that Angelina has perished. Both parents die of sadness; shortly afterward, Angelina's brother dies of cirrhosis. By the time Angelina and her son return to Mexico, she finds her parents' house empty.

Based on *Correo de Hiroshima*, the play *Nikkei... Correo de Hiroshima* was adapted by the Mexican playwright Javier Márquez and directed by Akiko, who also choreographed it, designed the costumes, and took part in the performance (the other actors were Laura Jaimes and Arturo Tames, as well as the dancers Viridiana Manjarrez and Ammi Villanueva). The play belongs to a type of sensorial theater in which the audience is temporarily deprived of its sense of sight (during the play's first half, viewers are blindfolded) to raise their senses. Their sense of smell is stimulated by burned tires, food, incense, and the dust flying from a coop of aroused chickens. Through live music and appeals to the senses, the audience listens to the plot, which includes letters between Angelina and her mother. When fanned with large hand fans, they also feel the wind of warplanes and hear birds fluttering over their heads. These methods cause viewers to experience an impending sense of nuclear annihilation (an advertising poster describes Hiroshima as "the face of a hell on earth"),[36] as it surrounds them with sensorial stimuli that resemble the horrors of war. It makes the audience more aware of life's fragility and the dreadful consequences of war and indolence. During the play's second half, the actors, by narrating the story through their dance and performance, try to convey the benefits of peace, nuclear disarmament, and unity among nations.

Nikkei... Correo de Hiroshima takes place in Mexico, Japan, and the United States. At its beginning, the audience listens to the story of the nineteenth-century Japanese who emigrated to the United States and Mexico to improve their lot in life. In Soconusco, one of these immigrants falls in love with a Mexican woman with whom he has two children. Their daughter Angelina, after reaching adolescence, becomes a Kibei (Nisei who studied in Japan) and, while studying medicine in Japan, seeks to understand her father's culture. While there she meets her Japanese husband and moves to Hiroshima, whence she narrates, in an epistolary format, the development of the Pacific War to her mother, Oliva. As in the novel, Angelina and her mother exchange letters for over five years in which they confide their hopes and fears. Then, after surviving Hiroshima's atomic bombing, Angelina and her son return to Mexico only to learn that her parents, not having received correspondence from her since the bombing, had died of sadness believing that she perished.

In *Nikkei... Correo de Hiroshima*, Akiko resorts to *Butoh* and *Nihon buyō* dances.[37] The play starts with projected black-and-white images of bomb victims in Hiroshima. Then, the author Camposeco gives a brief talk about the play's historical context, including Japan's pervasive poverty and overpopulation that caused the first emigration of workers to Hawaii's sugarcane and pineapple plantations. Through photographs, the audience first learns of Japanese emigration to California; then, after the 1888 treaty with Mexico, to Chiapas in 1897, where the Enomoto group failed to create a coffee plantation. Young Japanese bachelors leave hoping to save enough money before returning to Japan. Whether drawing on picture brides or returning to find brides in Japan, some marry Japanese women. Others marry Mexican women. Camposeco explains that his novel is based on the story of the Toyohara family, whose members he met as a child. After pointing at a large photograph of the Toyoharas projected on a screen and asking the audience to put on blindfolds, the author reveals that they were his Nikkei neighbors in Chiapas.

Still blindfolded, the audience hears Akiko and other actors reading sections of the letters between Angelina and her mother. Moving the setting to the United States in 1945, one hears jazz music in the background and the bomb-carrying *Enola Gay* taking off for Hiroshima. Years earlier, when the mother heard the news about the attack on Pearl Harbor, she wondered why Japan would take such an action and expressed her surprise in a letter; by contrast, Angelina celebrated it as a great victory. Meanwhile, Angelina's parents, receiving regular radio news about the war, begin to build a medical office for Angelina and her husband, expecting them to arrive soon in Chiapas. At the play's climax, during the description of the atomic attack in Hiroshima, the audience hears an explosion followed by a cloud of smoke over the stage. At that moment, the audience at last removes their blindfolds and hear Angelina (Akiko), a syllable at a time and in terrible pain, uttering words like *cold, ashes,* and *pain,* as well as sentences like "glass on the floor, on my body" and "blood on arms, legs." Angelina, sitting on the floor, slowly stands up. In a most impressive scene, the audience can see Angelina moving her arms, dancing slowly, as if in pain, with a face mask of herself on the back of her head. She drags her feet surrounded by dying and dead people. She tries to help the wounded to no avail, as their skin is hanging from their arms. Angelina runs out on the street and finds people monstrously burned, almost faceless. She screams, calling out her husband's and son's names, then suddenly hears a little girl singing the "Kimigayo" (The Emperor's Reign), the Japanese national anthem.

On stage, the mother, breathless, almost crying, with a light beaming over her head, learns of what has transpired in Hiroshima. Fearing for her husband's sanity, she states that he is covering his face with his hands, is completely silent, and refuses to listen or answer questions. Oliva then asserts that the uncertainty of not receiving news is most painful to her. In the next scene, the light beam moves over the mother who, aware of the bombing of Nagasaki, is crying in disbelief. The audience then hears the Japanese emperor's declaration of surrender on the radio. One of the mother's letters reveals that, after the first bomb, her father never spoke again and quietly died in his armchair.

The narration then moves to Hiroshima, two weeks after the bomb, with a description of those stricken by radiation and its effects, like hair loss, vomiting, and diarrhea. Angelina sits on the floor, coughing. With the light beaming on her head, she explains that seemingly healthy people, assisting with the casualties, later died. As she loses weight and her hair, she wonders whether she too will perish from the radiation. She suddenly stands and sings in Japanese. Identifying with Japan, she questions whether she will ever return to Mexico and see her family again. Feeling weak, she shifts to singing in Spanish about her yearning for Tapachula, when suddenly she decides to return with her son. Once in Tapachula, Rosita, her former neighbor, tells her that her parents and brother passed away. Angelina rereads one by one all the letters sent by her mother to her. At the play's end, she appears dressed in a kimono, a green beam of light shining over her and music playing in the background. She walks slowly and then falls to her knees. She sheds part of her kimono and the stage turns dark.

Like the previous plays, *Nikkei… Correo de Hiroshima* dwells on the transpacific, where issues of national identity and loyalty are explored, this time against the painful background of war.

EL AUTOMÓVIL GRIS AL ESTILO BENSHI JAPONÉS: A SILENT MEXICAN FILM MEETS A LOST JAPANESE PERFORMANCE GENRE

Continuing with the transpacific movement of cultural practices, with her *benshi* (also *katsudō-benshi* or *katsuben*) work in *El automóvil gris al estilo benshi japonés* (2019), Akiko educates her Mexican audience about a relatively recent Japanese cultural tradition of which today few Japanese are aware.[38] At the same time, she adds further innovation to the world of Mexican theater. The play is staged, in the Japanese *benshi* tradition, by an on-screen projection of the Mexican silent film *El automóvil gris* (The gray automobile, 1919), directed by Enrique Rosas (1877–1920). Akiko, dressed like a geisha in a kimono, and the Afro-Caribbean actor Fabrina Melón, also in costume, perform in *benshi* style, singing and dancing. They narrate the first part of the film's story as they dance, make comments, and provide simultaneous voicing for all the film's characters.[39] At a certain point, Akiko uses large puppets with different voices. In the background, a pianist contextualizes the drama by playing from a recent piano score composed from musical pieces of the silent Japanese and Mexican film era.

A century after the debut of *El automóvil gris*, *El automóvil gris al estilo benshi japonés* pays homage to director Enrique Rosas by transforming and enriching his film through Japanese *benshi* techniques. The outcome is a new product, neither Mexican nor Japanese, but a playful and evocative dialogue between the two different languages and cultures as they interact. Through this performance, the culturally hybrid product establishes nonhegemonic, transpacific, and epistemological bridges between Mexico and Japan, with no apparent hierarchical taxonomies. It is, somehow, a cross-cultural comparative study in search of common denominators between different worldviews. Incidentally, in her particular performance of Japaneseness, Akiko affects a strong Japanese accent in a Facebook video advertising *El automóvil gris*.[40]

In 1933, Enrique Rosas's heirs added sound to *El automóvil gris* and blended the different episodes (some had been lost) to summarize the story in a single film. In the mid-1950s, it was rerecorded with an improved soundtrack. Based on a true story, the action in *El automóvil gris* was filmed in the same 1915 locations were the original crimes took place and where the thieves were arrested. In fact, an actor and script coauthor, Juan Manuel Cabrera, was the police inspector in charge of the investigation. Others were actual robbery victims who played themselves. Rosas's film reenacts the crime spree committed by the Gray Automobile Gang, a group of Spaniards and Mexicans who robbed wealthy homes in the Mexico City of the Mexican Revolution.

In the opening scene, eight criminals are planning a robbery and swear unity regardless of the situation. Afterward, they abduct Ernestina, a woman walking down the street, and put her in their gray Fiat. Finding herself trapped inside a bedroom in the thieves' headquarters, she realizes that one of the thugs is her own boyfriend—he rapes her later. The assailants, wearing military outfits and showing authentic search warrants, manage to enter several homes. It turns out that the original gang included a police officer who, because of the country's tumult, was able to obtain search warrants to look for hidden weapons. Among the many evil deeds, the criminals murder an innocent boy who witnesses one of their robberies, and they torture an elderly man so he reveals where he keeps his money. Eventually, the thieves begin to be captured or killed one by one. In court, those caught are given the death penalty. The film closes with the newsreel clips filmed by Rosas on celluloid of their actual execution being witnessed the many spectators.

The real-life gang included five Mexicans and three Spaniards, one of whom was the leader. The inspiration for Ernestina was Alice, the daughter of a Frenchman who was kidnapped as she walked down the street. The criminals, after raping her, asked for ransom. Once citizens began to openly accuse the authorities of complicity, the criminals began to be arrested. While six, the powerless ones, were executed, their leaders were pardoned; some of the detainees, after agreeing to confess, were murdered in jail. This political intrigue, however, is not included in the film.

As stated, *El automóvil gris al estilo benshi japonés* entails a *benshi* performance, combining film, theater, and music. This interdisciplinary expression is much to Akiko's liking. During the Japanese silent film era, the *benshi* figure developed. Since Japanese audiences were used to narrators relating the story being performed as in Noh and Kabuki theater, with the advent of silent films in the late nineteenth century (early Japanese films were mostly filmic adaptations of Kabuki plays), the live, auxiliary function of a *benshi* performer who presented, voiced, and commented the moving visuals came to be expected. Seated or standing by the screen, this live narrator introduced, related, and interpreted the film's storyline in a dramatic, theatrical style. He or she lent a voice to all characters, male or female. They also explained the foreign (mostly American) cultural differences in the film and gave, in an engaging manner, coherence to the fragmented storylines. Their creative interpretations could include, for example, the recitation of poems not included in the film. Because no microphones were used, those who worked as *benshi* had to project their voices into large spaces, in coordination with the live music performed with the traditional Kabuki theater instruments.

In their day, *benshi* were a bigger theater draw than actors themselves. Posters advertising the films often included their photographs. With the introduction of "talkies," however, *benshi* became obsolete—their popularity prolonged the silent film era in Japan, which lasted until the mid-1930s. Today, very few *benshi* remain in Japan, but Akiko and Compañía Teatro de Ciertos Habitantes (Theater Company of Certain Citizens) decided to resurrect these Japanese cultural performers in Mexico. The *benshi* style of narration, interpretation, and (at times) misinterpretation—albeit respecting the spirit and essence of the original work—becomes a point of departure for cross-cultural encounters and dialogues.

Often resorting to the trope of the Pacific Ocean as a transnational, communicating bridge, Akiko's theatrical innovations not only enrich the Mexican cultural scene but also contribute to a mutual, transpacific understanding, beyond worn-out, racialized stereotypes and misplaced fantasies. By remembering transpacific historical events and migrations, as well as the exchange of cultural practices, traditions, and ideas (folktales, *benshi*, theater, dance, music) between Mexico and Japan, her plays are hybrid cultural products that articulate new dialogues and showcase surprising commonalities between supposedly distant worldviews. The loci of enunciation in Akiko's work are both her country and her ethnic homeland, as if attempting to think from both places simultaneously. She has contributed to reimagining Mexico as a historical contact zone between East and West and to reposition it as one of the countries in the Pacific Rim, Pacific Basin, or—as it is called today—the Transpacific. The numerous descriptions of Manzanillo, in the literature by and about Mexican Nikkeijin, as the tiny, underdeveloped port where Japanese immigrants landed is symptomatic of the fact that, at that time, Mexico was not focused on looking east. With time, however, these geopolitical perspectives are rapidly changing thanks to new economic and sociopolitical developments. Akiko's performance art, from a cultural standpoint, is an attempt to contribute to a Western reopening to the once-familiar East of the Manila galleon era while avoiding the pitfalls of (self-)Orientalization.

Conclusion
Another Past Is Possible

There are no major formal innovations in the cultural production by Japanese Mexicans (mainstream Mexican poets and artists have also been influenced by Japanese literature and art), as is also the case with cultural production by Japanese Peruvians and Japanese Brazilians. Actually, Japanese Mexican cultural production does not deviate significantly from the rest of Mexican cultural production. Moreover, because it is, for the most part, quite recent, Japanese Mexican cultural artifacts do not present a substantial chronological evolution in their themes or worldviews. Japanese Mexican writers' and artists' depiction of progressive cultural integration, much as their celebration of cultural difference and denunciation of historical grievances and oppression, does not meaningfully differ from works by other ethnic groups in Mexico and the rest of Latin America.

While in this study I have selected what I consider the most representative aspects and works of Japanese Mexican cultural production—literature, performance, and visual arts—several other works merit critical studies.[1] A further study could also be done on the sympathetic view of the Nikkei Other in Mexican cultural production.[2] The previous chapters have explored Mexican Nikkeijin's cultural construction of their own collective identity through writing, visual arts, and performance. Some texts, like Akane's poetry, lean at times toward Nihonjinron discourse, an ideological fantasy focusing on the uniqueness of the Japanese ethos in contrast with that of Westerners. Others, like *Los samuráis de México*, recycle colonialist concepts like Japanese spirit, virgin lands, natives, and colonization to re-create the Nikkei experience in Mexico. By contrast, Nakatani's memoirs, still belonging within the commonplace of the success story, implicitly challenge Nihonjinron discourse and official mandates of improving Japan's image abroad. Finally, Nishizawa's and Akiko's respective artistic discourses, far from self-Orientalizing mystifications or exoticizations of their cultural difference, rearticulate a hybrid third space through a transpacific dialogue between Mexican and Japanese cultures. Together, these works provide evidence of the ideological and identity heterogeneity of this ethnic group. There is, for example, a wide gap between Nakatani's support of Japanese imperialism and his refusal to acknowledge Japan's defeat in World War II and the utopian socialism practiced by several of the pioneers in Chiapas; or between Nonaka's deep cultural integration into Mexico's mainstream society and Nakatani's refusal to request Mexican naturalization or his lack of non-Nikkeijin friends.

Several analyzed texts, written by both Japanese immigrants and their descendants, single out the episode of their forced World War II relocation as a watershed event in the history of the Japanese Mexican community. The trauma it caused (e.g., deaths during transportation, depression, homelessness, destitution, loss of property, family separation, imprisonment) to Japanese immigrants and to their Mexico-born descendants was an eye-opening reminder of the limitations of their tenuous Mexican citizenship, even for veterans of the Mexican Revolution like Nonaka, many of whom were recruited owing to the assumption of their Japanese military prowess. The sudden association of their ethnicity and phenotype with espionage, enemies of the state, or a fifth column, together with the Mexican government's willingness to abide by Washington's demands, despite the general support of the Mexican population for Japan during the war, brought great disappointment and anxiety to this community. However, the forced relocation also led to major employment changes for northwestern Mexico's Nikkei community. As Ota Mishima explains, as a result first of agrarian reform, then relocation, "a population devoted to agriculture and fishing, became urban and commerce-oriented."[3] Decades later and on a different plane, the critics' stereotyping of Nishizawa's art by exaggerating its Japanese characteristics suggests that Nikkeijin's Mexican cultural citizenship may still be in question. By highlighting not only commonalities such as the trauma of relocation or the tendency to write first-person success stories but also the diversity within Nikkei cultural discourse, this study has tried to expose this type of stereotypical cultural essentialism that deploys a static ontological notion of Japaneseness.

In a 2020 article "La historia negra de los japoneses en México y una petición de perdón" (The Black History of the Japanese in Mexico and a Petition for an Apology), Jumko Ogata Aguilar, a Universidad Nacional

Autónoma de México undergraduate of Japanese origin, leads the demand for an official apology from the Mexican government for its mistreatment of her Nikkei ancestors in Mexico during World War II.[4] This demand counters traditional politics of Latin American Nikkei communities, which, not having enjoyed a civil rights movement struggling for social justice and equal rights similar to that in the United States, have typically opted for keeping a low profile. Ogata Aguilar, a Sansei from Veracruz with Nikkei and African ancestry, who also considers herself a Chicana for having been raised in California, has imported an American-style, ethnic minority protest tradition to Mexico. She speaks out for a community "that suffered huge civil rights violations . . . their bank accounts were frozen, their businesses impounded, and they were imprisoned though they were Mexican citizens."[5] Ogata Aguilar considers the current silence an "open wound" in the collective trauma of the Nikkei community: "We have to do away with those feelings, take them out, have a collective catharsis. What happened was, above all, a racist issue . . . We have to come up with another history that revaluates that past so as to avoid repeating it."[6]

Also in this same article, the journalist Carmen Morán Breña interviews Sergio Hernández, a researcher from the Instituto Nacional de Antropología e Historia (National Institute of Anthropology and History), and Shinji Hirai, a Japanese anthropologist. Hernández discloses that the Nikkei community in Mexico—along the Pacific coast and the US border (mostly Baja California, Sonora, and Chihuahua), and the central region of the country—was suspected of harboring spies or collaborators of the Empire of Japan. Hernández concludes that the Nikkei relocation during the war should at least be taught in schools because most Mexicans, including the Nikkeijin, are unaware of it.

The piece proceeds to emphasize that the Mexican government, unlike those of Peru and other Latin American countries, refused to send its Nikkeijin to internment camps in the United States. They were instead permitted, with limitations, free movement in those cities where they relocated. Hernández adds, however, that relocation caused a social and economic trauma to the displaced, particularly those who were unable to sell their properties, so had no money upon arriving in Guadalajara or Mexico City. Thankfully, mutual-aid committees run by Nikkeijin who were long-term residents of these cities, like Nakatani, offered them assistance. As Nakatani proudly ascertains, at the conclusion of his memoirs, many descendants of those displaced are now successful professionals. Hernández also seeks an official apology from the Mexican government: "Three decades after it occurred in the United States, the Japanese movement not only obtained an apology, but also compensation. An apology was partially offered in Peru, during Alan García's government. In Brazil, the initiative did not go forward. I believe that Mexico owes them an apology, but it is they who must decide to request it. The Mexican people, in any case, should know about this part of its history."[7]

Indeed, long after US president Ronald Reagan apologized in 1988 to Japanese Americans for their internment during World War II, Peru's President Alan García apologized in 2011 to Japanese Peruvians for the 1941 looting of their property. To date, no official apology has been issued by the Mexican government. Although Mexico's current president Andrés Manuel López Obrador has recently asked the Chinese, the Yaqui, and Mayan communities for forgiveness for his country's past abuses, to my knowledge the Nikkeijin have not received a similar apology.

Tomás Hirata, a Nikkeijin from Veracruz interviewed in the article, agrees that an official apology would help this community that "saw its honor eroded . . . to reconcile its feelings, something that is currently not entirely understood."[8] By contrast, and more in line with Latin American Nikkei communities' traditional response (or lack thereof), Alejandro Hirashi, a Nikkei researcher at the Universidad Autónoma Metropolitana, disagrees with the initiative of demanding an official apology: "Contexts determine international historical relations and outside of them, and ignoring them makes current reality incomprehensible. [Seeking an apology] escapes a certain logic and gives relevance to certain aspects that have nothing to do with a political or cultural program. . . . It is better to explain what happened, to investigate, to support the humanistic and literary research that sprang from these relations. They have to do with the formation of both countries. Education spares us from having to ask and from offering excuses at a time when relations are ideal."[9]

An interview with Ogata Aguilar is included in an article by journalist Ariadna García (2020), "Exigen disculpa para japoneses en México" (Apology Demanded for Japanese in Mexico), in the Mexican newspaper *El Universal*. Shocking were the hostile, racist, and xenophobic remarks in the comment section that conflated Mexican Nikkeijin with the Empire of Japan during World War II, although Ogata Aguilar twice explained that her demand is unbeknownst to the Japanese government. Several readers cannot accept that this third-generation Nikkeijin is Mexican or that the relocated Mexican Nikkeijin were falsely accused of being Japanese spies or collaborators. As the historian Jerry García points out: "Many of their rights were violated, even though they had nothing to do with the war. They could only get around with government permission. They were watched by the police."[10]

It is my hope that this study contributes to the recovery of Nikkei social, historical, and cultural heritage in Mexico. It is also my intention to rescue the persecution of Mexican Nikkeijin during World War II from oblivion. After all, their scapegoating cannot be solely attributed to then US government's demands for their relocation. If, as Bhabha argues, "increasingly, 'national' cultures are being produced from the perspective of disenfranchised minorities" (1994, 5–6), the study of Asian minority discourses in Mexico should produce new readings of this country's racial relations, national identity, and recent history.

Notes

INTRODUCTION

1. In this book, I use *Nikkei* as an adjective and *Nikkeijin* as both a singular and a plural noun.
2. There is also a Spanish talavera sculpture of Samson opening the jaws of a lion at the top of the fountain, as well as ceramics from Puebla, porcelain from Germany and England, and mirrors, stone sculptures, and aquatic elements such as mother-of-pearl, a mermaid playing a violin, and three Tritons.
3. Tuba was introduced to Mexico via the Manila galleons and is still popular in the Colima, Jalisco, Michoacán, and Guerrero.
4. *Anitos* can also refer to the human-like carved figures (the *taotao*) of these spirits.
5. "Los dos procesos de destilación (el árabe y el asiático) llegaron a México (por diversas rutas, probablemente) y fueron utilizados a lo largo de la costa del Pacífico para obtener aguardiente" (Valenzuela Zapata et al. 2008, 113).
6. In a related study, Valenzuela-Zapata and coauthors emphasize the importance of documenting the influence of Mongolian- and Chinese-style stills in Korea during the Mongol period to demonstrate "that the Mexican stills, which closely resemble the Asian prototypes and whose level of resemblance in technique is similar to that of Korean ones, certainly offer still another case of transfers/diffusions of the techniques of the Asian prototypes to a wider world" (2013, 104).
7. During World War II, Matsumoto, a naturalized Mexican citizen, offered his Hacienda Batán as a refuge for those Nikkeijin whom the Mexican government, at the request of the US government, forced to relocate to Mexico City. *Nikkeijin*, borrowed from Japanese 日系人, refers to a Japanese immigrant or descendant not residing in Japan. The term became popular during the 1940s, particularly after World War II. Previously, other terms were used to refer to Japanese immigrants and their descendants, including *Nihonjin* or *Nipponjin*,

Hōjin, and *zaigai* or *kaigai dōhō* (overseas brethren). Japanese Mexicans were referred to as *Zaiboku Hōjin* (Japanese residing in Mexico). However, as is customary, for clarity's sake I refer to all Japanese immigrants and their descendants as *Nikkeijin*, because the differentiations could lead to confusion for non-Japanese-speaking readers.

8. In Reyes Estrada's novel *La gallina azul*, based on interviews with Japanese Mexicans, the narrator's father, an Issei named Zenzo Yamada, makes a living in Ures, Sonora, selling this type of shaved ice.
9. Another Japanese Mexican family, the Nishikawas, also claims to have invented Japanese peanuts.
10. The word *chamoy* may derive from the Mandarin word for "apricot"; the Cantonese *see mui* (crack seed); or from *tsampoy*, a Filipino treat of salted fruit.
11. Nonaka, the memoirist studied in Chapter 1, opened a toy factory in Mexico City, and the Kasuga family (of the poet studied in Chapter 3) started an inflatable plastic toy business in the late 1950s. It was so successful that they ended up exporting to other Latin American countries.
12. Ultraman was a popular Japanese *tokusatsu* science fiction television series created by Eiji Tsuburaya in 1966–1967. Its hero, also named Ultraman, became a pop culture phenomenon in Japan.
13. See my "Worlding and Decolonizing the Literary World-System: Asian–Latin American Literature as an Alternative Type of *Weltliteratur*" (2018).
14. As the literary scholar Ignacio Sánchez-Prado notes, Latin America has the "paradoxical status of belonging both to the Global South (or the Third World, or the postcolonial world) and to Western culture" (2018, 8).
15. See my *Imaging the Chinese in Cuban Literature and Culture*; *The Affinity of the Eye: Writing Nikkei in Peru* (2013); *Dragons in the Land of the Condor: Writing Tusán in Peru* (2014); and *Japanese Brazilian Saudades: Diasporic Identities and Cultural Production*.
16. This is the case with much of the fiction by the Mexican author Mario Bellatin (1960), for instance, as I explain in "The Death of the Author through False Translation in Mario Bellatin's Orientalized Japan" (2013). For other examples, see my "Biopolitics, Orientalism, and the Asian Immigrant as Monster in Salazar's *La medianoche del japonés* and Rodríguez's (2021) *Asesinato en una lavandería china*."
17. "México fue visto como un lugar de gran esperanza por sus vastos territorios, clima templado y actitud amistosa hacia los japoneses, además de que no había prejuicios raciales contra ellos. Con frecuencia se dijo que ambos pueblos pertenecían a la misma familia ancestral" (as quoted by Nakatani Sánchez 2002, 48).
18. For more information on the dark episode of the deportation of Nikkei in Peru to internment camps in the United States, see the first chapter of my book *The Affinity of the Eye: Writing Nikkei in Peru* (2013).

19. The pejorative term *coolie*, which originally referred to unskilled hired workers in India, China, and East Asia, was later applied to Chinese and other Asian emigrant contract laborers employed by colonial powers, particularly after the abolition of the black slave trade. Although I am aware of the derogative origin of the term, I write it in quotations only the first time I use it in the study.
20. In his biography *Casi un siglo de recuerdos* (Almost a Century of Memories, 1994), Federico Imamura recalls: "Many Japanese left the coal mining area. Some had well-established businesses like those of certain furniture makers from Monclova that I remember. The entire area suffered the closings of certain businesses or the hasty transfer of owners of others, thereby exacerbating unemployment" ("Muchos japoneses salimos de la zona carbonífera, algunos tenían negocios bien establecidos como unos muebleros de Monclova que recuerdo, así que la zona entera resintió el cierre o el cambio apresurado de varios negocios agudizándose el desempleo") (Murray 1994, 194). Likewise, Selfa Chew, in *Mudas las garzas*, records how the village of Palau, in Coahuila, never recovered after the Japanese were relocated: "The Japanese-owned businesses stayed closed" (2007, 98).
21. "Al parecer, el gobierno mexicano y el norteamericano lo conservaron como rehén para cangearlo por ciudadanos de los países aliados atrapados en Japón al estallar la guerra" (Hernández Galindo 2011, 109).
22. "Reconocemos que no es justo que pueblos como el chino, que bajo el santo consejo de la moral confuciana se multiplican como los ratones, vengan a degradar la condición humana justamente en los instantes en que comenzamos a comprender que la inteligencia sirve para refrenar y regular bajos instintos zoológicos, contrarios a un concepto verdaderamente religioso de la vida... Las señoritas de San Francisco se han negado a bailar con oficiales de la marina japonesa, que son hombres tan aseados, inteligentes y, a su manera, tan bellos, como los de cualquiera otra marina del mundo. Sin embargo, ellas jamás comprenderán que un japonés pueda ser bello" (Vasconcelos 1948, 29).
23. Much to the dismay of the Chinese emperor, it included children: "In 1744, Emperor Qianlong forbade all the Chinese and Portuguese in Macau from selling children. Nevertheless, the sale continued. Chinese men, women, and children were sent aboard vessels that stopped in Lisbon, along other entrepôts on Spanish and Portuguese world trade circuits, including Mexico and Brazil"(Lee 2018, 29–30).
24. In June 1873, Peru was the first Latin American country to establish diplomatic relations with Japan, but on unequal terms.
25. Viscount Enomoto Takeaki was Japan's foreign minister when the two countries established diplomatic relations. Enomoto, a samurai and former admiral of the Tokugawa shogunate's navy, fought against the Meiji government but later served in it, becoming a founder of the Imperial Japanese Navy. He actively encouraged emigration to settler colonies in the Pacific Ocean and the

Americas by creating a section for emigration within the Foreign Ministry. Later, he helped create the private Colonial Association to encourage further emigration abroad.

26. "Llegaron a México alrededor de 10,000 japoneses. Por otra parte, los japoneses que habían arribado a Estados Unidos fueron objeto de leyes discriminatorias y ello fomentó el flujo de estos a México" (Falck Reyes 2020, 22).

27. "Aderezaron las revueltas con su valentía y heroísmo en el anonimato" (Suárez 2019, n.p.). Besides Fusaichi Otakara, Emanuel Suárez mentions Kisaburo Yamane, who joined Victoriano Huerta's army in 1911, and afterward joined Venustiano Carranza's forces as a military telegrapher. He was promoted three times. He also fought for Álvaro Obregón's army.

28. "En México se publicaron en total cuatro periódicos japoneses entre 1925 y 1941: el Nichiboku Shimbum, el Mehiko Shimpō, el Mekishiko Shimpō y el Mehiko Jihō. Es posible que haya habido uno más en Veracruz en 1935" (Miura 2018, 7).

29. In *Mudas las garzas*, Chew mentions a group of approximately fifty Nikkeijin interned at Rancho Villa Aldana, in Chihuahua. "Deprived of food and sanitary conditions," they sent a letter to the Mexican president requesting to be allowed to relocate to Mexico City at their own expense (Chew 2007, 118).

30. "Justificar las medidas discriminatorias y represivas contra los migrantes y atemorizar a la población para que se sumara a la lucha contra Japón" (Hernández Galindo 2011, 30).

31. In his biography, Federico Imamura mentions several of these individuals, some of them elderly, whose lives were destroyed by the forced relocation.

32. For more information on the Japanese Brazilian terrorist group Shindō Renmei's intraethnic violence against those in the community who publicly acknowledged Japan's defeat in World War II, see chapter 4 of my book *Japanese Brazilian Saudades: Diasporic Identities and Cultural Production* (2019).

33. Similar patterns arose throughout Latin America. Although the Peruvian Marxist thinker and activist José Carlos Mariátegui (1971, 1994) presented the Chinese university system as a model to follow and celebrated the cultural progress led by the nationalist movement in mainland China, his image of overseas Chinese living in Peru during the 1920s was quite negative. The predisposition to admire the achievements of modern Asian nations but not those of Asian immigrants has also been pointed out by Cristina Rocha in her study of Zen Buddhism in Brazil. She argues that, whereas Brazilian writers faithfully followed European Orientalists' interpretations of Japanese culture, including those of Buddhism and haiku, they ignored Brazilian Nikkeijin's Buddhist practices and haiku writing as a potential direct source of knowledge: "While the Brazilian cultural elite were drawn toward fantasies of lost wisdom in ancient Japanese classical ages long past, they did not view Japanese immigrants in Brazil as legitimate carriers of this heritage" (2013, 201).

34. For more information on how Asian fictional characters sometimes feel overworked, exploited, and imprisoned in their own ethnic communities, see my 2020 article "The Nikkei Community as Prison in Higashide's *Adios to Tears* and Yamashita's *Brazil-Maru*."
35. "El Sr. Baba, nuestro propio paisano, se aprovechaba del desamparo y la necesidad de nosotros pues como dije solo podíamos ingresar al país si contábamos con un permiso y un ofrecimiento de trabajo . . . explotando a varios jóvenes japoneses que trabajaban para él, le producía sin duda buenas ganancias, ya que no nos pagaba ni sueldo ni prestación alguna. Estábamos atrapados" (Murray 1994, 65). This is also explored by the Chinese Peruvian Siu Kam Wen in his novels *La vida no es una tómbola* (*This Sort of Life*, 2008) and *El verano largo* (The Long Summer, 2009), among other writings, as well as by the Japanese Peruvian Seiichi Higashide in his memoirs *Adios to Tears* (1981) and Karen Tei Yamashita in her novel *Brazil-Maru* (1992). For more information, see my "The Nikkei Community as Prison in Higashide's *Adios to Tears* and Yamashita's *Brazil-Maru*" (2020).

CHAPTER 1

1. Shinpei Takeda's *El México más cercano a Japón* made the official selection of the Los Angeles Asian Pacific Film Festival, BorDocs Film Festival, and Canada International Film Festival. He has written and filmed about Japanese Mexicans and Burmese refugees, and he directed another documentary focusing on atomic bomb survivors living in Latin America. His films have been shown at various festivals, including the Nippon Connection in Frankfurt in 2011.
2. Daniel Salinas Basave has collaborated with publications such as *Síntesis.tv*, *San Diego Red*, and *El Norte de Monterrey*, and was cofounder of *Diario Frontera de Tijuana*. He has received many awards, most recently the Certamen Internacional de Literatura "Sor Juana Inés de la Cruz" in 2015 for his essay "Bajo la luz de una estrella muerta."
3. Reyes Estrada, in her novel *La gallina azul*, based on interviews with Japanese Mexicans, also mentions how an Issei named Zenzo Yamada joined the revolutionary forces during the Mexican Revolution and became cavalry lieutenant in the Guillermo Prieto Brigade (2016, 35).
4. The "Plantación Oaxaqueña," owned by the Tabasco Plantation Company SA, was located fifteen and a half miles from Santa Lucrecia, in the Municipality of Suchilapan, Cantón de Minatitlán, in the State of Veracruz (Secretaría de Fomento, Colonización e Industria 1913, 726).
5. "Al perder de esta manera sus derechos ciudadanos, la población de japoneses fue sometida a procesos de represión selectiva y a acusaciones en masa desde señalarlos personas *non gratae* hasta considerarlos espías del imperio japonés . . . fue tratada como un ejército de quintacolumnistas bajo las órdenes del imperio japonés que planeaba una invasión continental" (Hernández Galindo 2011, 33).

6. According to Jerry García, Nonaka became "one of the few Japanese officially recognized and awarded medals for his contribution to the Mexican Revolution" (2014, 58).
7. "Nonaka vive en paz y sin rencores con México aunque nadie le pidió perdón o siquiera una disculpa por haberlo sacado de su casa y obligado a dejar Tijuana" (Salinas Basave 2019, 227).
8. "Suele arriesgar la vida como un soldado más y su carreta ambulancia se abre paso entre un enjambre de balas perdidas" (Salinas Basave 2019, 19).
9. The *ama* ("sea women") gatherers or Japanese divers were women who could dive to depths of thirty feet and hold their breath for up to two minutes. For four hours a day, they would dive naked or wearing a loincloth or white diving costume in search of abalone, octopus, lobster, sea urchin, seaweed, and pearls. Many of these women were divers until old age. The tradition is believed to be more than two thousand years old.
10. For Salinas Basave, his work is "a tribute to the emigrant. Tijuana is an emigrant city" ("Un tributo al migrante, Tijuana es una ciudad migrante" (Martínez 2019, n.p.).
11. For an analysis of Herbert's work, see my "Necropolítica, espectrología china e impunidad en *La casa del dolor ajeno* de Julián Herbert" (2019).
12. "El gobierno mexicano advertía de una supuesta invasión japonesa con el objeto de que la población apoyara la política norteamericana y aceptara una alianza estratégica con ese país; alianza que no era bien vista por la mayoría de la población" (Hernández Galindo 2011, 30).
13. "Con mucha tristeza por dejar el terruño y más que nada a mis padres y hermanos, salí de Japón en compañía de Yinkuro, mi hermano mayor, y de mi tío Shiotaro M. Nonaka, hermano de mi papá, en un barco de ruta Japón-Panamá, con escala en Hawái y Salina Cruz, México. La razón de este viaje no era la aventura, sino la necesidad económica, debido al desmedido crecimiento de la población. Durante el viaje casi no sentíamos cansancio, por tantas ilusiones y proyectos que planeábamos" (Nonaka 2014, 15).
14. "Una suerte de barrendero zen" (Salinas Basave 2019, 77).
15. "A falta de personal médico y de estar observando el trabajo de los cirujanos, aprendí cómo usar el bisturí y a suturar heridas, o hacer curaciones a pacientes recién operados, sin descansar, sin dormir o dormir unas horas, sin días de descanso, sin días de fiestas nacionales, sin fiestas de fin de año, sin días de semana santa" (Nonaka 2014, 20–22).
16. "A menudo resultan ser más eficientes y trabajadores que los mexicanos" (Salinas Basave 2019, 64).
17. "El gobierno norteamericano no obstaculizaba mayormente el flujo de armas" (Nonaka 2014, 32).
18. "Tome el dinero, y además, usted, doctor, se viene con nosotros, y será nuestro doctor, así es que póngase su saco y su sombrero, y vámonos" (Nonaka 2014, 31).
19. "Vámonos, la Patria necesita gente como usted, doctor" (Nonaka 2014, 31).

20. "Al día siguiente que llegamos ya casi estaba por iniciarse el mes de mayo, y los maderistas comandados por Pascual Orozco y Francisco Villa estaban preparándose para atacar la plaza. La mañana del día 8 de mayo empezó el tiroteo (esta fue la única vez que actué como soldado, en acciones posteriores estuve incorporado al servicio médico)" (Nonaka 2014, 34–35).
21. "Recuerdo cuando [Madero] quiso tomar la plaza de Casas Grandes, aparte de la tropa revolucionaria, traía como unas cien personas tipo campesinos, armados con escopetas, rifles calibre 22, carabinas 30-30 y otros con machetes. Sin embargo, cuando los maderistas cruzaron el río Bravo a tomar la plaza de Ciudad Juárez, había más de mil hombres perfectamente armados, eran de distintas nacionalidades, como italianos, alemanes, mexicanos, americanos blancos, afroamericanos y tejanos" (Nonaka 2014, 35–36).
22. "Yo soy jefe de un grupo, y nos estamos matando unos a otros de la misma raza, pero ellos pertenecen al ejército federal, a la gente de Porfirio Díaz, el dictador, y para él, los mexicanos no tenemos garantías, ni justicia ni igualdad, somos esclavos de los ricos extranjeros y entre nosotros los mexicanos tenemos gente muy competente para desempeñar cualquier trabajo por delicado que sea, pero para el presidente Díaz, que apoya sólo a los ricos extranjeros, los mexicanos no existimos. Por eso estamos matando a los partidarios y a la gente de Porfirio Díaz. ¿Me entendió, mi doctor Nonaka?" (Nonaka 2014, 63–64).
23. "Cada doctor que tenga o esté trabajando en un consultorio, si no se presenta en una hora, será clausurado su consultorio y también perderá su cédula profesional, así es que mande usted a miembros de la tropa de su confianza a que hagan efectiva la orden" (Nonaka 2014, 38).
24. "Confío en usted, señor Nonaka. Desde que me curó la herida en Casas Grandes supe que usted no me fallaría. Sé bien que el hospital se queda en buenas manos" (Salinas Basave 2019, 97).
25. "Y ahora, mi capitán Nonaka . . . muchachito, quiero que aquí el general Máximo García te dé una carta donde te nombra como Jefe Principal de los dos trenes, para el conocimiento de todos los trabajadores que viajan en los trenes, para que te obedezcan y te respeten, te recomiendo que tengas mucho cuidado con los heridos. Nos vemos en Ciudad Juárez . . . mi Doctor Nonaka" (Nonaka 2014, 42).
26. "Nonaka es comisionado a la Brigada Madero como jefe de enfermeros, tiene 18 personas a su cargo y su superior jerárquico es Máximo García, el director del hospital en Ciudad Juárez" (Salinas Basave 2019, 117).
27. "Antes de terminar, el general Villa nos dijo:
—No voy de regreso a Columbus con los gringos, porque me viene siguiendo el general Pershing. Es gringo y viene con muchos soldados. Por favor, no vayas a entregar los heridos a los americanos. El señor cura ya sabe todo, le expliqué lo mismo que a ti; confío en ti, porque sólo tú eres firme, muchachito. Hasta otra vista. —Y se fue con su gente" (Nonaka 2014, 47).

28. "Hacerle un favor al fugitivo más buscado puede costarle la vida al recién casado" (Salinas Basave 2019, 143).
29. "En el México de 1917 solo vale estar en buenos términos con Obregón y con Carranza" (Salinas Basave 2019, 152).
30. "Faltó dinero, pero tan pronto como llegue a la ciudad de Chihuahua se los mando, y también voy solucionar su problema, se los prometo. Al cabo de ocho días llegó el dinero, $200.00 para cada doctor. A mí me mandó un oficio felicitándome por mi buen servicio y $500.00 en una bolsita de lona" (Nonaka 2014, 59).
31. "Salvé vidas de oficiales, soldados y civiles, yo calculo que fueron un poco más de dos mil personas. Trabajé en hospitales o en los campos de batalla como enfermero de la Cruz Roja, sin descansar fines de semana o días festivos . . . a cada enfermero le tocaban más de 40 heridos a cada uno, a mí me tocaban mucho más, porque decían que yo era más cuidadoso y no tan brusco en las curaciones" (Nonaka 2014, 60–61).
32. "Ese enfermero delgadito de ojos rasgados y cara de niño es una suerte de ángel redentor que busca la mirada de los heridos cuando les pide confianza y fortaleza o simplemente toma con firmeza sus manos para ayudarlos a bien morir" (Salinas Basave 2019, 114).
33. "Siendo de los de abajo, en donde se trabaja mucho por poco dinero, está en contra de la brutal explotación del hombre por el hombre, sigue deseoso de transformarse en líder de una causa que redima a la clase a la que pertenecen él, los pobres y olvidados de la sociedad, y si existe alguien más que luche por un país más justo, será una persona a seguir, así Villa sigue de cerca la figura y las ideas de Francisco I. Madero y se le une" (Nonaka 2014, 63).
34. See the video posted on YouTube by the Secretaría de Cultura de Chihuahua, "Presentación del libro El samurái de la Gráflex, de Daniel Salinas Basave," October 31, 2020, https://www.youtube.com/watch?v=NMmQHHAQSkE.
35. Edited by Jesús Vargas Valdés himself under the title *Máximo Castillo y la Revolución en Chihuahua* (Máximo Castillo and the Revolution in Chihuahua, 2004).
36. "A partir de entonces Estados Unidos consideró a Japón como rival militar y a la migración japonesa en el continente americano un serio problema, 'un nuevo peligro amarillo' mucho más peligroso que el que representaban los migrantes chinos" (Hernández Galindo 2011, 24).
37. "Es un legado importantísimo. Da una nueva perspectiva sobre la ciudad de Tijuana, que históricamente ha estado vinculada con la leyenda negra. Las fotos de Nonaka, de 1923 a 1942, nos muestran una Tijuana diferente, centrada en manifestaciones culturales, cívicas, deportivas, y cómo se transforma de pueblo a ciudad . . . Antes de 1923, cuando abre su primer estudio, toda la fotografía de Tijuana es turística, por turistas y reporteros. Pero gracias a las fotos de Nonaka hoy podemos reescribir la historia de Tijuana y presentarla desde otro punto de vista. Él registró que Tijuana tenía inquietudes sociales y culturales" (De Ávila 2015, n.p.).

38. "Sus imágenes se han constituido en clásicas para conocer la Tijuana de ese periodo" (Rivera Delgado 2014, 7).
39. "No sabía nada de fotografía, solo iba aprendiendo, le buscó la manera, es increíble lo que hizo con sus primeras fotos, me dijo alguna vez que él quería que se viera en ellas a Tijuana como se mira a través de una ventana y que los turistas dejaran de hablar mal de ella" ("Lanza Daniel Salinas libro" 2019 n.p.).
40. "Encarna el mito fundacional de Tijuana" (Salinas Basave 2019, 26).
41. "Para los gobiernos del continente, esta población, sin importar edad ni sexo, fue tratada como un ejército de quintacolumnistas bajo las órdenes del imperio japonés que planeaba una invasión continental. Es importante señalar que un gran porcentaje de esta población había nacido en los países que los alojaron y no hablaba fluidamente el idioma japonés" (Hernández Galindo 2011, 33).
42. "Al valor de los jóvenes militares mexicanos que murieron durante la invasión norteamericana a México en 1847 en el castillo de Chapultepec" (Hernández Galindo 2011, 28).
43. "Revelaron los intereses imperiales de Japón en la zona y aceleraron la descomposición de las relaciones entre ambas potencias" (Hernández Galindo 2011, 44).
44. "Los puentes naturales para desarrollar los contactos comerciales que Japón necesitaba en los países donde radicaban" (Hernández Galindo 2011, 43).
45. "De repente, sus ojos rasgados lo han transformado en el villano de la historia, el agente secreto, el sospechoso, el espía al servicio del emperador Hirohito de quien es preciso cuidarse" (Salinas Basave 2019, 213).
46. "A lo de Guadalajara el gobierno no quiere llamarle campo de concentración, pero la verdad no se le puede denominar de otra forma" (Salinas Basave 2019, 219).
47. "Sólo había dos limitaciones: no traspasar el perímetro que el mismo gobierno había señalado para cada una de las casas de concentración, y no transitar de noche. Y nos entregó a cada familia un mapa con el área marcada de la que, nos advirtió, teníamos prohibido salir o seríamos consignados a las autoridades o llevados directamente a prisión" (Reyes Estrada 2016, 72).
48. "Kingo está quebrado por dentro, emocionalmente devastado. Nunca imaginó que el ejército mexicano le pagaría de esa forma y que Cárdenas no respondería a sus llamados" (Salinas Basave 2019, 220).
49. "Aquella purga anti-japonesa es un acto vilmente racista y anticonstitucional, pues las garantías constitucionales de ciudadanos mexicanos están siendo pisoteadas" (Salinas Basave 2019, 218).
50. "Kingo Nonaka es un mexicano con todas las de la ley, que ha vivido dos terceras partes de su vida en México y tiene una esposa y cinco hijos mexicanos. Hace 35 años dejó de vivir en Japón, habla español perfectamente y en esa lengua piensa y escribe. Cierto, nunca ha renegado de su origen ni de sus antepasados, pero Kingo Nonaka no tiene nada que ver con esa guerra imperialista ni se regocija con el ataque a Pearl Harbor" (Salinas Basave 2019, 217).

51. "En Estados Unidos, décadas después de la guerra, el gobierno reconoció los errores jurídicos y morales causados por la concentración y el despojo del que fueron objeto los inmigrantes, les pidió una disculpa pública y les otorgó una indemnización. En México hasta la fecha no ha ocurrido nada semejante" (Hernández Galindo 2011, 59–60).
52. "La actitud de los japoneses migrantes frente a su país de origen y frente a la guerra es un fenómeno muy complejo que debe ser estudiado con cuidado, pues podemos encontrar una enorme diversidad de posiciones y sentimientos que incluso dividieron fuertemente a las comunidades japonesas en el continente" (Hernández Galindo 2011, 30).
53. "Finalmente, la espada del samurái cae al suelo y el Emperador firma la rendición incondicional. Kingo Nonaka se sumerge en el mutismo y durante varios días no pronuncia palabra" (Salinas Basave 2019, 223).
54. "En su vejez recibirá condecoraciones y el homenaje del gobierno que en algún momento lo persiguió" (Salinas Basave 2019, 15).

CHAPTER 2

1. See Sidney Xu Lu's *The Making of Japanese Settler Colonialism: Malthusianism and Trans-Pacific Migration, 1868–1961*. See also my forthcoming article "Were Issei in Brazil Imperialists? Migration-Driven Expansionism in Nikkei Literature."
2. "Fueron leídos por los propios japoneses, que se convencieron de que podían presentarse ante Occidente de esa manera" (Funabiki 2017, 59).
3. Emma Nakatani, in an interview with Yoshigei Nakatani's daughter-in-law Mercedes Martínez Torres, learned that, unlike many of his compatriots, he never became a Mexican citizen out of loyalty to Japan. Yet he would tell Mercedes: "I am more Mexican than Japanese.... When I hear the Mexican national anthem and I see the Mexican flag go by, I become very emotional and I want to cry; I feel much more emotion than when I see the Japanese flag" ("Yo soy más mexicano que japonés... Cuando oigo el himno nacional mexicano y veo pasar la bandera mexicana, siento mucha emoción y quiero llorar; siento mucha más emoción que cuando veo la bandera japonesa"; Nakatani Sánchez 2002, 84).
4. "Tu padre tiene bien merecido ese reconocimiento. El jamoncillo que él y tu madre introdujeron en la zona ha dado de comer a mucha gente; se establecieron negocios que florecieron teniendo como negocio principal precisamente el jamoncillo, que se reconoce como emblema del lugar" (Reyes Estrada 2016, 196).
5. "Los japoneses estamos hechos para sufrir, para enfrentar las pruebas estoicamente, no podemos llorar ni gemir, debemos enfrentar las pruebas que nos impone la vida con serenidad y paciencia, yo no podía llorar entonces y mi madre menos aún... Con esa serenidad entregaban las madres japonesas a sus hijos, por miles, para salir al frente a morir en los conflictos armados del Japón" (Murray 1994, 47).

6. "Sabía también que si fracasaban mis planes buscaría, en honor a mis antepasados, la forma de morir por mi propia mano y con dignidad, en cuyo caso tampoco regresaría. La posibilidad de regresar derrotado al Japón tampoco era posible, sería señalado e indigno y rechazado por siempre por los míos" (Murray 1994, 46). Imamura repeats this idea a few pages later: "After all, we Japanese are used to traveling with a one-way ticket only. There is no possibility of return or failure for us. We must always triumph or honorably die with for our ideas" ("Después de todo los japoneses estamos acostumbrados a viajar solo con pasaje de ida, no existe para nosotros la posibilidad del retorno o el fracaso, debemos de triunfar o morir con honor por nuestras ideas siempre"; Murray 1994, 53).
7. "Quería hacer fortuna porque no podría morir sin regresar a mi tierra" (Nakatani Sánchez 2002, 265).
8. "Como hombre de bien; es decir, como un hombre que logró cumplir con los valores inculcados en su infancia, a pesar de haber salido de su país natal a los 22 años de edad" (Nakatani Sánchez 2002, 8).
9. In my article "Were Issei in Brazil Imperialists?," I argue that the creation of Shindō Renmei is the missing link between imperialism and migration-driven expansionism.
10. "Yo hacía el propósito de no ir porque Zuyako se estaba cansando, pero ellos me iban a buscar y yo caía en la tentación" (Nakatani Sánchez 2002, 175).
11. "Nosotros seguíamos jugando, en ocasiones dejábamos de trabajar tres días; nos confiábamos porque ya trabajaban obreros mexicanos, les habíamos enseñado y jugando de vez en cuando íbamos a inspeccionar si trabajaban bien los muchachos" (Nakatani Sánchez 2002, 213).
12. "Nadie quería trabajar" (Nakatani Sánchez 2002, 248).
13. "Los japoneses concentrados, unos luchaban en buscar la manera de vivir, otros, lo poco que traían lo terminaban en el juego" (Nakatani Sánchez 2002, 249).
14. "En 5 de febrero había una escuela japonesa para recaudar fondos, para su sostenimiento hacían fiestas continuas, los niños bailaban y los padres ofrecían sobres con dinero ... Mis hijos y mi esposa también lo hacían, les regalaban sobres con dinero, pero yo los entregaba para beneficio de la escuela: así cooperaba y nunca invitaron a mis hijos para que ahí cursaran su primaria" (Nakatani Sánchez 2002, 259).
15. "¿Por qué mi padre tenía ese corazón tan criminal?" (Nakatani Sánchez 2002, 109). Eventually, Kigey does provide for the family, even though he continues to humiliate his wife by inviting one of his lovers to his birthday party. On occasions, Kigey behaves like a good father: when Nakatani falls seriously sick, he unexpectedly pays him a visit and spends two nights caring for him.
16. "La gente que trabajaba en esas fábricas como ganaban bien cogían malos vicios, la mayoría de estos obreros venían de Osaka, eran personas maduras por eso mi madre me llamó para que regresara al restaurante, ella sabía que los que trabajaban el botón siempre terminaban mal" (Nakatani Sánchez 2002, 134).

17. "Soy menor de edad y por ese motivo no me gusta intervenir pero siempre veo en mi padre y en mi hermano un espectáculo inmoral" (Nakatani Sánchez 2002, 138).
18. "Una noche, el más viejo de todos me despertó dándome una patada y me dijo, 'he perdido todo mi dinero y quiero que tú juegues en mi lugar, creo que por ser primera vez tengas suerte,' yo le dije, 'no sé jugar,' 'yo te dirijo.' Esta fue la primera vez que yo cogía una baraja, esto fue lo que ocasionó mi desgracia, toda una amargura de mi vida y todo el sufrimiento de mi familia por muchos años" (Nakatani Sánchez 2002, 148).
19. For example, all Nikkei workers at the button factory where he worked left or were fired; a man named Yokohama plagiarizes his countryman's invention formula; other relatives and acquaintances are gamblers, thieves, or alcoholics who abandon their children; a man named Tsuru betrays Japan by committing fraud in the Mexican oil industry; and an employee of the Japanese embassy in Mexico steals the guns kept there "para una emergencia" ("for an emergency") (Nakatani Sánchez 2002, 236) to sell them at the market.
20. "Aquí hay muchos japoneses y han empezado a murmurar, dicen que ellos tienen mucho tiempo de radicar en Mazatlán y han trabajado honradamente, que aquí todos los respetan y que ahora llega gente de su raza a ponernos en mal y que no lo van a permitir" (Nakatani Sánchez 2002, 240).
21. "[Nakagaki] un día llegó y me dijo, 'Tengo ganas de ir a jugar,' me enseñó $500 que traía, era casi fin de año, 'señor Nakatani, usted conoce esos lugares, lléveme.' Yo no quería pero él insistía" (Nakatani Sánchez 2002, 274).
22. "Este día no pude cantar, mi pensamiento en el problema de estas mujeres y pensaba 'si no las ayudo jamás podrán salir de ese infierno', por eso yo estaba dispuesto pero tenía miedo, en ese entonces había gente mala" (Nakatani Sánchez 2002, 162).
23. "Sentí obligación de ayudarlo pues era el padrino de mi cuarta hija" (Nakatani Sánchez 2002, 249).
24. "Ahora que llegaste tú y tu esposa y haz [sic] hecho tan buena obra las cosas cambiaron, haz [sic] vuelto a realzar nuestro apellido" (Nakatani Sánchez 2002, 297).
25. "Aquí en este lago se suicidan muchos muchachos por amor" (Nakatani Sánchez 2002, 167).
26. "En Japón existe una leyenda de este animal, no se puede ver pero la gente que se orinaba a donde estaba la cría del Tanuki se vengaba y se apoderaba del cuerpo de la persona, los doctores no curaban este mal. Yo seguía con temperatura demasiado alta, le decía a mi mamá que quería comer arroz y frijoles pero el que pedía eso era el Tanuki porque en mis ratos de lucidez no recordaba nada" (Nakatani Sánchez 2002, 114).
27. In Japan *itako*, also known as *ichiko* or *ogamisama*, are blind women who train to become spiritual mediums through severe ascetic practices. They practice divination and communicate with *kami* (Japanese Shinto spirits) and the spirits of the dead.

28. "Tanto tiempo comí arroz y lo que me gustaba y ahora me voy" (Nakatani Sánchez 2002, 115).
29. The literary school of *costumbrismo* arose in nineteenth-century Spain. *Costumbrista* authors tried to interpret, often from a moralizing, critical, or satiric perspective, the mannerisms, customs, local color, folklore, and daily life of Spaniards.
30. "En Japón en cada barrio había grupos de chicos rebeldes y les gustaba pelear contra grupos contrarios pero se turnaban y únicamente peleaban dos y al que ganaba lo hacían jefe del grupo" (Nakatani Sánchez 2002, 177).
31. "Junto a él había un jarrón con ceniza y ardía, eso era una costumbre en Japón, entre la ceniza se ponía una especie de plancha para que siempre estuviera caliente y poderla ocupar para desarrugar las solapas de un quimono" (Nakatani Sánchez 2002, 146). Throughout the memoirs, Nakatani takes time to explain the differences between Japanese and Mexican customs. We learn that, in Japan, instead of knocking on the door, people would loudly announce their presence; couples were considered married (common-law) after cohabitating for two years; Nikkei immigrants would fall from beds because they were used to sleeping on tatami mats, thin mattresses, or floor cushions; they would ceremoniously pour sake instead of holy water on the new factory machinery; they gave money in envelopes to friends traveling abroad; they ate red snapper at farewell parties; and they wore a wool girdle to prevent abdominal pain. He also explains the customs of attending public baths (*onsen*) and having Buddhist family altars (*butsudan*) at home.
32. "De dos pueblos venían como 150 alumnos pero estos niños viviendo en Japón, llevaban sangre coreana. Hace siglos de parte del imperio fueron a visitar a este país trayendo aproximadamente como 20 personas para ocuparlos en trabajos humillantes; a lo largo del tiempo esta raza aumentó, ya eran aproximadamente como medio millón pero estaban repartidos en todo Japón buscando su propia vida. Esta gente cuando tienen familia no pueden registrarla como raza japonesa y a estas personas se les da el nombre de Shingemin; llevando este apodo y cuando había discusiones con ellos se desquitaban llamándoles por Shingemin, yo que llevaba más amistad con ellos pensaba por qué habían tanta distinción, me dolía tanta ofensa" (Nakatani Sánchez 2002, 113–14).
33. "Para ver si logran liberarse de ese infierno" (Nakatani Sánchez 2002, 167).
34. "Me entristeció ver cómo a diario golpeaban a los coreanos porque faltaban al trabajo, y yo decía dentro de mí 'por qué los japoneses tratan de esa forma a esa pobre gente'" (Nakatani Sánchez 2002, 168).
35. "Yo me sorprendí porque eran negros hombres muy grandes y fuertes y muy gruesos y los trataban muy mal; yo pensé cómo era posible que hubiera tanta distinción y me dolía el alma" (Nakatani Sánchez 2002, 204).
36. "Pequeña pero había mucha unión" (Nakatani Sánchez 2002, 217).
37. "Hay ocasiones en que estas mujeres no llegan a su destino, en el barco se llegan a enamorar de algún pasajero y huyen con él; por este motivo, nunca

vienen solas, sean señoras o señoritas. También se han suscitado suicidios, se arrojan al mar" (Nakatani Sánchez 2002, 203). Similarly, in Reyes Estrada's novel *La gallina azul*, we learn about a picture bride Akira who, even though she was already married before departing, fell in love with a man named Takumi who was emigrating to Brazil and later became pregnant by him (Reyes Estrada 2016, 45–46). By contrast, Selfa A. Chew, in *Mudas las garzas*, speculates: "The women who had married a figure printed on paper wondered if their husband in the flesh would be handsome, thin, strong, sweet, austere, as he looked in his photo. To several, that made no difference. It was the change of scenery, the emotion of entering an unknown world that had made them accept their marriages. Within a month's journey, all of them had raised their hopes for a better life in America" (2007, 46).

38. "Mutaguchi ganaba bastante y todos los días eran banquetes en su casa. Su esposa se llamaba Victoria, yo la admiraba, era una mujer muy prudente cuando su esposo estaba en la mesa con sus invitados, ella siempre estaba en la cocina esperando a que su esposo le pidiese algo, a cada momento la llamaba Toya, se le había hecho una costumbre aunque no la necesitara" (Nakatani Sánchez 2002, 223).

39. "Ya teníamos tres años de casados, mi hijo tenía 2 años y nació una niña, por nombre le pusimos Alicia. A mí no se me quitaba el vicio del juego, me reunía con los paisanos, se me había arraigado tanto el vicio que los fines de semana que era cuando jugaba no llegaba a dormir a mi casa. Mi esposa preocupada hablaba a mis padrinos pensando que ahí estaría, pero ellos le contestaban que no y también se preocupaban" (Nakatani Sánchez 2002, 224).

40. They had seven children, but one of them, Sergio, died of meningitis when he was a year old.

41. "A Emma, que es el nombre de mi esposa, le gusta arreglarse el cabello" (Nakatani Sánchez 2002, 294).

42. Japanese immigrant Seiichi Higashide (1909–1997), author of the memoirs *Adios to Tears*, published in Japanese in 1981, is another notable case, this time in Peru and the United States. According to Hernández Galindo, Masao Imuro also emigrated to Mexico to flee the horrors of war (2011, 108).

43. "En Japón había mucho fanatismo y cuando llegaba el servicio obligatorio los muchachos se sentían hombres responsables y sentían alegría en su alma" (Nakatani Sánchez 2002, 187).

44. "¿Cómo van a salir al extranjero? ¿No saben que la patria necesita soldados?" (Nakatani Sánchez 2002, 190).

45. "Van al extranjero y tienen que triunfar" (Nakatani Sánchez 2002, 191).

46. "Mamá, ya me voy, espero triunfar y regresar, y si no, no podría volver" (Nakatani Sánchez 2002, 192).

47. "Con el tiempo ganó Japón y tomó Formosa, Corea y Manchuria. Con este triunfo Japón creció cincuenta veces más y así Okinawa entró al lado de Japón, y ellos pidieron que se les otorgara la bandera de nuestro país. Desde entonces

ustedes empezaron a aprender el idioma de nosotros. El kimono antes era un poco diferente, pero desde la guerra ahora es igual al de nosotros" (Nakatani Sánchez 2002, 201).

48. "La guerra de China y Japón. Por un lado, estábamos contentos, ganábamos bien, pero nos preocupaba la situación por la que atravesaba Japón" (Nakatani Sánchez 2002, 209).

49. "Ese matrimonio era americano, Nakatani, no me explico cómo pude encontrar a estar personas tan humanas que a pesar de que la política entre Japón y Estados Unidos está muy dura, ellos me ayudaron" (Nakatani Sánchez 2002, 228–29).

50. "A los japoneses que radicábamos en México nos preocupaba, sabíamos que aquí había bastante petróleo pero no se le vendería a Japón y sin esta materia no se podía hacer" (Nakatani Sánchez 2002, 235).

51. "¡Ojara prendió el radio y en las noticias oímos que Japón había bombardeado Hawai. Al escuchar la noticia sentimos una inmensa alegría . . . nos reunimos cuarenta personas, unos ya estaban enterados, otros no lo sabían. Ojara dijo: 'Les hablé porque la situación es seria y tenemos que pensar bien, somos vecinos de Estados Unidos pero México está con Japón; estamos aquí, no hay peligro pero este país es vecino de los americanos, ¿por qué Japón antes de declarar la guerra atacó?'" (Nakatani Sánchez 2002, 244).

52. "Así pasó un mes y con tristeza nos informamos que Japón retrocedía, un submarino japonés cerca de Los Ángeles disparó dos cañonazos pero cayeron en el mar, mucha gente lo vio. Estados Unidos enojado mandó una orden para que México rompiera relaciones con Japón y a nosotros nos tenían que concentrar, esa era la orden" (Nakatani Sánchez 2002, 245).

53. "Asegurar la estabilidad interna a través de la eliminación de la amenaza de una 'quinta columna' adentro de las fronteras del país; calmar el miedo de Estados Unidos a que Japón, directamente o a través de sus súbditos residentes en México, usara territorio mexicano para atacar su territorio; y finalmente para cumplir con las obligaciones contratadas en los acuerdos panamericanos de las décadas de los años treinta del siglo XX y los primeros años de los cuarenta de defender el hemisferio occidental así como promover la cooperación política y económica entre los Estados americanos" (Peddie 2006, 75).

54. "Después de cinco días empezaron a llegar los japoneses de provincias, pero los que más sufrieron fueron los de la Ciudad Juárez, Mexicali y Tijuana, no tuvieron tiempo de vender sus pertenencias; había mucha gente millonaria pero todo lo tenían invertido y efectivo traían poco, sus amistades les voltearon la espalda, les encargaron sus negocios pero ellos pensaron aprovechar la situación. Era el mes de enero, hacía mucho frío y sufrían pobrezas" (Nakatani Sánchez 2002, 246).

55. "Bajo esas condiciones, no todos aguantaron: un bebé y dos ancianos fallecieron en el camino. Los reubicados llegaron a sus destinos sin alimentos, alojamiento, trabajo, cansados, hambrientos y despojados de la vida que habían conocido" (Peddie 2006, 77).

56. Likewise, in Reyes Estrada's *La gallina azul*, the narrator's family feels betrayed by their Mexican neighbors when they are relocated to Guadalajara: the neighbors refuse to take care of their belongings and take advantage of their situation by trying to purchase their truck for very little money.

57. "Para solucionar este problema, Sanshiro Matsumoto 'puso a su disposición la Hacienda Batán de su propiedad,' un terreno en Contreras, al sur del Distrito Federal. Ahí se juntó a aproximadamente cien trasladados que carecían de un lugar para vivir. No obstante, con la llegada constante de más japoneses de los estados fronterizos y costeros, Batán no fue suficientemente grande para acomodarlos a todos. Según una lista sin fecha de la Secretaría de Gobernación, Batán era el hogar temporal de 569 individuos alojados en el edificio de una escuela japonesa ya cerrada, quienes dormían sobre colchones conseguidos por Heiji Kato. Esta situación obligó a los miembros del *Kyoeikai* a buscar una solución permanente; el resultado fue el establecimiento de un campo agrícola en la ex Hacienda de Temixco en el estado de Morelos" (Peddie 2006, 87). The Japanese consul Miura chose three men to lead the *kyoeikai*, or association, known in Spanish as the Comité de Ayuda Mutua: Sanshiro Matsumoto, founder of the flower shop Flor Matsumoto; Heiji Kato, general manager of El Nuevo Japón; and Kiso Tsuru, owner of the oil company La Veracruzana, founded by the Japanese government and the Imperial Army (Peddie 2006, 86). This Heiji Kato is the same one who hired Nakatani and lost all his frozen assets (Peddie 2006, 91).

58. "Delante de Cuernavaca, en un pueblo llamado Temixco, había una refinería pero había dejado de funcionar. Siete capitalistas japoneses lo rentaron y llevaron a gente concentrada que sufría pobreza. Había mucho terreno y pensaron sembrar arroz para aprovechar a esa gente pero les pagaban un sueldo miserable que apenas les alcanzaba para comer . . . tantas personas que sufrían y se aprovechaban porque tenían necesidad" (Nakatani Sánchez 2002, 254).

59. "Cuando salía a la calle siempre se oían comentarios de mi país, unos buenos y otros en contra. Nos unimos más de cinco compañeros para formar un Club de Patriotas, con los días fueron aumentando hasta que llegaron a tres mil entre mujeres y niños" (Nakatani Sánchez 2002, 251). Zenzo Yamada, in Reyes Estrada's *La gallina azul*, along with several other Nikkeijin, also refuses to believe that Japan has surrendered.

60. "Los japoneses que regresaron a Japón fracasaron y los que se quedaron en México, lograron hacer fortuna" (Nakatani Sánchez 2002, 259).

61. "Ahora, para mi desgracia, encontré una casa de juego de chinos en las calles de Dolores; ningún japonés iba a ese lugar, únicamente yo. Era gente desalmada, se drogaban, no sé de dónde sacaban dinero para jugar" (Nakatani Sánchez 2002, 282).

62. "Cuando concentraron a mi familia en México, el gobierno de Estados Unidos mandó muchos soldados a este lugar como vigilancia. Esta casa fue prefabricada para los soldados. Cuando terminó la guerra a mi padre le entregaron

el terreno y la casa la dejaron; aquí sembró mi padre y ganó mucho dinero" (Nakatani Sánchez 2002, 269).

63. "Tanaka tenía el rancho más grande y suficiente dinero, por eso se sentía importante y quería dominar a todos los que lo rodeaban" (Nakatani Sánchez 2002, 270).

64. "Pero el vicio aumentó, con la derrota de Japón muchos paisanos tomaban y jugaban; cuando Japón era Imperio todos trabajaban mucho y con ánimo por su país. Ahora sí hay quien trabaja, tienen buenas empresas y lo hacen para aumentar su capital" (Nakatani Sánchez 2002, 276).

65. "Ahora que Japón perdió se olvidaron de su patria" (Nakatani Sánchez 2002, 285).

66. "Yo aprendí a cantar esa que tú me has oído en algunas reuniones con tu papá . . . 'Aishinkoku,' era como cuarentaitantas estrofas, una canción bélica que lanza a los japoneses adelante, vamos a matar al que se ponga . . . Yo me aprendí las cuarentaitantas estrofas, cada estrofa con cuatro versos . . . Me la enseñó él, ¿para qué?, sí me acuerdo que a veces tenían reuniones entre ellos, entre el grupo de gente que era, que estaba por el lado bélico japonés" (Nakatani Sánchez 2002, 89).

CHAPTER 3

1. The fifteen-minute documentary short *Obachan* (2020), by Nicolasa Ruiz, focuses on the life of another former picture bride in both Mexico and Japan through a mix of original fragments, presented nonchronologically, from family recordings, anime, and Ruiz's own filming. The *obachan*, or grandmother, in the title is Fuku Kiyota. She left Japan in 1941 to marry a Nikkei immigrant in Mexico who was seventeen years her senior.
2. A softer and more polite way of expressing the same idea is *ganbatte*, usually spoken by women. By contrast, *ganbare* is a command and therefore sounds less polite.
3. "Al cruzar el mar / contra lo que decía / mi gente allá" (Kasuga [2015] 2016, 51).
4. "¡Haz lo que tienes que hacer!" (Kasuga [2015] 2016, 51).
5. "Sin los adornos / que se llevan por fuera, / concentrada estoy / en vivir sin mentiras / dentro de mi corazón" (Kasuga [2015] 2016, 52) ("Without the adornments / worn on the outside / I am focused / on living without lies / inside my heart").
6. The Popocatépetl (from the Nahuatl for "smoking mountain") volcano, located about forty-three miles south of Mexico City, is Mexico's second-highest peak.
7. Meaning "picture(s) of the floating world," *ukiyo-e* is a genre of Japanese art, mostly paintings and woodblock prints, which flourished from the seventeenth through the nineteenth centuries.
8. "Más y más mexicana" (Kasuga [2015] 2016, 69).
9. "¡Vamos a cantar juntos, / cantemos abuelita!" (Kasuga [2015] 2016, 92).
10. "Cada vez que el mexicano se confía a un amigo o a un conocido, cada vez que se 'abre,' abdica. Y teme que el desprecio del confidente siga a su entrega. Por

eso, la confidencia deshonra y es tan peligrosa para el que la hace como para el que la escucha ... El que se confía, se enajena; 'me he vendido con Fulano,' decimos cuando nos confiamos a alguien que no lo merece. Esto es, nos hemos 'rajado,' alguien ha penetrado en el castillo fuerte" (Paz 2003, 166).

11. "Ojos que gritan: / ¡Pinches inmigrantes! No vean, / Mejor díganlo" (Kasuga [2015] 2016, 60).
12. A note to one of the poems explains that *yae-zakura* means "multi-layered cherry blossom and is a symbol of strength, as compared to the delicate *sakura* like *sornei yoshiro*" (Kasuga 2016, 83).
13. In reality, it is difficult to translate the concept of *enryo* in a single word because it represents several things in Japanese culture (modesty, sacrifice, hesitation, example) for which there may not be as much emphasis in the Western world. The *Kōjien* provides the definition "restraining speech/actions toward people" (「人に対して言語・行動を控え目にすること」).
14. "La imaginería del *furusato* apelaba a la japonesidad más esencial, evocando nostálgicamente un pasado tradicional que desaparecía sometido a las fuerzas centrífugas de la internacionalización económica, cultural y política" (Guarné 2017, 24).
15. "Un discurso—inequívocamente esencialista—según el cual los japoneses han desarrollado un carácter extremadamente sensible a la naturaleza y una actitud de no oposición, de no resistencia a ella" (61).
16. "Reflexiono y decido / repetirlo a mis hijos" (Funabiki 2017, 23).
17. Incidentally, a similar criticism of Japanese culture resurfaces in Imamura's biography *Casi un siglo de recuerdos*: "I have always instilled in my daughters and my grandchildren that they must live precisely as in Mexico, more fully, in a more natural and humane way. The rigidity and inflexible discipline of Japanese life, after having lived here for so long, leaves us feeling that we exist, but have ceased to live" ("A mis hijas y a mis nietos les he inculcado siempre que vivan precisamente como en México, con más plenitud, en forma más natural y humana. La rigidez y la inflexible disciplina de la vida japonesa, después de haber vivido aquí por tanto tiempo, nos deja la sensación que existimos, pero habiendo dejado de vivir"; Murray 1994, 47–48).
18. "Puedo verlas, bellas son" (Kasuga [2015] 2016, 24).
19. "Conceptos estéticos como *ki* (élan), *iki* (elegancia), *sabi* (simplicidad rústica), *wabi* (rusticidad melancólica) y *mono no aware* (unidad empática) se consideran exclusivos de Japón y, por tanto, exponentes singulares de su cultura" (Befu 2017, 42).
20. In another poem, by contrast, she suddenly feels ashamed of her chapped hands and swiftly hides them from a store clerk.
21. A well-known example of wabi-sabi is *kintsugi*, that is, the use of gold lacquer to repair cracked pottery and highlight damage instead of hiding it.
22. "Si todavía llevo / uno en las entrañas" (Kasuga [2015] 2016, 57).

23. "Nunca mostró sus debilidades" (Chikaba 2016, 11).
24. "¡Soy tan solo una mujer!" (Kasuga [2015] 2016, 56).

CHAPTER 4

1. For additional information, Ueno also conducted numerous interviews with Nikkei descendants—six photographs at the end of the book show the large number of collaborators in Mexico City, Tapachula, Escuintla, and Acacoyagua.
2. This haiku was included in in his masterwork *Oku no Hosomichi* (*The Narrow Road to the Deep North*, 1689).
3. "Hierba de verano / combates de los / héroes / huellas de un / sueño" (Bashō 1966, 17). The original in Japanese: 夏草や兵どもが夢の跡 natsukusa ya tsuwamono-domo ga yume no ato.
4. "El aliento de los antepasados que dejaron su vida en México" (Ueno and Sakuya 2008, 17).
5. In Terui's version, the word *sueño* (dream) is replaced by *un andar* (a walk).
6. A similar approach to the indomitable pride and epic heroism of Nikkei pioneers is found in the 2008 Japanese Brazilian manga *Banzai! História da imigração japonesa no Brasil en mangá* (*Banzai! History of Japanese Immigration in Brazil in Manga*) by Francisco Noriyuki Sato and Julio Shimamoto (2008).
7. "Ustedes son los representantes de Japón. Muestren su fuerza y valentía a los mexicanos" (Ueno and Sakuya 2008, 38).
8. "Siento como que somos como personajes de novela" (Ueno and Sakuya 2008, 23).
9. "¡Vamos a sembrar el espíritu japonés *Yamato* en esta gran tierra mexicana!" (Ueno and Sakuya 2008, 28).
10. "Aquí demostraremos nuestro espíritu japonés *yamato*" (Ueno and Sakuya 2008, 49).
11. "A escola japonesa não é senão o lugar em que se adquire o espírito japonês pelo ensino da língua japonesa. Ademais, a aquisição do espírito japonês deve resultar . . . primeiramente, na continuidade do sistema familial japonês imbuído de grande respeito aos pais e à autoridade do chefe de família" (Tsukamoto 1973, 27–28).
12. "Aquí también quedó arraigado el espíritu japonés en la tierra mexicana" (Ueno and Sakuya 2008, 168).
13. "La entonces virgen" (Ueno and Sakuya 2008, 158).
14. A local farmer in a traditional Mexican sombrero—like, somewhat stereotypically, many of the Mexican characters in the manga—has to explain which crops are more suitable for the terrain and the proper season for planting. Their unfamiliarity with coffee-growing techniques is highlighted by the fact that the first time they drank coffee was aboard a ship that took them to Mexico.
15. "Estos jóvenes japoneses iban impregnados del espíritu Enomoto que se basaba en una nueva idea migratoria consistente no solo en amasar una fortuna,

sino también en convivir y atender con devoción a los nativos del lugar, con el objeto de establecer un asentamiento permanente para el beneficio del pueblo" (Ueno and Sakuya 2008, 2).

16. "Os imigrantes partilhavam juntamente com seus compatriotas de uma imagem positiva, solidamente desenvolvida, de si próprios como japoneses. Tal sentimento se manifesta explícita ou implicitamente na forma do 'espírito japonês' (*yamato damashi*) e na convicção de que o japonês é capaz de enfrentar e vencer a adversidade. Consideram-se aptos a trabalhar árdua e inteligentemente, a dominar a situação e a encontrar soluções adequadas. Essa auto-imagem positiva é ainda mais ressaltada no além-mar pela comparação do que consideram sua própria polidez 'civilizada' e finesse como os aspectos 'rudes' que eles encontram na cultura estrangeira. Nós, como 'povo,' somos distintos 'deles' que são considerados 'primitivos' (*geshijin*) ou 'selvagens' (*yabanjin*)" (Staniford 1973, 47–48).
17. "El éxito está garantizado" (Ueno and Sakuya 2008, 22).
18. Viscount Enomoto viewed independent immigrants as the ideal immigrant prototype because they bought land with their own funds.
19. "¡Haremos historia aquí! ¡Arrrranquemos!" (Ueno and Sakuya 2008, 46).
20. "¡Somos gente de primera que venimos a colonizar esta tierra para la gloria de Japón!" (Ueno and Sakuya 2008, 59).
21. "A construir nuestra colonia y ser útiles a Japón" (Ueno and Sakuya 2008, 92).
22. "El vizconde Enomoto, integrante de una noble estirpe del shogunato, vivió en Francia entre 1862 y 1867, cuando estudiaba tecnología naval de la Armada francesa. Durante estos años tuvo tiempo de charlar con muchos oficiales que habían formado parte de la intervención francesa en México, especialmente con el capitán Jules Brunet, que logró colocar en su imaginario la idea de un país mágico, abundante y misterioso. Además de escuchar testimonios fantasiosos sobre México, Enomoto se familiariza con las teorías del socialismo utópico de Charles Fourier" (Salinas Basave 2019, 51–52).
23. "No abandona sus ideas socialistas y en el fondo de su corazón sigue soñando con fundar una comuna regida por los principios del trabajo igualitario y la ética samurái" (Salinas Basave 2019, 52).
24. The cooperative was renamed Cooperativa Mutualista de Inmigrantes and in 1905, Sociedad Cooperativa Mexicano-Japonesa.
25. "La cooperativa fue la organización más importante fuera de Japón" (Ueno and Sakuya 2008, 101).
26. Among other books, Uchimura published *Japan and the Japanese: Essays* (1894) and *How I Became a Christian: Out of My Diary, by a "Heathen Convert"* (1895).
27. "El país de la esperanza" (Ueno and Sakuya 2008, 141).
28. As stated, in addition to all his evangelizing and literacy efforts, Matsuda also established a taxonomy of southwestern Mexico's flora (many Mexican plants include *Eiji* or *Matsuda* in their scientific names), discovering and classifying

six new genres and 750 varieties, and creating an herbarium with six hundred thousand samples. He also classified more than four thousand birds and reptiles. His research was so impressive that the Universidad Nacional de México named him "professor and researcher for life" ("catedrático e investigador vitalicio"; 159). Grateful, Matsuda built a botanical garden next to its campus. In 1961, Matsuda also received a doctoral degree from the University of Tokyo.

29. "Confío en que ustedes que van a radicar en nuestro país contribuirán a estrechar los lazos de amistad entre los dos países" (Ueno and Sakuya 2008, 22).
30. "Creo que al cabo de cien años nuestros descendientes deben de hablar español y japonés y sirvan de puente entre México y Japón" (Ueno and Sakuya 2008, 104).
31. The same can be said about communities of Chinese descendants in Latin America, which have strategically positioned themselves as useful links between China and their native countries.
32. In 1914, Terui brought from the city of Kamaishi the professor Jiro Murai, who studied at the Royal Spanish Academy. In Chiapas, he began to translate an English-Spanish dictionary that he bought in the United States, but he soon became ill with malaria and entertained the thought of returning to Japan. It took him three years to complete his project. The advent of the Mexican Revolution, however, prevented its publication. In 1925, eleven years after its completion, the bilingual dictionary (which includes kanji) was published in Tokyo.
33. "Nosotros, aun siendo residentes extranjeros, viviendo en la tierra mexicana, debemos compartir el mismo dolor de los mexicanos" (Ueno and Sakuya 2008, 125).
34. "El país de los samuráis . . . Japón" (Ueno and Sakuya 2008, 128).
35. "Seremos el puente de unión entre México y Japón" (Ueno and Sakuya 2008, 129).
36. "¡No les permito que ofendan a los ciudadanos de mi país, México!" (Ueno and Sakuya 2008, 143). Impressed with his lecture, Shiro Takemura, an agronomist in the audience, requested Fuse's advice on how to move to Mexico. Later, he launched the Chiapas ranch. A former assistant of Fuse at the University of Komaba, Masasuke Takada, also emigrated to Mexico, but Fujino's death ended the project. In 1916, Fuse's group resigned from the Fujino community administration; a year after Fuse's death in 1932, his Xalapa ranch, which he created in 1916, went bankrupt.
37. "¡Quién ayudó en el parto de tu hija! ¿Quién construyó la escuela? ¿Quién puso la luz? ¿Quién puso el puente a la entrada del pueblo? ¡Todo gracias a los japoneses! (Ueno and Sakuya 2008, 191).

CHAPTER 5

1. Among the many Nikkei visual artists in Mexico (including Japanese artists who live or have lived in Mexico), one could include the Issei Akio Hanafuji, Carmen Harada, Cinthia Miyake, Fumiko Nakashima, Kenta Torii, Kishio Murata, Kiyoto Ōta, Kunio Takeda, Hiroshi Okuno, Maho Maeda, Midori Suzuki, Miho Hagino, Pavel Oi, Shino Watabe, Shinzaburō Takeda, Sumi Mamano,

Tamiji Kitagawa, Yui Sakamoto, as well as the Nisei Carlos Nakatani (son of the memoirist Nakatani, in Chapter 2), the Nisei Taro Zorrilla, the Sansei Yuriko Rojas Moriyama, and the Nikkei Eiki Itō, Hisae Ikenaga, Kazuya Sakai, Kiyoshi Takahashi, Noriko Suzuki, Shiori Ando, Sukemitsu Kaminaga, Tadashi Ue, Taiyo Miyake, Tamiji, Tawaja, and Terumi Moriyama. In other artistic fields, one could include singers such as the Nisei Yoshio (son of the memoirist Nakatani, in Chapter 2), the Sansei Kenji Hiromoto, and the Nikkei Hansae Hirata. Among the musicians, the Issei Elisa Nivon, Emi Fujimaki, Keiko Kotuku, Kiyoko Neriki, Rie Watanabe, Yoshiko Nishimura de Kasouaki, Yuriko Kuronuma; the Nisei Nahoko Kabayashi and Yukari Hirasawa; and the Nikkei Héctor Murrieta, José Mitsumori Guerrero Kojima, Julio Mizzumi Guerrero Kojima, Keiko Niikura, Marimo Sugahara, Martín Yaasuo Guerrero Kojima, and Saburo Iida. Among the dancers, the Issei Mayuko Nihei, Sakiko Yokoo, and Tamiko Kawabe, and the Sansei Harumi Pérez Nakandakara. In the fashion world, one can include the Nikkei Armando Takeda and Naoko Kihara (Alejandro Takeda makes samurai armors and helmets). The Issei Ogiso and the Nikkei Alfonso Muray are experts in Japanese gardens; the Issei Masahiko Hiyama and Toshiaki Iida (father of Irene Akiko Iida), in Japanese calligraphy (*shodō*); the Issei Higurashi and the Nikkei Koichi Mitsui and Mushago Koji in the tea ceremony; the Issei Ken Kajitani, in kitsuke (the art of wearing the kimono; showcasing the artistic designs of the kimono and admiring the work of the person that did the dressing). The Nikkei Masako Kasuga is an Ikebana expert and the Nikkei Alejandro Ramírez Honda is a puppeteer.

2. "En esos largos días de campo, me fijaba en la más íntima nervadura de cada hoja de árbol, de cada hierba, de cada milpita. Me fijaba en los juegos de luz que hacen los rayos de sol, entre las copas de los árboles, en las sombras, en las flores y los frutos, y en los animales que tan distraídamente llevaba yo a pastar ... La pintura estaba en todas las formas de la naturaleza, en el soplo del aire, en el espíritu de esa tierra negra de la Hacienda de San Mateo" (Tibol 1984a, 88).

3. Among Nishizawa's other main solo exhibitions are "Exposición de Nishizawa y Celia Calderón," Casa del Arquitecto, Mexico City (1952); Salón de la Plástica Mexicana, Mexico City (1953); "Exposición de Taku Hon," Museo de Arte Moderno, Tokio, Japan (1963); "Las nubes y las piedras," Salón de la Plástica Mexicana, Mexico City (1963); "Taku Hon: calcas por Kojin Toneyama y Luis Nishizawa," Museo de Arte Moderno, Mexico City (1965); "Autorretrato y obra," Museo de Arte Moderno, Mexico City (1966); "Dibujos y grabados," Salón de la Plástica Mexicana, Mexico City (1969); "El paisaje," Salón de la Plástica Mexicana, Mexico City (1971); "Luis Nishizawa: Las vacas flacas, los sueños rotos, recuerdos y presencias," Museo de Arte Moderno, Mexico City (1972); "Las tintas de Luis Nishizawa," Galería de Arte Contemporáneo de Lourdes Chumacero, Mexico City (1975); "Retrato y obra," Galería Natalia Zajarías, Mexico City (1977); "El lenguaje del dibujo," Galería Natalia Zajarías, Mexico City (1979); Salón Nacional de Artes Plásticas, sección de invitados,

Palacio de Bellas Artes, Mexico City (1980); Galería Natalia Zajarías, Mexico City (1980); "Exposición de dibujos," Museo del Pueblo de Guanajuato, Guanajuato (1984); Casa de la Cultura de Chihuahua, Chihuahua (1985); Museo Regional de Querétaro, Querétaro (1986); Galería Natalia Zajarías, Mexico City (1987); Galería Misrachi, Mexico City (1987); "Cuatro décadas, Exposición Homenaje," Sala Nacional, Diego Rivera e Internacional, Palacio de Bellas Artes, Mexico City (1989); Casa de la Cultura México-Japón, Mexico City (1989); "Pago en especie," Casa de Cultura, Cancún (1995); Museo Nacional de Agricultura de la Universidad Nacional de Chapingo (2002); "Homenaje al Maestro Luis Nishizawa," Escuela Nacional de Artes Plásticas, Plantel Xochimilco, Mexico City (2004); "De paisajes y sueños," Luis Nishizawa 1918–2008, Homenaje por sus 90 años de vida, Museo Nacional de San Carlos, Mexico City (2008); "Orígenes, por Luis Nishizawa," Casa Redonda Museo Chihuahuense de Arte Contemporáneo, Chihuahua (2012); "Luis Nishizawa: Poeta del silencio," Museo de Arte de la SHCP, Antiguo Palacio del Arzobispado, Mexico City (2015); Museo Francisco Cossío, San Luis Potosí, México (2016); "Luis Nishizawa: Figurativismo y abstracción," Museo Naval México, Veracruz (2018); "Luis Nishizawa: Figurativismo y abstracción," Centro Cultural Ignacio Ramírez El Nigromante de San Miguel de Allende, Guanajuato (2018); "Luis Nishizawa, íntimo universo," Museo Casa del Risco, Mexico City (2019); "Luis Nishizawa, Arte sin fronteras," Museo de Arte de Celaya, Guanajuato (2019); retrospective in the gallery of the University of Colima; and "Ayer y hoy" at Teléfonos de México."
4. Including, among other private collections, San Francisco's Ruth Hermose Galleries, and, among other museums, the Museo Taller Nishizawa (Nishizawa Museum Workshop), the Centro Cultural Mexiquense (Mexican Cultural Center), and the Museo de Bellas Artes (Museum of Fine Arts) in Toluca, as well as in the Museo de Arte Moderno (Museum of Modern Art), Instituto Nacional de Bellas Artes y Literatura (National Institute of Fine Arts and Literature), and the Museo Carrillo Gil (Carrillo Gil Museum) in Mexico City. Other pieces can be found in the permanent collectios of the Culture Museum of the Mikubishi Company in Yokohama, the Museum of Modern Art in Kyoto, and the Shinanu Museum in Nagaon, Japan, in Bulgaria's National Gallery for Foreign Art.
5. Several other institutions were named after him, including the Centro Cultural Luis Nishizawa in Atizapán de Zaragoza, Edomex, the Galería Luis Nishizawa at UNAM, and the Centro Cultural Luis Nishizawa at the Campus Estado de México of ITESM.
6. "De un abuelo heredé la sensibilidad, de otro la disciplina, por lo que mi proceso plástico ha sido la dialéctica entre mis dos raíces" (García Barragán n.d., 47).
7. "Me parece asimismo no traicionar su origen nipón en esos mismos paisajes pues en unos más que en otros, y sobre todo en sus dibujos, se advierte el estilo sintético y de una suprema elegancia de líneas de los Hokusai e Hiroshige" (as quoted in García Barragán n.d., 58).

8. "El arte japonés no guarda secretos para Nishizawa, y es justamente en la pintura de paisaje donde ese conocimiento se manifiesta ostensiblemente . . . Una de las mayores contribuciones de Nishizawa a la pintura de paisaje en México se encuentra en las obras derivadas de lo japonés, sobre todo en aquellas de tonos alcanzados con los recursos que ofrecen el blanco y el negro" (Villa Guerrero 2014, 77).
9. "[Reserva e] impasibilidad orientales" (as quoted in García Barragán n.d., 64).
10. "Sí, sí quiero, es más, lo deseo hondamente, pero ahora quiero conocer más que nada mi país, entenderlo y poderlo expresar en cada pincelada mía" (as quoted in García Barragán n.d., 64).
11. "La contribución mayor de Luis Nishizawa a la pintura de paisaje en México se encuentra en las obras derivadas de lo japonés, sobre todo en aquellas de tonos alcanzados con uno o dos colores, con los recursos que ofrecen el blanco y negro, como colores primarios; son magníficas obras realizadas la mayoría de las ocasiones en grandes hojas de papel. Esta contribución se manifiesta en innumerables pinturas, de manera rotunda, en cuadros como el dedicado al *Popocatépetl* (1970), el cual bien podría ser el famoso Fujiyama, por la manera como su autor lo realiza; se levanta majestuoso, con un color rojizo, en medio de un fondo azul transparente como el aire que lo envuelve" (León Portilla de Diener n.d., 28).
12. Located in Izta-Popo Zoquiapan National park, on the border between Puebla and the State of Mexico, Iztaccíhuatl ("white woman," for its resemblance to a reclining woman) is the third-highest volcano in Mexico, after Orizaba and the Popocatépetl, its twin to the south, connected by the Paso de Cortés.
13. "Cuando coloco un sello en mis cuadros, a la usanza de la estampa japonesa, lo hago para que dé un toque de color. La marca equilibra el dibujo monocromo. Ese sello bermellón forma parte del cuadro" (Tibol 1984a, 91).
14. "Luis Nishizawa nos relata el impacto que causó en él la exposición de estampas del pintor nipón Ando Hiroshige, efectuada en el Palacio de Bellas Artes . . . Igual seducción ejerció Hiroshigue en el ánimo de Nishizawa, y a la par que Tablada, el pintor mexicano ha seguido mística y devotamente la trayectoria del maestro japonés. Ante esa dilección por aquel arte superior, Alfredo Zalce comparte con Luis Nishizawa unas 'tintas secas' japonesas y el artista empieza a experimentar en sus trabajos con tintas y técnicas niponas, actividad que poco a poco va permeando su producción en cuadros exactos de luz y síntesis" (León Portilla de Diener n.d., 60).
15. "Síntesis caligráfica a la manera oriental en sus paisajes" (Tibol 1984a, 7).
16. "Ahora me he quedado en una semifiguración donde el espacio cuenta considerablemente. Me gustan las atmósferas sugeridas, lo envolvente. Trato de que el espectador penetre en mi mundo. Generalmente el paisaje está ligado a la poesía. No se trata tanto, al menos para mí, de la forma que proporciona un volcán o una campiña, sino de elementos en juego con los que se busca una solución plástica, emotiva y poética" (Tibol 1984a, 91).

17. "El aire es vida" was initially exhibited in the lobby of Mexico City's Hospital de Cardiología y Neumología. Currently, it is displayed in the lobby of the Centro Médico Nacional Siglo XXI.
18. *La justicia* was painted in the main stairwell of the Mexican Supreme Court for the bicentennial of Mexico's independence in 2010.
19. Popular religiosity, for instance, is represented in his colorful, mixed technique painting *La pasión de Iztapalapa, núm. 1* (Iztapalapa's Passion No. 1) from 1950.
20. *La imagen del hombre* is displayed at the headquarters of the Secretaría de Educación Pública.
21. This motif is similar to those of his bronze sculptures *Niño pez* (Fish Boy) and *El espíritu siempre se renueva* (The Creative Spirit Is Forever Renewed, 2000), against a background of green tiles representing water.
22. "Aquí conviven pacíficamente su visión amorosa de la tradición japonesa y el recio concepto del mural mexicano. Resuena en mis oídos una frase que pronunció recordando a su padre el día de la inauguración: Su sangre aún tiene voz" (as quoted in Tibol n.d., 122).
23. "Un corazón oriental sumergido en el humanismo mexicano que tañe la estética del sacrificio" (Tibol 1984a, 94).
24. Nishizawa will again imitate the shape of a Mexican petate in his *Mural en cerámica II* (Mural in Ceramics II), displayed at the Escuela Nacional de Artes Plásticas. Other murals by Nishizawa are found at the Centro Cultural Martí, the Centro Cultural Universitario, the General Archives of the State of Mexico in Toluca, the Procuraduría General de la República, and the Secretaría de Educación Pública.
25. "Tomando en cuenta los grandes problemas que presentan algunas de las obras de los muralistas mexicanos para su conservación, mi obra mural la he realizado con materiales perennes, materiales que puedan estar en el interior o en el exterior de cualquier recinto; he realizado dos murales en cerámica, uno ya con veinte años de vida sin presentar ninguna alteración, otro en el Japón con el mismo material" (Nishizawa 1990, n.p.).
26. An Asian modern and contemporary artist born in Ibaraki Prefecture, Toneyama, whose work often takes Mexico as its subject, was featured at the Art Institute of Chicago and the Kokuritsu Kindai Bijutsukan (National Museum of Modern Art) in Kyoto. His work exhibited Mexican stylistics and was influenced by 1950s abstract expressionism. He was fascinated with performance folk arts from Michinoku, Japan, as well as by Mexican folk art (in 1974, he published *The Popular Arts of Mexico*). For his efforts to promote Mexican culture, he received the Order of the Aztec Eagle from the Mexican government in 1972. He also promoted mural art in Japan.
27. A related traditional Japanese technique is *gyo-tuku*, whereby fishermen documented their prized catch by laying paper or fabric with ink on the fish and rubbing it with their fingers.

28. At the Museum of Modern Art in Tokyo, the Salón de la Plástica Mexicana, in Mexico City, and at Mexico City's Museo de Arte Moderno.
29. "La principal influencia que tengo del paisaje es de Francisco Goitia, quien no era paisajista, pero su cuadro 'La Hacienda de Santa María' es una de las obras que más me han impresionado" (Villa Guerrero 2014, 74).
30. "Nishizawa eligió inicialmente la [opción] de un realismo mexicanista, muy influido por el refinamiento de Julio Castellanos en la ejecución" (Tibol 1984a, 5).
31. Including Luis Sahagún, who gave him one of his favorite books, *El libro dell'Arte de Cennino Cennini* (*The Book of the Art of Cenninno Cenninni*, 1859); Benjamín Coria, who told him about the advantages of an oil and tempera mixed technique; and Julio Castellanos, who translated Max Doemer's treatise on painting materials.
32. "Toda mi vida he anhelado ser tan sólo un artesano que pueda amasar sus sentimientos con el barro para que el fuego haga el milagro" (Nishizawa 1990, n.p.).
33. "Lo escuchábamos con verdadero deleite, eran las hazañas heroicas de los antiguos samuráis, relatos que enriquecieron mi imaginación y mi conocimiento del mundo... También nos cantaba canciones guerreras muy antiguas de los samuráis... Le recordaban su infancia y a pesar de que vino muy joven a México, siempre se educó y vivió dentro del espíritu de los samuráis. Todo lo que he podido lograr como pintor y como hombre lo hago para honrar a mi padre... Creo que todos tenemos en la vida una persona que le da sentido y que es la razón de lo que hacemos. Para algunos, es una mujer; para otros, un ideal; para mí, es mi padre" (Villa Guerrero 2014, 73). He likewise told Poniatowska that everything he had done in his life was to honor his father (Tibol 1984a, 90).
34. "La disciplina y la filosofía zen (el sentido del honor, la integridad personal, la lealtad y un profundo sentido del respto por el ser humano)" (Del Arenal 2014, n.p.).
35. "La pintura de Nishizawa empieza a ser auténtica porque brota con fluidez de su fuente interna—asiática y americana—como de manera similar corre la sangre de las dos razas por las arterias del pintor" (84).
36. "Metamorfosis pictórica realmente notable" (Anzures 1961, 5).
37. "Durante muchos años, Nishizawa mostró en su obra una fuerte preocupación por manifestarse 'mexicano,' así, entre comillas. Este prurito, verdaderamente pernicioso, le tenía como estancado... aquello que dio ese aliento de original a su pintura actual, de frescura, de verdadera higiene pictórico-artística; de brillo propio y singularidad, fue decíamos, que Nishizawa por fin ha decidido manifestar también en su obra, el sentimiento y su alma de oriental; pero esta vez de un modo natural y auténtico, es decir de japonés verdadero, sin comillas. Y ahora él mismo debe sentir que respira en una atmósfera limpia, sin compromisos a priori. Porque siendo naturalmente original; como se es, cuando se *es*, y no 'original' por fuerza, se aflojan las tensiones del espíritu; la angustia, elemento negativo, se desvanece y se puede entonces, por eso, llegar más fácilmente a la plenitud de expresión" (Anzures 1961, 5).

38. "La identificación con su raíz japonesa lo devolvió al cultivo de la imagen bella como reafirmación de dignidad, y a la práctica de un paisajismo con su monumentalidad y su esplendor implícitos" (Tibol 1984a, 12).
39. "Líneas muy depuradas, casi criptográficas" (Tibol 1984a, 12).
40. "Estas naturalezas muertas son meditaciones, son poemas, son mitologías en homenaje a sus ascendientes" (Tibol 1984a, 15).
41. "Es casi obligatorio, cuando se habla de Luis Nishizawa, mencionar el arte japonés y la filosofía zen. Se sabe que el artista, por sus antecedentes, por su propia sensibilidad, por sus lecturas, viajes y contactos con otros artistas, ha dirigido la mirada hacia la tierra natal de su padre, de donde ha recibido influencias que en nada se oponen a su formación cultural, eminentemente mexicana" (Rodríguez n.d., 149).
42. "A la semejanza de los maestros japoneses se atrevió a tratar a un humilde crustáceo con la dignidad con que algunos pintores europeos del pasado trataban, en sus retratos, a los gloriosos monarcas de entonces" (Rodríguez n.d., 152).
43. "El Ajusco desde el Xitle" (The Ajusco from the Xitle), "Humo sobre el Popocatépetl" (Smoke over Popocatépetl), "Milpa Alta" (High Clearing), and "La lluvia" (The Rain) (Rodríguez n.d., 150).
44. "Fluctuando siempre entre pasión dramática de México y la tendencia a las grandes abstracciones del arte japonés" (Tibol 1984a, 86).
45. For an examination of critical exaggeration of Japanese influences in José Watanabe's poetry, see the forthcoming *The Poetic Cosmovision of José Watanabe: An Analysis of the Poet, the Artistry and the Ancestry*, edited by Randy Muth, Alfredo López-Pasarín Basabe, and Shigeko Mato.
46. "El japonés Nishizawa expone un paisaje que dentro de la modalidad tradicional está bien logrado. Se nota en él una marcada influencia de Velasco" (García Barragán n.d. 48).
47. "Aunque mexicano por la madre y por su nacimiento, desciende de padre oriental, como su nombre lo indica. Podía no obstante esto no haber heredado ese temperamento detallista y cuidadoso que nos muestra en su pintura. Pero así es y de él se sirve para interpretarnos, con efectos de composición y de colorido muy mexicanos, el paisaje, las escenas costumbristas y los seres" (Tibol 1984a, 81).
48. "Todo ello es muy natural si consideramos que el artista, aunque mexicano por su madre y por su nacimiento, desciende de padre oriental. Podía, no obstante esto, no haber heredado ese temperamento detallista y cuidadoso" (as quoted in García Barragán n.d., 58).
49. "Son ejemplos característicos de la introducción de códigos que son propios de la cultura de la que por línea paterna proviene, la japonesa" (Del Conde n.d., 86).
50. "Sino del modo como instaura los elementos en el espacio, vivido a la vez como macrocosmos y como microcosmos, la dualidad patente en las filosofías del oriente. En estos casos el cuadro se arma de pocos elementos, dos o tres figuras, en tanto que el espacio en el que se disponen es un fondo abstracto que posee importante papel protagónico. Las relaciones de proximidad o

lejanía entre las figuras están dosificadas del mismo modo que como ocurre, por ejemplo, en los jardines japoneses, donde los árboles, plantas y piedras se disponen calculadamente de modo que integran ambientes asimétricos que realizan la importancia de cada cosa y su relación de contigüidad en cuanto a distancia y forma" (Del Conde n.d., 97–98).

51. There are many other examples of this type of criticism. Luz García Ordóñez assesses the reasons behind Nishizawa's predilection for atmospheric landscape thus: "The master had two bloodlines, the Mexican, and the Japanese, and that blend made him go looking for his roots. At one stage in his life, he went to Japan to paint, he took classes in Asian ink art, drawing and painting in the oriental manner, a technique called 'nihonga.' When he went to Japan, he found that there were ranges of opacity in his paintings . . . He adjusted the paper to the ink and added the pigment making a technical fusion, like the one in his blood. Thus, he applied the Asian method with that found in European techniques . . . So, when he went to the East, he fused the fluid techniques from there with the concrete ones from Europe, working within those two rhythms. This is why he strived for oriental atmospheric poetics, because the subtle field of the atmosphere is totally poetic." ("El maestro tenía dos líneas sanguíneas, la mexicana, y la japonesa, esa mezcla lo hizo ir a buscar sus raíces. En una etapa de su vida fue a Japón a pintar, tomó clases de tintas orientales, de dibujo y pintura a la manera oriental, de una técnica que se llama 'nihonga.' Cuando fue a Japón se dio cuenta de que tenían rangos de opacidad sus pinturas . . . acomodó el papel a la tinta y anexó el pigmento haciendo una fusión técnica, así como la que traía él en su sangre. Así, aplicó el método oriental junto con el método de las técnicas europeas . . . Entonces él, al ir a Oriente, fundió las técnicas fluidas de allá con las concretas de Europa, trabajando a esos dos ritmos. Por ello se esmeró por la poética atmosférica oriental, porque el campo sutil de la atmósfera es poético totalmente" Del Arenal 2015, n.p.) By the same token, Moyssén discovers a "Japanese taste" in the bright-colored mixography *Peces rojos* (Red Fish, 1976), *El pez y la luna* (The Fish and the Moon, 1978), and *Langosta* (Lobster, 1978), as well as in his abstract art (León Portilla de Diener n.d., 16) and in still lifes containing seafood (León Portilla de Diener n.d., 25). García Barragán points out Japanese artistic influences in the techniques used in landscapes such as *Serranía de la villa* and *Paisaje de Tlayacapan* (Landscape of Tlayacapan), where, in my view, there are no evident traces of such influences.

CHAPTER 6

1. At the time of Akiko's birth in Mexico City, no foreign first names were allowed in Mexico, so her parents called her Irene. Akiko, her Japanese name, is not in her birth certificate, but it is in her baptism certificate. Besides Irene Akiko Iida, she has used the stage names Sachikaze Irene and Hanayagui Irene. She now prefers to be referred to as Akiko.

2. There are other Nikkei actors in Mexico, including Noé Muruyama (1930–1997), who played roles in the Mexican soap operas *El pecado de Oyui* (Oyuki's sin, 1988) and *Esmeralda* (1997), as well as in the Mexican films *Sonatas* (1959) and *Cada quién su vida* (To Each His Life, 1960), and in the French film *La bataille de San Sebastian* (Guns for San Sebastian, 1968). The Issei Hiromi Hayakawa (born Marla Hiromi Hayakawa Salas; 1982–2017) acted in the television series and soap operas like *El Chema* (2016–2017), *La vida es una canción* (Life Is a Song), *Lo que callamos las mujeres* (What Women Don't Say, 2000–), and *A cada quien su santo* (Each with His Own Saint). She also took part in numerous theater plays as well as in the films *Skyrunners* (2009), *Mi falso prometido* (My Fake Fiancé, 2009), *Mi niñera es una vampira* (My Babysitter Is a Vampire, 2010), *Harriet the Spy: Blog Wars* (2010), *En la boda de mi hermana* (At My Sister's Wedding, 2010), *Alicia en el país de las maravillas* (Alice in Wonderland, 2010), *Geek Charming*, *Los Muppets* (2011), *Prom* (2011), *Alicia a través del espejo* (Alice through the Glass Mirror, 2016), and *Cita a ciegas* (Blind Date). The Nikkei Úrsula Murayama (1972–) has acted in the films *Sin azul* (Without Blue, 1999), *Hijos del viento* (Sons of the Wind, 1999), *El último profeta* (The Last Prophet, 1999), *Pelea de gallos* (Cock Fight, 2002), *Pequeño palacio* (Little Palace, 2003), *Las trece rosas* (The Thirteen Roses, 2007), *Padre no hay más que uno* (There Is Only One Father, 2019), *Rambo V* (2019); and *Terminator VI* (2019). She also participated in the television series and soap operas *Morir dos veces* (Dying Twice, 1999), *Esmeralda* (1999–2000), *Yacaranday* (2001), *Mi hijo Arturo* (My Son Arturo, 2003), *El comisario* (The Sheriff, 2006), *Caso Waninkof* (The Waninkof Case 2008), *Serie LQSA* (LQSA Series, 2020), and *La familia* (The Family). In addition, the Issei Seki Sano (1905–1966; a short chapter in Chew's *Mudas las garzas* is devoted to him) was an actor, stage director, choreographer, and Marxist activist who greatly contributed to the development of the theatre in both Japan and Mexico. Known as the "father of Mexican theatre," he influenced numerous directors and actors not only in Mexico but also in the rest of Latin America. It is also worth mentioning the Nikkei filmmaker Naomi Rincón Gallardo, living in Austria, and the Japanese actor Toshirō Mifune (1920–1997), who acted in the 1961 Mexican film *Ánimas Trujano*, the second Mexican film to be nominated for an Oscar and a Golden Globe in 1962.
3. "Mi deseo es comunicar a Japón lo mexicano y a México lo japonés."
4. Only music school graduates can join the Takarazuka Review (founded in 1913 as the theater troupe Takarazuka Shokatai). The Takarazuka Music School, whose motto is "Purity, Honesty, Beauty," accepts only forty new students per year who have passed a competitive entrance exam. Once accepted, young women take performing arts, ballet, singing, and Japanese dancing lessons for two years.
5. A multidisciplinary company, Akikompania combines music, theater, dance, and calligraphy. It also uses *benshi* (Japanese performers who provided live narration and dialogue for Japanese and foreign silent films) and Sensorama (a multisensory technology machine considered a precursor of virtual reality).

6. In 2001 Akiko was the protagonist of the play *El crepúsculo de la cigüeña* (Twilight of the Stork), by Kinoshita Junji and directed by Abraham Stavans. In 2002, she was coauthor, choreographer, and producer of the poetry and music show *Kai-on, sonidos del mar* (Kai-on, Sounds of the Sea). In 2004, she was the scriptwriter, composer, and benshi interpreter of the project *Cascada de hilo blanco* (White Thread Waterfall) and *Nací, pero . . .* (I Was Born, But . . .), dedicated to five silent-film Japanese filmmakers. With Diego Piñón, in 2005 she choreographed and danced in the Butoh dance *In-yo*. The following year, she participated in *Yogamoi* by David Henry Hwang and directed by Richard Viqueira, in Paris, France, and from 2009 to 2018, in the "opera for actors" *El gallo* (The Rooster), by Claudio Valdez Kuri. Akiko also choreographed and advised on the opera *Madame Butterfly*, directed by Juliana Faesler. She was an actor in the 2015–2016 play *Humboldt, México para los mexicanos* (Humboldt, Mexico for Mexicans), directed by David Psalmon, and in the 2017 play *Babel, reconstruyendo comunidad* (Babel, Reconstructing Community). In 2019, she participated in *Kanawa, corona de hierro: Abismo astral* (Kanawa, Iron Crown: Astral Abyss). Akiko has taught traditional Japanese dance (*Kabuki buyō* style) at the Liceo Mexicano Japonés and has also given lectures and participated in conferences in Mexico, Costa Rica, the United States, Japan, and South Korea.
7. Akiko received a grant from the coinvestment project FONCA. The play was performed more than 150 times and received an award for best children's play at the seventeenth annual Feria Internacional del Libro Infantil y Juvenil.
8. Susana Wein, born in Mexico City, has given theater workshops for children and adolescents. Her play *La comparsa caballuna* won the 1980 Seguro Social puppet theater contest.
9. *Momotarō* is often translated as "Peach Boy"; *momo* means "peach" and *tarō*, "the eldest son in the family."
10. In Japanese folklore, an *oni* is a stock villain, a massive, horned evil demon or ogre. They are typically red, blue, or white; wear tiger-pelt loincloths; and carry iron *kanabō*, a spiked or studded two-handed war club used by samurais.
11. "Fruta importante, pero sin raíz no hay fruta. Tú, mexicano. Yo, oyiichan, japonés. Tú fruta, no raíz, qué bueno dos cosas eres: mexicano y japonés. Doble ventaja, si tú aprovechas, esmeras, será muy afortunado para ti y todo el mundo" (Wein and Akiko Iida 1997, 8). In a different performance, the grandfather (played by José Juan De la O) states: "Sin raíces, no hay fruta" (Without roots, there is no fruit). He also tells his grandson Juan/Taro (played by either Hidemi Pérez or his replacement, Jessica Gámez) that he heard the Momotarō story from his own *ojiichan*.
12. Raijin is the demon of thunder; in a different version of the play, they tie up Juan, Momotaro, and Dog while another *oni* with an orange wig plays the drums.
13. In a different version of the play, they all sail on a small ship, rowing while Dog encourages them: "¡Gambaré!" ("Ganbare!" in the usual English spelling, often said to encourage people to succeed or wish them good luck).

14. In the original folktale, *kibi dango* refers to millet dumplings made from the flour of the *kibi* (proso millet) grain. The Peach Boy hero uses it to recruit the three animals.
15. In a different version of the play, after the bad world news are projected on the screen, the terrible Maoo, with his long horns and a big club in his hand, finally appears on stage singing "Maoo, el más malo de los malos" (Maoo, the worst of the bad).
16. "Para triunfar hay que luchar con virtud; si sólo tienes poder, tarde o temprano te irá mal" (Wein and Akiko Iida 1997, 47).
17. "El samurai Hasekura lideró el viaje acompañado por alrededor de 180 japoneses, arribando a Acapulco en 1614. Se sabe que algunos japoneses permanecieron en México. Siete años tardó Hasekura en realizar esta encomienda. Cuando en 1620 regresó a Japón, los cristianos eran severamente perseguidos" (Falck 2020, 21).
18. "El *daimyo* Date Masamune, señor de Aizu, designó al samurái Hasekura como su embajador ante la Corona española, seducido por el ambicioso franciscano fray Luis Sotelo. La expedición partió de Tsukinoura en 1613, recorrió México, Sevilla, Madrid, Roma, Génova, Sevilla, México y Manila, y volvió al Japón en 1620" (Iwasaki 2005, 141).
19. Throughout the play, the audience also hears "ethnic" music, indigenous pre-Hispanic music, Gregorian chant, and *cante jondo flamenco*.
20. In the Japanese-language version, Hasekura also sings in Japanese, but one can hear Spanish words and sentences pronounced with a Japanese accent.
21. "El tener que aceptar cosas que no entiendes por el idioma, costumbres, ideología. El no poder expresar lo que se siente o piensa."
22. Endō's other major novel, *Chimmoku* (*Silence*, 1966), is a fictionalized account of the adventures of Portuguese Jesuit missionaries in Japan and the subsequent martyrdom of their Japanese converts.
23. "Se ve reducido su impacto al quedarse en meras impresiones de ciertos momentos que, aunque atractivos no terminan por mostrar la escisión ni la herida del samurái . . . no puede evitar preguntarse qué hubiera ocurrido si la dramaturga escénica hubiese hurgado en las profundidades de la vida de Tsunenaga para no bordear de manera superficial la vida del guerrero" (Enríquez 2010, 5).
24. Whereas traditional Kabuki is performed only by men (including female roles), Nihon Buyō is often performed by women. And unlike traditional Kabuki, Nihon Buyō performers rarely speak. Sometimes mixing dance and pantomime, Nihon Buyō is a more refined style of dance than other Japanese traditional dances, and it is typically performed on a public stage. It encompasses several traditional Japanese dance styles, including *mai* (refined dance with few leaps or quick movements), *odori* (energetic dance, with leaps and dynamic movements), and *furi* (Kabuki dance gestures and pantomime).
25. "Los inicios del Kabuki datan del año 1600, cuando una sacerdotisa llamada Okuni presentó una danza de invocación en el reino de Izumo. En ese entonces,

el Kabuki era interpretado por mujeres, por lo que era llamado Onna o Yujyô Kabuki (Kabuki de damas de noche). Luego surgió el Wakasyu Kabuki (Kabuki de jóvenes) y posteriormente el Yarô Kabuki (Kabuki de bribones), en el que sólo participaban hombres, como sucede en la actualidad. No obstante, desde principios del siglo XX, con el movimiento de Shinbuyô (danza contemporánea), la danza japonesa sufrió una transformación en la que dejó de llamarse Kabukibuyô para independizarse, en 1924, bajo el nombre más amplio de Nihonbuyô, en donde participan indistintamente hombres y mujeres a diferencia del Teatro Kabuki" (n.p.).

26. "Porque solo saber no le bastó, fue que a su mente con letras forjó."
27. "Aun el tono aromatizante de la joven flor se habrá de marchitar."
28. In Reyes Estrada's *La gallina azul*, the Japanese Mexican narrator, André (Haruki) Yamada, has four brothers studying in Japan when World War II breaks out; one enrolls as a kamikaze.
29. "Cuando tu padre llegó a Tapachula del Japón, con Furukawa, Yamazaki, Exal y todos los demás, no hablaba ni pizca de español y llegó en la inopia, verdaderamente muerto de hambre. Solo tenía las tierras silvestres que el gobierno del Japón había comprado para ellos, los pioneros como les digo, aquí en el Soconusco. Pero bueno, lo que sí traían eran unas ganas inmensas de trabajar, que nos sorprendieron, y la tenacidad que tú conoces bien" (Camposeco 2018, 13).
30. "En fin, todo sea por la integridad del Japón y su destino, que están por sobre todas las cosas . . . Japón prevalecerá, su destino es sagrado, como nuestro Emperador" (Camposeco 2018, 15).
31. "Los Estados Unidos intentan llevar al Japón a un callejón sin salida, y allí aniquilar su potencial, destruirnos, humillarnos. No lo conseguirán, la fuerza y la voluntad de cada japonés está por encima de toda esa infamia" (Camposeco 2018, 23).
32. "La victoria de Pearl Harbor" and "la gran victoria de Bataan, hace un año, donde los arrogantes ingleses y los americanos tuvieron su merecido" (Camposeco 2018, 30).
33. "Disculpa que te hable de la situación actual del Japón como una japonesa, en realidad lo soy, sin que niegue mi origen mexicano, son también mis raíces. Estoy ante la vida con un pie sobre el Japón y el otro en México, en Tapachula precisamente, bien plantada en sus gentes, en ustedes; también de allá provengo" (Camposeco 2018, 16).
34. "'Las calles eran ríos de fuego, las gentes se incendiaban como cerillos. Al amanecer, largas filas de personas quemadas, cubiertas de ceniza, aturdidas, caminaban sin dirección alguna, como en filas de hormigas,' dice el periodista de Asahi" (Camposeco 2018, 36).
35. "Lo que vi me pareció una alucinación, ¡la ciudad era un infierno! La gente salía de los escombros, de entre las llamas y las cenizas, monstruosamente quemada. Se dirigían al Hospital por instinto. Por cada uno que estaba de pie, diez estaban tirados en el suelo, muertos o agonizando" (Camposeco 2018, 95).

36. "El rostro de un infierno a flor de tierra."
37. *Nihon buyō* or *nichibu* is a type of classical Japanese performing art that borrows elements from older dance genres and sometimes pantomime. It refers to a few dance styles, such theatrical *Kabuki buyō*, geishas' *kamigata mai*, and some Japanese dances with modern choreography like *sosaku buyō*.
38. *El automóvil gris al estilo benshi japonés*, performed with the Compañía Teatro de Ciertos Habitantes, was directed by the prestigious Mexican theater director and actor Claudio Valdés Kuri. Akiko cowrote the script, along with Sofía González de León, Enrique Arreola y Claudio Valdés Kuri, and was responsible, along with Carlos Guízar, for the makeup. The play received two awards: Best Innovative Theater Director in 2002, from the Asociación Mexicana de Críticos de Teatro, and Best Group Theater in 2002, by the Asociación de Periodistas Teatrales.
39. It was performed, in the corresponding national language, throughout the world. For its 2008 Australian premiere at the Melbourne International Arts Festival, it was performed in Spanish, Japanese, and English, all with English subtitles.
40. For instance, Akiko switches the /l/ and /r/ sounds (there is no phonemic distinction between the rhotic /r/ and the lateral /l/ in Japanese), pronouncing her first word *hola* with an /r/ sound and then *alcaldía* as "arcardía." She also purposely makes a gender mistake in the adjective in *obra muldisciplinario* (multidisciplinary play) and pronounces *gris* as "grisu" (since Japanese words always end in a vowel or an /n/).

CONCLUSION

1. Along with the visual artists and actors mentioned in Chapter 6, there are several authors and literary works that merit further study, including Antonio Murray's *Casi un siglo de recuerdos: Biografía de Federico Imamura* (*Almost a Century of Memories: Biography of Federico Imamura*, 1994); Carlos Nakatani's poetry collection *Papá extranjero: Breves exequias* (Foreign Dad: Brief Obsequies, 2000); María del Carmen Hernández Ibarra's short-story collection *Una ilusión compartida* (A Shared Enthusiasm, 2017); Kenichi-Benito Murray's (n. d.) *Crónicas de los pioneros japoneses en México* (Chronicles of the Japanese Pioneers in Mexico); José Ramón Sato Parra's *Decisiones de triunfo* (Decisions of Triumph); José Ramón Sato Parra and Manuel Campos Caravantes's *Nocturno a Culiacán: Poemas* (Nocturnal Poems to Culiacán); Kenichiro Kawaji's (n. p.) *El viento de la Sierra Madre* (The Wind of the Sierra Madre); and Arata Akachi's unpublished 1986 memoirs "Kaiko roku."
2. Among these works, one could include the Chinese Mexican borderlands poet, narrator, and scholar Selfa A. Chew and her *Mudas las garzas*; Reyes Estrada's *La gallina azul*; Nicolasa Ruiz's documentary short *Obachan* (2020); Araceli Tinajero's memoir *Kokoro, una Mexicana en Japón* (Kokoro, a Mexican Woman in Japan, 2012); and the Mexican Mario Bellatin's short story "Bola negra"

(Black Ball; 2005) and novellas *Biografía ilustrada de Mishima* (Illustrated Biography of Mishima, 2009), *El jardín de la señora Murakami: Oto no-Murakami monogarati* (Mrs. Murakami's Garden: Oto no-Murakami monogarati, 2001), and *Shiki Nagaoka: Una nariz de ficción* (Shiki Nagaoka: A Fictional Nose, 2001).

3. "Una población que era imminentemente agrícola y pesquera, pasó a ser urbana y comerciante" (Ota Mishima 1985, 117–18).
4. Published in the Spanish newspaper *El País* on November 8, 2020. Ogata Aguilar is not asking for reparations like the ones offered by the US government in the late 1980s.
5. "Que sufrió tremendos agravios en sus derechos civiles . . . Los desplazaron a la fuerza, les desposeyeron de sus negocios, inmovilizaron sus cuentas bancarias, fueron encarcelados y eran ciudadanos mexicanos" (Morán Breña 2020, n.p.).
6. "Hay que remover esos sentimientos, sacarlos afuera, hacer una catarsis colectiva. Fue, más que otra cosa, una cuestión racista . . . Hay que construir otras historias que revaloricen ese pasado, para que ayude a no repetirlo" (Morán Breña 2020, n.p.).
7. "Tres décadas después de que aquello ocurriera en Estados Unidos, el movimiento de japoneses no solo logró disculpas, también una indemnización. Se ha pedido perdón de alguna manera en Perú, en tiempos de Alan García. En Brasil, la iniciativa no prosperó. Yo creo que México les debe una disculpa, pero eso lo tienen que decidir y plantear ellos mismos. El pueblo mexicano, en todo caso, debe conocer esta historia" (Morán Breña 2020, n.p.).
8. "Que vieron como se perdía la honorabilidad de aquel pueblo . . . a reconciliar emociones, algo que en el presente no se percibe en toda su dimensión" (Morán Breña 2020, n.p.).
9. "Los contextos determinan las relaciones históricas de los países y fuera de ellos todo parece ajeno a la realidad actual. [Pedir perdón] escapa a cierta lógica y da relevancia a aspectos que nada tienen que ver con un programa político o cultural . . . Mejor es explicar lo que ocurrió, investigar, apoyar a la investigación humanística, literaria, que emanó de esas relaciones. Tienen que ver con la formación de ambos pueblos. La educación nos salva de pedir y ofrecer disculpas en un momento en que las relaciones son óptimas" (Morán Breña 2020, n.p.).
10. "Se cometieron muchas violaciones a sus derechos, a pesar de que nada tenían que ver con la guerra. Sólo se podían mover con permiso de la autoridad. Eran vigilados por la policía" (García 2014, n.p.).

Works Cited

Ahmed, Sara. 2015. *The Cultural Politics of Emotion*. New York: Routledge.
Akachi, Arata. "Kaiko roku." Unpublished ms.
Anderson, Benedict. (1983) 2006. *Imagined Communities: Reflections on the Origins and Spread of Nationalism*. London: Verso.
Ang, Ien. 2001. *On Not Speaking Chinese: Living between Asia and the West*. New York: Routledge.
Anzures, Rafael. 1961. "Segunda Bienal Interamericana de México / The Second Interamerican Biennial of Mexico, 1961." *Artes de México* 6 (34): 1–17, 19, 21–25.
Appiah, Kwame Anthony. 1997. "Cosmopolitan Patriots." *Critical Inquiry* 23 (3): 617–39.
Bashō, Matsuo. (1689) 1966. *The Narrow Road to the Deep North and Other Travel Sketches*. Introduction and translation by Nobuyuki Yuasa. Harmondsworth, UK: Penguin Books.
Befu, Harumi. 2017. "El *nihonjinron* como identidad nacional japonesa: Un análisis antropológico." In *Antropología de Japón: Identidad, discurso y representación*, edited by Blai Guarné, 39–52. Barcelona: Bellaterra.
Belleau, Janick. 2012. "Tanka by Women since the 9th Century." (Overview of tanka poetesses preceding the bilingual collection of ninety-one tanka *D'âmes et d'ailes / Of souls and wings*, Literary Award Canada-Japan 2010). Translated by Maxianne Berger. https://www.janickbelleau.ca/contenu/Overview_tanka_poetesses_from_the_bilingual_collection.pdf.
Bhabha, Homi K. 1994. *The Location of Culture*. London: Routledge.
Braccio, Gabriela. 2009. "Esteban Sampzon, un escultor filipino en el Río de la Plata." *Eadem Utraque Europa* 8 (June): 53–72.
Butler, Judith. 1988. "Performative Acts and Gender Constitution: An Essay in Phenomenology and Feminist Theory." *Theatre Journal* 40 (4): 519–31.

Buzard, James. 2005. *Disorienting Fiction: The Autoethnographic Work of 19th-Century British Novels*. Princeton, NJ: Princeton University Press.

Camposeco, Víctor Manuel. (1995) 2013. *Correo de Hiroshima*. Mexico City: Amaquemecan.

Carvalho, Daniela de. 2003. *Migrants and Identity in Japan and Brazil: The Nikkeijin*. London: Routledge Curzon.

Casanova, Pascale. 2007. *The World Republic of Letters*. Translated by Malcolm DeBevoise. Cambridge, MA: Harvard University Press.

Castillo, Máximo. 2004. *Máximo Castillo y la Revolución en Chihuahua*. Edited by Jesús Vargas Valdés. Chihuahua, Mexico: Nueva Vizcaya.

Ceniza Choy, Catherine, and Judy Tzu-Chun Wu. 2017. Introduction to *Gendering the Trans-Pacific World*, edited by Catherine Ceniza Choy and Judy Tzu-Chun Wu, 3–9. Leiden: Brill.

Chang, Jason Oliver. 2017. *Chino: Anti-Chinese Racism in Mexico, 1880–1940*. Urbana: University of Illinois Press.

Chao Romero, Robert. 2010. *The Chinese in Mexico 1882–1940*. Tucson: University of Arizona Press.

Cheah, Pheng. 2014. "World against Globe: Toward a Normative Conception of World Literature." *New Literary History* 45 (3): 303–29.

Chen, Kuan-Hsing. 2010. *Asia as Method: Toward Deimperialization*. Durham, NC: Duke University Press.

Chew, Selfa A. 2007. *Mudas las garzas*. Mexico City: Eon.

———. 2012. *Silent Herons*. Translated by Toshiya Kamei. Chicago: Berkeley Press.

———. 2015. *Uprooting Community: Japanese Americans, World War II, and the US-Mexico Borderlands*. Tucson: University of Arizona Press.

Chikaba, Aiko. 2016. "Prologue: The Life of Mitsuko Kasuga." In *Akane, Immigrant Poet: The Tanka of Mitsuko Kasuga*, edited by Aiko Chikaba and translated by Naoko Shin, Cynthia Viveros Cano, Carlos Ernesto Pierre-Audian Kasuga, and Aiko Chikaba, 128–241. Tokyo: Texnai.

Chong, José Luis. 2014. *Historia general de los chinos en México 1575–1975*. Mexico City: Turner.

Clifford, James. 1988. *The Predicament of Culture: Twentieth-Century Ethnography, Literature, and Art*. Cambridge, MA: Harvard University Press.

Cruz, Denise. 2017. "Notes on Trans-Pacific Archives." In *Gendering the Trans-Pacific World*, edited by Catherine Ceniza Choy and Judy Tzu-Chun Wu, 10–19. Leiden: Brill.

De Ávila, José Juan. 2015. "Un samurái en la Revolución Mexicana." *El Universal*, May 16. https://archivo.eluniversal.com.mx/cultura/2015/un-samurai-en-la-revolucion-mexicana-1100398.html.

Del Arenal Martínez del Campo, Mónica. 2014. "Luis Nishizawa (1918–2014)." *Revista Electrónica Imágenes* (Instituto de Investigaciones Estéticas). http://www.revistaimagenes.esteticas.unam.mx/luis_nishizawa_1918_2014#_ftn13.

———. 2015. "Entrevista a Luz García Ordóñez." *Revista Imágenes Estéticas*, July. http://www.revistaimagenes.esteticas.unam.mx/luis_nishizawa_1918_2014.
Del Conde, Teresa. N.d. "Las naturalezas muertas de Luis Nishizawa." In *Luis Nishizawa*, edited by Adriana León Portilla de Diener, 81–106. Mexico City: Treyma.
Díaz Álvarez, Lucía, dir. 2016. *Espero que estés bien*. Performed by Cassandra Ciangherotti, Irene Akiko Iida, and Roberto Kameta. Mexico City: Mexico, Instituto Mexicano de Cinematografía (IMCINE)/Nomadas. 15 min.
Dirlik, Arif. 1998. *What Is in a Rim? Critical Perspectives on the Pacific Region Idea*. Lanham, MD: Rowman & Littlefield.
Ellingson, Laura L., and Carolyn Ellis. 2008. "Autoethnography as Constructionist Project." In *Handbook of Constructionist Research*, edited by James A. Holstein and Jaber F. Gubrium, 445–66. New York: Guilford Press.
Endō, Shūsaku. *Silence*. (1966) 2016. Translated by William Johnston. New York: Picador.
———. (1980) 1982. *The Samurai*. Translated by Van C. Gessel. New York: New Directions.
Endoh, Toake. 2009. *Exporting Japan: Politics of Emigration to Latin America*. Urbana: University of Illinois Press.
Enríquez, Lucía Leonor. 2010. "El camino de un guerrero." *Paso de Gato: Boletín Mensual de Teatro* 4 (53): 5.
Falck Reyes, Melba. 2020. "Las relaciones México-Japán y la migración japonesa a Jalisco." In *Presencia japonesa en Jalisco*, edited by Melba Falck Reyes, 19–28. Guadalajara, Mexico: Universidad de Guadalajara/Japan Foundation.
Falck Reyes, Melba, and Héctor Palacios. 2009. *El japonés que conquistó Guadalajara. La historia de Juan de Páez en la Guadalajara del siglo XVII*. Guadalajara, Mexico: Universidad de Guadalajara/Biblioteca Pública del Estado de Jalisco "Juan José Arreola."
———. 2020. "Los primeros japoneses en Guadalajara." In *Presencia japonesa en Jalisco*, edited by Melba Falck Reyes, 31–74. Guadalajara, Mexico: Universidad de Guadalajara/Japan Foundation.
Fernández de Lizardi, José Joaquín. (1816–1831) 1976. *El periquillo sarniento*. Edited by Luis Sáinz de Medrano. 2 vols. Madrid: Nacional.
———. 2004. *The Mangy Parrot: The Life and Times of Periquillo Sarniento Written by Himself for His Children*. Indianapolis, IN: Hackett Publishing.
Foster, David William. 2016. *El Eternauta, Daytripper, and Beyond: Graphic Narrative in Argentina and Brazil*. Austin: University of Texas Press.
Franco, Sergio R. 2017. *Autobiographical Writing in Latin America: Folds of the Self*. Translated by Andrew Ascherl. Amherst, NY: Cambria Press.
Funabiki, Takeo. 2017. "El desasosiego identitario japonés: Razones históricas del Nihonjinron." In *Antropología de Japón: Identidad, discurso y representación*, edited by Blai Guarné, 53–69. Barcelona: Bellaterra.

García, Ariadna. 2020. "Exigen disculpa para japoneses en México." *El Universal*, November 6. https://www.eluniversal.com.mx/nacion/exigen-disculpa-para-japoneses-en-mexico?fbclid=IwAR3QoMh8kWlozhcNERci3zQYMVgn2pfjFo2-euK8U3at6zQAGUOQLxe4tAk.

García, Jerry. 2014. *Looking Like the Enemy: Japanese Mexicans, the Mexican State, and US Hegemony, 1897–1945*. Tucson: University of Arizona Press.

García Barragán, Elisa. N.d. "Luis Nishizawa: Paisaje en soledad." In *Luis Nishizawa*, edited by Adriana León Portilla de Diener, 47–80. Mexico City: Treyma.

García Luna, Margarita. N.d. "Luis Nishizawa, Master of His Craft." *Voices of Mexico: Science, Art, and Culture*: 33–38. http://www.revistascisan.unam.mx/Voices/pdfs/5508.pdf.

González, Fredy. 2017. *Paisanos Chinos: Transpacific Politics among Chinese Immigrants in Mexico*. Oakland: University of California Press.

González Navarro, Moisés. 1994. *Los extranjeros en México y los mexicanos en el extranjero: 1821–1970*. Vol. 2. Mexico City: El Colegio de México.

Gordon, Peter, and Juan José Morales. 2017. *The Silver Way: China, Spanish America and the Birth of Globalisation, 1565–1815*. London: Penguin Random House.

Guarné, Blai. 2009. "The Japanese Oxymoron: A Historical Approach to the Orientalist Representation of Japan." In *One World Periphery Reads the Other: Knowing the "Oriental" in the Americas and the Iberian Peninsula*, edited by Ignacio López-Calvo, 309–29. Newcastle upon Tyne, UK: Cambridge Scholars Publishing.

———. 2017. "Introducción: Una aproximación antropológica al esencialismo cultural japonés." In *Antropología de Japón: Identidad, discurso y representación*, edited by Blai Guarné, 9–36. Barcelona: Bellaterra.

Guzmán, Martín Luis. (1928) 1998. *El águila y la serpiente: Obras completas*. Vol. 1. Mexico City: Fondo de Cultura Económica.

Hall, Stuart. 1999. "Cultural Identity and Diaspora." In *Identity, Community, Culture, Difference*, edited by Jonathan Rutherford, 222–37. London: Lawrence and Wishart.

Heeh, Peter. 2013. *Writing the Self: Diaries, Memoirs, and the History of the Self*. New York: Bloomsbury.

Herbert, Julián. 2015. *La casa del dolor ajeno: Crónica de un pequeño genocidio en La Laguna*. Mexico City: Random House.

Hernández Galindo, Sergio. 2011. *La guerra contra los japoneses en México durante la Segunda Guerra Mundial: Kiru Tsuru y Masao Imuro, migrantes vigilados*. Mexico City: Ítaca.

Higashide, Seiichi. (1981) 2000. *Adios to Tears: The Memoirs of a Japanese-Peruvian Internee in US Concentration Camps*. Foreword by C. Harvey Gardiner. Preface by Elsa H. Kudo. Epilogue by Julie Small. Seattle: University of Washington Press.

Hoyos, Héctor. 2019. *Things with a History: Transcultural Materialism and the Literatures of Extraction in Contemporary Latin America*. New York: Columbia University Press.

Iida, Irene Akiko (theater actor and director, Akikompanía). 2021. Interview with Ignacio López-Calvo. March 3.

Iwasaki Cauti, Fernando. 2005. *Extremo Oriente y el Perú en el siglo XVI*. Lima: Pontificia Universidad Católica del Perú.

Kahara, Nahoko. 2010. "昔話の主人公から国家の象徴へ—「桃太郎」パラダイムの形成．—" (From Folktale Hero to National Symbol: The Making of Momotarō Paradigm in Japanese Modern Age). *Bulletin, Faculty of Music, Tokyo National University of Fine Arts & Music* (36): 51–72.

Kasuga, Mitsuko Esperanza. (2015) 2016. *Akane: los tankas de Mitsuko Kasuga, migrante japonesa en México*. Edited by Aiko Chikaba. Translated by Miwa Teresa Pierre-Audain Kasuga, Carlos Ernesto Pierre-Audain Kasuga, Chiso Homma, Aiko Chikaba. Versification by Cynthia Viverso Cano and Mara Pastor. Tokyo: Texnai.

———. 2016. *Akane, Immigrant Poet: The Tanka of Mitsuko Kasuga*. Edited by Aiko Chikaba. Translated by Naoko Shin, Cynthia Viveros Cano, Carlos Ernesto Pierre-Audian Kasuga, and Aiko Chikaba. Tokyo: Texnai.

Kasuga Osaka, Carlos Tsuyoshi. 2016. "Message for the English Edition." In *Akane, Immigrant Poet: The Tanka of Mitsuko Kasuga*, edited by Aiko Chikaba and translated by Naoko Shin, Cynthia Viveros Cano, Carlos Ernesto Pierre-Audian Kasuga, and Aiko Chikaba, 9–11. Tokyo: Texnai.

Kawaji, Kenichiro. N.p., n.d. *El viento de la Sierra Madre*.

Kim, Junyoung Verónica. 2017. "Asia–Latin America as Method: The Global South Project and the Dislocation of the West." *Verge: Studies in Global Asias* 3 (2): 97–117.

"Lanza Daniel Salinas libro sobre pionero de la fotografía en Tijuana." 2019. *El Imparcial*, November 11. https://www.elimparcial.com/tijuana/espectaculoslocal/Lanza-Daniel-Salinas-libro-sobre-pionero-de-la-fotografia-en-Tijuana-20191111-0026.html.

Lara Cisneros, Gerardo. 2014. *¿Ignorancia invencible? Superstición e idolatraía ante el provisorato de indios y chinos del arzobispado de México en el siglo XVII*. Mexico City: Universidad Nacional Autónoma de México, Instituto de Investigaciones Históricas.

Lee, Ana Paulina. 2018. *Mandarin Brazil: Race, Representation, and Memory*. Stanford, CA: Stanford University Press.

Lee-DiStefano, Debra. 2012. "Theory, Orientalism and a Perspective on Their Place in the Study of Asians in the Americas." In *Peripheral Transmodernities: South-to-South Intercultural Dialogues between the Luso-Hispanic World and "the Orient,"* edited by Ignacio López-Calvo, 12–22. Newcastle upon Tyne: Cambridge Scholars Publishing.

León Portilla de Diener, Adriana, ed. N.d. *Luis Nishizawa*. Photography by Javier Hinojosa. Design by Luis Almeida. Mexico City: Treyma.

Lesser, Jeffrey. 2007. *A Discontented Diaspora: Japanese Brazilians and the Meanings of Ethnic Militancy, 1960–1980*. Durham, NC: Duke University Press.

López-Calvo, Ignacio. 2013a. *The Affinity of the Eye: Writing Nikkei in Peru*. Tucson: University of Arizona Press.

———. 2013b. "The Death of the Author through False Translation in Mario Bellatin's Orientalised Japan." *Bulletin of Latin American Research* 32 (3): 339–53.

———. 2014. *Dragons in the Land of the Condor: Writing Tusán in Peru*. Tucson: University of Arizona Press.

———. 2008. *Imaging the Chinese in Cuban Literature and Culture*. Gainesville: University Press of Florida.

———. 2018. "Worlding and Decolonizing the Literary World-System: Asian–Latin American Literature as an Alternative Type of *Weltliteratur*." In *Re-Mapping World Literature: Writing, Book Markets, and Epistemologies between Latin America and the Global South*, edited by Gesine Müller, Jorge J. Locane, and Benjamin Loy, 15–31. Berlin: De Gruyter.

———. 2019a. *Japanese Brazilian Saudades: Diasporic Identities and Cultural Production*. Louisville: University Press of Colorado.

———. 2019b. "Necropolítica, espectrología china e impunidad en *La casa del dolor ajeno* de Julián Herbert." In *Narrativas de lo chino en las Américas y la Península ibérica*, edited by María Montt Strabucchi and Amelia Sáiz López, 55–70. Biblioteca de China Contemporánea. Barcelona: Bellaterra.

———. 2020. "The Nikkei Community as Prison in Higashide's *Adios to Tears* and Yamashita's *Brazil-Maru*." In *Literatura e (i)migração no Brasil/Literatura and (Im)migration in Brazil*, edited by Waïl S. Hassan and Rogério Lima, 397–412. Rio de Janeiro: Makunaima.

———. 2021. "Biopolitics, Orientalism, and the Asian Immigrant as Monster in Salazar's *La medianoche del japonés* and Rodríguez's *Asesinato en una lavandería china*." In *Beyond the West: Cultural and Literary Dialogues Between Asia and Latin America*, edited by Goriça Majstorovic and Axel Gasquet, 121–41. London: Palgrave Macmillan.

———. Forthcoming. "Were Issei in Brazil imperialists? Migration-Driven Expansionism in Nikkei Literature." In *The Japanese Empire in Latin America*, edited by Sidney Lu and Pedro Iacobelli. Honolulu: University of Hawai'i Press.

Lu, Sidney Xu. 2019. *The Making of Japanese Settler Colonialism: Malthusianism and Trans-Pacific Migration, 1868–1961*. Cambridge: Cambridge University Press.

Machuca, Paulina. 2018. *El vino de cocos en la Nueva España. Historia de una transculturación en el siglo XVII*. Zamora, Michoacán: El Colegio de Michoacán y Fideicomiso Felipe Teixidor y Monserrat Alfau de Teixidor.

MacRobie Fliss, Charles Joseph. 2012. "Communal Identity through Cultural Essentialism: The Evolution of the American Anime and Manga Fan Community and the Orientalism of Its Conception of Japan." Undergraduate honor's theses, College of William and Mary. https://scholarworks.wm.edu/honorstheses/472.
Mariátegui, José Carlos. 1971. *Seven Interpretative Essays on Peruvian Reality*. Translated by Marjory Urquidi. Austin: University of Texas Press.
———. 1994. "Siete ensayos de interpretación de la realidad peruana." In *Mariátegui total*. Vol. 1. Lima: Amauta.
Martínez, Teresa. 2019. "Rescata biografía de revolucionario." *El Norte*, October 12. https://www.elnorte.com/rescata-biografia-de-revolucionario/ar1793956.
Martínez Legorreta, Omar, ed. 2014. *Un episodio de la renovada relación méxico-china: Los primeros estudiantes chinos en México, 1974–1984*. Zinacantepec, Mexico: El Colegio Mexiquense.
Marx, Karl, and Friedrich Engels. (1848) 2005. *The Communist Manifesto*. Stirling, UK: Filiquarian Publishing.
Masterson, Daniel M., and Sayaka Funada-Classen. 2004. *The Japanese in Latin America*. Urbana: University of Illinois Press.
Miller, Roy Andrew. 1982. *Japan's Modern Myth: The Language and Beyond*. New York: Weatherhill.
Minh-Ha, Trinh T. 2011. *Elsewhere, Within Here: Immigration, Refugeeism and the Boundary Event*. London: Routledge.
Miura, Satomi. 2018. "La presencia de la prensa de los Nikkei en el contexto de México antes de la Segunda Guerra Mundial." In *Asociación Latinoamericana de Estudios de Asia y África, XIII Congreso Internacional de ALADAA*, 3–20. https://ceaa.colmex.mx/aladaa/memoria_xiii_congreso_internacional/images/miura.pdf.
Molloy, Sylvia. 1991. *At Face Value: Autobiographical Writing in Spanish America*. Cambridge: Cambridge University Press.
Morán Breña, Carmen. 2020. "La historia negra de los japoneses en México y una petición de Perdón," *El País*, November 8. https://elpais.com/mexico/2020-11-08/la-historia-negra-de-los-japoneses-en-mexico-y-una-peticion-de-perdon.html.
Moyssén, Xavier. N.d. "Introducción al arte de Nishizawa." In *Luis Nishizawa*, edited by Adriana León Portilla de Diener, 13–46. Mexico City: Treyma.
Muñoz, Rafael F. (1931) 2008. *Vámonos con Pancho Villa*. Mexico City: Era.
Murasaki, Shikibu. 1990. *The Tale of Genji*. Translated by Edward G. Seidensticker. New York: Vintage Classics.
Murray, Antonio. 1994. *Casi un siglo de recuerdos: Biografía de Federico Imamura*. Monterrey, Mexico: Castillo.
Murray, Kenichi-Benito. N.d. *Crónicas de los pioneros japoneses en México*. Translated by Makoto Toda. N.p.

Museo de Arte Moderno. 1965. *Taku Hon: Calcas por Kojin Toneyama y Luis Nishizawa*. Mexico City: Instituto Nacional de Bellas Artes.
Nakatani, Carlos. 2000. *Papá extranjero: Breves exequias*. Mexico City: Times Editores.
Nakatani Sánchez, Emma Chrishuru. 2002. "Estudio preliminar y notas a 'Novela escrita por Carlos Nakatani. Historia de su propia vida.'" BA thesis, Universidad Iberoamericana, Mexico City.
Nguyen, Viet Thanh, and Janet Hoskins. 2014. "Transpacific Power and Knowledge." In *Transpacific Studies: Framing and Emerging Field*, edited by Janet Hoskins and Viet Thanh Nguyen, 1–24. Honolulu: University of Hawai'i Press.
Nishizawa Flores, Luis. 1990. "Consideraciones de la técnica como libertad de expression." Discurso de ingreso a la Academia de Artes, June 5. https://academiadeartes.org.mx//wp-content/uploads/2019/09/DiscursoNishizawaLuis.pdf.
Nitobe, Inazō. (1900) 2008. *Bushido: The Soul of Japan*. N.p.: Floating Press. Digital file. http://www.kobobooks.com/ebook/Bushido-The-Soul-of-Japan/book-00YAKdlxPE6xX9gFcvI05A/page1.html.
Nonaka, Kingo. 2014. *Kingo Nonaka: Andanzas revolucionarias*. Edited by Genaro Nonaka García. Mexicali, Mexico: Artificios.
Nonaka García, Genaro. 2014. Introduction to *Kingo Nonaka: Andanzas revolucionarias*, edited by Genaro Nonaka García, 13–26. Mexicali, Mexico: Artificios.
Noriyuki Sato, Francisco, and Julio Shimamoto. 2008. *Banzai! História da imigração japonesa no Brasil em mangá*. São Paulo: NSP-Hakkosha.
Ota Mishima, María Elena. (1982) 1985. *Siete migraciones japonesas en México: 1890–1978*. Mexico City: El Colegio de México.
Paz, Octavio. (1950) 2003. *El laberinto de la soledad*. Edited by Enrico Mario Santí. Madrid: Cátedra.
———. 1985. *The Labyrinth of Solitude*. Translated by Lysander Kemp. New York: Grove Press.
Peddie, Francis. 2006. "Una presencia incómoda: La colonia japonesa de México durante la Segunda Guerra Mundial." *Estudios de historia moderna y contemporánea de México* (32): 73–101.
Peña Delgado, Grace. 2012. *Making the Chinese Mexican: Global Migration, Localism, and Exclusions in the US-Mexico Borderlands*. Stanford, CA: Stanford University Press.
Portal, Gastón, Anwar Safa, and Jorge Colón, dir. 2017. *Las trece esposas de Wilson Fernández*. Television series. Performed by Carlos Valencia, Martín Altomaro, Irene Akiko, et al. Mexico City: Animal de Luz Films.
Pratt, Mary Louise. 1992. *Imperial Eyes: Travel Writing and Transculturation*. London: Routledge.
Reyes Estrada, Cecilia. 2016. *La gallina azul: Historia de una familia japonesa en México durante la Segunda Guerra Mundial*. Mexico City: Ítaca.

Rico Bovio, Arturo. 2000. "Nishizawa o el rescate de la percepción." In *Luis Nishizawa. Paisaje*, edited by Adriana León Portilla de Diener, 5. Chihuahua, Mexico: Museo Chihuahuense de Arte Contemporáneo.

Rivera Delgado, Gabriel. 2014. "Prólogo: Kingo Nonaka y sus andanzas." In *Kingo Nonaka: Andanzas revolucionarias*, edited by Genaro Nonaka García, 3–8. Mexicali, Mexico: Artificios.

Rocha, Christina. 2013. "Zen in Brazil: Cannibalizing Orientalist Flows." In *Orientalism and Identity in Latin America: Fashioning Self and Other from the (Post)Colonial Margin*, edited by Erik Camayd-Freixas, 200–216. Tucson: University of Arizona Press.

Rodríguez, Antonio. N.d. "El dibujo en Luis Nishizawa." In *Luis Nishizawa*, edited by Adriana León Portilla de Diener, 135–58. Mexico City: Treyma.

Ruiz, Nicolasa, dir. 2020. *Obachan*. Performed by Fuyu Kiyota. Mexico City: IMCINE. 15 min.

Rustomji, Roshni. 2012. "Walking the Talk: Saris, Sarapes and Elephants in Green Suits." In *Peripheral Transmodernities: South-to-South Intercultural Dialogues between the Luso-Hispanic World and "the Orient,"* edited by Ignacio López-Calvo, 23–39. Newcastle upon Tyne: Cambridge Scholars.

Said, Edward W. 1983. *The World, the Text, and the Critic*. Cambridge, MA: Harvard University Press.

Salinas Basave, Daniel. 2019. *El samurái de la Graflex: De enfermero de Villa a cronista fotográfico de Tijuana*. Mexico City: Fondo de Cultura Económica.

Sánchez-Prado, Ignacio. 2018. *Strategic Occidentalism: On Mexican Fiction, the Neoliberal Book Market, and the Question of World Literature*. Evanston, IL: Northwestern University Press.

Schiavone Camacho, Julia María. 2012. *Chinese Mexicans: Transpacific Migration and the Search for a Homeland 1910–1960*. Chapel Hill: University of North Carolina Press.

Secretaría de Cultura de Chihuahua. 2020. "Presentación del libro El samurái de la Gráflex, de Daniel Salinas Basave." October 31. https://www.youtube.com/watch?v=NMmQHHAQSkE.

Secretaría de Fomento, Colonización e Industria, Mexico. 1913. *Boletín del Departamento del Trabajo* 1 (1).

Seijas, Tatiana. 2014. *Asian Slaves in Colonial Mexico: From Chinos to Indians*. Cambridge: Cambridge University Press.

Siu, Kam Wen. 2007. *La vida no es una tómbola*. Lima: Abajo el Puente.

———. 2008. *This Sort of Life*. Translated by Siu Kam-Wen. Introduction by Ignacio López-Calvo. Morrisville, NC: Lulu.

———. 2009. *El verano largo*. Lima: Abajo el Puente.

Siu, Lok. 2007. *Memories of a Future Home: Diasporic Citizenship of Chinese in Panama*. Stanford, CA: Stanford University Press.

Staniford, Philip. 1973. "Nihon ni itemo sho ga nai: O background, a estratégia e a personalidade do imigrante japonês no além-mar." In *Assimilação e integração dos japoneses no Brasil*, edited by Hiroshi Saito and Takashi Maeyama, 32–55. Petrópolis, Brazil: Vozes.

Sturken, Marita. 1997. *Tangled Memories: The Vietnam War, the AIDS Epidemic, and the Politics of Remembering.* Berkeley: University of California Press.

Suárez, José I. 2019. "The Dichotomy Christianity-Japaneseness: Shusaku Endo's Autobiographical Novel *The Samurai*." Paper presented at the Eleventh Conference on East-West Cross-Cultural Relations Dialogs in Transition: Luso-Hispanic Cultural Production and Global South Exchanges, May 9–12, Warsaw, Krakow, and Bielsko Biala, Poland.

Subrahmanyam, Sanjay. July 1997. "Connected Histories: Notes toward a Reconfiguration of Early Modern Eurasia." *Modern Asian Studies* 31(3): 735–62.

Taggart, Emma. 2018. "Wabi-Sabi: The Japanese Art of Finding Beauty in Imperfect Ceramics." *My Modern MET*, October 29. https://mymodernmet.com/wabi-sabi-japanese-ceramics.

Takeda, Shinpei, dir. 2008. *El México más cercano a Japón/The Closest Mexico to Japan.* Tijuana, Mexico: Atopus Studio. 48 min.

Tibol, Raquel, ed. 1984a. *Luis Nishizawa. Realismo, expresionismo, abstracción.* Mexico City: UNAM.

Tibol, Raquel. 1984b. "Prologue." In *Luis Nishizawa. Realismo, expresionismo, abstracción,* edited by Raquel Tibol, 3–4. Mexico City: UNAM.

———. N.d. "La obra mayor de Luis Nishizawa." In *Luis Nishizawa,* edited by Adriana León Portilla de Diener, 107–34. Mexico City: Treyma.

Tinajero, Araceli. 2012. *Kokoro, una Mexicana en Japón.* Madrid: Verbum.

Toneyama, Kōjin. 1974. *The Popular Arts of Mexico.* Translated by Richard L. Gage. Foreword by Carlos Espejel. New York: Weatherhill/Heibonsha.

Torres-Rodríguez, Laura. 2019. *Orientaciones transpacíficas: La modernidad mexicana y el espectro de Asia.* Chapel Hill: University of North Carolina Press.

Tsuda, Takeyuki. 2003. *Strangers in the Ethnic Homeland: Japanese Brazilian Return Migration in Transnational Perspective.* New York: Columbia University Press.

Tsukamoto, Tetsundo. 1973. "Sociologia do imigrante: Algumas considerações sobre o processo migratório." In *Assimilação e integração dos japoneses no Brasil,* edited by Hiroshi Saito and Takashi Maeyama, 13–31. Petrópolis, Brazil: Vozes.

Uchida, Jun. 2014. *Brokers of Empire: Japanese Settler Colonialism in Korea, 1876–1945.* Cambridge, MA: Harvard University Press.

Uchimura, Kanzō. 1894. *Japan and the Japanese: Essays.* Tokyo: Min'yūsha.

———. 1895. *How I Became a Christian: Out of My Diary, by a "Heathen Convert."* Tokyo: Keiseisha.

Ueno, Hisashi (author), and Konohana Sakuya (illustrator). (1994) 2008. *Los samuráis de México. La verdadera historia de los primeros japoneses en*

Latinoamérica. Translated by Koji Hashimoto et al. Mexico City: Seika University Business Promotion Section/Kyoto International Manga Museum/ Asociación México-Japonesa.

Valenzuela Zapata, Ana G., Paul D. Buell, María de la Paz Solano-Pérez, and Hyunhee Park. 2013. "'Huichol' Stills: A Century of Anthropology—Technology Transfer and Innovation." *Crossroads* 8: 157–91.

Valenzuela Zapata, Ana G., Aristarco Regalado Pinedo, and Michiko Mizoguchi. 2008. "Influencia asiática en la producción de mezcal en la costa de Jalisco: El caso de la raicilla." *México y la Cuenca del Pacífico* 11 (33): 91–116.

Vasconcelos, José. (1925) 1948. *La raza cósmica*. Mexico City: Espasa-Calpe Mexicana.

Villa Guerrero, Guadalupe. 2014. "El arte de Luis Nishizawa," *Revista Bicentenario* (Instituto Mora): 72–79. http://revistabicentenario.com.mx/wp-content/uploads/2014/07/BiC-23-Luis-Nishizawa.pdf.

Wein, Susana, and Irene Akiko Iida. 1997. *Juan, el momotaro (obra de teatro infantil inspirada en una leyenda japonesa)*. Mexico City: Corunda/Consejo Nacional para la Cultura y las Artes.

Yamashita, Karen Tei. 1992. *Brazil-Maru*. Minneapolis: Coffee House Press.

Yun, Lisa Li-Shen. 2004. "An Afro-Chinese Caribbean: Cultural Cartographies of Contrariness in the Work of Antonio Chuffat Latour, Margaret Cezair, and Patricia Powell." *Caribbean Quarterly* 50 (2): 26–43.

Index

Acacoyagua, 20, 131, 139–40, 142, 217n1
Academia de Artes, 150, 156, 158, 160–61
Acapetahua, 134
Acapulco, 3, 19, 91, 137, 176–79, 229n17
Africa, 15, 27, 28, 134, 195
   enslaved African labor, 16–17
Agua Prieta, 54
Aguilar Robles Maldonado, Fernando, 59
Ahuacatlán, 19
Aizu, 177, 229n18
Akachi, Arata, 231n1
Akane (Mitsuko Esperanza Kasuga), vii, 2, 36, 71–72, 82, 152
   Akane, Immigrant Poet, 96, 99, 102, 106, 119
   and diasporic nationalist discourse, 186–93
   and female agency, xiv, 34, 68, 86
   and "Suberihiyu," 97
Akiko Irene (Akiko Iida Naito), Hanayagui Irene, Sachikaze Irene, Irene Sachikaze, vii, ix, xiv, 220n1, 226n1, 228nn6–7, 228n11, 229n16, 231n38
   Akikompania, 166, 168, 227n5
   and *automóvil gris al estilo benshi japonés, El*, 169, 190–91, 231n38
   and *Babel, reconstruyendo comunidad*, 169, 228n6
   and *Contramarea, el regreso del samurái*, 176, 178, 180, 182, 184
   and *Crepúsculo de la cigüeña*, 168, 228n6
   and *Edén, Expresión de Gracia*, 169
   and *Espero que estés bien*, 166
   and *gallo, El*, 169, 228n6
   and *Humboldt*, 169, 228n6
   and *Juan, el momotaro* (book), 169–70
   and *Juan, el momotaro* (play), 168–69, 184
   and *KAI-ON, sonidos del mar*, 168, 228n5
   and *KANAWA, corona de hierro*, 168–69, 228n6
   and *Madre solo hay dos*, 166
   and *Mai-Sho-Gaku, trazos de fuego*, 168, 182–83, 185, 226n1
   and *Nikkei . . . Correo de Hiroshima*, 168, 185, 187–88, 190
   and *Ópera para actores*, 169
   and third space, 35, 37, 194
   and *trece esposas de Wilson Fernández, Las*, 166
Algudín, 56

Americans, 14, 26, 52, 54–55, 85, 186, 196
Americas, the, 25, 57, 61, 63, 76, 135, 176
  and Asian migration, 9, 21
  and globalization, 15, 18
anarchists, 140
Anderson, Benedict, 31
Ando, Shiori, 220n1
anime, 132, 145, 215n1
Anitos, 3, 199n4
Arabs, 93
  alambique, 4
  Arab-Latin American literature, 28
Argentina, 22
Arima, Rokutaro, 136
Arreola, Enrique, 231n38
Asahi, 125, 187, 230n34
Asahi, Mari, 169
Asia, 7–10, 14–15, 27
  aesthetics, 2, 6, 13–14, 28, 33, 147, 152–54, 161–64
  Asian communities, 4, 13–16, 18, 25–27, 30–33, 45, 197
  Asian communities in the Americas, 10, 70
  Asian Holocaust, The, 3, 6, 14, 26, 88
  Asianness, 2, 6, 11–13, 15–16, 29, 32–33, 161, 163, 165
  and coolie, 18, 201n19
  distilling, 3, 4
  East Asia, 3, 7, 15, 27, 68, 156
  immigrants, 1, 9, 12–13, 15, 200n7, 200n16, 201n19, 202n33
Asian–Latin Americans, 8, 25, 95
  Asian–Latin American approach, 28, 34
  cultural production, xiii, 10, 13–14, 165
  literature, xiv, 8, 10–14, 164, 200n13
Asociación de Periodistas Teatrales, 231n38
Asociación Japonesa de Tijuana, 60
Asociación Mexicana de Críticos de Teatro, 231n38
Asociación México-Japonesa, ix, 5, 25
Atlantic Ocean, 9, 15

atomic bomb, 64, 158, 183, 186–89, 203n1
Austin, J. L., 106
autoethnography, 81–82
Ávila Caballero, Adriana Berenice, 151
Ávila Camacho, Manuel, 22, 24, 61, 89
Ávila Espinoza, Emma, 70
Axis powers, 24, 61, 63, 89, 91
Awaji Island, 70, 77, 78, 80, 87
Aztecs, 130, 178–79, 223n26
Aztec gods, 157
Azuela, Mariano, 45

Baja California, 20–21, 46, 48, 57, 62, 195
Bashō, Matsuo, 108, 131–32, 217n3
Battle of Bataan, 186
Bellatin, Mario, 200n16, 231n2
benshi, 169, 190–92, 227n5, 228n6, 231n38
Bermejillo, 53
Bhabha, Homi, 10, 102, 197
Bible, 142
Borneo, 3
Brazil, 22–25, 37, 71–72, 135, 201n23, 202n33, 208n1, 209n9
  abolition of slavery, 16
  jacaranda trees, 4
  Japanese Brazilians, 12, 14, 92, 133, 139, 196, 215n1, 217n6
Briseño, América Teresa, 43
Brunet, Jules, 138, 218n22
Buddhism, 2, 46, 118, 167, 177, 183–84, 202n33, 211n31
Bulgaria, 150, 221n4
Bunraku theater, 182
bushidō, 68
Butler, Judith, 106–7
Butoh dance theater, 182–84, 188, 228n6

Cabrera, Juan Manuel, 191
cacahuate japonés, 5
cafés de chinos, 2
California, ix, xiii, 9, 46, 100, 172, 176, 188, 195
Calles, Plutarco Elías, 54
Camposeco, Víctor Manuel, 186–87

INDEX   247

Cape Mendocino, 176
Cape of Good Hope, 9
Cárdenas, 100–101
Cárdenas, Lázaro, 22, 60, 62, 207n48
Cardón, Bibiana, 49
Cardón family, 49
Caribbean, the, 9, 61, 190
Carranza, Venustiano, 41–42, 55, 202n27, 206n29
Casas Grandes, 50–53, 57, 205n21
Castellanos, Julio, 160, 224n30
Castillo, Máximo, 57, 206n35
Catholics, Catholicism, 18, 70, 101, 176–77, 179–82, 186
Celaya, 16, 157, 221n3
Center for Japanese Artists, 148
Centro Cultural Martí, 59–60, 157, 223n24
Centro Cultural Mexicano-Japonés, 164
Centro Cultural Mexiquense, 157
Centro Cultural Tijuana, 59–60
Cercas, Javier, 45
Cerritos, 100
chamoy, 5, 101, 119, 122, 200n10
Chang, Jason Oliver, 26
Chao Romero, Robert, 26
Chapultepec castle, 61, 207n42
Chávez, Ignacio, 65
Chávez Morado, José, 160
Chew, Selfa A., 9, 24, 26, 42, 91, 202n29, 212n37, 231n2
Chiapas, 35–36, 130–31, 134–38, 141, 143–44, 188–89
  author, 185
  indigenous people, 160
  Japanese in, 20, 44, 63, 146, 194, 219n32
Chicago's Institute of Applied Science, 58
Chihuahua, 48–51, 91, 202n29, 206n30, 206n34, 206n35
  Japanese in, 24, 195
  Mexican Revolution, 53, 56
  Secretaría de Cultura, 221n4

Chikaba, Aiko, editor, ix, 5, 96, 99–101, 119, 217n23
  Prologue, 105, 111, 116, 124
China, 6–7, 14, 25–26, 168, 200n16, 201n19, 202n33, 219
  anti-Chinese racism, 26, 68
  Chinese, 3, 6, 161, 167, 201, 219n31
  Chinese-style stills, 199n6
  in Cuba and descendants, 9, 16, 22, 43, 200n15
  in Japan and descendants, 84
  Manila Galleons, 10
  in Mexico and descendants, xv, 17, 20–21, 23, 26, 32, 57; artists and writers, xiii, 2, 231n2; Chinese exclusion act, 9, 12, 45, 196; contract laborers, 16, 18; transpacific politics, 12, 94
  painting, 133, 154, 156, 159, 164
  in Panama and descendants, 16, 28
  in Peru and descendants, 15, 200n15, 200n18, 201n24, 202n33
  Sino-Latin American communities, 2, 25, 28
  in United States, 23
  university system, 202n33
  war with Japan, 61 88–89, 185
China Poblana (Mirnha; Catarina de San Juan), 2–3
Chinatowns, 2, 28
Chinese Exclusion Act (Immigration Act of 1882), 9, 23
Chinese shan shui style, 156
chino, indios chinos, 3
chinos californianos, 9
Chong, José Luis, 26
Christ, 46
Christian church, 70, 138, 140–42, 177, 179, 181, 218n26
  missionaries, 137, 140, 177, 179, 181
  utopias, 36, 138–40, 146
Ciudad Juárez, 48–53, 90–91, 205, 213n54
  hospital, 57–58
  Nonaka the soldier, 44

Civitavecchia, 179
Coahuila, 20, 22, 41, 50, 201n20
coconut wine, 3, 4, 19
Cold War ideology, 8
Colima, 3–4, 69, 199n3, 221n3
Colón, Jorge, 166
Colonia Enomoto, 20, 130–31
Colonial Association, 202n25
Columbus, 54, 205n27
Comité de Ayuda Mutua, 24, 90, 214n57
Compañía Teatro de Ciertos Habitantes, 169, 192, 231n38
CONACULTA, 150
Confucianism, 17, 121, 201n22
Consejo Nacional para la Cultura y las Artes, 150
Constitutionalist Army, 42
Contreras, Berenice, 183
Convenio de Libre Ejercicio del Médico, Dentista y Farmacéutico, 145
coolie, 9, 15–17, 201n19
Cooperativa Mexicano Japonesa, 136, 138–39, 143, 218n24
Coria, Benjamín, 224n31
Coria del Río, 177, 179
Cortés, Hernán, 130
Coshida, 89
cosmopolitanism, 11
Costa Rica, 228n6
COVID-19 pandemic, 31
Cuauhtitlán, 147
Cuba, 9, 15–16, 22, 43, 177, 179, 200n15
Cuernavaca, 16, 24, 92, 214n58

Daoism, 157
Darío, Rubén, 14
Date, Masamune, 177–78, 229n18
dekasegi, 8, 12, 135
Departamento de Identificación de la Comandancia de Policía de Tijuana, 58
Díaz Álvarez. Lucía, 166
Díaz del Castillo, Bernal, 130
Díaz Ordaz, Gustavo, 64–65
Díaz, Porfirio, 19, 33, 52, 205n22

Doctor Atl (Gerardo Murillo), 160
Doemer, Max, 224n31
Duke of Argyle, 9
Dvořák, Antonín, 139

Edo period, 108, 131, 169, 182
Ejército del Noroeste, 42
Encío, Luis de, Fukuchi Soemon (or Hyoemon), 18
Endō, Shūsaku, 180, 229n22
Enfukuji Buddhist temple, 177
Engels, Friedrich, 11
England, 143, 199n2
Enola Gay, 188
Enomoto, Viscount Takeaki, 20, 201n25, 218n18
Enomoto colony, xiv, 20, 36, 130–42, 145–46, 188, 217n15
Nichiboku Takushoku immigrant association, 137
Ensenada, 25, 47, 58
Escuela Industrial de Mecánica Automotriz, 60
Escuela Nacional de Artes Plásticas, Academia de San Carlos, 148, 220n3, 221n3, 223n24
Escuela Secundaria y Preparatoria de la Ciudad de México, 167
Escuintla, 20, 134, 137, 139, 142, 144, 217n1
espionage, 16, 22–23, 35, 43–44, 61–63, 91, 195–96
ethnic Koreans (Shingemin, *Zainichi-Kankoku-jin*), 84–85, 211n32
eugenics, 33
Europe, 8, 15, 27, 36, 81, 176–77, 179
artists, 160, 164, 225n42, 226n51
farmworkers, 16
modernity, 6
Orientalists, 10–11, 13–14, 27, 202n33

Fabela, Isidro, 3
Facebook, 190
Faesler, Juliana, 228n6
Falck Reyes, Melba, 18, 20, 26, 177

Federal Bureau of Investigation (FBI), 15, 22
Fernandes, Gaspar, 18
Fernández de Lizardi, José Joaquín, 75, 81
Fierro, Rodolfo, 53–54, 57
fifth column, 20, 23, 43, 61, 89, 194
Flores, María de Jesús, 147
Formosa, 88, 212n47
Fourier, Charles, 138–39, 218n22
France, 138, 143, 218, 228n6
Franciscan missionaries, 177, 229n18
Franco, Sergio R., 34
Freemason, 58
Fuente del Risco, Casa del Risco Museum, 3
Fuji, 28, 108–9, 144, 152–53, 184
Fujimaki, Emi, 220n1
Fujimori, Alberto, 13, 30
Fujin, 184
Fujino, Tatsujiro, Fujino Emigrant Association, 141, 219n37
Fukazawa, Yukio, 148
Fukuchi, 19
Fukuoka Prefecture, 19, 45–46, 48, 54, 176
Fukuyama, 75
Fuse, Tsunematsu, 140–41

Galeana, 51
Gámez, Jessica, 228n11
ganbare, 98, 119–20, 122, 215n2, 228n13
García, Alan, 196, 232n7
García, Jerry, 21, 26, 50, 196, 204n6
García, Máximo, 53, 57, 205n25, 205n26, 206n35
García Barragán, Marcelino, 64, 155, 160, 164, 221n9, 222n10, 225n48, 226n51
García de Nonaka, Petra, 54
García Luna, Margarita, 150
geisha, 13, 77, 116, 190, 231n37
Genoa, 177
Gentlemen's Agreement (1907), 19, 23
Germany, Germans, 52, 89, 199n2

Global North, 7
Goa, 18
Goitia, Francisco, 159, 224n29
González, Fredy, 26
González, Sergio, 52
González de León, Sofía, 231n38
Grand Shrine of Izumo, 182
Great Depression, 21, 100
Guadalajara, 18–20, 26, 60–63, 75, 195, 207n46, 214n56
  displacement of Japanese, 16, 22, 24, 30, 35, 43, 48, 144
Guanajuato, 152, 157, 221n3
Guaraní, 14
Guatemala, 24, 131
Gueiya-Maru, 69
Guerrero, 199n3
Guízar, Carlos, 231n38
Gutiérrez, Victoria, 178
Guzmán, Martín Luis, 53

Hacienda Batán, 90, 199n7, 214n57
Hacienda San Mateo Ixtacalco, 147
Hacienda Temixco, 24, 91, 95, 214n57
Hacienda Xalapa, 141, 219n36
Hagino, Miho, 169, 219n1
haiku, 296–97, 100, 125, 154, 202n33, 217n2
  Bashō, 108, 131–32
Hall, Stuart, 11, 131
Hanafuji, Akio, 219n1
Hanayagui Academy of Traditional Japanese Dance, 167
Harada, Carmen, 219n1
Harada, Shinzo, 41
Hasekura, Tsunenaga Rokuemon (Felipe Francisco Faxicura), 19, 176–82, 229n17
Hashimoto, Koji, 130
Hatanaka, Mirian Lie, 98
Havana, 177, 179
Hawaii, 48, 65, 89, 92, 99, 185, 188
Hayakawa, Hiromi, Marla Hiromi Hayakawa Salas, 227n2
Heeh, Peter, 34

Heian, Heian-kyō period, 97, 133
Heraldo de Nisei, El, 108
Herbert, Julián, 45, 204n11
Hernández Galindo, Sergio, 22–23, 41, 43, 60, 63
  guerra contra los japoneses en México durante la Segunda Guerra Mundial, La, 16, 26
Hernández Ibarra, María del Carmen, 231n38
Herrán, Buenaventura, 53
Hideyoshi, Toyotomi, 177
Higashide, Seiichi, 203, 212n42
Higurashi, 220n1
Hijikata, Tatsumi, 183
Hirai, Shinji, 195
Hirasawa, Yukari, 220n1
Hirashi, Alejandro, 196
Hirata, Chioko, 77
Hirata, Hansae, 220n1
Hirata, Tomás, 196
Hirazawa, Yukari, 184
Hirohito, 62, 74, 125, 207n45
Hiromoto, Kenji, 220n1
Hiroshige, Andō, 151, 153–55, 221n7, 222n14
Hiroshima, 64, 92, 168, 183, 185–90
Hiyama, Masahiko, 220n1
Hokkaido, Republic of Ezo, 138
Hokusai, 108, 151, 153, 221n7
  Great Wave off Kanagawa, The, 173
Horiguchi, Kumaichi, 52
Hospital Civil y Militar de Ciudad Juárez, 49–51
Hospital Muguerza de Monterrey, 65
Huerta, José Victoriano, 52, 202n27
huichol, 3–4
Hwang, David Henry, 228n6
hybridity, 33, 123, 157–58

Ichikawa, 148
Ichiro, 80
Iida, Saburo, 220n1
Iida, Toshiaki, 167, 220n1
Ikenaga, Hisae, 220n1
Imamura, Federico (Sekio), 29, 70–71, 92, 201n20, 202n31, 209n6, 216n17, 231n1
imari porcelain, 3
immigrant literature (*imin bungaku*), 35, 95, 130
imperialism, 63, 67–68, 87–88, 94, 186, 194
  escaping, 36
Meiji, 139
migration, 20, 72, 74, 91, 133–34, 145
Imuro, Masao, 16, 26
Ina, 99, 118, 121, 125
Inazō, Nitobe, 68
India, 2–3, 18, 27, 30, 152, 184, 201n19
Indian Ocean, 9, 15
indio, 3, 26
Indonesia, 3
Instituto Nacional de Cardiología, 65
internment camps, 15, 22–23, 30, 63, 144, 195–96, 200n18
Isambo, 80
Ishino, 47
Isibasi, 75
Isla Mujeres, 61
Istani, 80, 86, 93
Italy, 52, 177, 179, 205n21
Itō, Eiki, 220n1
Iwadare, Teikichi Luis, 5
Iwakura, Tomomi, 179
Iwasaki Cauti, Fernando, 177, 229n18
Iztaccíhuatl, 148, 153, 222n12
Izumo Kingdom, 182–83, 229n25
Izumo, no Okuni, 182

jacaranda trees, 4, 90, 109–10
Jaimes, Laura, 187
Jalisco, 4, 26, 199n3
jamoncillo, 70, 208n4
Japan
  in Brazil, 12, 93, 217n6; cultural production, 67, 193; government pressure, 37, 71; "return" emigration, 167; Shindō Renmei, 25, 133, 202n32

calligraphy, 183
economy, 20
flag, 45, 52, 99, 137–39, 143, 164, 208n3
Foreign Ministry, 61, 91–92, 100, 130, 136, 145-46, 176–77
government, 4, 20–21, 43, 67, 70, 94, 136-38, 185; and migration, 73, 90, 130, 195–96; relations with Mexico, 23, 52, 196, 210n19, 214n57; Sacred Treasure of the Dragon Award, 125, 150
immigrant literature, 40. 27, 35, 69, 96, 121n
Imperial Court, 97
Japaneseness, 33, 67–69, 107–8, 113–18, 167–68; and Christianity, 181; cultural essentialism, 131–35, 145–46, 162, 165, 184, 189, 193–94; performance of, 102, 117, 190
Japanese-US relations, 23, 62–63, 67
language, 29, 61, 76, 129, 133, 141–42, 179, 182; new generations, 46; pronunciation, 231n40; singing, 189
in Latin America, 8, 67
market, 20
military, 17, 21–22, 133, 141, 186, 201n25
newspapers, 22, 28
peanuts, 5, 68, 76, 200n9
in Peru, 30, 193, 203n34
in United States, 20, 26, 196
Jasimoto, 75
Jayasaka, 76
Jesuits, 18, 181, 229n22
Juárez, Benito, 134
Junji, Kinoshita, 228n6

Kabayashi, Nahoko, 220n1
Kabuki theater, 169–70, 181–84, 191–92
  Kabuki buyō, 182, 228n6, 229n24, 230n25, 231n37
Kachigumi, 92–93, 139
Kadama, 94

Kagoshima, 176
Kajitani, Ken, 220n1
Kamaishi, 219
Kameta, Roberto, 166
Kaminaga, Sukemitsu, 220n1
Kasato-Maru, 9
Kasuga, Masako, 220
Kasuga, Mitsuko Esperanza (Akane), 34, 36, 96, 101, 104, 200n11
  Akane, Immigrant Poet, 96, 99, 102, 106, 119
Kasuga, Miwa Teresa Pierre-Audain, 96
Kasuga, Tsutomu (Carlos), 5, 36, 99–101, 104, 115, 200n11
Kasuga Osaka, Carlos Tsuyoshi, 119
Kasuga Osaka, Hermelinda Michiko, 97
Kato, Heiji, 69, 90–91, 214n57
Kawabata, Yasunari, 45
Kawabe, Tamiko, 220n1
Kawaji, Kenichiro, 130, 231n1
Kawakami, Héctor, 130
Kegong, Gao, 156
Keichō embassy, delegation, 9, 176–77, 179
Kihara, Naoko, 220n1
Kikawa, Junji, 133
kintsugi, 216
kirishitan, 176
Kishimoto, Tsuchihiko, 134
Kitagawa, Tamiji, 220n1
Kiyono, Saburo, 136
Kiyota, Fuku, 215n1
Kobe, 9, 71, 99
Kohashi, Tokichi, 134
Koji, Mushago, 220n1
Kōjien (Authoritative Japanese Dictionary), 115, 216n13
Korea, 7, 67, 84–85, 88, 199n6, 228n6
Kotuku, Keiko, 220n1
Kuronuma, Yuriko, 220n1
Kusakado, 132, 137
Kyōiku Chokugo (Imperial Rescript on Education), 133
Kyoto, 80, 110, 182, 221n4, 223n26
Kyūshū, 4, 19, 48

Laguna Guzmán, 44, 53, 57
Lake Pátzcuaro, 155
La Merced market, 5
La Oaxaqueña sugar plantation, 42, 62
Lara Cisneros, Gerardo, 26
Latin America and the Caribbean, 9, 12, 25, 27
Latin Americanness, 13, 28
Liceo Mexicano-Japonés, 109, 121, 228n6
Lie Hatanaka, Mirian, 98
Lisbon, 201n23
Little Tokyos, 28
López de Gómara, Francisco, 130
López Obrador, Andrés Manuel, 196
Los Angeles, 46, 85, 89, 203n1, 213n52

MacArthur, Douglas, 186
Macau, 18, 201n23
Maderistas, 51–52, 205n20
Madero, Francisco I., 42–45, 49–54, 56–57, 205nn20–21
    Madero Brigade, 53
    serving under, 5, 35, 66
Madrid, 176–77, 229n18
Maeda, Maho, 219n1
Makegumi, 139
Malthusianism, 73, 208n1
Mamano, Sumi, 219n1
mamekashi, 5
Manchuria, 88, 185, 212n47
manga, vii, xiv, 34–36, 129–46, 186, 217n6, 217n14
Manila, 2, 6, 18, 177–78, 229n18
Manila Galleon (*Galeón de Manila, Nao de China*), 3, 6, 9, 15, 18, 192, 199n3
Manjarrez, Viridiana, 187
mantón de Manila, 6
Manzanilla de la Paz, 4
Manzanillo, 20, 69, 100, 192
Mariátegui, José Carlos, 202n33
Márquez, Javier, 187
Martínez Legorreta, Omar, 26
Martínez Torres, Mercedes, 208n3
Marx, Karl, 11

Marxism, 1, 140, 202n33, 227n2
Masamune, Date, 177–78, 229n18
Masayoshi, Homma, 158
Matsuda, Eiji, 134–35, 141–42, 218n28, 219n28
    "Iglesia Evangélica Cristiana Independiente El Buen Pastor," 140
    La Esperanza ranch, 141
Matsumoto, Tatsuguro (Sanshiro), 4, 24, 90, 199n7, 214n57
    and jacaranda trees, 4, 90, 109–10
Mayans, 159, 196
Mazatlán, 78, 111, 210n20
Medina, Yolox, 183
Mehiko Jihō, 22, 202n28
Mehiko Shimpō, 22, 202n28
Meiji era, 130, 169
    government, 133, 135, 139, 201n25
    militarism, 146
Mekishiko Shimpō, 22, 202n28
Melón, Fabrina, 190
Méndez, Tenoch, 184
Méndez Rojas, Alejandro Néstor, 176
Méndez Rojas, David, 176
Mendoza, María Luisa, 151
mescal, 3–4, 19
Mexicali, 21, 25, 43, 49, 58, 90, 93, 213n54
Mexico
    Armed Forces, 112
    Aztecs, 178
    border with Guatemala, 24
    Central Mexico, 37, 148, 154, 160
    Civil Registry, 125
    flag, 157, 208n3
    government, 22–25, 47, 63, 138, 141, 194–96
    identity, 10, 12, 28, 34
    intelligentsia, 27
    Mexican-American War, 186
    Mexicanness, 69, 106–9, 113–14, 163, 168; Japanese, 12–13, 102, 123, 125; narratives of, 8, 28
    muralism, realism, 148, 157–58, 160
    Post Office, 150

relationship with United States, 66, 89, 91, 100–101, 134, 144, 200n18, 223n26
Revolution of 1910, 3, 34–35, 41–45, 49, 52–54, 134; citizenship, 194; Gray Automobile Gang, 191; Nikkei soldiers, 5, 21–22, 66, 203n3, 204n6; obstacle for Nikkei businesses, 136, 143–44; stopped immigration, 23
State of Mexico, 150, 152, 222n12, 223n24
Mexico City, 80, 93–95, 111, 144, 147, 166–67, 169–70, 199n7, 200n11
Axis powers citizens, 61
birthplace, 226n1, 228n8
daily life, 69, 85
displacement of Nikkei, internment, 16, 22, 36, 47–48, 59, 62–66, 101, 195, 202n29
exhibitions, collections, Fuente del Risco, 3, 220n3, 221nn3, 4
jacaranda trees, 3–5
Japanese consulate, 88–91, 136, 138
Japanese-US relations, Gentlemen's Agreement, anti-Japanese racism, propaganda, 23, 62–63, 67
largest Nikkei communities, 20
manga, 217n14
Manila galleons, 15
mural, 157
Nikkei gambling, 75–76
Nikkei newspaper, 108
Nonaka's photographs, 42–43
Otherness, 13
patron saint, 177
Popocatépetl, 215n6
robberies, 191
staying after relocation, 134, 24–25, 30
theater, 176–77
Michoacán, 155, 160, 199n3
Mifune, Toshirō, 227n2
Miguel, 18
miguelito, 5
Minatitlán, 20, 203n4

Ming Dynasty, 3
Minh-Ha, Trinh T., 152
Mishima, Yukio, 45, 231–32n2
Missako Ikeoka, Maria Cecília, 98
Mitsui, Koichi, 220n1
Mitsuma, 75
Mitsumori Guerrero Kojima, José, 220n1
Miyagi, 177
Miyake, Cinthia, 219n1
Miyake, Taiyo, 220n1
Mizzumi Guerrero Kojima, Julio, 220n1
"model minority" stereotype, 12
modernistas, 14, 27
Molloy, Silvia, 34
Monclova, 201
Mongolia, 199n6
Monterrey, 53, 65, 71, 203n2
Morelos, 91, 152, 214n57
Moriyama, Tamiji, 220n1
Moriyama, Tawaja, 220n1
Moriyama, Terumi, 220n1
Moromisato, Doris, 98
Motines, 2
Muñoz, Rafael F., 54
Murai, Jiro, 219n1
Murakami, Haruki, 45
Murasaki, Shikubi, 97
Murata, Kishio, 219n1
Muray, Alfonso, 130, 220n1
Murayama, Úrsula, 227n2
Murota, 138
Murray, Antonio, 231n1
Murray, Kenichi-Benito, 231n1
Murrieta, Héctor, 220n1
Muruyama, Noé, 227n2
Museo de Arte Moderno, 158, 220n3, 221n4, 224n28
Museo Taller Luis Nishizawa, 150, 221n4
Mutaguchi, 75, 86, 93, 212n38
Mutua, Comité de Ayuda Mutua (Japanese Committee of Mutual Aid), 24, 90, 214n57

Nagano Prefecture, 99–100, 116, 147
Nagasaki, 64, 92, 177, 183, 186, 189

Nagoya, 176
Nahuatl, 14, 215n6
Naito, Chiyoko, 167
Nakahara, Emilio, 42
Nakamura, Ricardo, 50–51, 53
Nakashima, Fumiko, 219n1
Nakatani, Alicia, 86
Nakatani, Armando, 80
Nakatani, Carlos (Yoshigei), Yoshio, 34–36, 70, 99, 132, 193–95, 220n1
   diasporic nationalist discourse, vii, 25, 101, 135, 186
   Japanese peanuts, 5
   and "Novela escrita por Carlos Nakatani," xiii–xiv 36, 68–69, 71–72, 82, 95, 121
   picture brides, 123
Nakatani, Graciela, 81
Nakatani, Gustavo ("Nakatani"), 5
Nakatani, Kigey, 70, 76–77, 209n15
Nakatani Ávila, Carlos (artist), 23, 220n1
Nakatani Sánchez, Emma Chishuru, ix, xv
Nakaune, Akihiro, 130
Nanbu, Kunio, 130
Narita, 158
National Art Museum of Urawa, 158
Negrete, Jesús, 56
Neriki, Kiyoko, 220n1
Nevado de Toluca, 148
New Galicia, 4, 18
New Guinea, 3
New Mexico, 54
New Spain, 3, 9, 26, 130, 176–78, 181
Nichiboku Shimbum, 22, 202n28
Nihei, Mayuko, 220n1
Nihonjinron, 35–36, 67–68, 76, 88, 112–17, 132–33
   Akane's tanka, 102, 119–20, 193
   Nakatane challenging, vii, 70–72, 75, 78, 95, 94
Niikura, Keiko, 220n1
Niimi, Seiichi (Don Santiago), 130–31, 133, 142, 145

Nikkeiness, 167
Nipponophobia, 29–30
Nishikawas, 93, 200n9
Nishimura de Kasouaki, Yoshiko, 220n1
Nishino, Tsuruo, 41
Nishizawa, Adriana, 149
Nishizawa, Kenji, 147, 194
Nishizawa Flores, Luis, vii, xiv, 35, 37
   exaggerating Japanese characteristics, 194
   exhibitions, collections, 220n3, 221n4
   Taku Hon, 159, 220n3
Nivon, Elisa, 220n1
Noh theater, 167, 178, 182, 191
Nonaka, Bunsishi, 48
Nonaka, Gloria, 42, 50–51, 55, 64–66
Nonaka, Iku, 46
Nonaka, José Genaro Kingo, vii, xiv, 34–35, 82, 194, 200n11
   Kingo Nonaka, 35–36
Nonaka, Shiotaro M., 48, 204n13
Nonaka, Tasuyo, 48
Nonaka, Yinkuro, 65, 204n12
Nonaka García, Genaro, 41–42, 46
   and "Introducción," *Kingo Nonaka*, 48
Noriyuki Sato, Francisco, 217n6
Northern Song dynasty, 156
Nuevo Japón, El, 69, 90, 214n57
Nuevo León, 5, 65

Oaxaca, 46, 48–49, 61
Obon festival, 121
Obregón, Álvaro, 54–56, 143, 202n28, 206n29
Ogata Aguilar, Jumko, 194–96, 232n4
Ogino, Shozo, 130
Ogiso, 220n1
Ohno, Kazuo, 183
Oi, Pavel, 219n1
Ojara, 75, 89, 213n51
Ojinaga, 53, 143
Okinawa, 4, 88, 212n47
   immigrants, 34, 71
   language (Uchināguchi), xi, 29

Okinawans, 16, 29, 85
picture brides, 88
Oku, 88
Okuno, Hiroshi, 219n1
Oquendo, 9
Order of the Secret Treasure, 125
Orientalism, 12–14, 16, 23, 31, 44, 132, 162–63
   European Orientalists' interpretations, 202n33
   Japanese, 146
   in Latin American literature, 200n13
Orientalization, 33, 132, 192, 194, 200n16
Orozco, José Clemente, 160
Orozco, Pascual, 51, 205n20
Ortiz Rubio, Pascual, 4, 60
Osaka, 18, 77–78, 97, 119, 167–68, 209n16
Osato, 180
Ōta, Kiyoto, 219n1
Otakara, Fusaichi, 4, 22, 41, 202n27
Otta, Renji, 134, 137
Our Lady of Guadalupe, 123

Pacific Ocean, 7, 166, 168, 192, 201n25
Pacific War, 55, 188
Páez, Juan de, 18–19
Palace of Fine Arts, 155
Palau, Coahuila, 201n20
Palenque, 159
Panama, 16, 28, 48, 150, 204n13
Panteón Jardín cemetery, 66
Paraguay, 4
Paredón, 53
Paricutín, 160
Pastor, Mara, 96
Patriots Club, 92–93
Paul V (pope), 177, 179
Paz, Octavio, 113
Pearl Harbor attack, 23, 25, 47
   reactions to, 55, 63, 89, 100, 186, 188–89, 207n50, 230n32
   relocation, 35, 43, 61
Peña Delgado, Grace, 26

Peña Nieto, Enrique, 148
Pérez, 18
Pérez, Hidemi, 228n11
Pérez Nakandakara, Harumi, 220n1
Pérez Otakara, Ricardo, 4, 22
Perote prison, 30
Pershing, John J., 54, 205n27
Peru, 14–16, 22–24, 46, 164, 200n18, 201n24, 202n33
   internment camps, 7, 61, 63, 100, 144, 195–96
   Nikkei mass migration, 135
   Nikkei writing, 71, 212n42
Philippines, 3, 7, 177, 186
   Filipinos, 3, 15, 18, 200n10
Phillip III, 177–78
picture brides (*shashin hanayome*), 85, 88, 100, 123, 167, 188
   Akane, 34, 98, 126
   miai kekkon, 98
   Obachan, 215n2
Pierre-Audain Kasuga, Miwa Teresa, 96
Piñón, Diego, 228n6
Plantación Oaxaqueña, 203n4
Poniatowska, Elena, 147, 224n33
Pope Paul V, 117, 179
Popocatépetl, El Popo, 108–9, 148, 153, 215n6
Pratt, Mary Louise, 81
Proudhon, Pierre-Joseph, 140
Psalmon, David, 228n6
Puebla, 2, 16, 152, 199n2, 222n12

Qianlong (emperor), 201n23
Qing dynasty, 3
Quechua, 14
Querétaro, 16, 221n3

raicilla, 4
Rajin, 184
Rakuyo-Maru, 99
Ramírez Honda, Alejandro, 220n1
Rancho Villa Aldana, 202n29
Reagan, Ronald, 196
Red Cross, 56–57

Rembrandt, Harmenszoon van Rijn, 160
Renan, Ernest, 31
Reyes Estrada, Cecilia, 41, 70, 92, 186, 214n56
  and *gallina azul, La*, 41–42, 186, 200n8, 203n3, 212n37, 230n28, 231n2
  Mexican Revolution, 203n3
  picture bride, 212n37
  rumors about Japanese fleet, 92
  yuki, 200n8
  Zenzo Tanaka, 70
Rincón Gallardo, Naomi, 227n2
Río Bravo, 205n21
Rio Grande, 52
Rivera, Diego, 160, 221n3
Rivera Delgado, Gabriel, 42–43, 53, 58–59
Rodríguez, Juan José, 200n16
Rodríguez, Rafael, 43
Rojas Moriyama, Yuriko, 220n1
Rome, 177, 180
Rosas, Enrique, 190–91
Rousseau, Jean-Jacques, 139
Royal Spanish Academy, 219n32
Ruiz, Nicolasa, 215n1, 231n2
Russian Empire, 21, 88
Russo-Japanese War, 73, 133, 141, 170

Sahagún, Luis, 224n31
Said, Edward W., 14, 107
Saint-Tropez, 177
Sakaguchi, 80, 93
Sakai, Kazuya, 220n1
Sakamoto, Yui, 220n1
Sakuya, Konohana, 129, 131, 140, 144
Salazar, Jorge, 200n16
Salina Cruz, 46, 48, 61, 204n13
Salinas Basave, Daniel, 41–45, 48–49, 52–56, 58–60, 62–63, 65–66
  samurái de la Graflex, El, 26, 36, 41, 44, 53–54
  Viscount Enomoto Takeaki, 138
Salón de la Plástica Mexicana, 150, 220n3, 224n28

Samejina, 46
Samson, 199
San Benito, 48
San Buenaventura, 54
San Diego, 58–59, 203n3
San Felipe de Jesús, 171
San Francisco, 9, 17, 100, 201n22, 221n4
San Juan Bautista galleon, 176
San Lúcar de Barrameda, 177
San Luis Potosí, 4, 100, 221n3
Sano, Seki, 227n2
San-Ou cooperative, 136, 139–40
San Pedro de las Colonias, 53
San Rafael, Chihuahua, 24
Santa Lucrecia, 46, 48, 203n4
Santo, El, 6
Santos, 9
San Ysidro, 59
São Paulo, 9, 139
Sato Parra, José Ramón, and Manuel Campos Caravantes, 231n1
Satsuma Domain, 88
Schiavone Camacho, Julia María, 12, 26
Secretaría de la Defensa Nacional, 42, 65
Seijas, Tatiana, 3, 26
Sendai Prefecture, 19, 176–77, 179
Seville, 177
Shan shui, 26, 156
Shigaraki, 161
Shihan-Natori School, 167
Shimamoto, Julio, 217n6
Shimizu, Rafael, 130
Shimizu, Roberto, 5–6
Shin, Naoko, 96
Shindō Renmei, 73, 92–93, 133, 202n31, 209n9
Shingemin, 84–85, 211n32
Shinohara, Chiyoka, 47
Shinpei, Takeda, 36, 41, 44, 46, 203n1
Shintoism, 92, 95
shōchū, 4
Silva, Catalina de, 19
Sinaloa, 12, 63
Singapore, 9
Sinicization, 16

Sino-Japanese War (first), 133, 170
Sino-Japanese War (second), 88
Siu Kam Wen, 164, 203n35
slavery, 2, 6, 9, 15, 18–19, 31, 52, 159
  African, 16–17, 201n19
  Asian, 3, 26
  slave market, 17–18
social Darwinism, 33
socialism, vii, 36, 129, 138–40, 146, 194, 218n22
Sociedad Colonizadora Japón-México, 20
Sociedad Cooperativa Mexicano-Japonesa, 136, 143, 218n24
Soconusco, 185, 188, 230n29
Sonora, 12, 20, 86, 93–94, 195, 200n8
Sontag, Susan, 45
Sosa de Puebla family, 3
Sotelo, Luis, 177, 179, 181, 229n18
South China Sea, 9
Spain, 2, 6, 9, 43–45, 130, 176–79, 191, 211n29
  newspapers, 232n4
  Spanish crown, 18, 177
  world trade circuits, 201n23
Spivak, Gayatri Chakravorty, 67
Sri Lanka, 3
Stavans, Abraham, 228n6
Sugahara, Marimo, 220n1
Sumoto, Sumoto-cho, 5, 70
Suzuki, Midori, 219n1
Suzuki, Noriko, 220n1
Suzuki, Waka, 136
Suzume, Odori, 179

Tablada, José Juan, 27, 155, 222n14
Tacubaya Gakuen, 167
Tajuko ranch 136, 138–39
Takada, Masasuke, 219n1
Takahashi, Kiyoshi, 220n1
Takahashi, Kumataro, 136
Takarazuka Kagueki theater company, 167
Takarazuka Music School, 167, 227n4
Takarazuka Review, 227n4
Takarazuka School of Arts, 168

Takarazuka Shokatai, 227n4
Takeda, Alejandro, 220n1
Takeda, Armando, 220n1
Takeda, Kunio, 219n1
Takeda, Shinpei, 41, 44, 46, 203n1
Takeda, Shinzaburō, 219n1
Takemura, Shiro, 219n1
taku-hon, 159
Tames, Arturo, 182, 184, 187
Tamiya, Nihei, 134
Tanaka, 94, 215n63
Tanaka, Asahiro, 42
Tanaka, René, 62
Tanaka, Zenzo (José), 41, 62
tanka, 86, 96–98, 100, 104–17, 119–22, 124–25
  melancholy, vii, 36, 102
  picture bride, 34
tanuki, 83–84, 210n26
Tapachula, 139, 185–86, 189, 217n1, 230n33
Tenopalco, 147
Tenshō embassy, 176
Tepito, 147
Terui, Ryojiro, 132, 136
Texans, 52
Tijuana, 43–47, 57–60, 204n19
  Diario Frontera de Tijuana, 203n2
  documentary photographer, 26, 36, 41
  Japanese associations, 25
  relocation, 35, 63, 65, 90
Tinajero, Araceli, 231n2
Toda, Isawo, 130
Tokugawa, Ieyasu, 177
  shogunate, 178, 201n25
Tokugawa Hidetada, 178
Tokyo, 92, 167, 186, 219n32, 224n28
  Tokyo International Biennial, 148
Toluca, 148, 150, 157, 221n4, 223n24
Tomomi, Iwakura, 179
Toneyama, Kōjin, 157–59, 220n3, 223n26
Torii, Kenta, 219n1
Torreón, 41, 45, 53
Torres-Rodríguez, Laura J., ix, 27
transatlantic, 7, 9, 27, 176

transculturation, 5, 29, 81, 144, 172
Tratado de amistad, comercio y navegación, 19, 45
Tsuburaya, Eiji, 200n12
Tsuji, Tadasu, 144
Tsukinoura, 177, 180
Tsuru, Kiso, 24, 26, 210n19, 214n57
tuba, 3, 199n3
Tuito, El, 4

Uchimura, Kanzō, 141, 218n26
Ue, Tadashi, 220n1
Ueno, Hisashi, 129
Ultraman, 6, 200n12
United States, 20–24, 48–49, 55–57, 61–63, 88–89, 185–88, 219n32, 228n6
   anti-Japanese, 17, 19, 23, 61, 67, 99, 200n18
   Asian communities in US, 30, 195
   compensations after Mexican Revolution, 143
   immigration into, 8, 22–23, 27, 46, 62, 195
   museums, 150
   phalanxes, 139
   Seiichi Higashide, 212n42
   Tsuchihiko Kishimoto and Tokichi Kohashi, 134
   government, 16, 47, 50, 61, 94, 101, 197, 199n7, 232n4
   hegemony, 8, 23, 26
   Pacific Fleet, 89
Universidad Autónoma Metropolitana, 196
Universidad Nacional Autónoma de México (UNAM), 148, 221n5
Universidad Nacional de México, 219n8
University of Komaba, 219n36
University of Tokyo, 186 219n28
Ures, 200n8

Valdés, Agustín, 51
Valdés Kuri, Claudio, 228n6, 231n38
Valley of Mexico, 148, 152, 155, 159
Valparaíso, 99

Vargas Llosa, Mario, 13
Vargas Valdés, Jesús, 57, 206n35
Vasconcelos, José, 17, 27
Vatican, 179
Velasco, José María, 150, 159, 164–65, 225n46
Venice, 179
Ventura, 18
Veracruz, 20, 22, 63, 176–77, 195–96, 202n28, 203n4, 221n3
Victoria, 86
Viejo Casas Grandes, 50
Villa, Francisco "Pancho," 5, 22, 35–36, 43–45, 49–51, 53–57, 62, 66
   manga, 143
   Salinas Basave, Daniel, 26, 41
Villa Aldama, 91
Villanueva, Ammi, 187
Villarreal, Andrés, 53
vino de coco, 3
Viqueira, Richard, 228n6
Virgin Mary, 179

waka, 97
Washington, DC, 21, 45, 63, 194
Watabe, Shino, 219n1
Watanabe, José, 164, 225n45
Watanabe, Rie, 220n1
Wein, Susana, 169, 228n8
Western Hemisphere, 90
Wilson, Woodrow, 54
world literature, 10–11
World War II, 22–23, 25–26, 29–30, 36–37, 46–47, 102, 144–45, 194–97
   anti-Japanese American sentiment, 34, 43, 61, 66, 76, 134, 136, 142
   Chinese in Peru, 15
   Hacienda Batán, 80–81, 126, 199n7
   imperialism and migration, 68, 72, 92, 95, 133, 139, 170, 202n32
   kamikaze, 230n28
   Nikkei . . . Correo de Hiroshima, 185
   Nikkei economic contributions, 16, 136, 143
   return to Japan, 93

Xalapa, 141, 219n36
Xi, Guo, 156

Yaasuo Guerrero Kojima, Martín, 220n1
Yamada, Shintaro, 137
Yamada, Zenzo, 62, 70, 200n8, 203n3, 214n59
Yamamoto, Asajiro, 136
Yamamoto, Yūzō, 136, 170
Yamane, Antonio, 42
Yamane, Kisaburo, 41–42, 202n27
Yamasaki, Tizuka, 98
Yamashita, Karen Tei, 37, 139, 203nn34–35
Yamato, 132, 217n10
Yaqui, 196
Yashuarama, Alberto Iwao, 46
Yasuhara, 47
"Yellow Peril" stereotype, 12, 16, 23
yin-yang symbol, 157, 161

Yokohama, 69, 99, 210, 221n4
Yokoo, Sakiko, 220n1
YouTube, 6, 206n34
Yuan dynasty, 156
Yucatán Peninsula, 32, 160
yuki, yukeras, yukeros, 4
Yukugama, 84

Zacatecas, 50, 53
Zacatula, 3
Zalce, Alfredo, 155, 160, 222n14
Zapata, Emiliano, 41
Zapotitlán de Vadillo, 4
Zen Buddhism, 44, 49, 156, 162–63, 202n33, 225n41
Zen garden, 158
Zepeda, Eva, 148
Zorrilla, Taro, 220n1
Zuyako, 74–75, 79, 83, 85–86, 209n10

www.ingramcontent.com/pod-product-compliance
Lightning Source LLC
Chambersburg PA
CBHW051213300426
44116CB00006B/560